The
ACCUMULATION
of FREEDOM

WRITINGS ON
ANARCHIST ECONOMICS

EDITED BY DERIC SHANNON, ANTHONY J. NOCELLA, II,
& JOHN ASIMAKOPOULOS

AK
PRESS
EDINBURGH · OAKLAND · BALTIMORE

The Accumulation of Freedom: Writings on Anarchist Economics
© 2012, edited by Deric Shannon, Anthony J. Nocella, II, and John
Asimakopoulos

This edition © 2012 AK Press (Oakland, Edinburgh, Baltimore)
ISBN: 978-1-84935-094-5 | eBook ISBN: 978-1-84935-095-2
Library of Congress Control Number: 2011936250

AK Press   AK Press
674-A 23rd Street   PO Box 12766
Oakland, CA 94612   Edinburgh, EH8 9YE
USA   Scotland
www.akpress.org   www.akuk.com
akpress@akpress.org   ak@akedin.demon.co.uk

The above addresses would be delighted to provide you with the latest AK Press distribution catalog, which features the several thousand
books, pamphlets, zines, audio and video products, and stylish apparel
published and/or distributed by AK Press. Alternatively, visit our websites for the complete catalog, latest news, and secure ordering.

Visit us at:
www.akpress.org
www.akuk.com
www.revolutionbythebook.akpress.org

Printed in the USA on acid-free paper.

Contents

PART 4. PRACTICE

PART 5. RESISTANCE

PART 6. VISION

Afterword

Acknowledgments

We would of course like to thank everyone at AK Press—especially Zach, Charles, Lorna, Jessica, and Kate—the contributors, and the many people who have written in support of the book. Without all of you this book would not be possible.

Deric Shannon

Since this book is about anarchist criticisms and alternatives to capitalism, I would like to take the time to thank people who have helped me along in the spirit of mutual aid. Without many of these people I would have gone without food and shelter, without others I would have gone without needed kindness and friendship, and without them all my life would certainly be emptier. First and foremost, thank you to Amney Harper for repeatedly saving my life. I will never forget my debt to you. Secondly, and in no particular order, I would like to thank: Amanda Rose Zody, Jacquelyn Arsenuk, Abbey Volcano, Joe Sutton, Jilly Weiss, Tyler Watkins, David Burns, Liz Burns, Kevin Blue, Andrew Salyer, Kevin McElmurry, E Marino, John Wyatt, Gloria Felts, Courtney Cook, Naitha Bellesis, Ryan Ramsey, Nic Lee, Judi Lee (my bestest), Jesse Lee, Ryan Lash, Andrew Jackson, Josh Young, Maria Yates, Matt Sharp, Brooke, Virgil Carstens (you handsome bastard), Delicia Garcia, Bill Armaline, Abe DeLeon, Li'l Jerry (I miss you), Chloe and Sofie, Chris Wendt, Joe Hill, Jessica Forgille, Randy Hull, my brothers—Rich and Dustin, my mother, father, and grandmother, and a host of others who shall remain unnamed. My apologies to anyone I have forgotten on this long list of people who have helped me out throughout the years.

John Asimakopoulos

I wish to acknowledge the brutal and incompetent nature of my employer who, in the words of the American Arbitration Association, fired me "arbitrarily and capriciously." That was the final push to make me the involved, anti-authoritarian activist I am today and foster the birth of the Transformative Studies Institute (www.transformativestudies.org) to retake academia from the corporate university. Resistance is NOT futile. I got my job back and you can get YOUR lives back too with organized direct action.

Anthony J. Nocella, II

First and foremost I would like to thank my friends Deric and John for this incredibly fun and creative collaboration. You both have been an inspiration to work harder for social justice and peace. Much appreciation to the criminology and sociology students, staff, and faculty at SUNY Cortland and Le Moyne College for their friendship and the projects we have worked on. A special thanks to my advisors Peter Castro, Richard Loder, Mecke Nagel, Piers Beirne, and Micere Githae Mugo for their ongoing support and wisdom. And I am forever grateful to Robert Rubinstein for his amazing friendship, support, and advice since day one at Syracuse University. I would like to thank my family and all the other teachers and professors who always believed in me and never said that I did not belong because of having disabilities. I also want to express my gratitude to everyone involved with the Central New York Peace Studies Consortium, American Friends Service Committee, Political Media Review, Institute for Critical Animal Studies, Save the Kids, and Transformative Studies Institute. I would like to thank my dear friend who I work with day in and day out on everything and who is always there to talk with, Sarat Colling. Finally, I would like to thank my friends in no specific order—Steve Best, Richard Kahn, Jeremy, Jay, Brian, Ben Gottschall, Andrew, Heather, Eden, Andy, Bister, Owen, Alma, Cameron Naficy, Shane, Sean, Patrick Hoyt, elana levy, Nick Cooney, Dave Lambon, Jason Bayless, Lisa Kemmerer, Roger Yates, Richard Twine, Richard White, Peter McLaren, Anastasia Yarbrough, Abe DeLeon, Luis Fernandez, Nancy Piscitell, Lisa Mignacca, Barron Boyd, Richard Kendrick, Mecke Nagel, Andrew Fitz-Gibbon, Caroline Kaltefleiter, Ali Zaidi, David Gabbard, Kevin Pieluszczak, Josh Calkins, Liat Ben-Moshe, Bill Armaline, Abbey Willis, Roxanne Dunbar-Ortiz, Ramsey Kanaan, Sean Parson, Ernesto Aguilar, David Rovics, Gregory Martin, Stanley Aronowitz, Ruth Kinna, Jeff Monaghan, Carl Boggs, John Alessio, Julie Andrzejewski, Glenn Rikowski, Mitch Rosenwald, David Graeber, Benjamin Frymer, Richard Van Heertum, Jeff Ferrell, Elsa Karen Marquez-Aponte, Ward Churchill, and Jeff Monson, as well as the 2003–2004 PARC crew, Syracuse Bicycle, AVP Auburn prison, and everyone at Hillbrook. I love you all!

This book is dedicated to all of the exploited and oppressed people struggling for freedom and dignity. Let us transform society, liberate ourselves, and be free!

To the global working class, may they unite and take what is theirs.

Preface
Ruth Kinna

Economics was once called the dismal science and is still often associated with dry, technical argument and the modeling of preferences based on assumptions of perfect knowledge and rational calculation. The language of economics—investment, fiscal stimuli, growth, productive efficiency, bull and bear markets—is quite familiar. And the practical implications of these terms are all too predictable and easily understood, particularly during periods of recession. But to many the content of the subject remains mysteriously abstract and its scope seems narrowly focused. The study of economics is too often limited to the analysis of capitalist markets, the murky dealings of international finance or, as the recent and spectacular collapse of the banks shows, with system failure.

Naturally, there have always been critical voices within the discipline, but it is only recently that the possibility of imagining how economies might work, or be made to work differently, has been stated so emphatically. Since the emergence of the global social justice movement, new lines of inquiry about the assumptions, values, and effects of the global economic system have been opened. The mantra that there is no alternative has been subject to fresh scrutiny. Its counterclaim, that other worlds are possible, has proved to be a powerful rival and is beginning to supplant it. The rise of unregulated movements of capital, the dominating presence of multi-national corporations, and the structuring of free trade to favor the most powerful are no longer regarded as inevitable, unstoppable, or spontaneous features of economic markets—much less, desirable. That the global economy is a badly regulated, ill-planned system which has been facilitated by a morally bankrupt and oppressive ideology—neoliberalism—is surely now clear.

Some of the most important critiques of the neoliberal dystopia to have appeared since 1999 have been informed by non-anarchist socialist and left-liberal positions. The work of Susan George, Peter Singer, Alex Callinicos, Joseph Stiglitz, and others provides a rich source of inspiration. But the anarchistic nature of the social justice movement and the grassroots actions that it has embraced also provides space for the discussion of explicitly anarchist approaches to economics. Some of this discussion might fill non-anarchists with horror, especially if it is assumed that anarchism stands only for the deregulation of the economy, the privatization of all services, and the rolling back of the state with little regard for issues of equality, participation, and creative flourishing. For most groups within the social justice movement, this brand of right-libertarianism is hardly better, though perhaps less hypocritical, than regulated neoliberalism. Its association with anarchism—which is fiercely contested—owes much to the influence of Murray Rothbard who described his uncompromising and radical defense of individual rights and free market distributions as anarcho-capitalist. Whether or not his identification with anarchism distorted the tradition, his position hardly exhausts the possibilities for an anarchist economics. On the contrary, anarchism offers a strong and rich heritage of anti-capitalist thinking, and it is these lines of thought which might usefully be revived.

Anti-capitalist anarchism is grounded in the belief that problems of inequality, alienation, exploitation, and aggressive competition stem from the complex relationship of political and economic interests. Sometimes this relationship is understood as a class relationship in which political elites (historically patriarchal, racist, homophobic, and religiously bigoted) are more or less subservient to the economically powerful. Others treat the interrelation as evidence of a more diffuse military-industrial complex, where similarly structured political, economic, and military interests coalesce. Either way, anarchists have generally argued that capitalism has developed alongside a process of political centralization and state formation. A clean divorce of politics from economics, releasing markets from government interference, is simply impossible—even assuming it is desirable. The absorption of politics into economics is equally problematic.

Typically, the acknowledgment of the interdependence of states and markets has encouraged anarchists to examine the sociological effects of capitalism as well as its economic operation. For example, on the question of exploitation, anarchists have highlighted the repressive character of the organization and management of production as well as pointed out the injustice of ownership and contradictions of individual property rights. Similarly, they have explored the expansion of capitalist markets by looking at the centrality of war and the militarization of everyday life in addition to analyzing capitalism's imperialist dynamic. This approach to capitalism has played an important role in shaping revolutionary strategies. Anarchists have uniformly rejected ideas of state control and central planning and tied the possibility of redirecting production towards the satisfaction of socially useful ends to a process of independent popular action. As Kropotkin argued in *The Conquest of Bread*, social transformation relies upon the ability of individuals working in local communities to find ways of securing their own sources of well-being: food, shelter, and clothing.

This tradition of thought has supported a variety of utopian visions, characteristically defined by calls for the decentralization of production and direct worker/community control. Some anarchists have also argued for the abandonment of international trade and the division of labor in favor of the close integration of agriculture and industry in local areas. Others, unmoved by the possibility of equalizing the burdens of labor and/or reducing the hours of labor, have called for the abandonment of work—and, potentially, the structuring discipline of time—and for its replacement by voluntary production ("productive leisure"). These principles have been adapted to suit a diverse set of arrangements. Perhaps the best known historical example of their application is the anarcho-syndicalist federation, but anarchists have also supported cooperative systems, models of reciprocal exchange based on contract and ethical ownership, and free communism. In recent years, a variety of ecological alternatives have also been explored.

Globalization has not rendered the anarchist approach to economics redundant. Indeed, debates about the relative power of states and corporations as drivers of neoliberal change have refocused attention on the complexity of these relationships and the ways in which power is configured locally. Renewed interest in state sovereignty has encouraged analysis of the compatibility of principles of local decision-making, individual autonomy, and universal rights. These analyses have been shaped by a growing awareness of the interdependence of states and a desire to move beyond the liberal-communist polarization of Cold War ideology. Nevertheless, thematically there is a significant overlap between these discussions and traditional anarchist concerns.

Naturally, neoliberal globalization has created new concerns about the organization of economic systems which anarchists need to address. One set centers on the character of corporate capitalism. Naomi

Klein's analysis identifies branding and outsourcing as its key features. Branding is associated with lifestyle consumption and the promotion of a vapid acquisitive culture. This is supported by seductive, highly manipulative marketing campaigns which help conceal the growing differentials between rich and poor. Outsourcing describes a system of global franchising. In the old manufacturing sectors of the advanced economies, it brings the casualization of labor and mass unemployment. In the production zones of the developing world, it combines the slavish, sweated practices of Victorian capitalism with the bureaucratic efficiency of labor camp regulation. Escaping from the corporatization of the economy presents unimaginable difficulties. For although "the consumer is king," the wheels of corporate global capitalism are oiled by a deregulated banking system which requires consistently high consumption to support its speculations. Even assuming the possibility of re-patterning mass consumption, sudden shifts are likely to provoke a crisis of confidence in the financial system, threatening the mortgages of those least able to support them—pensions and government welfare systems. The extent and grasp of the web in which individuals are caught has been exposed all too clearly by the bank-led collapse of the economy.

A second set of issues prompted by globalization center on the environmental and ecological costs of industrialization and modernization. These concerns also have a long history but the servility of kowtowing governments has lent them a new urgency. The signs of ecological collapse—increasing rates of extinction, climate chaos, and ozone depletion—are now frighteningly obvious. So is the political corruption that often accompanies corporate expansion. Shell's involvement in Nigeria and the execution of Ken Saro-Wira is an outstanding example of the influence that corporate interests can court. Less obvious are the longer-term effects of industrial production and, especially, agribusiness: for example, the routine contamination of food supplies which results from the demand to increase yields and eradicate the plant and animal diseases that are encouraged by industrial processes that are now employed as standard in agriculture. Also hidden is the amount of food waste generated by the need to meet the supermarket standards of the rich world. It is estimated that British households unnecessarily throw away approximately six million tons of food a year. But even this huge figure pales in comparison to the amount that gets lost between field and display shelf. The miraculous promises of GM technology to make good the food shortages that lead millions to die of malnutrition and starvation every year should be seen in this context rather than freak and unmediated crop failures. In the framework of global capitalism, the drive of so-called emerging economies in India and China to follow the industrial model will further exacerbate all of these problems.

A third set of concerns centers around the unfairness of global market regulation and, in particular, the Western bias of institutions such as the International Monetary Fund and the World Trade Organization. The imposition of a one-size-fits-all policy to deal with economic problems across the globe and the use of trade sanctions has helped increase inequalities and facilitated the virtual recolonization of poorer states. A related issue is the growing interstate rivalry for control of natural resources. As Noam Chomsky has demonstrated, for most of the postwar period democratic states have pursued imperial ambitions with the vigor of old empires, defending liberal freedoms at home to push exploitative agendas abroad. Overt military action has been taken to protect vital interests. Oil is now a security issue, as the invasion of Iraq and the race to control the Arctic gas and oil fields has shown. Water is another. Current predictions are that the combined effects of untreated waste, agricultural pollution, and the massive transportation of ever-dwindling supplies from the poor to the rich worlds will result in destruction and death on an unprecedented scale.

Finding a response to any of these issues is an enormous undertaking and the more original voices that can be heard the better. One way of developing a specifically anarchist approach to neoliberal globalization is to examine the issues it has thrown up by using the frameworks of analysis developed in the early years of Western capitalist expansion. This would mean taking seriously the claim that it is both possible and desirable to find a way of regulating economic behavior without relying on the coercive apparatus of the state. Such an approach might take inspiration from the principles of design that the earlier generation of anarchists proposed without relying on or being too constrained by the particular models they devised. Parecon is a productive and inspirational example that might be developed in several different ways.

In the course of pursuing anarchist alternatives, it seems likely that the pressing nature of current problems will require some hard political choices. Contrary to what skeptics believe, resistance is sometimes an option, and anarchists have a long history of practical, constructive experimentation in developing systems of mutual support. This tradition continues to thrive, as thousands of other grassroots actions and initiatives demonstrate. Yet should resistance and experimentation fail or where the immediate choice of policy alternatives makes them irrelevant, the conviction that an anarchist economic system is realizable is a source of strength. It should help anarchists identify their most preferred (or least worst) options and, ideally, contribute positively to the reshaping of non-anarchist preferences.

Anarchist Economics:
A Holistic View[1]

Deric Shannon, Anthony J. Nocella, II, John Asimakopoulos

In an online discussion titled "Anarchist Economics" one poster recently commented, "Anarchist economics?! Now, that's an oxymoron!" After further discussion, it became clear that this person, a long-time anarchist, operated under the assumption that "economics" is *capitalism*. While that may be true for the typical university "economics" class, there is a long history of economic analyses, models, and practices that are based on *anti*-capitalist principles.

Meanwhile, to many who are not even radicals, capitalism looks like it is on its last legs, or at the least like an undesirable way to organize humanity.[2] Hundreds of billions (!) of public dollars have been spent to help private and enormous failed businesses recover. And while corporations are bailed out of their problems, in typical capitalist fashion, workers bear the brunt of the world's economic troubles (in addition to being daily disempowered, taxed, then having our money get turned over to groups and people who are already powerful and wealthy). We have seen "austerity" for workers in the form of cuts to education, social provisions, and massive layoffs while the world's wealthiest continue to enjoy higher and higher profit margins.[3] Some top economists have even suggested that the current economic tumult may be worse than the Great Depression.[4] Hunger is on the rise, people are losing their homes, jobs are disappearing—capitalism is, yet again, in crisis.

In addition to this depression, we see evidence for possible catastrophic consequences if we continue to despoil and damage the entire nonhuman world and treat it as a mere collection of "resources" for human use—another grouping of commodities for sale under capitalism. Various non-class oppressions and relations of domination, confining notions of gender and sexuality—and "identity" more generally—are still strong elements in the ways that we organize socially, embedded in our institutions, including our economy. Our way of life, in many ways, is unsustainable.

It is within this context that we wish to put forward these contemporary writings on anarchist economics, with a sense of the history that undergirds these critiques of the status quo and visions of radically different futures and presents. Nevertheless, the ubiquity of conflations of "economics" with capitalism and markets warrants some work at definitions. Likewise, because anarchism is a *prefigurative* practice— a politics that seeks to lay the foundations of a future society in the present—a distinctly *anarchist* economics, we argue, will have some unique features of its own.

Anarchism and Economics

So if "economics" is not synonymous with "capitalism" or "markets," what is it? Why should anarchists be concerned with economics?

Merriam-Webster's Collegiate Dictionary defines economics as "a social science concerned chiefly with description and analysis of the production, distribution, and consumption of goods and services." Generally, as accepted historical narratives go, economics as a social science began with Adam Smith and his book *The Wealth of Nations*, and was further developed by the likes of Thomas Malthus and John Stuart Mill. These famous men of classical economics are perhaps best known for being proponents of private ownership of the means of production and for theorizing that markets tend toward stabilization (best exemplified in Smith's famous phrase "the invisible hand"—which carries with it the assumption that markets are the most efficient method for the allocation of resources). And so goes the narrative, then along came Karl Marx to challenge the assumptions of political economy and critique capitalist property relations, theories of value, and markets. And now the science is generally divided between different capitalist analyses and models and *Marxian* models and analyses.

There are a couple of problems with this historical narrative. First, like most historical narratives of the various social sciences, it locates the "beginning" of economics in post-Enlightenment era European history and ignores earlier contributions from people of different time periods and locations, such as the Indian teacher Chanakya, or the famous North African forerunner of sociology Ibn Khaldun. Secondly, it effectively reduces perspectives critical of capitalism to Marxism, suggesting a limited framework for anti-capitalist perspectives. This might reflect larger relations of power in society, as these histories tend to be written by Western scholars and Marxism (or, perhaps more accurately stated, "Marxism" as it was interpreted and practiced by Lenin and his descendants) was the ideology that won out in the anti-capitalist revolutions of the twentieth century in Russia and China. This common narrative, then, effectively erases anarchist contributions to economic thought.

We do not, however, want to suggest an easy relationship between anarchism and economics as such. Anarchism, after all, is not limited to its critique of capitalism and puts forward an understanding "that the war against capitalism must be at the same time a war against all institutions of political power," recognizing that "exploitation has always gone hand in hand with political and social oppression."[5] For anarchists, then, "economics" abstracted from the rest of social life presents a problem in terms of analysis. Indeed, economic life intersects with all other aspects of social life, including other forms of social domination—so within these pages the reader will often see various authors attempting to lay bare those connections, moving "economics" beyond mere production, distribution, and consumption.

There is also a problem with the kind of specialization of knowledge that words like "science" tend to communicate. Typically, science evokes specialists and experts, mirroring the hierarchical and competitive production of knowledge under capitalism in the academy. The rest of society is assumed to be looking to these "experts" for their analyses and for the best way forward. But anarchists have always stressed that people can run our own affairs without the need for experts or bureaucrats. The majority of those anarchists who have contributed to economics have not, in fact, been academic workers and have argued for economic arrangements that dispense with the need for experts to direct the rest of us.

Further, beyond the assumptions of economics as a social science, the view of work and production tied to workplaces as a separate sphere of life and an economy as a medium of exchange is anathema to some schools of anarchist thought. Some anarchists explicitly call for an end to the economy,[6] the abolition of work,[7] and free consumption that would preclude exchange value and the relations that arise from it. If we define "economies" or "economics" this way—to include the assumption of exchange relations and access to the social product being tied to work—it could be suggested that some strains of anarchism are advancing something altogether different from "economics." Nonetheless, anarchists have contributed to economic thought, despite historical portrayals that write them out—reducing the narrative to capitalism and its Marxian opponents—and we do aim to remedy this despite some of these tensions.

Indeed, as the libertarian wing of the socialist movement, anarchism played a key role in the development of economic analyses, practices, and visions of a future society that were anti-capitalist and non-Marxist. Proudhon's contributions in this regard are particularly salient, as he was a contemporary of Marx as well as an influence on his thinking (and anticipated many Marxist arguments before they were ostensibly "invented" by Marx).[8] Proudhon also advocated an anti-capitalist anarchist vision called *mutualism*, a market form of socialism, both as a strategy out of capitalism and a broad sketch of what a post-capitalist society might look like.

Likewise, Bakunin, Marx's bitter opponent in the First International, contributed greatly to socialist criticisms and analyses of capitalism.[9] These forays into economics were not limited to this time period, but continued through Kropotkin[10] before the Russian Revolution, Santillán[11] after the Spanish Civil War, and so on into the contemporary period. And we wish to stress that these principles, analyses, and forays into vision were not limited to "great men of history," but represented collective theorizing by a *libertarian* socialist milieu—the anti-authoritarian and anti-state wing of the socialist movement. Thus, comparing anarchism to "Marxism" is a bit of a misnomer, as "Marxism" reduces many different ideas, collectively produced, to the leadership of a single "great man of history"—Karl Marx.

As a result of this history, anarchism has an interesting (and sometimes tense) relationship with Marxism, and that is reflected in the contents of this book. Some anarchists reject any association with Marxism and there has certainly been plenty of ink spilled in mutual denunciations (in some historical moments, it has also led to spilled blood—particularly of anarchists at the hands of authoritarians who identified with Marx's work). Still others have argued for a historical continuity within anarchism and the anti-authoritarian, anti-state variants of Marxism constituting a libertarian socialism—or, in some contexts, a libertarian *communism*. However, while some have suggested that engagements between the traditions could be fruitful,[12] this has definitely not been done without anarchist critics.[13] Yet one can see various authors in this collection, and many places outside of it, using these terms—"libertarian socialism" or communism—to describe their position, often as a nod to the similar trajectories between anarchism and some variants of Marxian thought.[14]

The differences between anarchist and Marxist thought might also (partially) explain a lack of anarchism within the field of economics. Marxism, after all, tends to be centrally focused on economics—considering the economy the "base" of a society, giving rise upon those economic foundations to other social relations. Marx stated it thusly:

> In the social production of their existence, men [sic] inevitably enter into definite relations, which are independent of their will, namely [the] relations of production appropriate to a given stage in the development of their material forces of production. The totality of these relations of production constitutes the economic structure of society, the real foundation, on which arises a legal and political superstructure, and to which correspond definite forms of consciousness. The mode of production of material life conditions the general process of social, political, and intellectual life.[15]

Anarchism, on the other hand, is a critique of domination that typically is not reducible to economics—or even economics *and* political life. Rather, when anarchists theorize about other relations of ruling (such as patriarchy, racism, heteronormativity, and so on), they are usually not "subsumed under an analysis that is limited to a critique of the state-capitalist apparatus," but rather are seen as "social dynamics which are generated, reproduced and enacted within *and* outside this apparatus."[16] Anarchists tend to see forms of domination presenting themselves in society without the need to root them in the economy. Although some anarchists would suggest that class is *primary*,[17] most avoid the ranking implied in such statements and the Marxist theory of an economic base serving as the foundation for the rest of existing social relations.[18]

However, as anti-capitalists, anarchists have always been concerned with economics. We participated (and continue to participate) in revolutions and insurrections directed against capitalism and class society. We attempt to embody anti-capitalist values in the ways that we engage with other people and our world more generally. Since anarchists have always been preoccupied with the problem of capitalism and how we might move beyond it into communities of mutual aid and cooperation, it is necessary to start, in an anarchist economics, with that which we oppose in economics—capitalism.

Capitalism and the Anarchist Critique

Anarchism is a diverse set of anti-capitalist ideas and this diversity is reflected in the ways that various anarchists describe and critique capitalism. We will, no doubt, miss some things in this short introduction, but we do think that we can make some broad generalizations that are useful in situating the contents of such a volume. But first, if we may, we would like to offer two general caveats.

First, theory can only go so far in describing existing institutional arrangements and, importantly, the ways that they materialize in daily life. Capitalism is a resilient system, oftentimes changing features in reaction to class struggle as well as its own internal limitations. As opponents of capitalism, then, anarchists have been concerned not just with describing capitalism as it is, but also capitalism as it *may be*. That is, if we want to move beyond capitalism to something altogether different, then we need to understand how capitalism can recuperate struggles that seem at first glance to develop in opposition to it. This means attempting to analyze how capitalism has changed, and might change, in order to satisfy popular demands and still allow for the continuation of capital accumulation despite resistance to the system.

Secondly, it is a truism that social life is complex. We cannot possibly hope for theory to completely describe how a system operates that involves and affects billions of people. And we certainly cannot have those kinds of hopes for a single section in the introduction of a small edited collection. Nonetheless, we might try to describe in broad, general terms the features of the economic system we live under—capitalism—and why anarchists oppose it.

We could begin by simply saying that capitalism is the way the world is currently organized in terms of production, distribution, and consumption. But, again, that would not get at the ways that capitalism was organized historically, nor would it account for the ways that capitalism might reconstitute itself in reaction to attempts to dissolve the social relations that form it. Another approach might be to use a textbook definition. One popular sociology textbook defines capitalism as "a political economy characterized by an arrangement of production in which workers cooperate to produce wealth that is then privately owned by whoever hired the workers."[19] That is certainly descriptive, but misses out on some important nuances (and features that seem generalizable to capitalist society).

Rather, we propose understanding capitalism in terms of some major defining features. This allows one to analyze capitalism contemporarily, historicize aspects of its development, and speculate about its future (if it is to have one at all). It also allows for us to sketch an explanation of capitalism that accounts for debates among anarchists. These features are not meant to be exclusive to capitalism (indeed, some could arguably exist in a different kind of system of production and allocation) nor are they intended to be eternal. As mentioned before, capitalism is a resilient system and is capable of changing to accommodate the pressures of class struggle. These descriptive features also allow for illustrating anarchist *criticisms* of capitalism. With this in mind, we suggest understanding capitalism in terms of wage labor/exploitation, private property, markets, class society, and states.

Wage labor/exploitation is one of the basic constituent parts of capitalism. In order to access the social product, workers must rent themselves out for a wage. The value produced under capitalism by workers, minus whatever wage the capitalist pays, is then appropriated by the capitalist in the form of surplus value—this process is exploitation. Some anarchists refer to this set of relationships as "wage slavery" to point out a historical continuity between *owning* another person and what is, essentially, *renting* another person. Bakunin, in his famous analysis of capitalism, put it thusly:

> And once the contract has been negotiated, the serfdom of the workers is doubly increased; or to put it better, before the contract has been negotiated, goaded by hunger, he [*sic*] is only potentially a serf; after it is negotiated he becomes a serf in fact. Because what merchandise has he sold to his employer? It is his labor, his personal services, the productive forces of his body, mind, and spirit that are found in him and are inseparable from his person—it is therefore himself. From then on, the employer will watch over him, either directly or by means of overseers; everyday during working hours and under controlled conditions,

the employer will be the owner of his actions and movements. When he is told: "Do this," the worker is obligated to do it; or he is told: "Go there," he must go. Is this not what is called a serf?[20]

Not only do anarchists oppose wage labor and exploitation on the grounds that they are unfair, but these things are also against the material interests of working people and create a social relation of domination between the boss and the worker (which Bakunin so eloquently describes above). Indeed, many anarchists argue that the wage labor relation is *the* defining aspect of capitalism. One cannot be an anarchist in any coherent sense and advocate for wage relations and economic exploitation.

This social relation (exploitation) is made possible by private property. To be clear, anarchists make a distinction between *possessions* and private *property*. Possessions are personal items based on current occupancy or use (i.e., no anarchist advocates taking your home or your toothbrush). But private property allows for exploitation through ownership without *use*. Just as capitalists exploit workers through wage labor, so too do capitalists exploit workers through landlordism, claiming ownership of homes they do not live in and charging people for their occupancy. Likewise, capitalists do not *use* the means of producing goods, services, and so on in our society—workers do. Yet in a system of private ownership, capitalists reap the benefits of things that are *socially* produced by the rest of us. This is what led Proudhon to the now-famous statement, "Property is theft!"—arguing this declaration was just as logical as the belief that slavery is murder.[21] That is, *their property is essentially our loss.*

Another element of capitalist society as we know it is market relations. Generally, and likely because in dominant narratives Marxian economics are juxtaposed with capitalist models, we are told that for allocation we have a choice between central planning and markets. Anarchists, however, have typically called for some form of *decentralized* planning. To further complicate matters, under capitalism we have market allocation, but there are some anarchists who have suggested that we might have anti-capitalist, socialist markets.[22] This was the theory proposed by Proudhon—a market socialism in which self-managed worker-owned firms would compete in a market regulated by an "agro-industrial federation."[23]

Most anarchists, however, reject market-oriented visions, with some even suggesting that markets themselves are part and parcel of capitalist society. Jarach, for example, points out that there has been "a nearly total absence of Proudhon's economic ideas among anarchists for the last 150 years."[24] Bowman, in his treatment of communism, refers to Proudhonian visionary arguments as a form of "capitalism without capitalists" due to its retention of some fundamental aspects of capitalism.[25] This collection generally reflects those trends, treating markets (however deformed by the state) as a crucial part of capitalist society. And while many pieces take note of market-oriented anarchist visions of post-capitalist society, most are critical of those kinds of arguments.

Anarchists point out that these economic arrangements lead to the development of class society. While we are often told we are all equals under the law or that we all have equal power through voting, anarchists point out that these claims (which serve to justify and naturalize capitalist society) are absurd. Rather, we do not live in a society of equals. We live in a society of *classes*—with different material interests. The ruling class in capitalist society has an interest in maintaining capitalism while the rest of us have an interest in smashing capitalism and taking what rightfully belongs to us—everything.

Rather than a fetishized version of the worker as a (usually white and male) industrial (factory) worker and the capitalist as a (also usually white and male) factory owner (complete with a top hat), McKay explains anarchist class analysis by defining these two classes thusly:

Working class—those who have to work for a living but have no real control over that work or other major decisions that affect them, i.e. order-takers. This class also includes the unemployed, pensioners, etc., who have to survive on handouts from the state. They have little wealth and little (official) power. This class includes the growing service worker sector, most (if not the vast majority) of "white collar" workers as well as traditional "blue collar" workers. Most self-employed people would be included in this class, as would the bulk of peasants and artisans (where applicable). In a nutshell, the producing classes and those who either were producers or will be producers [editor's note: this would, then, include most students as well as those who engage in reproductive labor, such as child-rearing, housekeeping, etc.]. This group makes up the vast majority of the population.

Ruling Class—those who control investment decisions, determine high level policy, set the agenda for capital and state. This is the elite at the top, owners or top managers of large companies, multinationals and banks (i.e. the capitalists), owners of large amounts of land (i.e. landlords or the aristocracy, if applicable), top-level state officials, politicians, and so forth. They have real power within the economy and/or state, and so control society. In a nutshell, the owners of power (whether political, social or economic) or the master class. This group consists of around the top 5–15% of the population.[26]

It should be noted, however, that anarchist class analysis allows for some degree of "fuzziness." That is, not everyone fits neatly into these broad categories (though, we would argue, most people do). It should also be noted that some radicals, anarchists included, argue for the existence of a third class. Some refer to this as "the middle class," "the coordinator class," "the techno-managerial class," and so on. This is typically used to highlight the existence of people with a high degree of social power—often directly over working people—such as high-paid lawyers, tenured professors at elite institutions, and so on. This class is sometimes conceived as having their own sets of material interests, in opposition to the ruling class and the working class, and sometimes conceived as having similar interests as workers, but being placed above them in capitalist society due to their social power. Most anarchists, however, reject this view, arguing for a traditional two-class analysis.

We might juxtapose this anarchist class analysis with sociological analyses of class that often split society into a lower (or "under") class, working class, lower middle class, upper middle class, and upper class. Anarchists argue that there might be cultural differences to account for between better off members of the working class and those less well off, and at times differences in terms of their identification with the present society. However, we should recognize a unified (if not always united) working class as a better model for looking at the potential for rupture with capitalist society and where that rupture might come from.

Finally, anarchists point out that the social relations in capitalist society are protected and maintained by states. As Malatesta pointed out years ago, we are taught that states are "the representative…of the general interest: it is the expression of the rights of all, construed as a limit upon the rights of each" and that states are "moral…endowed with certain attributes of reason, justice."[27] Anarchists point out that actually the state protects property relations, allowing for the existence of private property (again, without occupancy and use). Without a police force and property laws to threaten (and use) force for rents and wage labor, what would stop us from just taking our homes, our workplaces, and our communities? Note, for example, the ways the police are used to attack people even in so-called "public" places during the existence of the various "Occupy" sites. Similarly, when was the last time the police were used to break up a strike by beating up the boss and carting *him* off to jail? Yet there is a history of the police repression of labor—indeed, of many individuals or groups attempting to take back and determine their own lives.

This is the *economic* function of the state—to protect private property and the accumulation of capital. Also, this is one reason why anarchists reject the Leninist suggestion that we seize the state (or in some interpretations, smash the existing state and create a new "workers' state"—complete with a vanguard party to run it). Its very existence implies a classed society. Anarchists argue that the state will not wither away of its own accord after a tumultuous period while it is controlled by benevolent leftists. Rather, we must rid ourselves of the state, not use it to attempt to further our own ends. It is one reason why anarchists advocate for direct action (rather than electoralism or participation in governance).

It should be noted that the state serves many more purposes beyond its economic functions protecting capital and capitalists, although it would require a book-length work to outline these functions. The state also draws boundaries around the public and private spheres, it forces identity categories on us from above, and it controls ever more aspects of social life well beyond simple economic relations (thus the need for an analysis that recognizes forms of domination related to, but not reducible to, class, capitalism, and economics). Anarchists might analyze it as an institution, as a set of social relations, or as some combination of those things (and anarchists *have* in the past advanced those sorts of analyses of the state), but for the purposes of attempting to abstract "economics" from other spheres of life, the state's function as a protector of capitalism and a recuperator of struggles (particularly as struggles get opportunistically channeled into electoral politics) is particularly salient.

Beyond these institutional features, other features of modern capitalism exist that we have declined to comment on. We want to encourage the reader, however, to consider the role of currency and money in capitalism. Further, it is questionable if modern capitalism could exist without debt, as Graeber skillfully points out (and in the process, he smashes many myths associated with capitalist economists).[28] One also might investigate pricing mechanisms and value as vital pieces of capitalism (some libertarian communists argue, for example, that destroying capitalism means likewise dispensing with the value form). However, due to spatial constraints, we limit our institutional analysis to the above features.

Anarchists also point out (the somewhat obvious fact) that part of how capitalism reproduces itself is through the participation of people in those social relations. That is, anarchists can often be found advocating for mass refusals and the withdrawal of our participation—sometimes in the form of general strikes; sometimes, as in the case of the illegalists, in the form of direct expropriations—with the support and participation of social movements or not; sometimes in the form of occupations and the taking of space; and still other times in advocating for creating alternatives to capitalist relations in the here and now; and so on. But the advocacy of these kinds of practices does lead to the question: If it is in our interests to abolish capitalism, why (and how) is capitalism continually reproduced in our social lives and why do we not destroy those social relations and begin writing a new future today?

Some of the possible answers to that question are contained within popular understandings of economics (which also might explain why anarchists are often loath to refer to our analyses as "economics" or our proposed alternatives as "economies"). Capitalism is justified by ideological assumptions about "human nature," what is "pragmatic," and just how wonderful and benevolent democracy can be. Given that mass media are largely owned and operated by wealthy corporations, our popular forms of entertainment are most often commodities produced under (and by) capital, our compulsory educational systems are run by the state, and so on, it might not be a surprise just how popular those kinds of ideological assumptions are and how infrequent critical thought enters into human relations (anarchists can also often be included in that).

For example, capitalism is often justified by a belief that it is "human nature" to be greedy, to want to accumulate wealth at the expense of others, to desire power over other people, and the like. Yet the vast majority of human social relations were spent in hunter-gatherer societies without any concept of private property, in collectivities that based their lives on personal possessions and forms of common, social resources (nothing that could properly be called *property*). Given that long history, how could it be "human nature" to want to dominate, to own, to compete for resources? Did we collectively just act against our natural wiring for the vast majority of our existence? The argument barely makes any sense, yet such ideas of "human nature" are common among people the world over. This is part of what prompted Emma Goldman to declare, "Poor human nature, what horrible crimes have been committed in thy name! Every fool, from king to policeman, from the flatheaded parson to the visionless dabbler in science, presumes to speak authoritatively of human nature. The greater the mental charlatan, the more definite his [*sic*] insistence on the wickedness and weaknesses of human nature. Yet, how can anyone speak of it today, with every soul in a prison, with every heart fettered, wounded, and maimed?"[29] Her larger point was that those things that we refer to as "human nature" are little more than our projections of our dominant institutions into our very *selves*. Thus, capitalism is not some naturally occurring system. It is a system that is constructed and one that can be dispensed with.

Similarly, economists often object to anarchist alternatives to capitalism as utopian (in the pejorative sense of the term) or not being pragmatic. They argue instead that alternatives to capitalism would never "work" (another word that requires some unpacking, which we will forego in this introduction). First, this ignores the vast majority of human social organization, which presumably "worked" (that is, we are still here and people sometimes struggled in the past, but other times we have surely thrived without capitalism).[30] This also ignores human experiences and experiments outside of capitalist relations that exist within capitalist society[31] or in revolutionary situations.[32] But more egregiously, it assumes that capitalism, even by its own ideological standards, is a system that "works." Given massive poverty, privation, and hunger; the routine destruction of landbases and the despoiling of the natural environment; massive worldwide wars; periodic crises such as the one we are experiencing while we pen this introduction—indeed, given that a tiny elite owns massive amounts of resources (multiple homes, dozens of luxury cars, servants and coteries, and the like) while most of us struggle to survive—can we really say this is a system that "works"?

But we are told that under democracy checks and balances are present in the form of state regulation of the economy that can address some of the failures of capitalism. This is sometimes why people refer to the study of capitalism as "political economy"—because there is no idealized "free market" that exists without state interference. But even a cursory look at recent history should demonstrate how absurd these deeply held beliefs about democracy are. Perhaps the best examples are when leftist governments are voted into power. In much of Europe we have a rather long history of socialist parties legislating regulatory mechanisms into the economy in order to create a kinder and gentler capitalism. And we can see with the current austerity just how lasting those reforms and regulations are (which is to say, not lasting at all—the state can dismantle any reform or regulation it sets in place at any moment. Therefore, we only keep what we take and defend). Further, as anarchists, we argue that a gentler form of exploitation is not enough. We want to run our lives and actively create and participate in our social relations without the kinds of restraints placed on us by hierarchical authority and power—in the context of the economy, identity, culture, our conceptual order, indeed *all* facets of social life.

Part of the danger of this particular ideological underpinning of capitalism is the creation of militant liberal alternatives that aim for much less than total social transformation. Militant reformism can serve as a recuperative mechanism to radical social mo(ve)ments, defanging possible transformations by functioning as the leftwing of capital. Thus the institutionalized Left historically (and contemporarily) is something that anarchists should be wary of if we wish different worlds instead of reformed versions of the existing order.

The preceding institutional analysis of capitalism was intended to describe the existing society, as well as give some insights into possible forms that a future capitalism might take. The analyses of the ideological assumptions in place to justify and naturalize capitalism are intended to destabilize the mythologies surrounding those institutional arrangements. Anarchists have, however, offered possible alternatives to capitalism in varying degrees of detail. These alternatives tend to be bound up with specific strategic and theoretical assumptions as well. Next we will look at some of these anarchist proposals, also noting anarchists' frequent reticence to advance visionary arguments in too much detail.

Anarchist Economics

As we said before, a distinctly *anarchist* economics is going to have some unique features of its own, and we have organized this anthology to reflect that. Firstly, anarchism has some interesting tensions in terms of post-capitalist vision. Secondly, as a largely *prefigurative* practice, a part of anarchist economic analysis must include investigations into current practices that might contain anarchic elements that could contain seeds of a future, post-capitalist economy (while, of course, also noting their limitations). It also means that we need ways to evaluate the resistance strategies we use to create ruptures in capitalism and to recognize the spaces in everyday life in which capitalism is *not* present. Finally, since anarchism is a holistic movement seeking to reconfigure the totality of social relations and not limited to the economy, our analyses of current practices need to include investigations into the affective and embodied experience of these practices. We begin with a look at the different proposals advanced by anarchists for a future society (and the processes used to create such a society).

To begin discussing the differences between the three main post-capitalist anarchist theories—mutualism, collectivism, and communism—we should first take note of a few things. First, as mentioned above, most anarchists reject mutualism outright contemporarily. While it played a historic role in laying the foundations of anarchist economics (as McKay eloquently lays out in his chapter), it has little impact on the existing milieu beyond those foundations (although one will occasionally find adherents to this market philosophy at various bookfairs and anarchist gatherings or, more often, on open anarchist Internet forums—and they *do* seem to be gaining steam as more and more people lose faith in capitalism). Beyond that, many anarchists are suspicious of visionary arguments and blueprints for the future, seeing anarchism as a conscious creation of the dispossessed and not a future that can be written within the context of the present. As Emma Goldman put it:

Anarchism is not, as some may suppose, a theory of the future to be realized through divine inspiration. It is a living force in the affairs of our life, constantly creating new conditions. The methods of Anarchism therefore do not comprise an iron-clad program to be carried out under all circumstances. Methods must grow out of the economic needs of each place and clime, and of the intellectual and temperamental requirements of the individual.[33]

Following this, some anarchists would eschew labels and "hyphenations" like "anarchist-communism," preferring to refer to their preference simply as "anarchy," or at times not refer to a preference at all.

There is also a strong tradition of revolutionary pluralism in anarchism. In the past, some anarchists would advocate for an "anarchism without adjectives," perhaps most famously advanced by thinkers such as Voltairine de Cleyre, to indicate a tolerance for many visionary (and strategic) differences. Similarly, there have been (and are) anarchists who advocate for specific proposals, but see a need for a deep humility and commitment to pluralism in terms of vision. One of the best examples of this can be found in the Italian anarchist Errico Malatesta, who advocated for anarchist-communism, yet stated:

One may, therefore, prefer communism, or individualism, or collectivism, or any other system, and work by example and propaganda for the achievement of one's personal preferences, but one must beware, at the risk of certain disaster, of supposing that one's system is the only, and infallible, one, good for all men [sic], everywhere and for all times, and that its success must be assured at all costs, by means other than those which depend on persuasion, which spring from the evidence of facts.[34]

Undoubtedly, this is also reflective of anarchist suspicion of visionary arguments and blueprints for a future society.

Finally, it should also be noted that the borders that we draw around these different visionary proposals are points of contention and debate. What we call "collectivism" here might be called a transitional phase for anarchist-communism by others. Still others argue for a minimalist definition of libertarian communism that would include things like some form of remuneration for labor time, onerousness of tasks, and the like—which contemporary anarchist-communists typically reject (but past anarchist-communists have, at times, advocated for). Yet we argue that contemporarily these categories have crystallized to have certain meanings among anarchists. Our attempt at defining them, then, is itself a heavily politicized project and we want to acknowledge that. Undoubtedly we will ruffle some feathers in the process, but the purpose here is to give some broad sketches and not have the final word on how these terms were defined historically or how they are commonly used today. Indeed, we hope that these defining strategies can serve as jumping off points for needed debates about the usage and meaning of these categories. This is also why these sketches are brief—an entire book could be written about each tendency. And we have no intention of doing that here, so some paragraphs on each tendency will have to suffice for the purposes of this collection.

Mutualism

As we mentioned before, Proudhon was an advocate of a form of market socialism called mutualism. Mutualism was an anti-capitalist model that saw mutual banks and credit associations as a way to socialize productive property and allow for a form of dual power for workers, particularly through the use of low-interest loans, charging only the necessary interest to pay for administration. Thus, Proudhon argued for mutualism not only as a post-capitalist vision, but also as a strategic orientation stressing the need to build alternative economic relationships in the here and now that would eventually replace capitalism. While mutualism is not typically advocated by anarchists anymore, we still owe much of our development of economics to Proudhon (ironically enough, Marxists also owe this debt to Proudhon). Nevertheless, it should be acknowledged that there are still some advocates of mutualism.

As Proudhon sketched it out, wage labor and landlordism would be abolished in a mutualist society. Rather, ownership would be based on occupancy and use. Therefore, all workers would have access to their own means of production—most organizing into cooperative, non-hierarchical firms. These self-managed firms would compete in a free market, regulated by a grand agro-industrial federation. Many mutualists have argued that these firms would function in ways similar to worker cooperatives contemporarily, but without some of the pressures of operating in the context of a capitalist and statist society. Further, rather than capitalists expropriating surplus value from workers, workers would keep or trade those products that they produce.

This would mean that distribution in a mutualist society would be "by work done, by *deed* rather than need. Workers would receive the full product of their labour, after paying for inputs from other co-operatives."[35] This is an important distinction, particularly as anarchists who advocate for communism argue for forms of distribution by *need* and parts of the debates over anarchist visionary arguments are centered on the distribution of the things that we produce. This also means that in a mutualist society, exchange relations would continue to exist, with self-managed firms exchanging goods and services in a market. For this reason, some anarchists—particularly communists—argue that mutualism would actually just be a self-managed form of capitalism, as it retains so many elements of capitalism (exchange relations, markets, and so on).

Some modern descendants of mutualism are Kevin Carson, Shawn Wilbur, some folks at the Alliance of the Libertarian Left or Center for a Stateless Society.[36] Many of these modern mutualists have altered features of Proudhon's arguments in key ways, influenced by the American individualists like Benjamin Tucker and Josiah Warren. Some of the aforementioned groups see anti-statists working together across broad economic spectrums—some of whom are socialist, others who advocate for forms of capitalism and could not therefore properly be called "anarchists" (if the term, which is admittedly broad and sometimes messy, is to have any consistent meaning at all). Thus, for example, lining the top of the web page for the Alliance of the Libertarian Left can be seen pictures of mutualists like Proudhon side by side with self-avowed capitalists like Murray Rothbard. Nevertheless, it is within these modern descendants where we see the ghost of Proudhon and echoes of his mutualist anarchism.

Collectivism

Collectivism is most often associated with Bakunin, who referred to himself as a "collectivist" to distinguish his theory from state-communists. While mutualism was a reformist and gradualist strategy that would try to *overgrow* capitalism over a long period of time, Bakunin saw a need for a revolutionary rupture with capitalism. Therefore, Bakunin argued for a revolutionary movement that would expropriate property, socializing it.

Collectivism, then, begins with the assumption of social ownership of productive property, like mutualism. The product of labor, however, would be gathered into a communal market. Bakunin's friend, Guillaume, when outlining Bakunin's vision called for a society where "items...produced by collective labor will belong to the community. And each member will receive remuneration for his [sic] labor either in the form of commodities...or in currency. In some communities remuneration will be in proportion to hours worked; in others payment will be measured by both the hours of work and the kind of work performed; still other systems will be experimented with to see how they work out."[37] Where communities used currency, it would be used to purchase items from the collective market.

And yet Dolgoff said of Guillaume that he "saw no difference in principle between collectivism and anti-state communism. The collectivists understood that full communism would not be immediately realizable. They were convinced that the workers themselves would gradually introduce communism as they overcame the obstacles, both psychological and economic."[38] Thus, in this way, the idea of remuneration was not seen as an end in Bakunin's collectivism, but rather a transitional phase into a system of "full communism," presumably where norms of remuneration would be done away with.

But it is not clear that Bakunin saw himself as anything other than a communist anarchist, which makes part of this project of definitions and categorization both difficult and, as we said, heavily politicized. Guillaume writes that "the term 'collectivists' designated the partisans of collective property" in the First International and that "(t)hose who advocated ownership of collective property by the state were called 'state' or 'authoritarian communists.'...To distinguish themselves from the authoritarians and avoid confusion, the anti-authoritarians called themselves 'collectivists'."[39] Nevertheless, the term "collectivism" is still widely in use among anarchists, who often distinguish between collectivism and communist anarchism on the basis of debates over remuneration and distribution.

Contemporarily, like mutualism, there are few anarchists who advocate for collectivism, as such. But echoes of some of these concerns over remuneration can be seen as some anarchists advocate for participatory economics (or "parecon"), a non-market libertarian socialism developed by Michael Albert and Robin Hahnel and also advocated by Chris

Spannos.[40] Indeed, Albert writes in his afterward for this anthology that "citizens should have a claim on society's economic product that increases if they do socially valued work longer or more intensely or under worse conditions." This is where we might see the descendants of collectivism in some ways. However, for advocates of parecon, it is typically not seen as a transitional phase into a full communism of free consumption, but an end unto itself, which differentiates it from Bakunin's theory. It differs in other key ways as well and curious readers are encouraged to read the many books on participatory economics that outline its theory.

Communist Anarchism

Communist forms of anarchism are the dominant tendency among anarchists (for those who identify with a particular economic tendency). Strategically, communist anarchists (sometimes referred to as anarcho-communists, anarchist-communists, or libertarian communists—with each of those terms connoting some strategic and theoretical differences) typically see a need for a revolutionary break with capitalism. Some envision, like Bakunin, this being a series of grand revolutionary events enacted by an organized working class. Others, however, see anarchism and communism more as processes than end goals, and often advocate for insurrectionary moments that would, perhaps, coalesce into revolutions.

Libertarian communists advocate for the social ownership of productive property and distribution on the basis of need or, perhaps better stated, an end to ownership and property relations altogether (i.e. the abolition of property). This anarchist communism argues for economic visions organized around the principle "from each according to ability, to each according to need," though the details of how to realize this objective are certainly debatable. Added to this, "communism" is also a contested term with a variety of meanings, both historically and contemporarily. This makes for a category that is difficult to pin down with simple definitions, but much of the early communist anarchist theory was written in reaction to the collectivist wages system.

Communist anarchists typically argue against any form of currency or remuneration. In Kropotkin's view, this was a wrong-headed idea from the start and one that could possibly lead to the redevelopment of capitalism:

In fact, in a society like ours, in which the more a man [*sic*] works the less he is remunerated, this principle, at first sight, may appear to be a yearning for justice. But it is really only the perpetuation of past injustice. It was by virtue of this principle that wagedom began, to end in the glaring inequalities and all the abominations of present society; because, from the moment work done was appraised in currency or in any other form of wage; the day it was agreed upon that man would only receive the wage he could secure to himself, the whole history of State-aided Capitalist Society was as good as written; it germinated in this principle.[41]

Kropotkin's view presented one way forward for a post-revolutionary society that has "taken possession of all social wealth, having boldly proclaimed the right of all to this wealth—whatever share they may have taken in producing it will be compelled to abandon any system of wages, whether in currency or labour-notes."[42]

This is important not only in terms of vision, but also inasmuch as it refers to the political *content* produced by anarchists during insurrectionary or revolutionary mo(ve)ments. That is, communist anarchists tended to be process-oriented. So instead of advocating for a revolutionary break, then a new organization of society along communist anarchist lines, Kropotkin suggested that workers, in the context of a revolution, would "demand what they have always demanded in such cases—communization of supplies."[43] Similarly, in Carlo Cafiero's report to the Jura Federation, he described anarchy and communism in immediate terms. For Cafiero, "liberty and equality are the two necessary and indivisible terms of the revolution."[44] Further, and again in the immediate sense, "Anarchy today is the attack, the war upon all authority, all power, every State."[45] Emma Goldman also suggested a process of creating communism that precluded commercial processes:

To make this a reality will, I believe, be possible only in a society based on voluntary co-operation of productive groups, communities and societies loosely federated together, eventually developing into a free communism, actuated by a solidarity of interests. There can be no freedom in the large sense of the word, no harmonious development, so long as mercenary and commercial

considerations play an important part in the determination of
personal conduct.[46]

Kropotkin was particularly adamant about this: "The Revolution will
be communist; if not, it will be drowned in blood, and have to be begun
over again."[47]

These descriptions of vision and process do nothing to talk about
many of the other tensions and disagreements among communist anarchists. There are those who believe that formal anarchist organizations are crucial to social struggle and those who think those kinds
of organizations become ends unto themselves and get in the way of
struggle. Some communist anarchists argue for an egoist anarchism
rooted in personal desire while others argue for a more social- and
collective-oriented approach to theory. There are communist anarchists
who identify with the Left and others who reject it, some who argue for
self-managed workplaces and others who advocate for the abolition of
work. Also, there are many who find themselves in some middle place
in these disputes. Again, this brief introduction is no place to expand
on these debates, but they should be accounted for so as not to leave
the reader with the assumption of the existence of some monolithic
communist anarchism, which, quite obviously, does not exist.

Other Unique Characteristics

Aside from the tensions around vision among anarchist communists,
collectivists, and mutualists, we argue that an anarchist economics is
also unique because of the prefigurative nature of anarchism. That is,
anarchists argue that the ways that we organize in the here and now
should *prefigure* the kind of world we wish to create, inasmuch as that
is possible. This means that a part of anarchist economics is an investigation of current practices that might contain anarchic elements.
Likewise, this means that an anarchist economics would be concerned
with evaluating anarchist resistance strategies as we attempt to create
ruptures in capitalism and eventually abolish it.

Finally, an anarchist economics would also concern itself with
the embodied experiences of people as they engage in these contemporary anarchic economic practices and forms of resistance. This
focus on the affective aspects of production and distribution is perhaps best described by Milstein's reformulation of the communist
maxim, "(f)rom each according to their abilities *and passions*, to each

according to their needs *and desires*."[48] While this is certainly accounted for in Marxist economic analyses of capitalism, particularly
Marx's focus on alienation, for anarchists this means paying close attention to the affective and embodied experiences of people engaged
in non-capitalist economic activity (however limited those activities
might be as they exist in embryonic form *under* capitalism).

The Contents of This Anthology

This anthology represents over three years of collecting and editing
contemporary writing on anarchist economics. We have tried to as-
semble a good cross-section of contemporary anarchist economics in
the form of analyses and critiques of capitalism, pieces on the history
of anarchist economics, contemporary pieces on vision, as well as those
unique aspects of anarchist economics we have outlined above. This
anthology, in those three years, has undergone huge amounts of editing, rewriting, and reformulating into this, its final version.

We have created sections for the book that quite often bleed into
each other. That is, the reader might see elements of critique in our
"analysis" section or elements of resistance in our "practice" section,
and so on. This phenomenon seemed unavoidable when compiling the
book as these elements of economics are often not neatly separated one
from the others. Nonetheless, we ask the reader's understanding that
the process of creating discrete sections for the book was seen by the
editors as both valuable (in order to identify commonalities in pieces),
but at the same time, in many ways, impossible.

We begin with two pieces in our "History" section. First, Chris
Spannos explores the history of anarchist economics to try to broadly
sketch the future. As he mines through anarchist writers and historical
examples, he brings out the principles from these sources by which
he believes a post-capitalist society is best served. Spannos provides
an important contribution in terms of looking into our history and
our present to make a case for a radically different future. Next, Iain
McKay looks specifically at Proudhon's contributions to radical economics. Perhaps one of the most interesting aspects of this piece is
just how much of socialist economic theory originated not with Marx
(as the traditional histories are written), but with Proudhon. McKay
draws out these contributions, as well as some of the visionary and
strategic commitments of Proudhon's *mutualism*.

Our "Analysis" section is opened by Abbey Volcano and Deric Shannon, who contribute a sort of "beginner's guide" to important concepts for understanding capitalism in the 2000s. They take seven elements of contemporary capitalism that anarchist beginners to economics might use to understand how our social system has changed and how we might best analyze it in our contemporary period. Next, Jeff Monaghan and D.T. Cochrane evaluate anarchist resistance strategies to capitalism. They argue that we might make models for evaluating how economic disruption campaigns and sabotage hurt capital—and amend our practice accordingly. In the next piece, Richard J. White and Colin C. Williams argue that capitalism is not the totalizing system that we often paint it as. Reflecting on the rising interest in elements of post-structuralism among anarchists (or "post-anarchism," as some people have come to call these forays into theory), they argue that we should note the places in our society that are non-monetized and that have avoided the alienating aspects inherent in capitalist social relations. Doing so, they create a counter-narrative to what they call the "capitalist hegemony thesis" that sees capitalism as inescapable (and perhaps link up nicely with socialist post-structuralist commitments to an "exodus" from capitalism typified by anarchist theorists like David Graeber and Stevphen Shukaitis, or autonomist Marxists like Antonio Negri and Michael Hardt).

John Asimakopoulos begins our "Critique" section demonstrating that crisis and inequality are inherent in capitalism. As such, he argues that we need mass movements to usher in alternatives to our system rather than attempts at "regulating" a broken institutional framework. Anarchists might use this analysis to illustrate how reforms are illusory and that smashing capital is a necessary requirement for creating a stable and humane social order. Robin Hahnel reformulates a talk he gave at B-fest in Greece in May of 2010, an annual anarchist gathering in Athens, explaining the current economic crisis. He also outlines libertarian socialist responses to the austerity measures imposed on countries like Greece by the European Union. Anarchists who have paid attention to mass responses to these measures in Greece, Spain, France, and beyond will benefit from Hahnel's analysis and recommendations for economic policy in the short term. Finally, William T. Armaline and William D. Armaline focus on educational institutions under contemporary capitalism. This political economic analysis is especially salient now given the militant resistance that has risen in response to tuition increases and funding cuts at universities all over the world—ranging from protests, property defacement and destruction, to the student occupation movements.

As we mentioned, since anarchism is a prefigurative practice, part of what makes an anarchist economics distinctly *anarchist* is a focus on alternatives and resistance enacted in the here and now. Our next two sections speak to this concern, beginning with our "Practice" section. First, Uri Gordon looks at common contemporary anarchist practices. This valuable piece investigates a wide variety of current economic practices of anarchists (and those that might contain *anarchic* elements) with a nonsectarian approach fitting for the diverse anarchist milieu. Secondly, Caroline Kaltefleiter takes a cultural studies approach to investigating everyday resistance strategies in a time of capitalist crisis. She argues that the everyday spaces created by café cultures, community currencies, and street actions provide examples of the spirit of community and mutual aid necessary to demonstrate alternatives to capitalism, while also noting some of the limitations in these practices.

In our "Resistance" section, Marie Trigona begins with a piece on Latin America's occupied factory movement. She argues that these "transnational manufacturing sites could be considered modern-day prisons" in many ways. That begs the question: What might self-management look like in this context? For this, she investigates the experiences of workers within *occupied* factories for a look at how self-management, in this embryonic form, might manifest itself. Next, Ernesto Aguilar writes about the resistance of people of color under global capitalism. Aguilar argues that through the standpoint of people of color, we are best able to analyze contemporary capitalism—and argue for a world organized on the basis of simple dignity. Aguilar's analysis is particularly valuable in that it investigates radical resistance movements by people of color that are not limited to ideological markers such as "anarchism," yet attempts to bridge these diverse experiences within the context of anarchist economics.

Our final section contains three pieces on possibilities for anarchist futures, titled simply "Vision." There has always been a tension around vision for anarchists, some of whom have been willing to broadly sketch what a post-revolutionary society might look like and others who have been critical of such exercises (indeed, some anarchists suggest that the very task of sketching a future might be authoritarian, making arrangements for a people who do not yet exist and without their participation). Nonetheless, these kinds of visionary writings have always accompanied the anarchist project and we include three pieces of contemporary anarchist vision here. First, Deric Shannon outlines a libertarian communist critique of mutualism. He broadly sketches this argument in terms of vision, but also responds to mutualist theory and practice. Next, Scott Nappalos tackles how distribution might work in an anarchist-communist society. Here the reader might see elements of arguments about "collectivism" (as it was expressed by Kropotkin) as Nappalos provides this plan with a critical response to suggestions for differential remuneration. Wayne Price argues for a humility of vision. Price references Malatesta's work, suggesting that a technique of experimentation is best in terms of anarchist vision. Though he certainly advocates for his own positions, he suggests that the anarchist method is not one of dogmatism and final answers, but of experimentation and humility.

We end with an afterward by Michael Albert. Albert is a well-known radical economist who helped develop participatory economics, an anti-authoritarian vision that has influenced many contemporary radicals—some of whom advocate for it, some of whom critique it, and many of whom do a bit of both. Albert argues that anarchists might develop a more detailed post-revolutionary vision, advocating for parecon while also suggesting that we might take a broader view in terms of strategy. He, no doubt, makes some controversial suggestions for practice that can serve as points for reflection and discussion for contemporary anarchists.

The editors of this collection put forward these pieces as discussion documents. That is, we, as editors, do not necessarily *agree* with everything put forward in this collection. However, we think an anthology of this sort, a collection of pieces on anarchist economics (broadly conceived), is long overdue. Furthermore, the kinds of discussions that these pieces can raise are potentially important in continuing to refine anarchist analysis and praxis. With this objective in mind, we give you this collection with the hopes that the contents prove useful in abolishing the existing hierarchical social order and the creation of new, egalitarian social forms that provide sustainable alternatives to the unsustainable and brutal world that we have all inherited.

Endnotes

1   Thanks are due to Nate Hawthorne, Gayge Operaista, and Zach Blue for helpful comments on this introduction.

2   One recent Rasmussen poll found that only 53 percent of Americans favor capitalism over socialism, down from just a year and a half before when 70 percent favored capitalism. While leaving the terms "capitalism" and "socialism" undefined is problematic for such a survey, particularly in an age of Glenn Beck style red-baiting, this loss of faith in capitalist fundamentalism in Americans tells us that a good portion of the population just might be open to alternatives—provided we are willing to broadly sketch them out. See Rasmussen, "Just 53% Say Capitalism Better Than Socialism," http://www.rasmussenreports.com/public_content/politics/general_politics/april_2009/just_53_say_capitalism_better_than_socialism (accessed October 10, 2010).

3   Jill Treanor, "World's Wealthiest People Now Richer Than Before the Credit Crunch," *The Guardian*, http://www.guardian.co.uk/business/2011/jun/22/worlds-wealthiest-people-now-richer-than-before-the-credit-crunch/print   (accessed September 2, 2011).

4   Eileen AJ Connelly, "Paul Volcker: Economic Crisis May Be Worse Than Great Depression," *Huffington Post*, http://www.huffingtonpost.com/2009/02/20/paul-volcker-financial-cr_n_168772.html (accessed October 10, 2010).

5   Rudolf Rocker, *Anarcho-Syndicalism: Theory and Practice* (Oakland: AK Press, 2004, Orig. 1938), 11.

6   See, e.g., Alfredo Bonanno, "Let's Destroy Work, Let's Destroy the Economy," The Anarchist Library, http://theanarchistlibrary.org/HTML/Alfredo_M._Bonanno__Let_s_Destroy_Work__Let_s_Destroy_the_Economy.html (accessed September 4, 2011).

7   See, e.g., Bob Black, "The Abolition of Work," The Anarchist Library, http://theanarchistlibrary.org/HTML/Bob_Black__The_Abolition_of_Work.html (accessed September 4, 2011).

8   Pierre-Joseph Proudhon, *What is Property?* (New York: Cambridge University Press, 1994, Orig. 1840).

9   See especially Mikhail Bakunin, "The Capitalist System," Anarchy Archives, http://dwardmac.pitzer.edu/anarchist_archives/bakunin/capstate.html (accessed September 4, 2011).

10 See especially Peter Kropotkin, *The Conquest of Bread* (Oakland: AK Press, 2008, Orig. 1892).

11 Diego Abad De Santillán, "After the Revolution," LibCom.org, http://libcom.org/book/export/html/33181 (accessed September 4, 2011).

12   For a good contemporary example, see Staughton Lynd and Andrej Grubacic, *Wobblies and Zapatistas: Conversations on Anarchism, Marxism, and Radical History*, (Oakland: PM Press, 2008).

13   Anarcho, "'Synthesised' Marxism and Anarchism? My Arse!," Anarchist Writers, http://anarchism.pageabode.com/anarcho/synthesised-marxism-and-anarchism-my-arse (accessed September 4, 2011).

14   In some cases this might also indicate being influenced by anarchist ideas, but not necessarily identifying *as* an anarchist for one reason or another.

15   Karl Marx, *A Contribution to the Critique of Political Economy* (Moscow: Progress Publishers, 1977, Orig. 1859), preface.

16   Uri Gordon, *Anarchism and Political Theory: Contemporary Problems*, The Anarchist Library, http://theanarchistlibrary.org/HTML/Uri_Gordon__Anarchism_and_Political_Theory__Contemporary_Problems.html (accessed September 4, 2011).

17   Lucien Van Der Walt and Michael Schmidt, *Black Flame: The Revolutionary Class Politics of Anarchism and Syndicalism* (Oakland: AK Press, 2009).

18   It should be noted that many Marxists reject this deterministic view as well, though this certainly is not the place for developing yet another interpretation of Marx's work.

19   Kenneth J. Neubeck and Davita Silfen Glasberg, *Sociology: Diversity, Conflict, and Change* (Boston: McGraw-Hill, 2005).

20   Bakunin, "The Capitalist System."

21   Iain McKay, ed., *Property is Theft: A Pierre-Joseph Proudhon Reader* (Oakland: AK Press, 2011).

22   See, e.g., http://mutualist.org/, for some modern examples of mutualist theory.

23   Ibid.

24   Lawrence Jarach, "Proudhon's Ghost: Petit-Bourgeois Anarchism, Anarchist Businesses, and the Politics of Effectiveness," http://theanarchistlibrary.org/HTML/Lawrence_Jarach_Proudhon_s_Ghost__petit-bourgeois_anarchism__anarchist_businesses__and_the_politics_of_effectiveness.html (accessed September 11, 2011).

25   Paul Bowman, "What is Communism?," http://www.anarkismo.net/newswire.php?story_id=1555 (accessed September 11, 2011).

26   Iain McKay, *An Anarchist FAQ: Volume 1* (Oakland: AK Press 2008), 185.

27   Errico Malatesta, "Anarchy," in *No Gods No Masters: An Anthology of Anarchism*, ed. Daniel Guérin (Oakland: AK Press, 2005), 356.

28   See David Graeber, *Debt: The First 5,000 Years* (Brooklyn: Melville House Publishing 2011).

29   Emma Goldman, "Anarchism: What it Really Stands For," http://sunsite.berkeley.edu/goldman/Writings/Anarchism/anarchism.html (accessed September 11, 2011).

30 For one interesting anthropological look at this question, see Marshall Sahlins, "The Original Affluent Society," http://www.eco-action.org/dt/affluent.html (accessed September 11, 2011).

31 See, e.g., Colin Ward, *Anarchy in Action* (London: Freedom Press 2001, Orig. 1973) and Peter Gelderloos, *Anarchy Works* (Berkeley: Ardent Press 2010).

32 See especially Santillán, "After the Revolution."

33 Emma Goldman, "Anarchism: What it Really Stands For," http://sunsite.berkeley. edu/goldman/Writings/Anarchism/anarchism.html (accessed October 5, 2011).

34 Errico Malatesta, *Errico Malatesta: His Life and Ideas*, Vernon Richards, ed., (London: Freedom Press 1984), 28-29. Quoted from Wayne Price, "Malatesta's Anarchist Vision of Life After Capitalism," http://theanarchistlibrary.org/HTML/ Wayne_Price__Malatesta_s_Anarchist_Vision_of_Life_After_Capitalism.html (accessed October 21, 2011).

35 Anarcho, "The Economics of Anarchy," http://anarchism.pageabode.com/anarcho/the-economics-of-anarchy (accessed October 21, 2011).

36 See, e.g., http://mutualist.blogspot.com/, http://libertarian-labyrinth.blogspot. com/, http://c4ss.org/, http://all-left.net/.

37 James Guillaume, "1876: On Building the New Social Order," in *Bakunin on Anarchy*, Sam Dolgoff, ed., (New York: Alfred A. Knopf, Inc., 1971), 361.

38 Sam Dolgoff, ed., *Bakunin on Anarchy* (New York: Alfred A. Knopf, Inc. 1971), 159.

39 Ibid., 158.

40 See, e.g., Michael Albert and Robin Hahnel, *Looking Forward: Participatory Economics for the Twenty First Century* (New York: South End Press, 1991); and Chris Spannos, ed., *Real Utopia: Participatory Society for the 21st Century* (Oakland: AK Press, 2008).

41 Kropotkin, *Conquest*, 195.

42 Ibid., 194–195.

43 Ibid., 102.

44 Carlo Cafiero, "Anarchy and Communism," in *Guérin, No Gods*, 293.

45 Ibid.

46 Emma Goldman, "What I Believe," http://dwardmac.pitzer.edu/Anarchist_ Archives/goldman/whatibelieve.html (accessed October 21, 2011).

47 Kropotkin, *Conquest*, 195.

48 Cindy Milstein, *Anarchism and its Aspirations* (Oakland: AK Press 2010), 53.

History

"Not whether we accomplish anarchism today, tomorrow, or within ten centuries, but that we walk towards anarchism today, tomorrow, and always."—Errico Malatesta

Examining the History of Anarchist Economics to See the Future

Chris Spannos

Situating "Anarchist Economics"

Beyond economy, an anarchist society should provide new socialization of children and future generations, stateless and self-governing adjudication and law-making, and cultural and ethnic diversity and equality—all based on mutual aid and participatory self-management in all spheres of life. But here, considering only the history of anarchist economics, imagine scenarios where the 1871 Paris Commune had not come to a tortured end; the Factory Committees and Soviets of the Russian Revolution had not fallen under Bolshevik control (1917–1921); the 1936-1939 Spanish anarchists had not been abandoned by the West, betrayed by the Stalinists, and shattered by the Fascists; the 1956 worker uprisings and council formations in Hungary and Poland had blossomed; the May 1968 uprising in France had carried forward its objectives rather than dissipating back into the normalcy of everyday life; that this century's worker takeovers in Argentina spread and continue marching forward; or that today's anti-authoritarian uprisings in North Africa and the Middle East continue to spread inspiration—beyond the mass occupations and general assemblies arriving in Europe and North America in 2011—and all win the day. What institutions should be employed to best realize the social and material objectives of a new anarchist economy?

Russian anarchist Pyotr Kropotkin (1842–1921) wrote his theory of mutual aid (1890–1896)[1] as a scientific endeavor combining observation, hypothesis, testing, and theorizing into a theory of evolution that had implications for how social and material relations should be ethically reorganized for a new society that he called anarcho-communism. Nowadays, fearing sectarian excess or mistakes, some doubt the value of vision such as he sought, but in the words of Italian anarchist Errico Malatesta (1853–1932), "Anarchy may be a perfect form of social life" but "we have no desire to take a leap in the dark." Malatesta suggested that people "meet, discuss, agree and differ, and then divide according to their various opinions, putting into practice the methods which they respectively hold to be the best," so that "that method, which when tried, produces the best results, will triumph in the end."[2]

So What Is an Economy and Why Do We Need One?

Consider any aspect of our material lives: our homes, workplaces, hospitals, or schools. Or consider the materials needed for leisure activities, making music, or playing any sport. All require complex interactions. Inputs combine into outputs. Wood, stone, and brick become homes. Tools craft guitars and baseball bats. Community gardens require shovels and rakes, which must be produced somewhere, with most of their inputs coming from yet another place and, after being assembled, require shipping and transportation before seeing use. An economy is needed for production, consumption, and allocation of the material means of life to serve both simple and complex human needs.

Any economy has a small set of defining institutions that, taken together, determine its broad character. For example, despite the possibility of great variation, a capitalist or "socialist" economy will have common attributes with others of like type such as property relations, divisions of labor, remuneration schemes, and allocation mechanisms. Specifically, capitalism has private ownership of productive assets, hierarchical divisions of labor, remuneration for property, output, or bargaining power, and markets for allocation. State socialist economies of the twentieth Century included state or public ownership of productive assets, hierarchical divisions of labor, remuneration for output or bargaining power, and central planning or markets for allocation. Referencing past anarchist and libertarian criticisms of capitalist and state socialist economic institutions as well as their positive proposals for reorganizing material life can help us formulate our own ideas.

Property Relations

Anarchists have traditionally rejected inequalities in power and privilege arising from private ownership of the means of production. For Russian anarchist Mikhail Bakunin (1814–1876), property meant that not only did those who owned productive assets have the right to live without working, but "since neither property nor capital produces anything when not fertilized by labor" the owners also had the power "to live by exploiting the work of ... those who possess neither property nor capital" and so were forced to sell their productive power to the "lucky owners of both."[3]

Writing in 1911 anarchist Emma Goldman (1869–1949) saw that property had "robbed" humanity of its "birthright," and turned the worker into a "pauper and outcast." Goldman wrote that the "student of economics knows that the productivity of labor within the last few decades far exceeds normal demand." "But," she asked of private property, "what are normal demands to an abnormal institution?"[4] In the twenty-first century, labor and technology produce much more than Goldman could probably have ever imagined and certainly far beyond the productive levels during the time of her writing. Yet workers are still cast out and even pauperized while outputs remain outside the control of producers themselves. One of the earliest self-proclaimed anarchists, Pierre-Joseph Proudhon (1809–1865) wrote *What Is Property? An Inquiry into the Principle of Right and of Government* in 1840 in which he queried:

> If I were asked to answer the following question: What is slavery? and I should answer in one word, It is murder, my meaning would be understood at once. No extended argument would be required to show that the power to take from a man his thought, his will, his personality, is a power of life and death; and that to enslave a man is to kill him. Why, then, to this other question: What is property! May I not likewise answer, It is robbery, without the certainty of being misunderstood; the second proposition being no other than a transformation of the first?[5]

Leaping from theory to practice for a two-month period between March and May 1871, the Paris Communards sought to consciously implement the practice of abolition of private property and attempted the administration of society for themselves and by themselves. As Karl Marx (1818–1883) expounded in his 1871 "The Civil War in France":

> The Commune, they exclaim, intends to abolish property, the basis of all civilization! Yes, gentlemen, the Commune intended to abolish that class property which makes the labor of the

many the wealth of the few. It aimed at the expropriation of the expropriators.[6]

Though Versailles troops ended the Paris Commune in a bloody massacre, the ideals inspired by abolition of privately owned productive property lived on. The son of a French Communard, anarcho-syndicalist Gaston Leval (1895-1978) became a militant fighter in the Spanish Civil War (1936-1939) and in his *Collectives in Spain* (1938) he described agrarian socialization and the orientation towards property during the formation of the Aragonese collectives:

> One of the first steps was to gather in the crop not only in the fields of the small landowners who still remained, but, what was even more important, also on the estates of the large landowners all of whom were conservatives and rural "caciques" or chiefs. Groups were organized to reap and thresh the wheat which belonged to these large landowners. Collective work began spontaneously. Then, as this wheat could not be given to anyone in particular without being unfair to all, it was put under the control of a local committee, for the use of all the inhabitants, either for consumption or for the purpose of exchange for manufactured goods, such as clothes, boots, etc., (for those who were most in need.)[7]

Leval wrote that in this reorganization small property had near completely disappeared so that in Aragon 75 percent of "small proprietors have voluntarily adhered to the new order of things."[8] Moreover, in the early months of the Spanish Civil War, anarchist, economist, and revolutionary Diego Abad de Santillán (1897–1983) presented his program for an anarcho-syndicalist society in *After the Revolution* (1936–1937). Quoting John Stuart Mill's rejection of society permitting "a class which does not work" while other people "are excused from taking part in the labor incumbent on the human species," Santillán said:

> Stuart Mill is right. We believe that such a society has no right to existence and we desire its total transformation. We want a socialized economy in which the land, the factories, the homes, the means of transport cease to be the monopoly of private ownership and become the collective property of the entire community.[9]

Anarchists have stood principled against private ownership and control of the means of production including rejecting not only workers selling their labor to capitalists, but also workers taking orders from managers or the state. Indeed, one of the defining features of so-called "socialist" economies of the twentieth century, contrary to anarchism, was state ownership and control of productive assets. The way state ownership was rationalized by "socialist" central planners and managers was by their asserting they knew best how to use those assets. Bureaucratic planners and managers believed that everyone else was unfit to make effective decisions. The statists claimed that people had false consciousness and little skill and were therefore not able to decide how best to plan their own lives. The bureaucratic planners and managers of these economies, what I and others call the "coordinator class," asserted that they alone were free from false consciousness and thus knew what was in the best interest of the people and, of course, this paternalistic rationale for state control over productive assets dovetailed nicely with the material interests of the elite. The negative effects of central planning on people were built into the economic institutions and affected the overall society.

So far I have briefly noted two orientations toward productive property: (1) private ownership of productive assets as in capitalism, and (2) state ownership of productive assets as in centrally planned and market "socialist" economies. We clearly need a third orientation toward property relations, "anarchist economy," which in accord with Bakunin, Goldman, and the Spanish anarchists, and others abolishes not only private ownership, but also state or other central control. In this new system, ownership could plausibly be conceived in either of two equally satisfactory and equivalent ways:

(1) The concept of ownership over productive assets is abolished so that ownership becomes a non-issue, meaning that no one owns productive property. Or...

(2) Society as a whole owns all productive property but again ownership conveys no special rights or privileges.

In either orientation class rule due to ownership of productive property is abolished and the way is cleared to also establish anarchist self-managed decision-making.

Class and Division of Labor

Class affects not only social and material relations, behaviors, and outcomes within the economic sphere of society, but also in other realms of social life. Of course variations exist across societies and cultures, but, broadly speaking, people in the same class, for example, the working class, typically have similar kinship arrangements, cultural tastes, and self-perceptions. They share common material positions in society, which affects their collective bargaining power and decision-making control over their lives both in relation to property and also within the division of labor. Classes typically conflict with one another. For example, the capitalist, coordinator, and working classes all have contrary interests due to their position in relation to the means of production and in the division of labor.

Anarchist treatments of class and the division of labor trace back to two primary historical and theoretical influences—the towering figures of Karl Marx and Mikhail Bakunin. Marx's work overwhelmingly emphasizes a two-class theory based on ownership relations while Bakunin had a three-class theory based not only on ownership, but also on the division between mental and manual labor. In his *Economic and Philosophical Manuscripts of 1844*, in the section on "Estranged Labor," Marx provided early rationale for the two-class theory:

> We have started out from the premises of political economy. We have accepted its language and its laws. We presupposed private property; the separation of labour, capital, and land, and likewise of wages, profit, and capital; the division of labour; competition; the conception of exchange value, etc. From political economy itself, using its own words, we have shown that the worker sinks to the level of a commodity, and moreover the most wretched commodity of all; that the misery of the worker is in inverse proportion to the power and volume of his production; that the necessary consequence of competition is the accumulation of capital in a few hands and hence the restoration of monopoly in a more terrible form; and that, finally, the distinction between capitalist and landlord, between agricultural worker and industrial worker, disappears and the whole of society must split into the two classes of *property owners* and propertyless *workers*.[10]

Bakunin took an additional step to see a third class between "the two classes of *property owners* and propertyless *workers*." He predicted the "Red Bureaucracy" that arose within the Russian Revolution and plagued the "Actually Existing Socialism" of the twentieth century based on the existence of this class. He specifically called into question the "dictatorship of the proletariat," while exposing the self-aggrandizing beliefs of the Coordinator Class. Bakunin wrote:

> Of course, production would be badly crippled, if not altogether suspended, without efficient and intelligent management. But from the standpoint of elementary justice and even efficiency, the management of production need not be exclusively monopolized by one or several individuals. ...The monopoly of administration, far from promoting the efficiency of production, on the contrary only enhances the power and privileges of the owners and their managers.[11]

Bakunin's theoretical concerns and forecasts were validated in the Russian Revolution (1917). In his pamphlet of 1918 titled "The Immediate Tasks of the Soviet Government," V. I. Lenin (1870–1924) wrote that it was necessary to learn how to harmonize the democracy of the working masses "with *iron* discipline while at work," and with "*unquestioning obedience* to the will of a single person, the Soviet leader."[12]

The betrayal of workers' control in the aftermath of the Russian Revolution is chronicled by libertarian socialist Maurice Brinton (1923–2005) in his 1975 pamphlet "The Bolsheviks and Workers Control 1917–1921." Brinton's criterion for evaluating the Russian Revolution was "workers' management of production—implying as it does the total domination [by] the producer over the productive process." For Brinton this was not "a marginal matter" but rather "the core of our politics" and "is the only means whereby authoritarian (order-giving, order-taking) relations in production can be transcended and a free, communist or anarchist, society introduced." He went on to write:

> In 1917 the Russian workers created organs (Factory Committees and Soviets) that might have ensured the management of society by the workers themselves. But the soviets passed into

the hands of Bolshevik functionaries. A state apparatus, separate from the masses, was rapidly reconstituted. The Russian workers did not succeed in creating new institutions through which they would have managed both industry and social life. This task was therefore taken over by someone else, by a group whose specific task it became. The bureaucracy organized the work process in a country of whose political institutions it was also master.[13]

What are the implications of this history for truly "communist or anarchist" class relations of the future? If an anarchist economy adopts property relations such as those proposed in the earlier section, i.e., either fully eliminating ownership of productive assets or having everyone own them equally, and in both cases everyone also having self-managed decision-making in proportion to how they are affected, then class hierarchies based on ownership or control of the means of production will be abolished. However, how does one accomplish that self-management at work? What about the division of labor? Is it enough to say like Bakunin that "the management of production need not be exclusively monopolized by one or several individuals?" There are many possibilities for how class rule in society could reemerge even with this as a guiding desire, unless a new economic model has institutional features and decision-making norms that propel classlessness, solidarity, and self-management, while suppressing possibilities for class rule coming back to haunt us.

The 1960s and 1970s saw many innovations in understanding class analysis and the division of labor, some of which elaborated on early attempts at a three-class analysis. One notable example was put forward in *Between Labor and Capital* (1979),[14] a book organized around the lead essay "The Professional-Managerial Class" by Barbara and John Ehrenreich. In summary, the Professional-Managerial Class (PMC), as the Ehrenreichs called it, was a third class between capitalists and workers with its own relations and interests. Broadly consistent with Bakunin's early formulation, the PMC approach differed from popular notions of the "middle class," in that it saw this third class as being structurally as important as capitalists and workers and defined not firstly by income, but by position. The PMC as the Ehrenreichs described it, included doctors, managers, "cultural workers," teachers, and others who do largely conceptual and empowering work.

The PMC thus differed from capitalists who own and control society's productive assets, as well as from workers who do mostly manual labor on assembly lines, agricultural work, sales, busing tables, and so on. The relations and antagonisms between capitalists, the PMC, and workers persist and, according to the Ehrenreichs, cause us to need to consider "the historical alternative of a society in which mental and manual work are re-united to create whole people."[15] What is consequential for anarchism is that this insight provides a jumping off point for envisioning how the division of labor can be altered to allow and even entail classlessness.

Also consistent with the classical anarchist thrust towards a three-class theory, Michael Albert and Robin Hahnel made their own contribution in the same book. In their essay, "A Ticket to Ride: More Locations on the Class Map," they outlined their proposal for a three-class analysis introducing what they called the "Coordinator Class," thereby laying the groundwork for what would eventually become their vision of a classless participatory economic system.[16] To Paraphrase Albert and Hahnel, the Coordinator Class, like the PMC, is positioned above workers who do rote and un-empowering tasks and who want higher wages, better working conditions, more control over their work, and so on, and positioned below capitalists who own the means of production and want to lower wages while extracting more labor and progressively weaken the bargaining power of workers in order to gain more profit. Standard two-class analysis highlights ownership relations but fails to emphasize a highly significant actor within economics: the Coordinator Class. On the one hand, coordinators have authority and power over workers. They do mostly empowering and conceptual work, and so benefit from their elite position. On the other hand, workers do mostly rote and executionary work. This matters, not only in the unjust distribution of desirable conditions, but also because the kinds of work we do helps shape and inform our capacities for decision-making and participation both in our workplaces and also in the institutions of society more broadly. This modern approach to class and the division of labor points to the need for innovation, not only regarding ownership, mental, and/or manual labor, but also empowerment in terms of the labor we perform and the decisions we make.

In later works, Albert and Hahnel refine their vision, which includes, among other aspects, a positive reorganization of the workplace so that everyone has in their work a comparably empowering array of responsibilities. Combining tasks to equalize empowerment ensures that no single group, or class, monopolizes decision-making power nor gets complacent or apathetic doing only rote tasks.

Remuneration Schemes

Society needs and values things. Whether something as simple as a kite for a child or something more complex like a hospital or telecommunications system—people produce what others desire and in the process sacrifice socially valuable time and energy that could have been used for other ends, whether producing something else, or simply socializing in diverse ways. People also work under more or less desirable conditions, with better or worse tools, with more or less innate gifts such as bigger muscles or more stamina. People can also work longer or harder than one another, have better training, or have more effective workmates. So what should compensation be?

Under capitalism bargaining power determines incomes. Production and consumption seeks, first, to aggrandize those at the top. Obviously anarchists reject this. But the principle of remuneration proposed by Marx for socialism where income is proportional to contribution, where again contribution is determined by the luck of better genetics, tools, workmates, or land—all circumstances out of our control—is likewise out of touch with anarchist notions of justice.

We saw in the section on property how private ownership of the means of production forces workers to sell their own labor and how state ownership of productive assets forces workers to give up control over their own labor. In both cases workers have little bargaining power with capitalists or the state to negotiate fair remuneration for their work. Another method based on the communist principle of remuneration according to need is proposed by Kropotkin in his anarcho-communist work, *The Conquest of Bread* (1892).[17] For Kropotkin if private ownership of productive property in capitalism produces scarcity of goods for those at the bottom, then the new economy, based on abolition of private ownership of productive assets combined with the introduction of mutual aid and voluntary cooperation, should distribute the abundant fruits of society's productivity to all based on what they need. Anarchists quickly reject the principle of remuneration according to contribution, because hierarchies emerge due to some having better tools or genetics, or producing in a sector of more value. The fact that some produce more or less due to circumstances largely out of their control should not be cause for them to receive more or less income. But what about remuneration according to need?

Historically, it was during anarchist experimentation in the Spanish Civil War that we first saw the mass application of remuneration according to need. Gaston Leval described the scenario:

> It is the first time in modern society that the anarchist principle "to each according to his needs," has been practiced. It has been applied in two ways: without money in many villages in Aragon and by a local money in others, and in the greater part of collectives established in other regions. The family wage is paid with this money and it varies according to the number of members in each family. A household in which the man and his wife both work because they have no children receives, for the sake of argument, say 5 pesetas a day. Another household in which only the man works, as his wife has to care for two, three or four children, receives six, seven or eight pesetas respectively. It is the "needs" and not only the "production" taken in the strictly economic sense which control the wage scale or that of the distribution of products where wages do not exist.[18]

Applying this method of remuneration in the real world, especially under near impossible circumstances during a time of internal and external war, is quite a remarkable achievement. But we should note that it is amending remuneration for hours worked with a need component, not simply remunerating need, which would deliver income regardless of work.

In Marx's "Critique of the Gotha Program" (1875) he proposes, "In a higher phase of communist society...after labor has become not only a means of life but life's prime want; after the productive forces have also increased with the all-around development of the individual, and all the springs of co-operative wealth flow more abundantly—only then can the narrow horizon of bourgeois right be crossed in its entirety and society inscribe on its banners: From each according to his ability, to each according to his needs!"[19] This is an ethical proposal for a morally good society. Yet there remains a fuzzy middle ground between theory and practice where many interesting and important questions hide. For example, how do we know what is desirable for society without knowing the relative benefits of alternative allocations of society's human and natural resources? How are costs determined and shared equitably? To the extent remuneration according to need means "take what you feel you need" and "anything goes" it is not only utopian, but also dysfunctional, hiding the relative benefits and costs of alternative options that we must choose among. Such sentiments should be tossed into the "anti-social waste basket." Determining incomes in a socially responsible way means introducing another remuneration method different from "people can have what they want and do as they choose." In fact, the real underlying desire of most advocates of remuneration for need is that people should get a responsible amount of the social product and do their fair share of the labor that is required to produce the social product. But of course, how do we know how much income and how much labor are responsible and fair?

Anarchists might seek the answer by looking at the work of a valued doctor, lawyer, or artist. In the third volume of his *Political and Social Writings*, Greek philosopher Cornelius Castoriadis (1922–1997) asked, "What sense is there in saying that the competency of a good surgeon is worth exactly as much as—or more, or less, than—that of a good engineer? And why is it not worth exactly as much as that of a good train engineer or good teacher?"[20] Or, more directly, why is a surgeon not remunerated less than a garbage collector?

Castoriadis saw that "competence," "merit," and "intelligence," were similar to the luck of better tools or workplace circumstance and was just as much out of our control as genes inherited from the genetic lottery, and so was not deserving of more income (even if society paid for the education to nurture its development). But don't producers of great value need the incentive of high income? Castoriadis wrote:

> To the extent that someone has a gift, the exercise of this gift is in itself a source of pleasure when it is not hindered. And as for the rare exceptionally gifted individuals, what really matters is not monetary reward but creating what they are irresistibly driven to create. If Einstein had been interested in money, he would not have become Einstein—and it is likely that he would have made a rather mediocre boss or financier.[21]

Or, as Lucy Parsons (1853–1942), founding member of the International Working People's Association (IWPA) and co-founder of the Industrial Workers of the World (IWW), said in her speech on "The Principles of Anarchism," "The grandest works of the past were never performed for the sake of money."[22] She was aware that there is a social reward for the scientist who makes an important discovery, the artist who brings great joy, or the surgeon who saves a life that is beyond the realm of material value. Saving a life or making a discovery, like all other work, should receive material compensation for how long one does it, how hard one does it, and the onerousness of conditions under which one does it. That is, work is rewarded for longer hours, greater intensity, or being less pleasant or more onerous or dangerous, though this remuneration is of course tempered by payment according to need in cases of ill health, age, or some other condition that inhibits us from working.

Allocation

Every economy needs a way to decide how to distribute inputs and outputs for the production and consumption of the material means of life. This is called allocation. As a simple example, consider books. Two basic ingredients for books are ink and paper. The printer needs to order both, which in turn requires ink and paper producers to consume pigments, dyes, solvents, and additives, and paper finishing according to weight, size, and other physical properties. Without an allocation system, books could not be made, medicine could not cure, schools would not be built, nor computers assembled. Indeed, society would attain very little, if it would exist at all. So allocation needs to facilitate the democratic and non-wasteful distribution of inputs and outputs for production and consumption.

Since I have presented some components of anarchist economic theory and practice in prior sections of this chapter, we already have filters for easily ruling out allocative options that do not satisfy anarchist criteria and see other possibilities that provide as close an approximation of the best possible anarchist economic system as we can imagine today.

The first allocation mechanism is the one we find in capitalism. The main institutions that define capitalism are private ownership of productive assets, which we rejected in the section on property, hierarchical divisions of labor, which we jettisoned in the section on divisions of labor, unfair compensation for work, which we decided against in the section on remuneration, and finally market allocation, which we now consider.

Markets entail buyers and sellers each trying to "buy cheap and sell dear." Markets pit people against one another and the deciding factor is who has the most bargaining power. For example, in the labor market, "Mr. Money Bags" wants to hire "Lucy the Laborer" at very low wages, speed up her work, worsen her conditions, lengthen her workday, and so on. Lucy wants to avoid being thusly fleeced by the capitalist, and so she seeks to raise wages, reduce the pace of work, improve conditions, shorten the workday, and so on. This is class struggle. But even when selling products, or buying items, the same motives prevail, getting as much as you can while paying as little as you can.

Beyond the site of exchange, moreover, if someone purchases a car at a dealership, even though the buyer and seller alone negotiate the cost, many others are affected as soon as the car leaves the parking lot and carbon dioxide emissions increase greenhouse gasses propelling global climate change. Many people are excluded from decisions that in fact affect them.

Because market transactions such as buying and selling favor those with more power, wealth, and privilege—over long periods of time they warp production and consumption in elites' favor. Overall, on a society-wide scale, this means that markets bias transactions toward more private rather than public outcomes, for example private health care, education, and transportation, rather than more public forms. For these and additional reasons, markets are antithetical to anarchism.

Another allocation possibility, even easier for anarchists to reject, is central planning. Centrally planned "socialist" economies are defined by state ownership and control of productive property, corporate divisions of labor in the work place, and central planners and managers who comprise the "Red Bureaucracy" that Bakunin spoke of. Most anarchists would oppose this system on principle, arguing that it is authoritarian, and they would be right.

Anarchist rejection of central planning and markets is appropriate but a question arises when we tell people we must get rid of each. What have we to offer in their place? Well, we know that formations of neighborhood assemblies, workers' councils or soviets, and industrial syndicalism sprout up everywhere that people seek to take control over the material means of life and self-manage society. However, if uprisings create new institutional forms then what happens when these forms grow and blossom? What role will they play in the future society beyond their role to escape the past and present one? Will they be good only as vehicles of struggle or will they constitute the foundation of the new society and help create new social and material relations while being the glue that holds it all together?

Providing context for the historical model of the soviet, German anarcho-syndicalist theorist and historian Rudolf Rocker (1873–1958) sketched the origins and goals in his essay "Anarchism & Sovietism":

> The idea of soviets is not a new one, nor is it one thrown up, as is frequently believed, by the Russian Revolution. It arose in the most advanced wing of the European labour movement at a time when the working class emerged from the chrysalis of bourgeois radicalism to become independent. That was in the days when the International Workingmen's Association achieved its grandiose plan to gather together workers from various countries into a single huge union, so as to open up to them a direct route towards their real emancipation. Although the International has been thought of as a broad based organisation composed of professional bodies, its statutes were drafted in such a way as to allow all the socialist tendencies of the day to join with the sole proviso that they agree with the ultimate objective of the organisation: the complete emancipation of the workers.[23]

An institutional tradition providing "emancipation of the workers" is offered as anarcho-syndicalism which allows for all means of production, consumption, and allocation of the material means of life to be brought under direct control and administration of, for, and by the workers themselves. Industry is organized into federations locally, regionally, and nationally. The Paris Commune offered an early glimpse into "what could have been" as Friedrich Engels (1820–1895) informed us in his introduction to Marx's "The Civil War in France," which he wrote on the twentieth anniversary of the commune and also twenty years after Marx published his original text:

On April 16 the Commune ordered a statistical tabulation of factories which had been closed down by the manufacturers, and the working out of plans for the carrying on of these factories by workers formerly employed in them, who were to be organized in co-operative societies, and also plans for the organization of these co-operatives in one great union.[24]

The opening of the twentieth century saw syndicalism reemerge again when factory committees and soviets rose up in the Russian Revolution, providing a nucleus for workers' control that was, however, crushed by the Bolsheviks. In September of 1920, Italian workplace takeovers spread across auto factories, steel mills, breweries, steamships and much more, involving at its peak 600,000 workers in massive assemblies.[25] Syndicalism later achieved one if its highest points during the Spanish Civil War. Along with federated and self-governing assemblies across urban neighborhoods and rural villages, the Spanish anarchists attempted the syndicalization of industry as outlined by Gaston Leval:

Each industry is centralized in the Syndical Administrative Committee. This committee is divided into as many sections as there are principal industries. When an order is received by the Sales Section it is passed on to the production section whose task it is to decide which workshops are best equipped to produce the required articles. Whilst settling this question they order the required raw materials from the corresponding section. The latter gives instructions to the shops to supply the materials and finally, the Buying Section receives details of the transaction so that it can replace the material used.[26]

For Dutch astronomer and Marxist Anton Pannekoek (1873–1960) council organization was both the means by which workers would struggle to take self-managed control over society and the form in which they would administer that new society themselves. Written in the 1940s, Pannekoek's book *Workers' Councils* proposes that council allocation could occur on a grand scale and

will be possible only by combining all the factories, as the separate members of one body, into a well organized system of

production. The connection that under capitalism is the fortu-
itous outcome of blind competition and marketing, depending
on purchase and sale, is then the object of conscious planning.
Then instead of the partial and imperfect attempts at organization of modern capitalism, that only lead to fiercer fight and
destruction, comes the perfect organization of production, growing into a world-wide system of collaboration. For the producing
classes cannot be competitors, only collaborators.[27]

Sharing similar institutional aspirations, especially after being influenced by the 1956 uprisings against Soviet bureaucracy in Hungary
and Poland, Cornelius Castoriadis published his 1957 classic "Workers' Councils and the Economics of Self-Managed Society." Although
Castoriadis, like Brinton, was not an anarchist, his vision was one of
the first to deal with the economics of what Brinton called an anarchist
or communist society. His essay was republished as a pamphlet by the
London Solidarity Group in 1972, and their preface states: "To the
best of our knowledge [until Castoriadis] there had been no serious
attempts by modern libertarian revolutionaries to grapple with the
economic and political problems of a totally self-managed society."[28]

In Castoriadis' vision of a self-managed society, economic life is
organized by federated workers' councils, council administration, and
economic planning. To avoid the command structures and bureaucracy
of centrally planned economies, the councils were to "collect, transmit
and disseminate information collected and conveyed to them by local
groups." The center and periphery of a council society, as Castoriadis proposed, was to have a "two-way flow of information" and there
would also be a reorganization and transformation of work including
the division of labor. For Castoriadis, equitable and full participation
in the economy was key. However, there is a problem with one of the
main institutional features that Castoriadis proposed to facilitate allocation, which was what he called "The Plan Factory," where data
for possible economic plans would be calculated and then voted on.
Castoriadis assumed this was simply a technical matter and therefore,
despite his intentions, overlooked the qualitative aspects of how removing these decisions from workers and consumers could lessen the
autonomy and self-management of both while empowering those in
the Plan Factory. While Castoriadis was a pioneer in championing a

non-market worker council vision, much has been learned by others who have developed more effective planning procedures that allow for greater council self-management than his early model from 1957. The same problem of how to realize the fullest possible means of self-management and autonomy in economic planning appeared in anarchist Murray Bookchin's (1921–2006) vision of libertarian municipalism. Influenced by communal and assembly formations from both the Paris Commune and Spanish Civil War, Bookchin proposed a network of councils whose members are elected from face-to-face democratic neighborhood assemblies which would coordinate decision-making on city, municipal, and "confederal" levels by sharing responsibilities and accountability through recallable community delegates and mandated representatives. The problem for autonomy and self-management arises when Bookchin proposes the "municipalization of the economy" where he stated this would "bring the economy as a whole into the orbit of the public sphere, where economic policy could be formulated by the entire community."[29] Two problems arise. All decisions are by majority vote, yet not all decisions in fact affect everyone equally. But even more, suddenly people in neighborhood assemblies have more decision-making say about what should go on in a workplace and in production and consumption than the workers who work there or those who want their goods. As a consequence workers and consumers lose their ability to cooperatively negotiate with one another about what to produce, how to produce it, and where it should be distributed throughout society. Individual and collective autonomy and self-management, where people decide their own objectives and have decision-making say to the degree they are affected are rendered obsolete for the worker in Bookchin's vision.

Anarchist allocation should deliver many traditional anarchist and libertarian socialist values such as classlessness, autonomy, self-management, solidarity, mutual aid, and diversity, and also, since we are talking about economics and the material means of life, equity and efficiency. We have embarked on an introductory overview of some of the most common and effective ways that people have sought to take control over their lives throughout recent history. Any model that offers itself up for the future should be composed of the best features from the past, as well as some new and original attributes to overcome problems that plagued previous efforts, and should weave all this into a synthesis where the new whole is greater than the sum of its parts. We have looked at a few historical and theoretical methods used for economic allocation, such as markets and central planning. Now, let us consider the modern-day participatory economic model and its method of decentralized participatory planning as offered by Michael Albert and Robin Hahnel. It should be noted, however, that the simple sketch provided here, like many of the models offered throughout this chapter, has been spelled out in much greater detail in many books.[30]

The method of decentralized participatory planning uses many institutions familiar from past struggles but in a new context and serving a new purpose. Allocation takes place in an institutional setting where balanced job complexes—the new division of labor in which we all have a fair apportionment of empowering tasks—and remuneration for duration, intensity, and onerousness of work deliver classlessness and self-managed decision-making over production and consumption. The council organization of society and the syndicalization of industry provide the means for people to directly control the economic system, but with a few new twists. For example, self-managed councils provide workers with means to negotiate what to produce and how to produce it with self-managed consumers' councils who propose what they want to consume. The decentralized workers' and consumers' councils together cooperatively and comprehensively negotiate economic plans, without any central authority and with self-management. Where markets pushed the negative costs of economic activity onto the weaker party and privatized the positive aspects of a transaction for the more powerful participant, decentralized participatory planning considers the full positive and negative costs and consequences of economic decision-making, including apportioning benefits and costs justly. Councils arrive at a plan seeking to minimize waste and obtain maximum results from the least amount of socially valued effort and resources.

Closing Comments

Any history of anarchism or "anarchist economics" is bound to be incomplete and will require many more pages and authors than present in this single chapter. Indeed, when put into future practice, on a society-wide scale, we will all be its authors. On my own here though, instead of providing a catalog or chronology, and without being definitive, I have tried to pull out the best and most well-known parts that

I am aware of, with the space available, and without assuming any prior knowledge about anarchism that the reader may or may not hold, to give an introduction to what could be called "anarchist economics" as well as to point towards how these different historical tendencies may relate to one another, providing building blocks for an emancipatory society. If closer scrutiny reveals, as I believe, that participatory economics fulfills anarchist economic aims as outlined above, then we can advocate and seek it, along with complementary and revolutionary changes in other spheres of life. Otherwise, in accord with Malatesta, we can "meet, discuss, agree and differ, and then divide according to [our] various opinions, putting into practice the methods which [we] respectively hold to be the best," so that "that method, which when tried, produces the best results, will triumph in the end."

Endnotes

1   See Peter Kropotkin, *Mutual Aid: A Factor of Evolution* (London: William Heinemann, 1902, Orig. 1890–1896).

2   Errico Malatesta, *Anarchy*, http://theanarchistlibrary.org/HTML/Errico_Malatesta__Anarchy.html#toc7 (accessed October 26, 2011). Although this quote from Malatesta is from his original 1891 text, a better translation then that found in the Anarchist Library online appears in Charles Bufe, *The Heretic's Handbook of Quotations* (Tucson: See Sharp Press, 2001). It is from this more recently published text that I quote Malatesta from for this chapter.

3   Mikhail Bakunin, "The Capitalist System," http://dwardmac.pitzer.edu/anarchist_archives/bakunin/capstate.html (accessed October 26, 2011).

4   Emma Goldman, "Anarchism: What it Really Stands For," http://dwardmac.pitzer.edu/Anarchist_Archives/goldman/aando/anarchism.html (accessed October 26, 2011).

5   Pierre Joseph Proudhon, *What is Property? An Inquiry into the Principle of Right and of Government*, http://etext.virginia.edu/toc/modeng/public/ProProp.html (accessed October 26, 2011).

6   Karl Marx "The Civil War in France," http://www.marxists.org/archive/marx/works/1871/civil-war-france/ch05.htm (accessed October 26, 2011).

7   Gaston Leval, *Collectives in Spain*, http://dwardmac.pitzer.edu/anarchist_archives/leval/collectives.html (accessed October 26, 2011).

8   Ibid.

9   Diego Abad De Santillán, *After the Revolution*, http://zinelibrary.info/files/After%20the%20Revolution.pdf (accessed October 26, 2011).

10   Karl Marx, *Economic and Philosophical Manuscripts of 1844*, http://www.marxists. org/archive/marx/works/1844/manuscripts/labour.htm (accessed October 26, 2011), original emphasis.

11   Mikhail Bakunin quoted by Sam Dolgoff in *Bakunin on Anarchism* (Montreal: Black Rose Books, 1980), 424.

12   V. I. Lenin, "The Immediate Tasks of the Soviet Government," http://www. marxists.org/archive/lenin/works/1918/mar/28.htm (accessed October 26, 2011), original emphasis.

13   Maurice Brinton, "The Bolsheviks and Workers Control 1917–1921," http:// www.spunk.org/texts/places/russia/sp001861/bolintro.html (accessed October 26, 2011).

14   Pat Walker ed., *Between Labor and Capital* (Brooklyn: South End Press, 1979).

15   Ibid., 17.

16   Ibid., 243.

17   Peter Kropotkin, *The Conquest of Bread*, http://dwardmac.pitzer.edu/anarchist_ archives/kropotkin/conquest/toc.html (accessed October 26, 2011).

18   Leval, *Collectives in Spain*.

19   Karl Marx, "Critique of the Gotha Program," http://www.marxists.org/archive/ marx/works/1875/gotha/ch01.htm (accessed October 26, 2011).

20   Cornelius Castoriadis, *Political and Social Writings. Volume 3: 1961–1979. Recommencing the Revolution: From Socialism to the Autonomous Society*, David Ames Curtis, ed. and trans., (Minneapolis: University of Minnesota Press, 1993), 223.

21   Ibid.,224.

22   Lucy Parsons, "The Principles of Anarchism," http://www.lucyparsonsproject.org/ writings/principles_of_anarchism.html (accessed October 26, 2011).

23   Rudolf Rocker, "Anarchism & Sovietism," http://www.scribd.com/doc/56870772/ Anarchism-Sovietism (accessed October 26, 2011).

24   Frederick Engels, "On the 20th Anniversary of the Paris Commune," http:// www.marxists.org/archive/marx/works/1871/civil-war-france/intro.htm (accessed October 26, 2011).

25   Tom Wetzel, "Italy 1920," http://workersolidarity.org/?p=122 (accessed October 26, 2011).

26   Leval, *Collectives in Spain*.

27   Anton Pannekoek, *Workers' Councils*, http://libcom.org/library/workers-councils-1-pannekoek (accessed October 26, 2011).

28   Cornelius Castoriadis, "Workers' Councils and the Economics of Self-Managed Society," http://www.lust-for-life.org/Lust-For-Life/WorkersCouncilsAndEconomics/WorkersCouncilsAndEconomics.htm (accessed October 26, 2011).

29   Murray Bookchin, "The Ghost of Anarcho-Syndicalism," http://dwardmac.pitzer.
      edu/Anarchist_Archives/bookchin/ghost2.html (accessed October 26, 2011).

30   For example, see Michael Albert and Robin Hahnel, *Quite Revolution in Wel-
      fare Economics* (Princeton: Princeton University Press, 1991); Michael Albert
      and Robin Hahnel, *Looking Forward: Participatory Economics for the 21st Cen-
      tury* (Brooklyn: South End Press, 1991); Michael Albert and Robin Hahnel, *The
      Political Economy of Participatory Economics* (Princeton: Princeton University Press,
      1991); Michael Albert, *Life after Capitalism* (London: Verso, 2004); Robin Hahnel,
      The ABC's of Political Economy (London: Pluto, 2002); Robin Hahnel, *Economic
      Justice and Democracy* (New York City: Routledge, 2005); and Chris Spannos, ed.,
      Real Utopia: Participatory Society for the 21st Century (Oakland: AK Press, 2008).

Laying the Foundations: Proudhon's Contribution to Anarchist Economics[1]

Iain McKay

Anyone sketching the positive vision of libertarian economics would, undoubtedly, include such features as common ownership of land, socialization of industry, workers' self-management of production, and federations of workers' councils. Such a vision can be found in the works of such noted revolutionary anarchists as Mikhail Bakunin, Peter Kropotkin, and Rudolf Rocker.

What may be less well known is that these ideas can be found in the works of Pierre-Joseph Proudhon (1809–1865), the first person to proudly proclaim himself an anarchist and, consequently, the founder of anarchism as a named socio-economic theory: "the land is indispensable to our existence, —consequently a common thing"; "all accumulated capital being social property, no one can be its exclusive proprietor"; "democratically organised workers' associations"; "industrial democracy"; "that vast federation of companies and societies woven into the common cloth of the democratic and social Republic"; "an *agricultural-industrial federation.*"

As with later anarchists, Proudhon rejected the twin evils of capitalism ("monopoly and what follows") and nationalization ("exploitation by the State") in favor of "a solution based upon equality,—in other words, the organisation of labour, which involves the negation of political economy and the end of property." This insight, from 1846, is at the heart of anarchism.

First a point of clarification. The term "anarchist economics" contains two related concepts. One is the anarchist critique of capitalism, the other the suggestions for how an anarchist economy would function. Both are interrelated. What we are opposed to in capitalism will be reflected in our visions of a libertarian economy just as our hopes and dreams of a free society will inform our analysis of the current system. Both need to be understood as both are integral to each other.

This dual perspective can be found in the ideas of Proudhon. Here I will sketch both aspects of the Frenchman's anarchist economics, showing how the critique of property fed into his positive vision of libertarian socialism and vice versa. In so doing, I will also be shedding light on a key anarchist thinker who is better known for a few quotes than for his substantial contributions to both the critique of capitalism and of our visions of anarchy.

What Is Property?

Proudhon's fame and influence was secured in 1840 when he wrote *What Is Property?* and answered "theft." This book contains a searing critique of private property as well as sketches of a new, free society: anarchy. Rejecting both capitalism and (authoritarian) communism, Proudhon called for a "synthesis of communism and property," a "union" which "will give us the true form of human association." "This third form of society," he stated, "we will call *liberty*."

Proudhon's critique rested on two key concepts. Firstly, property allowed the owner to exploit its user ("property is theft"). Secondly, that property created oppressive social relationships between the two ("property is despotism"). These are interrelated, as it is the relations of oppression that property creates which allows exploitation to happen and the appropriation of our common heritage by the few gives the rest little alternative but to agree to such domination and let the owner appropriate the fruits of their labor.

Proudhon's genius and the power of his critique was that he took all the defenses of, and apologies for, property and showed that, logically, they could be used to attack that institution.

To claims that property was a natural right, he explained that the essence of such rights was their universality and that private property ensured that this right could not be extended to all. To those who argued that property was required to secure liberty, Proudhon rightly objected that "if the liberty of man is sacred, it is equally sacred in all individuals; that, if it needs property for its objective action, that is, for its life, the appropriation of material is equally necessary for all." To claims that labor created property, he noted that most people have no property to labor on and the product of such labor was owned by capitalists and landlords rather than the workers who created it. As for occupancy, he argued that most owners do not occupy all the property they own while those who do use and occupy it do not own it.

Proudhon showed that the defenders of property had to choose between self-interest and principle, between hypocrisy and logic. If it is right for the initial appropriation of resources to be made (by whatever preferred rationale) then, by that very same reason, it is right for others in the same and subsequent generations to abolish private property in favor of a system which respects the liberty of all rather than a few. ("If the right of life is equal, the right of labour is equal, and so is the right of occupancy.") This means that "those who do not possess today are proprietors by the same title as those who do possess; but instead of inferring therefrom that property should be shared by all, I demand, in the name of general security, its entire abolition."

Property allows the creation of authoritarian social relationships and exploitation. For Proudhon, the notion that workers are free when capitalism forces them to seek employment was demonstrably false. He was well aware that in such circumstances property "violates equality by the rights of exclusion and increase, and freedom by despotism." It has "perfect identity with robbery" and the worker "has sold and surrendered his liberty" to the proprietor. Anarchy was "the absence of a master, of a sovereign" while "proprietor" was "synonymous" with "sovereign" for he "imposes his will as law, and suffers neither contradiction nor control." Thus "property is despotism" as "each proprietor is sovereign lord within the sphere of his property" and so freedom and property were incompatible.

Hence the pressing need, if we really seek liberty for all, to abolish property and the oppressive social relationships it generates. With wage-workers and tenants, property became "the right to use [something] by his neighbour's labour" and so resulted in "the exploitation of man by man" for to "live as a proprietor, or to consume without producing, it is necessary, then, to live upon the labour of another." Like Marx, but long before him, Proudhon argued that workers produced more value than they received in wages:

> Whoever labours becomes a proprietor ... And when I say proprietor, I do not mean simply (as do our hypocritical economists) proprietor of his allowance, his salary, his wages, —I mean proprietor of the value he creates, and by which the master alone profits ... *The worker retains, even after he has received his wages, a natural right in the thing he has produced.*"

The capitalist also unjustly appropriates the additional value (termed "collective force") produced by cooperative activity:

> A force of one thousand men working twenty days has been paid the same wages that one would be paid for working fifty-five years; but this force of one thousand has done in twenty days what a single man could not have accomplished, though he had laboured for a million centuries. Is the exchange an equitable one? Once more, no; when you have paid all the individual forces, the collective force still remains to be paid ... which you enjoy unjustly.

Property meant "another shall perform the labour while [the proprietor] receives the product." So the "free worker produces ten; for me, thinks the proprietor, he will produce twelve" and so to "satisfy property, the worker must first produce beyond his needs." Little wonder "property is theft!"

His classic work did not limit itself to critique and gave a few sketches of an anarchist economy. Property would be socialized as the "land cannot be appropriated" and "all capital, whether material or mental, being the result of collective labour, is, in consequence, collective property." People "are proprietors of their products—not one is proprietor of the means of production." Thus "right to product is exclusive" while "the right to means is common." Workers' control would prevail as managers "must be chosen from the workers by the workers themselves, and must fulfill the conditions of eligibility. It is the same with all public functions, whether of administration or instruction." So whether on the land or in industry, Proudhon's aim was to create a society of "possessors without masters."

The following year saw Proudhon pen a second memoir (*Letter to M. Blanqui*) in which he clarified certain issues raised in the first memoir and answered his critics. He again argued for socialized property and use rights for "wealth, *produced by the activity of all*, is by the very fact of its creation *collective* wealth, the use of which, like that of the land, may be divided, but which as property remains *undivided*." Proudhon aimed to "reduce" property "to the right of possession" and "organise industry, associate workers" in order to "apply on a large scale the principle of collective production." He called this "non-appropriation of the instruments of production" the "destruction of property." Thus use rights replace property rights with common ownership ensuring individuals and groups controlled the product of their labor, the labor itself and as the means of production used. In short: "I preach emancipation to the proletarians; association to the workers."

System of Economic Contradictions

Proudhon's next major work was 1846's two-volume *System of Economic Contradictions*. It was this work which first saw his use of the term "mutualism" to describe his libertarian socialism. This term was not invented by him but by workers in Lyon during the 1830s. Proudhon stayed there in 1843 and was deeply influenced by the workers' ideas and practice.

This book is best known for Marx's 1847 reply *The Poverty of Philosophy*. While Marx does make a few valid points against Proudhon, his distortions, selective quoting, quote tampering, and other intellectually dishonest practices drain it of most of its value. Suffice to say, reading Proudhon's work quickly shows a radically different thinker than the one readers of Marx would expect.

It must be stressed, given the prevalent myths begat by Marx to the otherwise, that Proudhon supported large-scale industry. Indeed, he explicitly rejected a return to small-scale production as "retrograde" and "impossible." He also supported workers' associations, unsurprisingly once you understand that Proudhon locates exploitation within capitalism firmly in production as a consequence of wage labor. As this analysis informs his vision for an anarchist economy, it is worth discussing—particularly as, ironically, Proudhon was the first to expound many of the key concepts of Marxist economics.

First, Proudhon stressed that labor did not have a value but what it created did and so produces value only as *active* labor engaged in the production process:

> Labour is said to have value, not as merchandise itself, but in view of the values supposed to be contained in it potentially. The value of labour is a figurative expression, an anticipation of effect from cause ... it becomes a reality through its product.

Second, consequently, when workers are hired there is no guarantee that the value of the goods produced equals their wage. Under capitalism wages *cannot* equal product as the proprietor secures a profit by controlling both product *and* labor:

> Do you know what it is to be a wage-worker? It is to labour under a master, watchful for his prejudices even more than for his orders ... It is to have no mind of your own ... to know no stimulus save your daily bread and the fear of losing your job.
>
> The wage-worker is a man to whom the property owner who hires him says: What you have to make is none of your business; you do not control it.

Third, this hierarchical relationship allowed exploitation to occur:

> the worker ... create[s], on top of his subsistence, a capital always greater. Under the regime of property, the surplus of labour, essentially collective, passes entirely, like the revenue, to the proprietor: now, between that disguised appropriation and the fraudulent usurpation of a communal good, where is the difference?
>
> The consequence of that usurpation is that the worker, whose share of the collective product is constantly confiscated by the entrepreneur, is always on his uppers, while the capitalist is always in profit ... political economy, that upholds and advocates that regime, is the theory of theft.

In short, the capitalist firm "with its hierarchical organisation" means that workers had "parted with their liberty" and "have sold their arms" to a boss who controls them, appropriates the product of their labor and, consequently, the "collective force" and "surplus of labour" they create. This produced the economic contradictions Proudhon analyzed. Thus, for example, the introduction of machinery within capitalism "promised us an increase of wealth" but it also produced "an increase of poverty" as well as bringing "us slavery" and deepening "the abyss which separates the class that commands and enjoys from the class that obeys and suffers." Such contradictions could only be resolved by abolishing the system that creates them.

His analysis of how exploitation occurred in production and the oppressive nature of the capitalist workplace feeds directly into Proudhon's arguments for workers' associations and socialization ("to unfold the system of economic contradictions is to lay the foundations of universal association"). As "all labour must leave a surplus, all wages [must] be equal to product" and "[b]y virtue of the principle of collective force, workers are the equals and associates of their leaders." The association of the future would be based on free access ("should allow access to all who might present themselves") and self-management ("to straightway enjoy the rights and prerogatives of associates and even managers"). Hence "it is necessary to destroy or modify the predominance of capital over labour, to change the relations between employer and worker, to solve, in a word, the antinomy of division and that of machinery; it is necessary to ORGANISE LABOUR." Here we see how critique feeds directly into the vision of a free economy.

This argument was rooted in Proudhon's awareness that societies change and develop. He denounced "the radical vice of political economy" of "affirming as a definitive state a transitory condition, —namely, the division of society into patricians and *proletaires*." The "period through which we are now passing" was "distinguished by a special characteristic: WAGE-LABOUR." Just as capitalism had replaced feudalism, so capitalism and its system of property rights would be replaced by an economy based on *associated* labor and socialized property: mutualism.

These two volumes were primarily a work of critique, with positive visions few and far between. What there is shows a keen understanding of the necessity to transform the relations of production, to seek a solution *at the point of production* to the exploitation and oppression of capitalism. However, the work's focus was destructive and not constructive—he explicitly stated that he would "reserve" discussion on the organization of labor "for the time when, the theory of economic contradictions being finished, we shall have found in their general equation the programme of association, which we shall then publish in contrast with the practice and conceptions of our predecessors." The February revolution of 1848 forced him to do just that.

Solution of the Social Problem
Proudhon considered his work of the 1840s as essentially critique, although tantalizing glimpses of his vision of libertarian socialism do come through. The February revolution of 1848 saw him develop his positive theories on anarchist economics and politics as he sought to

influence it towards libertarian ends or, as his first work after the revolution put it, to formulate the *Solution of the Social Problem*. For, as he correctly predicted, "either property will overrule the Republic or the Republic will overrule property."

He stressed that to be permanent the revolution had to move from just political changes to economic transformation. He urged that "a provisional committee be set up to orchestrate exchange, credit and commerce between workers" and this would "liaise with similar committees" across France in order that "a body representative of the proletariat be formed . . . in opposition to the bourgeoisie's representation." And so "a new society [would] be founded in the heart of the old society," created only "from below" as "the organisation of labour must not emanate from the powers-that-be; it ought to be SPONTANEOUS."

This would be achieved by means of a "Bank of the People." Its aim was "to organise credit democratically" and this "organisation of credit" was considered as the means to achieve the organization of labor, with socialized credit producing socialized property. Thus "the Exchange Bank is the organisation of labour's greatest asset" and allowed "the new form of society to be defined and created among the workers." Significantly he linked his ideas to the working-class self-activity going on around him, pointing to those workers who "have organised credit among themselves" and the "labour associations" which have grasped "spontaneously" that the "organisation of credit and organisation of labour amount to one and the same." By organizing both, the workers "would soon have wrested alienated capital back again, through their organisation and competition." Mutual banks would support "all efforts of associations of workers, and organisations of workers" to ensure that "all the workshops are owned by the nation, even though they remain and must always remain free." Workers' control would "make every citizen simultaneously, equally and to the same extent capitalist, worker and expert or artist," this being "the first principle of the new economy, a principle full of hope and of consolation for the worker . . . but a principle full of terror for the parasite and for the tools of parasitism, who see reduced to naught their celebrated formula: *Capital, labour, talent!*"

Proudhon took care to base his arguments not on abstract ideology but on the actual practices he saw around him. He was well aware that banks issued credit and so increased the money supply in response to market demand. As such, he was an early exponent of the endogenous theory of the money supply. He recognized that a money economy, one with an extensive banking and credit system, operates in a fundamentally different way than the barter economy assumed by most economics. He saw that income from property violated the axiom that products exchanged for products and that interest reflected no sacrifice which required payment as the rich person "lends it ... precisely because the loan is not a deprivation to him; he lends it because he has no use for it himself, being sufficiently provided with capital without it." For both economic and ethical reasons we "must destroy the royalty of gold; we must republicanise specie, by making every product of labour ready money."

It must be stressed that in today's economies neither credit nor money is backed by gold. So Proudhon has been vindicated when he mocked bourgeois political economy for arguing that "the idea of abolishing specie is supremely absurd, as absurd as the thought of abolishing property!" Only partially, though, as credit has not been republicanized via a mutual bank to achieve the organization of labor.

For all his talk of "the organisation of credit," the socialization of property and organization of labor remained his goals with the mutual bank seen as a means to achieve that end. In December 1849 he irately denied that he sought the "individual ownership and non-organisation of the instruments of labour" stating categorically that he had "never penned nor uttered any such thing" and had "argued the opposite a hundred times over." He "den[ied] all kinds of proprietary domain" and so did "precisely because I believe in an order wherein the instruments of labour will cease to be appropriated and instead become shared." The previous year he had publicly presented this vision in a manifesto:

> Under the law of association, transmission of wealth does not apply
> to the instruments of labour, so cannot become a cause of inequal-
> ity ... We are socialists ... under universal association, ownership
> of the land and of the instruments of labour is *social* ownership ...
> We want the mines, canals, railways handed over to democratically
> organised workers' associations ... We want these associations to
> be models for agriculture, industry and trade, the pioneering core
> of that vast federation of companies and societies woven into the
> common cloth of the democratic and social Republic.

As in the Paris Commune of 1871, this "organising [of] the workers' mutual solidarity" would be based on elected delegates whom the voters can "recall and dismiss" for the "imperative mandate and permanent revocability are the most immediate and incontestable consequences of the electoral principle." Like the Commune, any assembly would "exercise executive power, just the way it exercises legislative power through its joint deliberations and votes," through "organisation of its committees."

All through the revolutionary period we see the interplay between critique and vision, with each informing the other. Under capitalism "a worker, without property, without capital, without work, is hired by [the capitalist], who gives him employment and takes his product" and his wages fail to equal the price of the products he produces. "In mutualist society," however, "the two functions" of worker and capitalist "become equal and inseparable in the person of every worker" and so he "alone profits by his products" and the "surplus" he creates.

General Idea of the Revolution

Proudhon's hectic activity during the revolution saw him vilified by the Right and imprisoned on spurious charges. In prison he wrote another classic of libertarian politics, his 1851 *General Idea of the Revolution in the Nineteenth Century.* This was considered by Proudhon as a constructive summary for social change, the positive complement to the critiques of 1846.

Its aim was modest: "Capitalist and landlord exploitation stopped everywhere, wage labour abolished, equal and just exchange guaranteed." As would be expected, "the organisation of credit, the deprivation of the power of increase of money" was a focal point of his book but it was just *one* part of a series of reforms which included "the limitation of property" and "the establishment of workers companies." Proudhon, Marxist myths notwithstanding, did not aim *just* to abolish interest, he aimed to abolish the extraction of surplus from the workers in *all* its forms.

Socialization still played a key part of his vision of a free society and Proudhon made various suggestions on how to achieve it. Rental payments "shall be carried over to the account of the purchase" of the resource used and once the property "has been entirely paid for, it shall revert immediately to the commune." In the case of housing, such payments would result in "a proportional undivided share in the house he lives in, and in all buildings erected for rental, and serving as a habitation for citizens." Thus land and housing would become socialized as the property "thus paid for shall pass under the control of the communal administration" and for "repairs, management, and upkeep of buildings, as well as for new constructions, the communes shall deal with bricklayers companies or building workers associations."

Proudhon spent considerable space arguing for workers' associations (while attacking centralized state-run association). Either, he argued, the worker "will be simply the employee of the proprietor-capitalist-entrepreneur; or he will participate in ... the establishment, he will have a voice in the council, in a word, he will become an associate." Under capitalism, "the worker is subordinated, exploited: his permanent condition is one of obedience and poverty." Under libertarian socialism, "he resumes his dignity as a man and citizen, he may aspire to comfort, he forms a part of the producing organisation, of which he was before but the slave ... he forms a part of the sovereign power, of which he was before but the subject." Without association people "would remain related as subordinates and superiors, and there would ensue two industrial castes of masters and wage-workers, which is repugnant to a free and democratic society."

In short, "all workers must associate, inasmuch as collective force and division of labour exist everywhere, to however slight a degree" and so "association, due to the immorality, tyranny and theft suffered, seems to me absolutely necessary and right." Otherwise, capitalists would continue to "plunder the bodies and souls of the wage-workers" which would be "a violation of the rights of the public, an outrage upon human dignity and personality."

Significantly, his practical suggestions for workplace self-management map *exactly* to his previous arguments (particularly his comments from 1846). Thus "every individual employed in the association ... has an undivided share in the property of the company" as well as "the right to fill any position" for "all positions are elective, and the by-laws subject to the approval of the members." Wages would be equal to output as "each member shall participate in the gains and in the losses of the company, in proportion to his services" and "the collective force, which is a product of the community, ceases to be a source of profit to a small number of managers and speculators: it becomes the property of all the workers." Thus there would be a new form of economic organization based on "the co-operation of all who take part in the collective work" with "equal conditions for all members."

Public utilities would be under the "initiative of communes and departments" with "workers companies … carrying the works out." This decentralization, this "direct, sovereign initiative of localities, in arranging for public works that belong to them, is a consequence of the democratic principle and the free contract."

This associative socialism would be universal, for there "will no longer be nationality, no longer fatherland, in the political sense of the words: they will mean only places of birth. Whatever a man's race or colour, he is really a native of the universe; he has citizen's rights everywhere."

The Federative Principle

With the revolution crushed, first by the onslaught of the Right and then by President Louis-Napoleon's coup d'état of December 1851, Proudhon's work was naturally affected as there was little working-class self-activity to inspire him and he was constantly under the watchful eyes of the emperor's censors and police.

His first major work, published anonymously initially, was the *Stock Exchange Speculator's Manual* whose title hid a subversive message—the abolition of wage-labor, the end of the capitalist company, and the advocacy of producer and consumer associations. It asked how "the ownership and management of companies" instead "of remaining individual" could become "collective" so ensuring the "emancipation" of the workers and "a revolution in the relationship between labour and capital." It concluded:

> Workers' associations are the home of a new principle and model of production that must replace current corporations…. There is mutuality … when in an industry, all the workers, instead of working for an owner who pays them and keeps their product, work for each other and thereby contribute to a common product from which they share the profit … extend the principle of mutuality that unites the workers of each association to all the workers' associations as a unit, and you will have created a form of civilisation that, from all points of view—political, economic, aesthetic—differs completely from previous civilisations."

The message of 1840, one of the core concepts of anarchist economists, remained at the fore of Proudhon's ideas and the Frenchman added another expression to the arsenal of hope within anarchist theory: "industrial democracy."

Proudhon's next work in 1858 was his magum opus, his *Justice in the Revolution and in the Church*. Economic justice required that labor be "reconciled by its free nature with capital and property, from which wage-labour banished it." This meant: "The land to those who cultivate it"; "capital to those who use it"; "the product to the producer." Such a self-managed economy "cannot cause a distinction of classes" and "makes society, as well as [economic] science, safe from any contradiction."

The early 1860s saw Proudhon turn increasingly to political issues, notably the questions of federalism, centralism, and nationalism. However, he always recognized the links between the economy and the political structure and so his 1863 *The Federative Principle* discusses economic reforms in a federal system as "political right must have the buttress of economic right."

Building on his previous ideas for "universal association," he argued for the necessity of an "agricultural-industrial federation" as "industries are sisters; they are parts of the same body; one cannot suffer without the others suffering because of it. I wish that they federate then, not to absorb one another and merge, but to mutually guarantee the conditions of prosperity that are common to them all and that none can claim the monopoly of." Without this, there would be "economic serfdom or wage-labour, in a word, the inequality of conditions and fortunes." The agricultural-industrial federation "tends to approximate more and more equality" as well as "guaranteeing work and education" and "allow[ing] each worker to evolve from a mere labourer to a skilled worker or even an artist, and from a wage-earner to their own master." He termed "this political-economic guaranteeism" and considered it both as "the highest expression of federalism" and "the strongest barrier to feudalism of the land and capital, toward which unitary powers inevitably go."

Proudhon died in January 1865. On his deathbed, enthused by the rebirth of the labor movement, he dictated *The Political Capacity of the Working Classes*. He outlined the economics and politics of mutualism, and his continued support for "the mutualist and federative theory of

Property, the critique of [property] which I published twenty-five years ago," and reaffirmed the necessity for free access and association:

> in virtue of the principle which characterises it, the ranks of the Association are open to whomever, having recognised the spirit and the goal, asks to join; exclusion is contrary to it, and the more it grows in number the more advantages it gains. From the point of view of personnel, the mutualist association is therefore by nature unlimited, which is the opposite of all other associations…. [It] admits … everyone in the world, and tends towards universality … one is required to contribute neither money nor other valuables … the only condition demanded is to be faithful to the mutualist pact; —once formed, its nature is to generalise itself and to have no end.

He, as before, attacked both capitalism and state socialism as neither expressed "the great hopes that the workers' Democracy had placed in the idea of the association." Instead he urged self-management and re-iterated "the importance accorded in the New Democracy to workers' associations which are deemed to constitute economic agencies and mutual institutions." Cooperatives ("workers' companies") continued to play a key role in his vision of a free economy: "The revolution, in democratising us, has launched us on the paths of industrial democracy."

Conclusion: From Proudhon to Kropotkin

Anyone familiar with Proudhon's work can quickly see the debt later anarchists owe him. His placing of anti-capitalism alongside anti-statism defined anarchism. His critique of property, his analysis of exploitation occurring in production, and his rejection of wage labor, all fed into revolutionary anarchist (and Marxist) analysis of capitalism. His arguments for self-management, socialization, possession, use rights, and socio-economic federalism are all found in the works of Bakunin, Kropotkin, and other revolutionary anarchists. As he summarized in 1851:

> socialism is … the elimination of misery, the abolition of capitalism and of wage-labour, the transformation of property, the

decentralisation of government, the organisation of universal suffrage, the effective and direct sovereignty of the workers, the equilibrium of economic forces, the substitution of the contractual regime for the legal regime, etc.

The key differences with libertarian communist theory are on means (revolution replacing reform) and on the extension of the critique of wage *labor* into an opposition to the wages *system*. This involved developing a stronger critique of competition and a greater awareness of the problems associated with market forces than can be found in Proudhon (who, myths notwithstanding, was well aware of the negative sides of markets and so recommended various institutional means of limiting them and their impact). It also meant raising ethical objections to distribution by labor cost, recognizing that needs are not proportional to a person's ability to labor, and that some, due to illness and age, simply cannot work at all.

By the mid-1870s, most anarchists had embraced distribution according to *need* rather than Proudhon's according to *deed* (labor). The rationales for this move to (libertarian) communism were elegantly and convincingly expounded by Kropotkin in many works (most obviously, *The Conquest of Bread*). Yet in terms of the critiques of capitalism, property, and wage labor, and of the positive vision of a decentralized, self-managed, associated, and federated libertarian socialism, the links are obvious. The only significant difference is the rejection of Proudhon's socialism based on a market in the *products* of labor in favor of one inspired by the maxim "from each according to their abilities, to each according to their needs."

It is for these reasons that Bakunin proclaimed Proudhon "the master of us all" and his own ideas simply "Proudhonism widely developed and pushed right to these, its final consequences."

ENDNOTES

1   All quotes are from Iain McKay, ed., *Property is Theft! A Pierre-Joseph Proudhon Anthology* (Oakland: AK Press, 2011).

Part 2
Analysis

"Oh, Misery, I have drunk thy cup of sorrow to its dregs, but I am still a rebel."—Lucy Parsons

Capitalism in the 2000s: Some Broad Strokes for Beginners

Abbey Volcano and Deric Shannon

Capitalism, the economic system that we live under, is not in stasis. It is not a monolith, exhibiting the same features in all places and times. Rather, over the years capitalism has assumed different forms in different historical, cultural, and geographical contexts.

Indeed, in broad strokes, one can see how the features of capitalism have historically changed—now in its current neoliberal globalized form and perhaps morphing into some newly emerging form post-crisis. Even if we took a fairly small slice of history, this is not too difficult to demonstrate.

Consider, for example, a single bounded region like the United States (that's where we're from, so it's a history we are familiar with) before the Fair Labor Standards Act made the eight-hour day the law throughout the nation (as a piece of New Deal legislation). Consider what life was like for most working people then and how the economy functioned. This was well before bloated bureaucracies like OSHA (the Occupational Safety and Health Administration) gave working people the limited safety standards we have had since the '70s. It was also before New Deal legislation that gave workers some limited forms of social assistance under other poorly run state bureaucracies.

Workers, at times, worked ten-to-twelve hour workdays—sometimes even more. The state, while always involved in the economy under any form of capitalism (indeed, capitalism cannot exist without a state managing existing class antagonisms), did not provide many of the benefits we've come to expect in the 2000s. It was a time of child labor, black lung disease, and companies, at times, owning the entire town that a given set of workers lived in. It was a time when private security firms like the Pinkertons might be brought in to physically assault or in some cases even kill, striking workers. It was a past where racist and sexist assumptions about "worthy" workers had effects on who might be unionized, who might be hired for certain jobs (or hired at all), and who could serve as floating pools of cheap labor for our capitalist masters (not that these practices don't still exist—rather, they too have changed form).

It was under these conditions that the Great Depression of the 1930s emerged and, eventually, New Deal policies took effect that changed the nature of American capitalism. What emerged was a Keynesian[1] form of capitalism that emphasized social spending in ways unimaginable before the Depression. Still, after this initial Keynesian-ism, we saw the rise of a capitalism associated with economists from the Mont Pelerin Society, whose membership included Ludwig von Mises (a particularly dystopian right-wing economist) and Milton Friedman (economic advisor to Ronald Reagan). In this shift, we can see the rise of neoliberal globalization and, especially, criticisms of anything standing in the way of privatization and profit-seeking at any cost.

It was in this neoliberal context in which the current "crisis" (more on the use of this particular word later) emerged. And so we are left to analyze capital on the brink of yet another historical change. Questions about what form capitalism might take next and, more importantly, how best might anarchists and other anti-authoritarians analyze, fight, and end capitalism, are the motivating force behind this essay. Here we give anarchist beginners to economics seven ideas that we consider important for analyzing capitalism in the 2000s. This is not intended as a high and mighty economistic analysis for people with a good handle on economics. It is intended for beginners. Nor is it intended as a complete list or set of concerns. Such a project would require an entire book.

Rather, we give seven broad categories for thinking about mod-ern capitalism for anarchists to put to use in understanding how the economy functions, how we might talk about it, and how we might best organize to smash capitalism to bits. What follows then, again in broad strokes, are some suggestions for anarchists when looking at capitalism at this emerging new stage—and what we hope might be the beginning of its end.

Globalization from Above

The dominant narrative of globalization is one of increasing inter-dependence and cooperation through trade. So the story goes, kind and benevolent institutions like the World Bank (WB), the World Trade Organization (WTO), and the International Monetary Fund (IMF) would see to the development of co-called Third World nations through capital investment programs. Through large-scale free trade agreements like NAFTA, capital would be able to move freely, aiding in development by providing jobs to workers in underdeveloped nations that desperately needed the money. Further, this process would force state industries into the private sector where wise entrepreneurs could develop them without the interference of incompetent state bureaucrats. This would lead to more even development and prosperity for the underdeveloped world.

And, of course, what goes unstated in this dominant narrative is that the opposite is what is actually taking place—that is, poorer nations have been steadily becoming poorer at the expense of enriching already (over)developed nations. And this process continues.

The IMF, WB, and WTO (in its role in supervising international trade) require structural adjustment programs to the countries that apply for their loans. What these "structural adjustments" mean are privatization of social services and increasing deregulation of their economies. Essentially, then, these nations are under threat from these institutions—either implement more "free" market policies, or don't have access to these loans. Thus, poorer nations are blackmailed into opening their markets to foreign investors who have a greater stake in making a buck than in seeing the economies of these countries develop. Rather than developing these nation's economies, it eviscerates them and makes loads of money for foreign investors, most typically from (over)developed nations (though with payoffs and perks for local elites). Now similar demands are being made on (over)developed nations in the form of "austerity measures" in order to receive aid for their ailing economies (see Hahnel's chapter in this collection)—in some cases leading to increased resistance to capital in these nations (e.g., the general strikes in France and Spain, the student occupation and protest movements in England and Italy, and so on).

In addition, capital mobility hardly led to a global economic arrangement where workers would compete on some (non-existent) "level playing field" for jobs, leading to greater productivity that benefited everyone. Rather, it caused what many economists call a "race to the bottom," where workers in the most tenuous economic circumstances are forced to work for wages well below the standards set by union victories in (over)developed countries. In other words, if a given union fought for, and received, decent wages in a factory in an (over)developed nation, the company could simply pack up and move its factory to an underdeveloped nation without the same history of union organizing and battles (and, in many cases, where the governments of those nations actively allow or help union-busting efforts). In this way, they're able to make huge sums of money that would otherwise have gone to paying workers a decent wage—thereby raising the net incomes of savvy capitalists and further impoverishing workers without many choices. What occurred, then, was specifically a globalization *from above*. Sure, capital and business could move around freely. But where was the promise of "globalization" for working people and the poor? Indeed, when workers try to have the same mobility—particularly workers of color from the global South—they are labeled "illegals," etc., and subject to arrest and deportation. Also, the economies of these underdeveloped nations became subject to the whims of international capital, typically located within (over)developed nations. This set the stage for the same kinds of paternalistic manipulations that were part and parcel of the colonial project—now a purer *economic* imperialism (or what has been referred to as *colonization by proxy*).

Anarchists still need to shift the discourse from "globalization" to something altogether different (or, perhaps, a "globalization" of a distinctive kind)—which is what the alterglobalization movement has been trying to do, with perhaps its most spectacular effort at the Battle of Seattle in 1999. What was new and unique in this mobilization was the broad support that we had in opposition to the WTO in particular, and globalization from above in general, from indigenous groups, unions and worker's rights organizations, feminists, environmentalists, students, etc. (and, of course, these groupings included anarchists). Keeping these networks alive has been a challenge for anarchists, as has finding the best ways to argue for a confrontation, rather than a reconciliation, with capital and the state within them. One of the important strategic debates among anarchists today continues to be our role in such movements and mobilizations, their importance, and how we might also mobilize in our workplaces and communities against these impoverishing institutions and social relations.

"I have found a flaw"

In late October 2008, Alan Greenspan admitted to a congressional committee that he was partially wrong, in the now famous sentence: "I have found a flaw."[2] Greenspan, chairman of the Federal Reserve from

1987 to his retirement in 2006, is known as a cheerleader for deregulation, one of the main components of neoliberalism, also known as the "Washington Consensus" (funny choice of words since "consensus" is pretty much the exact opposite of how this new form of economic [dis]organization came into play). Greenspan was censured for the subprime mortgage and credit crisis of 2007, with *Time* magazine placing him as number three in a list of twenty-five people to blame.[3] Although Greenspan did admit that he was wrong (saying that he had "put too much faith in the self-correcting power of free markets and had failed to anticipate the self-destructive power of wanton mortgage lending"), he refused to take personal blame for the crisis.[4] We agree with him here (he's not personally to blame). The entire global economic system, at its roots, is horribly flawed and blaming one person (or twenty-five people) is an easy way to get around a basic critique of capitalism as a system (and what was supposed to be its current savior: neoliberalism).

As an attempt to save capitalism, the philosophy that Greenspan advances (neoliberalism) advocates for expanding "free" trade, deregulating markets and economies by removing government oversight, and privatizing everything from water to schools and parks, as a process aimed at reversing Keynesian economic policy. As a result of the influence of neoliberal ideas, the response to the current crisis of capitalism in the (over)developed world in our current period has been austerity measures. The common themes here have been raising the retirement age, increasing school tuition, cutting funds available to potential students, and so on—in short, cutting social spending.

These austerity measures affect an enormous part of the population—the working classes are tightening our belts and watching whatever is left of welfare become even less available. At this point, more and more people are seeing flaws in the way our economies are (dis)organized and this is an important opportunity for radical movements, as there is a sort of "permanent working class insecurity" now.[5] Radical critique of the economy is becoming more and more palatable to hitherto "happy" citizens. As anti-capitalists, we have a better chance of getting our ideas across to other working-class people since none of us can any longer rely on good (or even "acceptable") wages and working conditions for ourselves or our children. We need to move beyond our often insular and inward focus and turn outward to the working class (of which we are a part). Today class is becoming an important topic again—and as anti-capitalists we need to help put class and anti-capitalism back on the agenda. And we need to break through the commonly held illusion that supposed "experts" like Greenspan are doing anything more than weaving myths for our age's new ruling religion.

David Graeber said in his recent Void network interview:

> In terms of the specifics, yes, all that we're seeing is the run-off of a huge housing bubble, centered on the US, but global in its scope, that opened the door for an almost unimaginable succession of financial scams, in fact, the most extraordinary and all-encompassing set of financial scams in the history of the world. Yet the perpetrators of these scams—the international banking class—are still being treated as the arbiters of economic morality. How did we end up here? Why is anyone taking the pronouncements of these crooks in any way seriously? That's the question we should be asking.[6]

These are also questions we need leveled at wealthy class warrior "experts" like Greenspan. In an age where Keynesianism is increasingly seen as somehow "left-wing," we must point out how multinational corporations and the super-wealthy few have, through neoliberal policies, avoided the kinds of tax responsibilities that could easily fund much more generous social programs and public sector works than we have seen in even the most liberal of social democracies. And, as anarchists, we need to point out how even those social democracies fall short of providing alternatives to exploitation, crisis, war, poverty, hunger, and all of the ill effects inherent in capitalist society. In this way, we can link our analysis of the current situation to broad visions of libertarian communist futures.

Polls Show Increased Interest in Socialist Alternatives

There have been a handful of significant polls in the United States conducted recently that have shown that people are becoming more interested in socialist alternatives, especially young people. One poll shows that younger Americans are evenly divided: 37 percent prefer capitalism, 33 percent socialism, and 30 percent are undecided.[7] This is a fundamental ideological shift that's taking place, replacing the Cold War anti-communist hysteria with people openly expressing support for so-cialist alternatives. This is huge for the United States and shows that there is ample space for anarchists to tell people about our own versions of socialism—libertarian alternatives—and perhaps make some headway in putting forward anarchist economic visions. The political climate probably hasn't been better for us in the United States in (many of) our lifetimes.

How do we take advantage of this? We believe that anarchists need to express class struggle values. By "class struggle" we don't mean "class first" or "class-centric." Rather, "class struggle" means that we are fighting against class exploitation and we are explicitly anticapitalist. Further, society will be changed by ordinary (extraordinary?) working people—not politicians, not wealthy capitalists, and not tenured pro-fessors and other "experts"—if we are to have a liberatory future. Again, this doesn't mean that we should reduce the struggle against all forms of domination to class. We do not believe that all other hierarchies will automatically dissolve or wither away if we overthrow capitalism. It means that all oppressions intersect in complex ways (more on this later) and all forms of domination are unique.[8] Class is unique in that we advocate for a struggle between the classes to resolve the contradic-tions in (and abolish) capitalist society. Too often, radicals forget this unique feature of class and strategize to fight against "classism" rather than struggling to end class society altogether (as if we just wanted capitalists to treat us nicer under capitalism).

With these polls we can see that younger folks in the United States are turning toward a more positive view of socialism and that many don't know what they prefer. A large part of this confusion comes because there is not enough education of what, exactly, socialism even is. Thus, popular education is a strategy that we need to start having a larger stake in. We live in a time when people are looking for answers, people are either precariously employed or under- or unemployed, and people have a direct interest in understanding alternatives to capital-ism. If we aren't providing visions of these alternatives, we can be sure that people with wealth and power and their lackeys running news media will happily provide ready-made "explanations" that reinforce the widespread confusion about socialism in the United States.

A part of this task, too, means updating our class analysis. We need to abandon the fetishized, historical view of the working class as a group of rugged (usually white and male) factory workers. Too often we rely on these ideas of the "normal, average worker" that fail to take into account the ways that capitalism (and, by extension, the workforce) has changed and the ways that feminists, anti-racists, and others have intervened to update our ideas of who is included in the class. We aren't just factory workers (in large portions of the United States, the factories have been moved elsewhere). We are service employees, line cooks, people who do reproductive labor like raising children and keeping house. We are unemployed people and students who are waiting for the time we are pushed out into the workforce. And, yes, we are also the hyper-alienated and lazy ones, avoiding work as we can and attempting to build our lives outside of monetized capitalist relations and the boredom and alienation inherent in the capitalist workplace.

The Meaning of "Crisis"

As Asimakopoulos explains in this collection, capitalism is prone to periodic "crises." This isn't necessarily a new insight—a system based on capital investments creates "bubbles" in expanding industries (i.e., housing, the "dot com boom," etc.) that cannot last, but that investors want to make a quick buck off (or a few million, for that matter). When these bubbles "burst" (when they are no longer profitable), investors stop raking in profits and this can lead to economic downturns—to recessions or, in the case of the current crisis, depressions.

But what do we mean with this discourse of "crisis?" A quick look at the ultra-rich doesn't show a drastic reduction in comfort and lifestyle. And while unemployment, poverty, precarity, and privation are affecting larger sections of the world's population, those problems are business as usual for a significant portion of the world. And yet we declare capitalism in "crisis" now. For children working in sweatshops, for entire countries struggling with food insecurity and hunger, for continents grappling with an AIDS crisis that disproportionately affects our most marginalized populations, for trafficked women and children, for queer youth struggling to obtain basic resources and kicked out of their homes by fundamentalist parents, for those people living with the legacy of colonization and slavery—for the majority of the world's inhabitants—capitalism IS the crisis. But the discourse of "crisis" isn't employed until it starts hurting the collective bottom line of the wealthy.

This, in and of itself, can be used as an opportunity to discuss the need for socialist alternatives. And the truth is that capitalism requires these "crises" to function. People talk about events like the 1987 stock market crash, the Asian financial crisis of 1997, and the dot-com and housing bubbles and bursts as though they are anomalies. These things are regular features of capitalism. And those not at the top tiers of our global class system (about 95 percent of the world) are experiencing crisis every single day—a constant crisis of sorts. So the discourse surrounding crises themselves seem to uphold that capitalism is more or less functioning the rest of the time. More and more people are coming to the realization that this is not the case—and we need to be pressing this point as we battle against austerity. If we want to avoid "austerity," we need to smash capitalism to pieces. No amount of good-hearted reform or Keynesian policy is going to substantively address the *social* crisis that *is* capitalism.

The Feminization of Poverty

A useful concept coined by feminists in recent years is the "feminization of poverty." "Feminize" is a verb; it is a process by which something becomes more "feminine." The "feminization of poverty" refers to the fact that poverty is becoming more prevalent among women. This is a clear example of hierarchies intersecting and becoming more than a sum of their parts and shows us that feminist concerns must be linked to an anti-capitalist practice. This concept also highlights how contemporary capitalism affects those most marginalized—particularly if we move those margins to the center of our analysis. So we might investigate the experiences of women of color when speaking of the feminization of poverty—or the racial feminization of poverty.

One obvious example would be the maquiladora workers in Mexico along the US border. Under globalization from above, the labor of women of color guarantees maximum profitability—many of these women are working in either the informal sector or in unregulated assembly plants in export processing zones where the words "workers' rights" are nonexistent. As well, "while women have always been an important source of labor power, their active recruitment in low-paid labor, mainly in the service industry, is a new feature of globalization."[9] This recruitment is largely based on companies seeing women of color in these precarious circumstances as a pliable and easily controllable workforce—one that is in no danger of forming unions or otherwise acting collectively to improve their condition. Any study of anarchist economics needs to take into account how different hierarchies interact with each other—in this case how colonization, white racism, patriarchy, and capitalism act together.

A distinctly *feminist* anarchism allows us to account for these changes in capitalism and, likewise, to build on feminist analyses of *reproductive* labor—the labor that goes into day-to-day tasks like cooking, cleaning, child-rearing, and so on and is still commonly the domain of women. Often this labor is unpaid, un(der)valued, and *invisible* in capitalist society, yet it is necessary to keep the system going. And part and parcel of the ways that the patriarchal family inscribes women as caretakers and mothers, we see huge economic imbalances between single female-headed households and single male-headed households (by "household" we are referring here to families with children, but we want to point out that "family" is a loaded term and that folks *should* be free to associate in whatever familial way they fancy). Further, poor women (again, mostly women of color), whose precarity is an influencing factor in this part of the labor marker, are hired to perform reproductive labor for rich white women.

Add to all of this the ways that poor women in our society are blamed for an enormous amount of "social ills"—from being too fertile, too "lazy," "welfare queens," and the like (yet again, especially women of color) and we get a particularly virulent mixture of marginalization and loathing.[10] When theorizing the struggle against capitalism, anarchists need to make sure we don't follow in the same steps of capitalists and continue to invisiblize reproductive work and the other issues that women specifically face in this violent and cruel system. For a consistent politics, anarchism needs feminism (and feminism needs anarchism).

An Intersectional Analysis

Global capitalism since 2000 has borne down hardest, as always, on the people existing within the "dangerous intersections" of our institutional arrangements. While this is nothing new, many radicals still think in terms of a reductionist theory that seeks a single source for social domination. Likewise, many argue for the *strategic* privileging of some forms of hierarchies over others. We think these approaches are wrongheaded and ultimately self-defeating and advocate for anarchists putting the idea of intersectionality that emerged from black feminism to use.

The theory of intersectionality argues that forms of institutionalized domination intersect and are connected into a whole and that they cannot be teased apart theoretically or strategically and one declared the "primary contradiction."[11] Rather, social life is complex and when thinking strategically, the form(s) of domination that is most salient will depend on context (e.g., geographical, historical, the social locations of the people involved in a given struggle, etc.). This lends itself nicely to anarchist analyses, as we oppose domination in all of its forms and need not be limited by reductionist theories of domination.

The uses of this kind of analysis should be obvious. It opens up new windows for us to frame our political practice, taking into account complexity and the interactions of various (and unique but interwoven) forms of hierarchy and control. Yet while we advocate for borrowing this analysis from feminism, we also suggest synthesizing it with (and building a *critique* of it from) anarchism. Too often an intersectional analysis is utilized in terms of *identity*, but is lacking a commitment to smashing existing hierarchical *institutions* such as the state and capitalism. Likewise, anarchists can historicize intersectionality to demonstrate how geographically contingent forms of domination have emerged in a given locale—and by extension the best ways that we might struggle against them.

Whether it's maquiladora workers in Juarez or seed activists in India; poor and homeless queer youth of color all over the world and especially in places with new draconian legislation disciplining non-normative sexual and gender practices, like Uganda; or indigenous populations fighting for autonomy against the imperial project of capital (including capital's indigenous representatives); anarchists can only strengthen our analysis by recognizing the intersections of the hierarchies we have inherited and the tapestry they weave together to create a totality. By moving the margins to the center of our theory and practice we can struggle against hierarchies in ways that move us all forward rather than benefiting the most privileged among us and leaving others behind. And when developing an anarchist economic analysis we can note the political economy's connections at the institutional level with other hierarchies and argue for a holistic politics that refuses reduction and demands an end to *all* forms of oppression.

The Now More-than-Obvious Unsustainability of Capitalism

We've tried throughout this chapter to thread together an analysis of capitalism in the 2000s that takes into account the ways that the economy interacts with other forms of domination in our global society. But where we've been lacking so far, and where anarchist alternatives might make important interventions in terms of vision, is the economy's connection to ecology. Eighty percent of the world's forests are gone.[12] Humans have consumed, in the last fifty years, more resources than the entirety of human history before them.[13] There is near-universal agreement among climatologists that ozone depletion is due to human activities and the consequences of continuing these activities are potentially apocalyptic in scope.[14]

Perhaps one of the most salient contributions to radical theory in recent years by anarchists has been their showing the ways that environmental destruction is part and parcel of capital's growth economy. Given that resource depletion is one among many parts of this global ecological catastrophe, how can we expect an economic system based on treating the entire nonhuman world as various groupings of commodities to profit from to effectively address the environmental crisis? How can the imperial and expansionist project of capital accommodate concerns about the destruction of our habitats? How can an economic system that buttresses industries like factory farming and nonhuman animal harvesting be consistent with reducing or eliminating our collective ecological footprint?

Of course, we believe that capitalism can in no way be compatible with building an environmentally sustainable future, nor can it be used to fix the problems we have already created. But these are exactly the kinds of attempts that are being made under capitalism in the 2000s. Indeed, rather than try to tackle the ways that capitalism is intimately connected to environmental devastation, our rulers are attempting to create the illusion that we can address the environmental crisis while maintaining (and *using*) the conditions necessary for (their) capital accumulation. So we are seeing an increased interest in market "solutions" and cynical attempts at "greening" capitalism.

The latest proposed market-based solution being aggressively advanced is creating emissions markets (called "cap and trade"). The idea is that businesses responsible for large amounts of carbon emissions would be given a sort of stock market for those emissions. Those businesses would be given a "cap," or a limit on how much they can pollute, and the stocks (that represent carbon emissions) will be able to be bought and sold and traded in order to create profitability for being environmentally "conscious." This is the brilliant scheme of the same market fundamentalists who brought us the dot-com bubble (and burst) and the subprime mortgage bubble (and burst). Guess who stands to profit by the millions from such an arrangement?

In any case, the problems that got us into this in the first place (the market expansionism inherent in capitalism, the resource depletion in a system based on profit, etc.) are being offered back to us as possible "solutions." And this is just the tip of the iceberg of new schemes of supposed "conscious consumption"—these attempts at trying to make people believe that we can consume away the problems that are endemic in a consumer-oriented society in a consumption-oriented system. Anarchist visions of a decentralized future, of an economy based on popular participation rather than profit, and of a social order free of institutionalized domination give us responses to these kinds of popular mystifications. When analyzing capitalism in the 2000s, we can and should critique the creation of this new bubble, point out whose interests it serves, and be willing to provide possible alternatives to the system of profit, ownership, and markets that got us into this position in the first place.

Toward a Post-Capitalist 2000s

We've tried here to examine some major facets of capitalism in the 2000s that we think are important to the development of a contemporary anarchist critique of political economy, as well as some concepts that we believe can help along the way. There's likely much missing here—for example, an analysis of the origins of this current crisis, the effects of increased digitization on capital mobility and investment, the ways that permanent precarity might structure contemporary class struggle, and so on. However, in the context of a chapter-length piece (and the small amount of space for developing these ideas), we thought that these seven were the best that we could offer in terms of space, knowledge, and interest.

The relevance of anarchist economic analyses can be measured inasmuch as they can be used to create tangible resistance to domination. It is our hope that this particular piece can further struggles against capitalism and hierarchies of all kinds. It is this post-capitalist future that motivates us to write, study, and struggle. It is the power of possibility that often gives us the desire to even get out of bed in the morning in a world like ours where possibilities are so often pushed to the margins in favor of a boring, violent, and fundamentalist belief in the necessity *and* superiority of the status quo. It is our hope that we can add to our resistance strategies against capital, but more so that we can aid in toppling capitalism altogether and creating a livable future for ourselves, each other, and the many inhabitants that we share this world with. Anarchist economics, to be worthy of the name, should be a part of that larger project.

ENDNOTES

1   Keynesianism is a form of capitalism (named after economist John Maynard Keynes) that advocates for robust government intervention and a strong public sector in order to stabilize a predominantly private-sector economy.

2   *Guardian*, October 24, 2008, "Greenspan—I Was Wrong About the Economy. Sort of," http://www.guardian.co.uk/business/2008/oct/24/economics-credit-crunch-federal-reserve-greenspan (accessed August 28, 2010).

3   *Time*, "25 People to Blame for the Financial Crisis," http://www.time.com/time/specials/packages/completelist/0,29569,1877351,00.html (accessed August 28, 2010).

4   *New York Times*, October 23, 2008, "Greenspan Concedes Error on Regulation," http://www.nytimes.com/2008/10/24/business/economy/24panel.html (accessed August 28, 2010).

5   Greg Albo, Sam Gindin, and Leo Panitch, ed., *In and Out of Crisis: The Global Financial Meltdown and Left Alternatives* (Oakland, CA: PM Press, 2010).

6   Http://voidnetwork.blogspot.com/2010/05/exclusive-interview-of-david-graeber-by.html (accessed August 28, 2010).

7   *Rasmussen Reports*, April 9, 2009, "Just 53% Say Capitalism Better Than Socialism," http://www.rasmussenreports.com/public_content/politics/general_politics/april_2009/just_53_say_capitalism_better_than_socialism (accessed August 28, 2010).

8   J. Rogue and Deric Shannon, "Refusing to Wait: Anarchism and Intersectionality," Nov. 11, 2009, http://theanarchistlibrary.org/HTML/Deric_Shannon_and_J._Rogue__Refusing_to_Wait__Anarchism_and_Intersectionality.html (accessed August 29, 2010).

9   Delia D. Aguilar and Anne E. Lacsamana, ed., *Women and Globalization* (Amherst,

NY: Humanity Books, 2004).

10   Diane Dujon and Ann Withorn, *For Crying Out Loud: Women's Poverty in the United States* (Boston: South End Press, 1996).

11   See especially Patricia Hill Collins, *Black Feminist Thought: Knowledge, Consciousness, and the Politics of Empowerment* (New York: Routledge, 2000).

12   "Environmental Facts," Better World Club, http://www.bikeroute.com/EnvironmentalFacts.php (accessed December 13, 2010).

13   U.S. EPA, Sustainable Materials Management: The Road Ahead (2009).

14   "Surveyed Scientists Agree Blobal Warming is Real," January 20, 2009, CNN.com, http://edition.cnn.com/2009/WORLD/americas/01/19/eco.globalwarmingsurvey/ (accessed December 13, 2010).

Fight to Win! Tools for Confronting Capital

D. T. Cochrane and Jeff Monaghan

Context: How to Assess Success or Failure?

Social change does not just happen, it must be created, provoked, necessitated. Transforming systems that perpetrate injustice cannot depend upon determined forces, but rather requires the forces that we create. There is a long history of grassroots movements undertaking campaigns to challenge the political and corporate elite. Operating according to Utah Phillips' dictum—"You've got to mess with people day and night"—diverse tactics have been employed against diverse opponents, with a wide range of successes and failures.

Even when campaigns or movements are not explicitly organized under an anarchist banner, there are anarchistic influences wherever people collectively confront power in an effort to leverage control of their communities. Despite the well-known antagonism between anarchists and Marxist theory, ideology, and ideals, many anarchists nonetheless retain an adherence (often unintentional) to Marx's political economy. Yet much of what anarchists find objectionable in Marxist theory—the determinism, the misinterpretation of state power, the vanguardism—was, for both the great thinker and his followers, a direct consequence of his economic theory. The labor theory of value is the vital component of Marx's scientific socialism that foresees the necessary collapse of capitalism. Of course, Marx asserted that "men [*sic*] make their own history" but he followed that up with "they do not make it as they please."[1] He sought to discover the laws of historical motion, and no matter how he wished to empower individuals, he believed they remained ultimately constrained by the material realities of being. All of this, of course, is deeply contrary to anarchists who generally respond to existing conditions in an ad hoc and amalgamationist fashion rather than based on theoretical prescriptions. This means an antinomy exists between a general anarchistic adherence to Marxist political economy and their adoption of strategies and tactics on the fly. For anarchists, as long as there is oppression, the only necessity is struggle. The forms of that struggle, the short-term aims and even the longer term goals, are not rigid or predetermined. Anarchists have generally rejected the idea that there is or ought to be a pure or inherently revolutionary strategy or tactic. This is one of the reasons self-identified anarchists, or those who adhere to principles that would be considered anarchistic—autonomy, egalitarianism, solidarity, and so on—can be found in diverse social justice organizations and movements. In this chapter we make use of a non-Marxist theory of value and capital in a way that informs and supports the ad hoc perspective on struggle and fighting to win. However, our primary purpose is to propose a method based on this theory as a means for social justice activists to assess their particular campaigns. Such assessment is, we believe, important if people in particular campaigns are to understand their own efficacy and if they are to be part of a larger movement in pursuit of a humane post-capitalist world.

Further, we argue, such an analysis is a needed component of an anarchist economics. Although economics, as a science, is typically centered on production, distribution, and exchange, anarchists have long rejected the disciplinary reduction that tries to separate economics from politics. Production, culture, distribution, sexuality, communication, exchange, gender, and race—as just a few social institutions—are irreducibly intermixed. Our analysis attempts to deal with this reality. In this way, we seek to theoretically catch up to practices on the ground, where anarchists are attempting to change our social worlds and take control of our lives through a praxis that does not isolate economics. Anarchists engage with production, distribution, and exchange as inalienable facets of life, and therefore subject to demands of equal access for all, with neither privilege nor exclusion.

Political-economic disruption campaigns (PEDCs) are among the most commonly adopted strategies that organizers within social justice movements use to confront dominant institutions, particularly corporations. These campaigns are incredibly diverse. Some have explicitly radical goals. Others have concrete and immediate aims. Some align themselves with broader justice movements, while others are narrowly focused on local issues. Some make use of old and familiar tactics. Others are tactically unpredictable and creative. Some espouse an absolute commitment to nonviolence. Others engage in property destruction, kidnapping, and assassination.

Whether employing boycotts or marches, coordinated public actions or autonomous clandestine disruptions, public outreach or direct action, these struggles have shaped the politics, imagination, and participants of the global justice movement. Whether these campaigns aim to reform or negotiate certain corporate activities, evict them from particular spaces, or aim to explicitly shut down their operations, they all target the political-economic body of corporate power: capital.

However questions emerge: Have these campaigns had an impact? If so, what kind of impact? How can the success or failure of particular campaigns and tactics be assessed? Can these disparate campaigns be drawn together to inform and inspire anti-capitalist struggles?

A challenge posed to any movement that confronts dominant political economic entities is the difficulty of evaluating the actual effects of a campaign. We argue that organizers can rely upon a readily available tool for "empiricizing" political-economic disruption campaigns: the capitalists' own quantitative references. Employing the concept of "differential accumulation" developed by political economists Jonathan Nitzan and Shimshon Bichler, we examine the financial fortunes of corporations targeted by these diverse campaigns.[2] As we detail later in this chapter, differential accumulation is a framework for evaluating the financial position of a corporation—or corporate coalition, against various benchmarks. Although there are many tools for evaluating financial positions, we argue that this model is useful because it allows us to evaluate campaigns from the vantage point of capitalists. In this sense, it provides us with an idea of what these corporations feel and fear. To demonstrate this method, we will use differential accumulation to "empiricize" three different campaigns: the anti-sweatshop movement, the Take Down SNC-Lavalin! campaign, and the Stop Huntingdon Animal Cruelty (SHAC) campaign. We will consider the diverse organizing strategies employed by these groups/movements within the differential accumulatory contexts of their targets. We suggest that among the advantages of this perspective for PEDCs are that it: a) provides a means of before-the-fact assessing actions and tactics employed by similar campaigns; b) allows for an after-the-fact assessment of chosen actions and tactics; c) makes organizers cognizant of the actual processes underlying capitalist accumulation, improving their ability to disrupt "business as usual."

These cases, like any other parts of the global justice movement, are complex and we are not interested in casting judgment on "successes" or "failures" in general. The model and opinions that we present are not definitive and are, by design, offered to illustrate only the economic damages from the perspective of the targeted capitalists. We readily acknowledge that there are many perspectives from which to view victories or defeats. What our analysis offers is a preliminary quantitative perspective on diverse tactics of strategically organized campaigns as a means of judging their impact on the targets. This allows us to assess the contexts in which different strategies and actions have challenged the ability of corporations to accumulate. The campaigns discussed below also display ways that organizers can create spaces and possibilities for themselves and broader global justice movements.

"Differential Accumulation" as an Analytical Tool

The concept of differential accumulation has been developed by Jonathan Nitzan and Shimshon Bichler over the last decade and was applied most fully in their book *The Global Political Economy of Israel*. In developing what they call the "power theory of capital," Nitzan and Bichler argue that capital is a strategic power institution.[3] Their theory stands in contrast with both the neoclassicist "utility theory of value" and Marxist "labor theory of value." Profit and its transformation into capital cannot be understood on the basis of either neoclassical "factors of production" or Marxist accounts of surplus value. Both theories employ reductionism based on "impossible entities"—"utils" and socially necessary, simple, abstract labor, respectively. Contrary to the bottom-up conceptions of capital and accumulation, Nitzan and Bichler hold that capital is "finance, and *only finance*."[4] Understood as an institution of power, capital represents the complex assemblages of assets under the control of particular capitalist entities, including the means of production. Capitalists are able to manipulate these assemblages in order to increase, or—more importantly, as Nitzan and Bichler argue—to sabotage production in an effort to accumulate. This process includes much more than ongoing immiseration of the worker, or the development of new, more efficient methods of production. Specific activities such as lobbying or marketing, but also broader social realities such as racism or nationalism, can become part of capital as they play a role in processes of accumulation.

According to Nitzan and Bichler, "the accumulation of capital represents neither material wealth, nor a productive amalgamate of 'dead labor', but rather the *commodification of power*." In this sense, "capitalised profit represents a claim not for a share of the output, but for a *share of control over the social process*."[5] Capital is the translation of control over the diverse social processes—including labor and production—into a divisible, vendible quantitative representation while accumulation is the augmentation of that control. Given that power can only be understood as a relation between two entities, capitalists judge their accumulatory success in relative terms. In other words, they think differentially. The model of differential accumulation was developed to compare how capitalist actors fare in relation to each other.

In contrast to absolute accumulation, which has no meaning once we reject the transcendent entities of neoclassical or Marxist value theory, the guiding logic of capital is to "beat the average [and] their (capitalists') yardstick is the 'normal rate of return', their goal—to exceed it."[6] Differential accumulation can be calculated by the rate of growth of capitalization of one capitalist entity (or capitalist coalition) less the rate of growth of the average capitalization. In other words, it is a calculation of how corporations have compared against an average (whether it is their industry, or the particular market, or the market as a whole). For example, if a firm accumulates at a rate of 10 percent during a boom when their competition averaged 15 percent growth, that firm's differential accumulation—despite its growth—has been negative. In other words, they have experienced relative *deccumulation* and their share of total social profits has decreased. On the other hand, if that same firm shrinks by 5 percent during a recession while their peers have lost 10 percent, the differential accumulation—despite an absolute loss—is positive. They have increased their share of capitalization and, despite the appearance of losses, have grown in relation to their peers-competitors. To increase your relative financial magnitudes is "to increase your relative power to shape the process of social change."[7] This means that both growth and loss can serve the interests of particular firms and moments of crisis or depression are not inherently contrary to the interests of capital. Nitzan and Bichler stress that capital income does not depend on the growth of industry, but "on the strategic *control* of industry."[8]

The business press is suffused with language of "beating the average." Beating the average means growing more powerful. It is to this end that capitalists function, undertaking exercises of massive social upheaval, in an effort to outperform their rivals. This means the primary struggle of capitalism is the intra-capitalist struggle. As Nitzan and Bichler note, "The very essence of differential accumulation is an intra-capitalist struggle simultaneously to restructure the pattern of social reproduction as well as the grid of power."[9] Every other facet of society becomes collateral damage, rewarded or punished as part of diverse accumulatory endeavors.

As an example of how differential accumulation works as an analytical tool, we offer a demonstration concerning the pharmaceutical industry. Figure 1 displays two series, one absolute—the average capitalization of US pharmaceutical firms that are among the largest 500 firms, the other differential—the ratio of pharma's average capitalization to that of the 500 largest firms.[10] The chosen basis of comparison is based on another concept of Nitzan and Bichler's—dominant capital. Their perspective means capital should not be treated as a singular entity with universally shared interests. Rather, each corporation or corporate coalition will have particular interests depending upon what sorts of assets they control and what means are available in their efforts to augment their control. Within capital, they identify dominant capital as "the largest and most profitable corporate coalitions at the core of the social process."[11] Our aggregate of the 500 largest US firms, as measured by market capitalization, is a proxy for dominant capital.

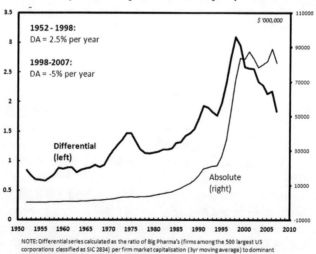

NOTE: Differential series calculated as the ratio of Big Pharma's (firms among the 500 largest US corporations classified as SIC 2834) per firm market capitalisation (3yr moving average) to dominant capital's (500 largest corporations) per firm market capitalisation.
SOURCE: Compustat via Wharton Research Data Services.

Figure 1. Big Pharma Accumulation: Differential or Absolute?

The absolute series, measured in millions of dollars, on the right hand axis, shows incredible growth from 1952 until 1999. From 1999 on, it appears to stagnate at its high level of capitalization. The differential series gives a different picture of what happened to Big Pharma after 1998. Instead of simply stagnating, we can see that pharma lost ground to other dominant firms in the accumulatory struggle. In 1952, the average member of Big Pharma was smaller than the average member of dominant capital (the ratio is less than one), while by 1998, the average pharma firm is three times larger. Their rate of differential accumulation was 2.5 percent per year, a stunning performance against the largest, most powerful firms. By 2007, however, they had fallen to less than twice as large, differentially deccumulating 5 percent per year. The differential perspective motivates different questions than the absolute. In fact, once we dismiss as ridiculous and/or unworkable the transcendent entities of absolute accumulation, the absolute can provoke no questions. In order to answer the questions that emerge from the differential picture, we need to look at the entire field of social processes that bear on accumulation, and not solely to labor and production. The pharmaceutical industry is heavily dependent upon intellectual property rights and marketing. It works to forge personal relationships with physicians. Much of the research that goes into its most profitable drugs emerges from government or university labs. A lot of money is spent developing "copycat drugs." All of this and much more needs to be considered in trying to explain how Big Pharma grew, and why it has fallen. For those involved in PEDCs, this dependence of capital upon complex social processes means disruption of production is not strictly necessary to disrupt accumulation. Rather, targeting any of the processes upon which the firm depends may have an impact. This confirms the street-level adoption of strategies and tactics that have always been anarchists' modus operandi, over the attempt by Marxists to adhere to strategies informed by their pet theory.

Given the importance of capital accumulation for the capitalists' understanding of their own success, it provides us with a means of judging the success of PEDCs that target individual corporations. Although the differential perspective is not the only means to judge success, it does allow an assessment from the capitalists' own perspective: did the PEDC hurt its targets? If a campaign's actions are associated with particular moments of differential deccumulation, or, more importantly, an entire campaign is associated with a trend of differential decumulation, then it seems, all else equal, fair to judge the campaign a success, even if specific goals and outcomes have not been achieved. Of course, caution is always required when trying to tie accumulatory movements to a specific cause, given the complex multitude of forces acting upon and being enacted by any given corporation. Nonetheless, if due caution is taken, campaigns should not hesitate to declare victory when such decumulatory trends are associated with the campaign. In the context of the global justice movement, where confrontational action is a permanent practice of addressing diverse injustices, we can use this model as a method to evaluate campaigns that challenge capitalists, large and small.

Using case studies of three disparate campaigns, all of which included participants who expressly identified as anarchists, we hope to draw some examples and lessons about what actions have worked against what sorts of corporations. Specifically, we will first consider the anti-sweatshop movement's targeting of Nike. A widespread campaign that included a range of political perspectives, from liberal to anti-capitalist, the campaign was one of the precursors to the Northern anti-globalization movement. Secondly, we will examine the 'Take Down SNC-Lavalin!' campaign. Undoubtedly unfamiliar to most, it was a small, short-lived campaign that took place in eastern Canada and Quebec. Despite its local character, it nonetheless managed to exact a toll on its target, a leading global engineering corporation. Finally, we will analyze the SHAC campaign that has recently been the subject of an intense governmental crackdown on so-called "eco-terrorism," precisely because of the huge impact it was having on its target. The conclusions we draw are tentative but we hope they encourage discussion about possibilities and strategies/tactics for fighting (and beating) capitalists. We especially hope to show that if campaigns are knowledgeable about their targets and willing to be flexible in terms of tactics, they can exact a sizable toll on the financial fortunes of targeted corporations. This is true both for well-organized, broad-scale campaigns as well as those that consist of just small groups of disciplined and dedicated organizers.

Case Study 1: Anti-Sweatshop Targeting of Nike

In the mid-1990s, Nike became the paragon of corporate exploitation. The sweatshop emerged as the symbol of global corporations' valuation of profits over workers, the environment, and human dignity. Although, the charge had been leveled against the company since the late 1980s, it was only in 1996 that it began to stick. The close association between the shoe designer-marketer—it can hardly be called a shoemaker—and sweatshops emerged from a more general campaign against the use of child labor by American corporations that began to build momentum during the early 1990s. In 1996, the Apparel Industry Partnership, a presidential taskforce with both industry and non-industry participants, convened to draft an agreement on job conditions. In April 1997, the group reached an agreement that, among other things, set minimum age and maximum hour requirements. However, it was too late for Nike, as the "swoosh" emerged from tight competition with Kathy Lee Gifford as the face of sweatshops.

Nike had been a corporate wonderkind. Just one of many shoe companies of the 1980s, its innovative branding allowed it to rise above the pack. It hitched its wagon to Michael Jordan, whom it then marketed as no other athlete had ever been before. Air Jordans became a must-have item, particularly for inner-city youth. In the process, following the logic of accumulation, it sought to boost earnings by pushing down costs. To this end, it began to ship jobs to low-wage zones in Asia. It was hardly unique in this. However, its own success would bring blowback as its high profile led anti-sweatshop activists to focus their attention on the sportswear company that claimed to be about more than shoes.

The campaign against Nike was almost entirely focused on public education, although participants also sought to shame both CEO Phil Knight and Jordan personally. Actions were usually little more than public spectacles, picketing and flyering. At the time of publishing *No Logo*, Naomi Klein could find only one incidence of vandalism against a Nike Town outlet.[12] Yet, as can be seen in Figure 2, between 1996 and 1997 the actions taken against Nike had a huge impact on its accumulation. The company differentially accumulated 13.5 percent per year from 1981 to 1996, then from 1996 to 1999 it differentially deccumulated at a stunning 28 percent per year. Similar to the graph for Big Pharma, this graph charts Nike against dominant capital. In 1986, Nike was barely 10 percent the size of an average member of this group. By 1996, it was 21 percent larger than the average member. Then, in 1999, it's just half the size. Since 1999, despite the continued pressure on the company, accumulation has resumed. Nike may have,

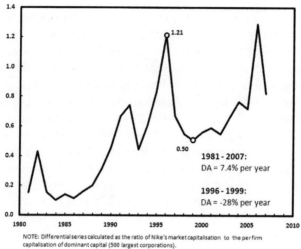

NOTE: Differential series calculated as the ratio of Nike's market capitalisation to the per firm capitalisation of dominant capital (500 largest corporations).
SOURCE: Compustat via Wharton Research Data Services.

Figure 2. Anti-sweatshop Campaign: Taking a Toll on Nike

paradoxically, benefited from the growth of the "anti-globalization" movement as it moved from a criticism of specific companies to corporations and capitalism more generally. Nike became just another corporate miscreant among many.

Nike was susceptible to the tactics adopted by the anti-sweatshop movement because of its dependence on public image. It was a pioneer of advertising that did not directly pitch its product. Instead, it touted a "lifestyle" and then associated itself with that lifestyle. It championed women's right to participate equally in sports. It had ads with Tiger Woods observing that there are still some courses from which he is banned because of the color of his skin. Its philanthropic endeavors provided sports equipment to impoverished children. This carefully constructed image was so thoroughly at odds with the realities of sweatshops that simply exposing their involvement tarnished it. As one of the world's best-known brands, they were also susceptible to "culture jamming": defacing billboards, using corporate logos and slogans in sarcastic and subversive counterattacks. Once Nike's use of overseas sweatshops became general knowledge, any defaced billboard or advertisement served as an instant reminder. Although Nike had positioned itself head and shoulders above its competition in terms of the social appeal of its shoes, it nonetheless faced intense competition.

It was not difficult for consumers to switch to another brand. Culture jamming has been rightly criticized as a limited and non-revolutionary tactic. However, as we noted above, there is no pure or revolutionary tactic. Although tactics must accord with the principles of the organizers, their only other criterion is effectiveness and for this campaign, it appears to have been effective. Of course culture jamming will not, in and of itself, foment revolution, but neither will any other tactic. The effectiveness of culture jamming is limited to corporations dependent upon their image. The campaign against Nike was so effective that it even warranted a mention in its annual report to investors. Forced to explain Nike's poor performance in 1997, Knight cited "labor practices" and the "alarmed" consumer. Although Knight promised that both media and consumers were being "informed," we can see that the message took a few years to get through. In fact, although Nike began to recover in 1999, it wasn't until 2001—the year resistant movements refocused on antiwar efforts and away from corporate misdeeds—that it resumed its early growth levels.

Although Nike managed to escape the accumulatory purgatory into which it was relegated, the anti-sweatshop campaign managed to inflict significant damage. Klein demonstrates how common the differential perspective is, although lacking any theoretical component, when she compares Nike's performance to that of Adidas.[13] During the campaign against Nike, Adidas managed to overtake them and has remained larger, if only just, ever since. This highlights one of the consequences of PEDCs: they may benefit others. Adidas is just as implicated in the use of sweatshop labor as Nike, yet it avoided the same sort of scrutiny and has been the differential benefactor of Nike's decline. However, as long as capitalism remains, there will necessarily be those who benefit from one corporation's differential decline. As with the particular tactics of political economic disruption, PEDCs themselves are not inherently anti-capitalist. Rather, their purpose is to insert us into the accumulatory process, to become risk factors that must be accounted for.

Case Study 2: Take Down SNC-Lavalin!

Organized under the explicitly anti-capitalist hallmarks of the People's Global Action, the Take Down SNC-Lavalin! campaign was a collaboration between Ottawa's Catapult! Collective, June 30th in Toronto, and Block the Empire in Montreal. The target, SNC-Lavalin, was a provider—through subsidiary SNC TEC—of ammunition to the US occupation in Iraq. The campaign featured various tactics, including public education, confrontational marches, covert information gathering from SNC workers, public spectacles and symbolic actions, and calls for autonomous direct actions.

In Ottawa, several marches targeted the SNC office building as part of a campaign that highlighted war profiteering in general. The high-profile "snake marches" took place in the downtown core, and disrupted traffic and business around the buildings housing US defense corporations, including Raytheon and General Dynamics. On the international day of solidarity with Iraq in 2005, Catapult! members scaled the façade of SNC's Ottawa office building to call attention to all manner of exploitive practices, including the production of munitions, the degradation of the environment, and their destructive mining and biotech projects around the world. In Montreal, members of Block the Empire tried to install a photo exhibit featuring images of occupied Iraq entitled "Your Bullets, Iraqi Lives," in the lobby of SNC's corporate headquarters, a building that the company shares

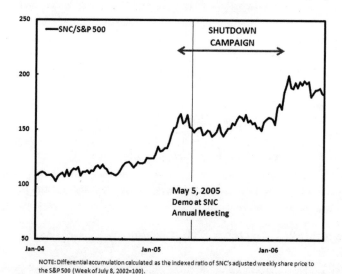

Figure 3. Take Down SNC-Lavalin!: Relative to the S&P 500

with the US consulate. In Toronto, organizers crashed a banquet hosted by SNC-Lavalin. A diverse collection of activist organizations participated in a protest outside SNC's 2005 Annual General Meeting, which drew national media attention. As news stories noted, the protest overshadowed the company's otherwise "promising outlook."

We have charted the differential status of SNC relative to the S&P 500[14]—as a proxy for dominant capital—from 2002 until 2006. The campaign lasted from early 2005 until early 2006. Our data indicates that SNC experienced a significant change in its accumulatory trend over this period. As can be seen in Figure 3, SNC enjoyed significant accumulation in the period before the campaign began. In the year prior to the first week of April 2005, SNC gained 53.5 percent relative to the S&P 500. Over the course of the campaign their accumulation stagnated. Eventually the campaign lost its momentum and stopped mobilizing when it realized one of its goals: SNC's divestment from its arms-producing entity SNC TEC. At that point SNC resumed its upward accumulatory trend. As noted above, there is no absolute "average" against which capitalists judge their success, this too is contingent. As such, we also charted SNC's performance against an index composed of two of its sectoral competitors—fellow Canadian engineering firm Aecon and a US firm of roughly the same size, Jacobs Engineering.

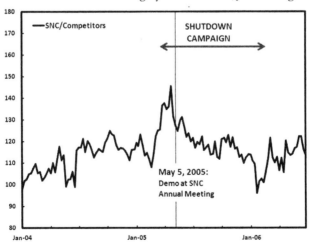

NOTE: Differential accumulation calculated as an indexed ratio of SNC's adjusted weekly share price to a weighted composite of two sectoral competitors (Aecon and Jacobs Engineering Group) (Week of July 8, 2002=100). The composite of the two firms was weighted for their market capitalizations.
SOURCE: Yahoo! Finance

Figure 4. Take Down SNC-Lavaline!: Relative to Competitors

This shows even more clearly SNC's differential fate over the duration of the campaign. From its apex, the week of April 25, 2005, to its nadir, the week of January 23, 2006, SNC-Lavalin differentially *decumulated* 34 percent. In the context of SNC's global reach, its engagement in several sectors, and its political connections, this frozen (or declining) period is of significant interest. Why did SNC-Lavalin's trend of accumulation stall? Were investors frightened by public associations with war profiteering? Did they prefer the relative anonymity of other potential investment opportunities? Did they fear the confrontational style of the Take Down SNC organizers? Did they worry that more disruptive direct actions were to come? These are all possibilities that require further consideration.

Both graphs demonstrate that accumulation continued beyond the start of the campaign, and resumed before what we've identified as the end—the aforementioned sale of SNC TEC. The continuation of accumulation beyond the start of the campaign is not surprising. A single march criticizing SNC-Lavalin was unlikely to be considered a threat to accumulation. However, the beginning of the campaign was particularly intense. With actions in the three aforementioned cities the campaign appeared to be widespread. Activists in Halifax and Vancouver also incorporated criticism of SNC into their antiwar efforts. The resumption of accumulation before what we've identified as the end of the campaign is also unsurprising. For various reasons, the campaign lost steam and began to peter out. The resumption of accumulation shows that market participants felt the PEDC against SNC was no longer a threat. Perhaps this occurred because a forthcoming sale of SNC TEC was suspected which would defuse criticism of SNC-Lavalin as a "war profiteer." The market let the campaign know it was over. Nonetheless, we conclude that the campaign had an impact and managed to hit SNC-Lavalin where it hurt and should be considered a factor in the company's decision to sell its munitions production.

Two features of SNC-Lavalin allowed the chosen tactics of the Take Down campaign to be successful. First, SNC TEC was a relatively minor production segment as a percentage of SNC's earnings. SNC's primary business is engineering-related. Although its engineering and other activities also provide grounds for criticism, they are not directly implicated in war. Second, although SNC-Lavalin is one of Canada's largest corporations, with operations and political connections all over the world, the corporation is little known. This made them susceptible to a public education campaign that brought both the public and media spotlight to bear upon them, particularly when it focused on the company as a "war profiteer." The relative unimportance of SNC TEC for earnings made it more likely SNC-Lavalin would judge the gains of diverting the public glare to outweigh any decline due to the loss of SNC TEC's profits.

SNC TEC was sold to General Dynamics, whose business is almost entirely military-related. Notably, we do not believe a similar naming and shaming campaign aimed at them is likely to succeed in the same way. While SNC-Lavalin and its investors were not prepared to be decried as "war profiteers," General Dynamics undoubtedly is. Any investors with moral or practical objections to "war profiteering" have already placed their capital elsewhere. This does not mean a campaign against General Dynamics is impossible, just that it could not rely on the same tactics. The fact that SNC TEC was sold to General Dynamics and continues to produce bullets sold to the US military means that the success of the Take Down! PEDC was certainly limited. Nonetheless, it is significant that a short campaign organized by a couple dozen people spread throughout three cities managed to have this impact on a multi-billion-dollar corporation. Take Down SNC-Lavalin! succeeded in injecting itself into the accumulatory efforts of SNC-Lavalin and its success required their capitulation, however limited.

Case Study 3: Stop Huntingdon Animal Cruelty (SHAC)

The SHAC campaign officially began in 1999 and has developed into an international campaign, comprised of several dozen active groups. Although many organizers are associated with other elements of the animal rights and animal liberation movements, the SHAC campaign is organized with the exclusive objective of shutting down the vivisection firm Huntingdon Life Sciences (HLS).

Since the beginnings of the SHAC campaign, organizers have scored numerous victories against HLS. Through their relentless antagonism they provoked several banks and financiers to pull loans and scared hundreds of business partners into terminating contracts and severing business relations. In the words of HLS Chairman Andrew Baker they engendered a widespread view of HLS as "a pariah" of the business world. Strategically, SHAC has identified secondary and tertiary targets and taken direct action against them as well. Secondary targets include the banks that have given financial support to HLS, while tertiary targets include the customers of secondary targets. The intention has been to provoke a decumulatory fear in the financiers so they would sever ties with HLS, rather than risk losing other customers. SHAC stresses that their efforts focus on publishing material about animal abuse and issuing action alerts through their websites and mail lists. Their websites and publications publicize this material and participating groups, to varying degrees, encourage individuals to undertake a broad array of tactics to confront these targets. These have included business disruptions, encouragement of autonomous actions, large and small rally demonstrations, property destruction, letter-writing campaigns, ethical investment strategies, boycott organizing, and so on.

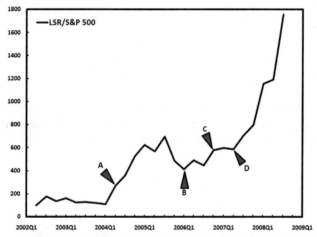

NOTE: Differential series calculated as the indexed ratio of the market capitalization of Life Sciences Research (formerly Huntington Life Science) to the S&P 500 (2002 Q2 = 100).
SOURCE: Compustat via Wharton Research Data Service; Yahoo! Finance

Figure 5 SHAC Crackdown: 'Eco-terrorism' and Accumulation

The most well-known tactic associated with SHAC is the "home demonstration." These involve activists confronting vivisectors, financiers, and corporate executives at their residences. These non-violent but highly confrontational tactics are meant to bring attention and shame upon their targets (and their families) in an attempt to undo the privacy and secrecy that are important components of the political economy of the vivisection industry. The wide range of direct action targets was a central motive underlying the corporate-state suppression campaign against SHAC. In fact, our research indicates that it was precisely the success of their tactic that provoked the government's heavy-handed suppression.

The public visibility of organizers involved in SHAC made them a scapegoat upon which the government could hang every direct action committed by environmental and animal liberation groups and autonomous cells. Politicians, media, and prosecutors in the United States and United Kingdom have frequently made the association between groups affiliated under SHAC and actions undertaken (and claimed) by autonomous individuals and groups, such as the Animal Liberation Front (ALF). The government has claimed that because SHAC affiliated groups provide information about animal abusers, they are facilitating or even interchangeable with the ALF.

Citing "eco-terrorism," the corporate-state suppression campaign against SHAC developed over several years. Our graph depicting the differential accumulation of HLS has marked four notable moments in the state-corporate suppression campaign targeting SHAC. These dates are: "A"—the indictment of the US SHAC 7; "B"—the conviction of the US SHAC 7; "C"—the signing of the enhanced US Animal Enterprise Terrorism Act (AETA), an amplified version of the Animal Enterprise Protection Act under which the SHAC 7 were charged; and "D"—Operation Achilles that targeted organizers of SHAC and the general animal liberation movement in the United Kingdom and other Western European countries.

Our graph begins in 2002 after HLS moved their headquarters to the United States under the shell company Life Science Research. After SHAC UK successfully prevented HLS from accessing capital markets in the United Kingdom, by targeting both the banks that provided loans and the "market makers" needed to participate in equity markets, the corporation moved to the United States in an attempt to access new pools of investors and capital. HLS also hoped to benefit from stronger privacy protections accorded to US investors compared to their UK counterparts to prevent SHAC from targeting their capital sources.

As seen in Figure 5, from 2002 to 2003, HLS accumulation was stagnant. This suggests that following the HLS move to the United States, the SHAC campaign was successful in halting the corporation's differential growth. However, in late 2003, coincident with the US government's increasing criminalization of the activities of SHAC USA organizers, HLS began to accumulate. With the indictment of the SHAC 7, HLS experienced a sharp rise in differential accumulation. This accumulatory trend became more turbulent in early 2005, perhaps over uncertainty concerning the verdict in the SHAC 7 trial, although SHAC UK was also still active. A renewal of accumulatory growth was associated with the SHAC 7's conviction. After the conviction, HLS's accumulation was upward, but still turbulent. Undoubtedly this was because SHAC's international presence meant the US government's legal maneuvers had not completely neutralized SHAC. The passage of the AETA marks an intensification of the upward trend, indicating an expectation that this was another nail in the coffin of SHAC. With the initiation of Operation Achilles, the United Kingdom aligned its criminalization of environmental and animal liberation with the United States. This released HLS from most of the perceived risk of SHAC's direct action and the corporation's differential accumulation skyrocketed.

Aside from the debate about whether or not these criminal proceedings had a neutralizing effect on the campaign, our data suggests that the corporate-state campaign against SHAC and the imprisonment of activists was perceived as a victory for HLS by market participants. The accumulatory trend illustrates the logic behind the corporate-state counter-campaign targeting SHAC. In contrast to the early period of the graph—where SHAC was inflicting significant disruption against HLS and its allies, preventing any differential accumulation—the final portion of the graph indicates that the surge in capital accumulation coincided with the corporate-state suppression campaign of so-called "eco-terrorists." Freed from the threat of disruption, HLS achieved significant differential success following the state's efforts to neutralize and demobilize the SHAC campaign. This evidences the earlier success of the SHAC campaign to seriously impact the accumulatory efforts of its target. Further, it indicates how far capital can and will go to remove a threat that is truly hitting it where it hurts.

The success of SHAC's PEDC seriously threatened the future of HLS. The UK government had to intervene with loans and special dispensations when banks and other business service firms refused to do business with the vivisection firm. This special consideration was vital for HLS's continued viability and should be considered as an important and valued part of HLS's capital. These interventions are evidence of SHAC's determination, combativeness, and innovative tactics.

SHAC has provided organizers with important lessons on how PEDCs provoke the anxieties of capital. Investors have a twofold fear: 1) fear of being personally targeted; 2) fear that the fear of others will drive down the value of the stock. With their success in isolating HLS within the business "community," SHAC demonstrated how activists can leverage the naked commitment of capital to accumulation. Although the banks' managers who swore not to do business with HLS almost certainly personally despised being forced to capitulate, that was of no consequence; one segment of capital will not make a principled stance in defense of other segments. Short of a threat to capitalism itself, the accumulatory process means capitalists are more than willing to sacrifice their compatriots if doing otherwise risks their own accumulation.

Conclusions

Aside from damaging that which capitalists covet most—profits!—PEDCs are also integral to movement building. Whether we succeed in closing sweatshops, put a stop to the manufacturing of weapons, or halt the destruction of nonhuman life, we are actively challenging those accumulating rewards at the expense of others' suffering. While confronting our enemies, anarchist organizers must also consider the forms, structures, and practices that we undertake to prefigure a radically different society. Neither concrete PEDC goals nor prefigurative practices can take precedence, and fighting to win is about both.

Marxists and the traditional left have for too long fixated on sectarian identities and dogmatic programs at the expense of challenging dominant forces that, especially for those of us from privileged backgrounds, live next door. We must acknowledge that resistance to corporate globalization takes infinite forms and struggles, and not all anti-corporate campaigns are anti-capitalist. One of the leading organizations in the movement against Nike, and sweatshops in general, was United Students Against Sweatshops (USAS). Not only were they not anti-capitalist—although active members certainly were—they intentionally mimicked the hierarchical structure of the corporations they targeted. This resulted in a leadership structure that privileged the type of male-dominated, competitive, and non-participatory environments that anarchists are committed to eliminating. Similarly, animal rights activism, including SHAC, has been criticized for not making connections with other forms of violence and oppression. Despite such legitimate critiques, are committed anarchist organizers to forsake these (and similar) movements?

We think not. Capitalism has evidenced a remarkable resilience. The differential process results in plasticity that demands anti-capitalists work with (or at least support) allies who may not share our organizing principles or prefigurative ideals. This does not require compromising our principles. It is possible to balance vigilance towards centralizing tendencies that reproduce hierarchical and non-participatory power structures, avoid the exclusionary and reactionary divisiveness that limits movement building, and work short-term with allies who share the limited goals of a PEDC. Anarchists, not hampered by excessive theoretical prescription, can work toward short-term outcomes that will have real and desirable consequences, even if just to set capital back on its heels for a moment. Fighting to win is a twofold process of both damaging the existing power structure and prefiguring a humane post-capitalist society.

Participants in PEDCs need to recognize the limitations of such endeavors in terms of challenging capitalism itself. Given the differential nature of accumulation, there will always be capitalist beneficiaries of PEDCs. Capital always flees to another, who welcomes its arrival. We believe Nitzan and Bichler's theory of differential accumulation offers the best means of understanding precisely how anti-capitalists can effect change within capitalism through the confrontation of capital. The theory draws attention to the qualitatively complex structures and processes that constitute accumulation. It also makes us aware of how far our interjections into the accumulatory process can go. Any victory that fails to topple the ethical justification and juridical apparatus of private property that make possible capital and accumulation will always be a partial victory. That means no particular campaign need be criticized as such, for we are always aware that it is.

If we understand capital as the quantification of claims over qualitatively complex social processes, we cannot treat all corporations as the same. The high diversity of social assets that are drawn upon to make profits means each corporation will have different vulnerabilities. The same tactics cannot be reflexively used against different targets.

Diversity of tactics becomes not an ethical position, but a tactical necessity. While public awareness may be sufficient against some targets, others may require direct action.

Part of any transition will be a transformation of the political economic hierarchy. The vested interests will not simply disappear under the weight of their own contradictions. We can mess with them all we want, but if we cannot affect their ability to accumulate and augment control over social processes, then we have no hope of moving beyond the capitalist status quo.

ENDNOTES

1   Karl Marx, *The Eighteenth Brumaire of Louis Bonaparte*, 1852, www.marxists.org/
    archive/marx/works/1852/18th-brumaire/ch01.htm (accessed June 3, 2009).

2   See Jonathan Nitzan and Shimshon Bichler, *The Global Political Economy of Israel*
    (London: Pluto Press, 2002). With the exception of their newest book, *Capital As
    Power* (2009), Nitzan and Bichler make their work freely available at bnarchives.net.

3   Nitzan and Bichler, *The Global Political Economy of Israel*, 31.

4   Ibid., 36. Emphasis included. We do not want this to be conceptually blurred
    with Marx's notion that finance represents the "highest form of capital." Our
    contention is that finance is the only form of empirically identifiable capital, not
    merely a subset. For Marx, finance capital was mixed among other functions of
    capitalism but was ultimately a fiction against the reality of material production,
    which is anchored in the labor process. The Marxist labor theory of value states
    that production is where labor is exploited and surplus value expropriated, and
    where capital accumulation takes place. This allowed Marx to distinguish different
    segments of capital based on the M-C-P-C'-M' breakdown of the capital
    flow. Only P is productive. C, representing merchant capital, and M, representing
    finance capital were considered parasitic. However, these distinctions cannot be
    made empirically—how do we distinguish which of Caterpillar's profits are due
    to the parasitic Cat Finance and which are due to its production units, which
    produce for customers who depend upon loans from Cat Finance? This breakdown
    of capital is a theoretical tale that cannot help us in trying to understand
    contemporary capitalism.

5   Ibid. Emphasis included.

6   Ibid., 37.

7   Ibid., 38.

8   Ibid., 45. Emphasis included.

9   Ibid., 41.

10   Both series have been smoothed as three-year moving averages to facilitate their demonstrative use.

11   Ibid., 40.

12   Naomi Klein, *No Logo: Taking Aim at the Brand Bullies* (Toronto: Knopf Canada, 2000), 367.

13   Ibid., 378.

14   Unlike the Big Pharma and Nike graphs, ratios using the S&P 500 are indexed. Therefore, the individual numbers have no meaning. They are only meaningful in longitudinal comparison, like with the consumer price index.

Escaping Capitalist Hegemony: Rereading Western Economies

Richard J. White and Colin C. Williams

"[O]n the left, we get up in the morning opposing capitalism, not imagining practical alternatives. In this sense, it is partly our own subjection—successful or failed, accommodating or oppositional—that constructs a 'capitalist society.'"[1]—J.K. Gibson-Graham

"To re-read a landscape we have always read as capitalist, to read it as a landscape of difference, populated by various capitalist and noncapitalist economic practices and institutions—that is a difficult task. It requires us to contend not only with our colonized imaginations, but with our beliefs about politics, understandings of power, conceptions of economy, and structures of desire."[2]—C.C. Williams

Introduction

This chapter contests the widely held belief that we exist in a "capitalist" world, one in which goods and services are produced, distributed, and organized around the unadulterated pursuit of profit in the marketplace. That this belief is both misguided and mistaken is testament to the powerful economic discourse which colonizes the mind and imagination into believing that capitalism is omnipresent, particularly so in the Western economies. In 1898, Kropotkin observed:

[I]t is certain that in proportion as the human mind frees itself from ideas inculcated by minorities of priests, military chiefs and judges, all striving to establish their domination, and of scientists paid to perpetuate it, a conception of society arises, in which conception there is no longer room for those dominating minorities.[3]

It is the desire to free the mind from the ideas inculcated by a dominant minority within economics that informs the particular focus of this chapter. To this end the chapter will develop a critical challenge to a central economic discourse—the commodification thesis—on two important grounds. The first is related to questioning the empirical data that claims to offer support to such a dominant thesis. The second involves critically unpacking the regime of representation and discursive construction that effectively serves to legitimate the vested interests of capital and constrain the actions of anarchist (and other) economic agents and policy makers who desire to engage with and harness meaningful alternative economic practices.

From a critical perspective, rethinking "the economic" is to engage in a process that is highly subversive and long overdue. As this chapter argues, such a commitment allows greater focus and clarity to emerge on a heterodox range of alternative/post-capitalist economic practices, practices that are firmly embedded in the economic fabric of the contemporary world, and particularly so in the "advanced" economies of the West. Importantly, the very act of identifying dynamic, routine, non-capitalist practices as existing in the here and now offers a practical and tangible opportunity to abandon the market without the need to envisage, design, or agitate for a completely new alternative economic system to capitalism. The chapter concludes by drawing on some key implications that a rereading of economic practices has for transforming the way in which we should think about our economic futures.

A Capitalist Hegemony?

One mode of work, that in which "goods and services are produced by capitalist firms for a profit under conditions of market exchange"[4] can claim to have hegemonic status within the popular imaginary of "the economic." In contemporary economics, capitalism alone, as Gibson and Graham argue, has been constituted as:

> large, powerful, persistent, active, expansive, progressive, dynamic, transformative; embracing, penetrating, disciplining, colonizing, constraining; systemic, self-reproducing, rational, playful, self-rectifying,; organized and organizing, centred and centering; originating, creative, protean; victorious and ascendant; self-identical, self-expressive, full, definitive, real, positive, and capable of conferring identity and meaning.[5]

This narrow economic discourse is maintained still further by the popular representation of this capitalist sphere that perceives the market as *increasing* its dominant status within the economy. The market, it is argued, is expanding inexorably at the expense of the other two principal modes of producing and delivering services and goods in society, namely the "community" and the "state." As Castree et al. argue: "that this is a predominantly capitalist world seems to us indisputable... there's scarcely a place on the planet where this mode of production does not have some purchase...this system of production arguably now has few, if any, serious economic rivals."[6] Significantly, such a reading is not only widely held by those of a neoliberal bent, and who would openly welcome such economic totalitarianism, but it is also evident in the very language of those who actively resist it.[7] For one illustration of this, consider Buck's reading of "the economic" when he argues that:

> *The neo-liberal economic system in which life (anarchic or otherwise)* takes place, has much to do with the setting of life. It is with and in this system that anarchists must vie for living room. Hence, the need for economic thought among anarchists.[8]

To begin to address this economic scenario critically, it is constructive to visualize this capitalist hegemony in context with "alternative" spheres of work (those "alternative" spheres which are believed to be washed over and increasingly eroded away by a relentless sea of capitalism). In Figure 1, the shaded area represents those goods and services that contain two intrinsic qualities, namely that they are (1) produced for exchange, and (2) that this exchange is monetized and imbued with the profit motive (i.e. to make or to save money). It is this form of exchange that is interpreted by a capitalist hegemony thesis to be continually expanding at the expense of other forms of

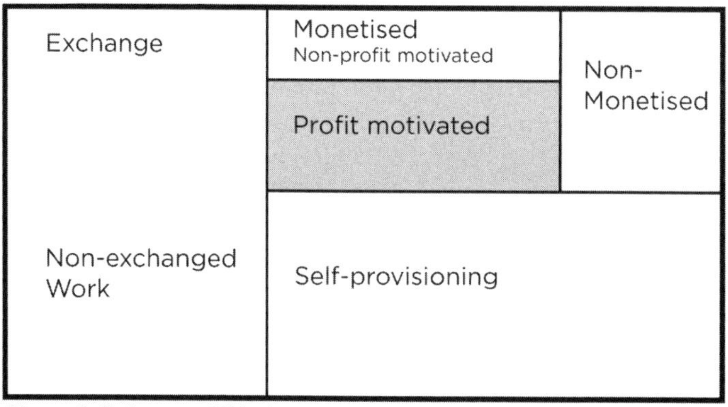

Exchange	Monetised Non-profit motivated	Non- Monetised
	Profit motivated	
Non-exchanged Work	Self-provisioning	

Figure 1: Spheres of Work

work and exchange. The alternative spheres of work are defined by the qualities that they *lack* in comparison to the capitalist form of exchange. So alternative forms of work would be seen where the work is non-exchanged, non-monetized, and/or where the work is monetized and not undertaken primarily for profit-motivated rationales.

Such a dominant reading of the economy through this capitalist lens has troubling implications on many levels. Arguably the most significant of these is that this reading is so powerful that it effectively channels thought and visions of possible forms and modes of economic organization as taking place *within* and not beyond, or outside of, a capitalist framework of economic management and organization. Thus any critical project which seeks to envision the very possibility of harnessing truly alternative non-capitalist futures of work and exchange to displace this capitalist sphere are dismissed out of hand as naive, implausible (not to say impossible), misguided, yet another example of puerile utopia. Though there may be alternative approaches that rearrange the economic deck chairs on the capitalist ship, there are no real alternatives *to* capitalism itself. The sobering outcome of this is that, as Frederic Jameson writes,

> [i]t seems to be easier for us today to imagine the thoroughgoing deterioration of the earth and of nature than the breakdown of late capitalism; perhaps that is due to some weakness in our imaginations.[9]

A Call to Unleash Our Economic Imaginations

To imagine capitalism's supersession is neither utopian nor impractical. An increasing global body of anarchist, critical, post-capitalist, and post-development academics and activists have successfully begun to problematize the meta-narrative of capitalist hegemony and exposed the spurious empirical grounds that this hegemonic status is embedded in. Regarding the latter, Williams observed:

> Given the overwhelming dominance of this belief that a commodification of the advanced economies is taking place, one might think that there would be mountains of evidence to support such a stance. Yet one of the most worrying and disturbing

findings once one starts to research musings on this subject is that hardly any evidence is ever brought to the fore by its adherents either to show that a process of commodification is taking place or even to display the extent, pace or unevenness of its penetration.[10]

While appreciating the difference and diversity within and between these approaches, collectively many have also sought to recognize, value, and harness heterodox economic practices *that are already part of contemporary society.* This has been crucial in allowing a meaningful space for thinking critically about how to better imagine, create, and construct these non-capitalist forms of work and organization in the future.[11]

Two key strategies have been employed to upset the theoretical and symbolic signs that construct capitalist hegemony as both "natural" and "inevitable." The use of discourse analysis has been employed to critique the notions that objects/identities are inherently stable and fixed.[12] Such a subversive and radical focus has been employed to destabilize the binary opposition which is employed by modern societies to establish and differentiate "order" (i.e., capitalist work practices) and "disorder" (i.e. non-capitalist work practices). The binary opposition works to effectively continually suppress the latter category (non-capitalist) and promote the former (capitalist). However, to attempt to challenge this binary opposition on its own terms (promote non-capitalist work practices by attaching monetary value to domestic work, for example) is extremely problematic given the powerful organizational complexity within this binary hierarchy. This is apparent when a wider framework of understanding is sought, where one can perceive, for example, the multiple ways that the binary opposition links formal work with the masculine, the rational, the objective, the productive, and informal work to the "other" (including, but not limited to, the feminine, the emotional, the subjective, the non-productive).

Another strategy harnessed to expose the unstable and fuzzy nature of economic exchange has been to indicate ways in which formal and informal economic spaces are *not* mutually exclusive or necessarily oppositional in nature. Gibson and Graham, for example, argue that the household can be interpreted as a place where goods and services can be produced, just as a factory setting can also act as a reproductive space.[13] A further related significant approach has been to show how formal and informal economic spaces are intimately connected. For example, research has shown how non-commodified work is often undertaken in a more creative, empowering, and non-routine nature within households that are relatively market-orientated. To recap, some of the more searing critiques that have challenged and subverted the hierarchical economic binaries in modern thought have emerged from attempts to (a) revalue the subordinate category, (b) reinterpreted the sites of production/consumption/reproduction, and (c) highlight the interconnectedness of the binary opposition.

Academics looking to promote non-capitalist economic futures have also embraced a more Foucauldian approach to challenging and deconstructing commodification ideology. This is evidenced in two ways, firstly by those who adopt a genealogical analysis of the processes and (dis)continuities by which a particular discourse is constructed, and secondly by critically analyzing the way theories, systems of meanings, and unwritten rules effectively exclude, censor, and restrict, and thereby can be used effectively to perpetuate injustice and violence.[14] To offer a more detailed look at this, in his provocative post-structualist work *Encountering Development: The Making and Unmaking of the Third World*, Escobar embraces such a Foucauldian approach when focusing on (deconstructing) the postwar discourse on development.[15] In his own words:

> To speak development, one must adhere to certain rules of statement that go back to the basic system of categories and relations. This system defines the hegemonic worldview of development, a worldview that increasingly permeates and transforms the economic, social, and cultural fabric of Third World cities and villages, even if the languages of development are always adapted and reworked significantly at the local level.[16]

Through harnessing a historical narrative, he demonstrated how post–World War II societies in Asia, Africa and Latin America became synonymous with terms such as "backward," "poor," "illiterate," "under-nourished," and "under-employed," and thus became seen to be in need of Western assistance. The problems of the Third World under such a Western diagnosis, it is argued, could only be remedied by a dose of industrialized First World economic development. Thus the development policies that became powerful and effective postcolonial mechanisms of control were, from the very beginning, created and enforced principally to serve the interests of the industrialized nations of North America and Europe. Importantly, those disadvantaged the most by this Western hegemonic discourse (e.g., peasants, women) were also—on the face of it—arguably the least able to transcend and think beyond the grand narratives and structures produced by this discourse. However, encouragingly, Escobar draws on examples of individuals and "hybrid cultures" that have transformed the development regime of representation. These individuals and cultures have effectively repositioned themselves as active agents (of resistance) in the face of this professionalization of development, and have successfully created alternatives in the face of modernity's crisis. One of the central conclusions he makes is about how best to move beyond this apparently hegemonic discourse:

> instead of searching for grand alternative models or strategies, what is needed is the investigation of alternative representations and practices in concrete local settings, particularly as they exist in context of hybridization, collective action and political mobilization.[17]

A powerful call to move away from capitalocentric readings of the economic and envisage a rich and dynamic alternative economic spectrum comes through the work of joint authors Gibson and Graham.[18] Adopting a similar approach to Escobar by harnessing a Foucauldian critique, Gibson-Graham's work has also consistently harnessed a Derridan framework of deconstruction. This has made a deep and powerful impact on rethinking (and encouraging others to rethink) conventional representations of capitalism as the naturally dominant form of economy and thus contributes to an anti-capitalist politics of economic invention. The author(s) engage with a process of "unearthing," "of bringing to light images and habits of understanding that constitute "hegemonic capitalism" at the intersection of a set of representations."[19] One only has to think, for example, of how people and nations are categorized and positioned within linear representations of Western capitalism to see the (imposed) configurations of power in the world. This established configuration interprets the most formalized economies as being the most "advanced and progressive," and the most informal/non-capitalist economies as those that are by reference "backward, under-developed."

To reimagine and rethink the capitalocentric economic landscapes of the Western countries through a pluralistic economic lens that allows for the recognition of diversity and difference in commodified and non-commodified spheres of work, for example, has two key implications. In the first instance it openly allows for the possibility of future alternative economic work practices. Secondly, it openly suggests that alternative economic work practices are very much situated in the present and thus represents alternative non-capitalist economic spaces as both existing and emerging. The pedagogical-inspired economic "iceberg model" (figure 2) that they employ is particularly effective in demonstrating the plurality of economic activities that are situated within society. The model makes visible those rich and diverse economic activities that, within the capitalist hegemony thesis are effectively "[r]educed to... another shadowy zone, often hard to see for lack of adequate historical documents, lying underneath the market economy; this...elementary

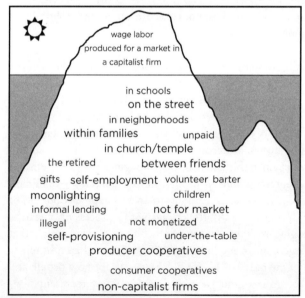

Figure 2. The Economic Iceberg

basic activity which went on everywhere and the volume of which is truly fantastic...a layer covering the earth."[20]

The effectiveness of this model can be discerned on many levels, not least as Gibson and Graham themselves argue, in that the model

> opens up conceptions of economy and places the reputation of economics as a comprehensive and scientific body of knowledge under critical suspicion for its narrow and mystifying effects.[21]

The prevalence of alternatives to capitalism in contemporary society certainly illustrates an impressive range of possibilities to exit and abandon the market: alternative models *are* being practiced and enabled within the current economic framework. Moreover, as we will argue later, these alternative work practices are *expanding* in the Western world relative to exchanged and monetized work.

A criticism of this argument may be that it is too idealistic—how can these disparate economic practices form a coherent and robust challenge to capitalism? To take one example: how can regular, routine, household work provide us with the tools to take on the grand façade of capitalism? Byrne et al. make a strong case for arguing in the affirmative:

> We can view the household as hopelessly local, atomized, a set of disarticulated and isolated units, entwined and ensnared in capitalism's global order, incapable of serving as a site of class politics and radical social transformation. Or we can avoid conflating the micro logical with the merely local and recognize that the household is everywhere; and while it is related in various ways to capitalist exploitation, it is not simply consumed or negated by it. Understanding the household as a site of economic activity, one in which people negotiate and change their relations of exploitation and distribution in response to a wide variety of influences, may help to free us from the gloom that descends when a vision of socialist innovation is consigned to the wholesale transformation of the "capitalist" totality.[22]

When one is encouraged to perceive the market from this perspective, which removes capitalism from its core position at the center of the Western imaginary, then this re-signification brings to the foreground the possibility of post-capitalist futures. The market as conceived by Byrne and represented so effectively in Gibson-Graham's economic iceberg model becomes one of many types of economic practice. It is divested of its "inherent" and naturalized dominant status that it has enjoyed. Importantly, such a rereading of capitalism hegemony is also firmly supported by the empirical work that has focused on the emerging diversity of economic trajectories. This discussion becomes the focus of the next section.

Understanding Dominant Economic Trajectory: One of Plurality and Difference

Two central arguments can be discerned within the capitalist hegemony thesis: first, that non-exchanged work is contracting relative to monetized exchanges and second that, monetized exchanges are becoming increasingly commodified: i.e., undertaken for profit-motivated purposes. Any critical investigation of this thesis then should rightly be expected to find robust evidence in support of these two arguments.

A Critical Focus on Non-Exchanged Work in Western Economies

Time-budget studies have become an important way of making detailed records of how people allocated their time. From this it is possible to highlight the comparative proportion of time individuals allocate to paid work and non-exchanged work. Given the claims of the capitalist hegemonic thesis, one could rightfully expect paid work to take up a (significant) majority of time in the Western "advanced" economies. Table 1 however illustrates a very different scenario. When focusing on the allocation of working time across twenty different Western countries, time spent in unpaid domestic work (i.e. non-exchanged work) accounts for 43.6 percent. Indeed, the proportion of time spent on non-exchanged work exceeds this figure in France (45.3 percent), Norway (46.7 percent), and Finland (44.6 percent). What to conclude from this: it appears that limits of the market to a claim on time are far more restricted and uneven than allowed for by market advocates or those who have opposed its encroachment but still see the commodification process as inevitable and unstoppable. In light of this evidence, how can we reconcile such a statement as "the pervasive reach of exchange-value society makes it ever more difficult to imagine and legitimate non-market forms of organization and provision"?[23] Or, equally, the pronouncement by Castree et al.

> that this is a predominantly capitalist world seems to us indisputable…there's scarcely a place on the planet where this mode of production does not have some purchase…this system of production arguably now has few, if, any, serious economic rivals.[24]

Country	Paid work (minutes per day)	Non-exchanged work (minutes per day)	Time spent on non-exchanged work as % of all work
Canada	293	204	41.0
Denmark	283	155	35.3
France	297	246	45.3
Netherlands	265	209	44.1
Norway	265	232	46.7
UK	282	206	42.2
USA	304	231	43.2
Finland	268	216	44.6
20 countries (avg.)	297	230	43.6

Table 1. Allocation of Working Time in Western Economies

This finding, though, is not unexpected. For example, consider Polanyi when he spoke of the "great transformation,"[25] one which had seen economic life becoming "progressively disembedded from its societal and cultural matrix."[26] Polanyi was quite careful—and well justified—not to exaggerate the extent of the shift in balance from economic activity taking place in the non-market sphere and the market.[27]

However, when the other powerful meta-narrative of capitalist expansion—that of becoming ever more expansive, totalizing, and hegemonic—is considered in reference to the evidence, then even such notions of a "great transformation" seem to be exaggerated. Again drawing on longitudinal data produced based on the time-use survey, there appears to be little evidence that economic activity has moved from non-waged work and into paid work. In Western countries such as the United Kingdom, the United States, France, Finland, and Denmark, paid work now occupies a *lower* share of people's total working time than it did forty years ago (see Table 2).

Country	1960–73		1974–84		1985–present	
	Mins per day	% of all work	Mins per day	% of all work	Mins per day	% of all work
Paid Work	309	56.6	285	57.3	293	55.4
Subsistence Work	237	43.4	212	42.7	235	44.6
Total	546	100.0	497	100.0	528	100.0

Table 2: Subsistence work as a percent of total work time across 20 countries, 1960 to present. Source: Gershuny (2000, Table 7.1)

Non-monetized Exchange

Further suspicion about the legitimacy of the capitalist hegemony thesis can be found in the problematic fact that non-exchanged work is extremely prevalent in the Western world. The belief that non-monetized exchange is being systematically overcome by market-based transactions embodied in Harvey's statement that "[m]onetary relations have penetrated into every nook and cranny of the world and into almost every aspect of social, even private life"[28] again begs the obvious question: where is the evidence?

When a concerted attempt is made to gather robust empirical data to support such a central tenet this proves extremely difficult. In many Western countries there is a significant amount of work that takes place on an unpaid basis, whether through more formal, voluntary-based groups or organizations, or through informal networks of reciprocal support, such as mutual aid or unpaid community exchange. In 2001, for example, the Home Office Active Citizenship Survey identified that within the previous twelve months around 3.7 billion hours of volunteering had taken place. Given that twenty-seven million people work full-time for an average of thirty-five hours per week, this 3.7 billion hours of volunteering equates to just over two million people being in work on a full-time basis. Alternatively, it indicates that in the UK up to one hour is spent working on a non-monetized basis for every fourteen hours spent working in formal employment.

These statistics quite clearly indicate that the capitalist hegemonic belief that argues that these economic spaces are marginal, residual, and disappearing is at best grossly exaggerated. The reality is that non-monetized exchange (that is to say unpaid community work, mutual aid, or more formal voluntary work) continues to occupy prevalent and important spaces within the contemporary economic landscapes in Western society.

Not-For-Profit Monetary Transactions

Zelizer observed that "a powerful ideology of our time [is] that money is a single, interchangeable, absolutely impersonal instrument—the very essence of our rationalizing modern civilization."[29] Certainly, the assumption that monetary exchange is principally profit-motivated cuts deep across economic discourses ranging from anarchism to neo-classicalism.

This crude view of monetized exchange is often promoted across this range too, and is common to those who welcome such a (natural) development, and those who cite this as another reason to resist and push against any further capitalist advances being made in society. Yet there are many "alternative economic spaces" that exist as sites where not-for-profit monetary transactions are commonplace including, but not limited to, garage sales,[30] car boot sales,[31] charity shops,[32] and local currency experiments such as Local Exchange and Trading Scheme.[33] What quickly becomes apparent when looking at the complexity of monetized exchange in contemporary society is that "money is neither culturally neutral nor socially anonymous"[34] and thus as Zelizer writes,

> The classical economic inventory of money's functions' and attributes, based on the assumption of a single general-purpose type of money, is unsuitably narrow. By focusing exclusively on money as a market phenomenon, it fails to capture the very complex range of characteristics of money as a social medium…certain monies can be indivisible (or divisible but not in mathematically predictable proportions), nonfungible, nonportable, deeply subjective and qualitatively heterogeneous.[35]

It is also worthwhile reflecting on the public sector, a sector which is not oriented towards profit and still accounts for about 30–50 percent of GDP in Western economies.[36] Even if the public sector is no longer as significant as it has been in terms of being a provider of goods and services, it is important not to make the mistake of assuming that the provisions for these goods and services have been taken up by the capitalist sector. The growth of the not-for-profit sector has been seen in many Western economies, which represents around five percent GDP. Drawing on data gathered by the Johns Hopkins Comparative Nonprofit Sector Project (CNP), Salamon and Sokolowski examined the not-for-profit sector in twenty-four countries.[37] In terms of economic impact this is a "$1.1 trillion industry that employs 19.5 million full-time equivalent (FTE) paid workers in the twenty-four countries on which data are so far available."[38] As Table 3 shows, on average the nonprofit sector grew by 24 percent between 1990–1995, compared to just an 8 percent rise in employment. In the United States, the growth in employment stood at 8 percent during this time, whereas the growth in employment in the nonprofit sector was 20 percent. In Europe (UK, Netherlands, Germany, France), whereas growth in the total economy grew by 3 percent, the nonprofit sector increased by 24 percent. Given such trends—far from reinforcing the link between the profit-motivated and monetary exchange—it could be more properly suggested that this relationship is diminishing.

Within the private sector, it is unquestioningly assumed by the supreme representation of enterprises (themselves assumed to be coherent, predictable, ordered, organized sites) that any monetary transactions are always and necessarily market-like, and therefore driven principally by profit-motive rationales. Yet this relationship has also come under the critical spotlight, with studies demonstrating that such an assumption is not entirely robust, and there are examples of private-sector enterprises that are not always driven by the necessity to make profit and do retain sub-capitalist economic constructions and practices.[39] To take one example, in seeking to open a conversation about what a corporation is, O'Neill and Gibson-Graham analyzed the Australian-based multinational BHP.[40] The research questioned the capitalist notions of "the company" in a way that ultimately "[p]roduce[d] a decentred, 'disorganized' representation of the enterprise." The researchers highlighted the unpredictable, social and open nature of the enterprise—and decoupled the essentialist arguments of these entities, including the logic that they are only driven by profit-motivated concerns. This itself was seen to be significant not only in undermining popular representations of enterprise discourses, but in the act of producing a more nuanced reading that has "the potential to liberate the political and geographical imagination, and to proliferate alternative possibilities for regional futures and corporate-community relationships."[41]

Country	Nonprofit Sector 1990–95 Change		Total Economy* 1990–95 Change	
	Net	As % of 1990 level	Net	As % of 1990 level
France	157,202	20%	-329,000	-2%
Germany	422,906	42%	2,163,875	8%
Hungary	12,200	37%	-25.641	-1%
Israel	19,182	15%	395,237	33%
Japan	450,652	27%	7525,680	14%
Netherlands	41,623	7%	240,000	5%
UK**	119,068	28%	-202,058	-1%
US*	1,360,893	20%	1,872,817	3%
EU Total/Avg. (4 Countries)	740,800	24%	1,872,817	3%
Other Total/Avg. (4 Countries)	1,842,927	25%	15,976,069	14%
Total/Average	2,583,727	24%	17,848,886	8%

*) Total non-agricultural employment, updated: January 20, 2000.
**) Excluding sport and recreation, unions, and parts of education.
NOTE: Except for Israel and the Netherlands, all 1990 figures come from Johns Hopkins Comparative Nonprofit Sector Project, Phase I, and have been adjusted where necessary to make them comparable with the 1995 figures.
Table 3. Changes in Nonprofit Sector FTE Employment, by Country, 1990–1995

The result of this critique is one that argues that it is simply not the case, despite all the popular assumptions to the contrary, to say that we live in a capitalist world. When all the estimates are taken into account, significantly less than half of the Western economies can be properly said to be aligned with commodity production driven by capitalist profit-motivated monetary rationales and relationships (see Figure 3).

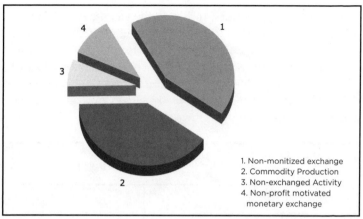

1. Non-monitized exchange
2. Commodity Production
3. Non-exchanged Activity
4. Non-profit motivated monetary exchange

Figure 3: Distribution of Work in Western Societies

Explaining the Persistence of Alternative Economic Practices

There are several approaches which have been adopted to explain the persistence of alternative economic practices in Western economies. One view argues that the growth of these non-capitalist practices is a result of a new emergent stage of capitalism, which discards social reproduction functions back into the non-capitalist realm.[42] De-commodification, in this approach, is the result of the flexibilization and deregulation of production, a trend that has resulted in the breakdown of the postwar welfare states and economic regulations.

But to explain the presence of alternative economic practices in such stark structural economic terms is, we argue, extremely problematic. Once the extent of the non-capitalist sphere has been identified, and the heterogeneous rationales that underpin it have been explored, then such an explanation is found inadequate. For example, UK-based research using Household Work Practice surveys has shown that although higher-income households lead more marketized lives, they engage in a higher level of alternative economic practices.[43] In contrast to lower-income households, the type of informal work practices that they engage in are more creative, rewarding, fulfilling, and non-routine. Moreover, another principal finding is that the majority of higher-income populations choose to engage in such work, compared to lower-income populations, which undertake such work out of economic necessity. Such findings suggest the need for any explanations of the persistence of alternative economic practices to incorporate agency-orientated narratives in addition to economistic discourses, if more accurate and robust readings are to be forthcoming.

For Cahill, "the anarchist looks about him or her and sees *protest and resistance* against the dominant economic system."[44] A more agency-orientated reading of the continued presence/relevance of alternative economic practices would focus on them as being preserved by successful cultures of resistance in the face of increasing disillusionment and dissatisfaction with capitalism and its hegemony.[45]

From this reading, non-capitalist economic practices have been interpreted as "spaces of hope"[46] that contain intrinsic values such as pleasure and satisfaction that are absent from commodified formal spaces.[47] Certainly, it must be said that not only is capitalism far from complete, but it is struggling to defend its ground in what is, and continues to be, a deeply contested process.

Conclusion

The American anarchist Howard Ehrlich argued, "We must act as if the future is today."[48] What we have hoped to demonstrate here is that non-capitalist spaces are present and evident in contemporary societies. We do not need to imagine and create from scratch new economic alternatives that will successfully confront the capitalist hegemony thesis, or more properly the capitalist hegemony *myth*. Rather than capitalism being the all powerful, all conquering, economic juggernaut, the greater truth is that the "other" non-capitalist spaces have grown in proportion relative in size to the capitalism realm.

This should give many of us great comfort and hope in moving forward purposefully for, as Chomsky observed: "[a]lternatives have to be constructed within the existing economy, and within the minds of working people and communities."[49] In this regard, the roots of the heterodox economic futures that we desire *do exist in the present*. Far from shutting down future economic possibilities, a more accurate reading of "the economic" (which decenters capitalism), coupled with the global crisis that capitalism finds itself in, should give us additional courage and resolve to unleash our economic imaginations, embrace the challenge of creating "fully engaged" economies. These must also take greater account of the disastrous social and environmental costs of capitalism and its inherent ethic of competition. As Kropotkin wrote:

Don't compete!—competition is always injurious to the species, and you have plenty of resources to avoid it! Therefore combine—practice mutual aid! That is the surest means for giving to each and all to the greatest safety, the best guarantee of existence and progress, bodily, intellectual, and moral....That is what Nature teaches us; and that is what all those animals which have attained the highest position in the respective classes have done. That is also what man [*sic*]—the most primitive man—has been doing; and that is why man has reached the position upon which we stand now.[50]

A more detailed and considered discussion of the futures of work, however, is beyond the scope of this chapter. What we have hoped to demonstrate is that in reimagining the economic, and recognizing and valuing the non-capitalist economic practices that are already here, we might spark renewed enthusiasm, optimism, insight, and critical discussion within and among anarchist communities. The ambition here is similar to that of Gibson-Graham, in arguing that:

The objective is not to produce a finished and coherent template that maps the economy "as it really is" and presents... a ready made "alternative economy." Rather, our hope is to disarm and dislocate the naturalized dominance of the capitalist economy and make a space for new economic becomings—ones that we will need to work to produce. If we can recognize a diverse economy, we can begin to imagine and create diverse organizations and practices as powerful constituents of an enlivened noncapitalist policies of place.[51]

If the chapter has succeeded in doing this then it will have achieved its principal objective.

Endnotes

1   J. K. Gibson-Graham, *The End of Capitalism (As We Knew It): A Feminist Critique of Political Economy*, new ed. (Oxford: Blackwell, 2006), xv–xvi.

2   C. C. Williams, *A Commodified World? Mapping the Limits of Capitalism* (London: Zed, 2005), 226.

3   P. Kropotkin, "Anarchism: Its Philosophy and Ideal," (San Francisco: Free Society,

1898) http://dwardmac.pitzer.edu/Anarchist_archives/kropotkin/philandideal.html.

4   A. J. Scott, "Capitalism, Cities and the Production of Symbolic Forms," *Transactions of the Institute of British Geographers*, NS 26 (2001): 11–23.

5   Gibson-Graham, *The End of Capitalism* (Minneapolis: Minnesota Press, 2006), 4.

6   N. Castree, N. M. Coe, K. Ward, and M. Samers, *Spaces of Work: Global Capitalism and the Geographies of Labour* (London: Sage, 2004), 16–17.

7   See Comelieau, *The Impasse of Modernity* (London: Zed, 2002); J Rifkin, *The Myth of the Market: Promises and Illusions* (Dartington: Green Books, 1990); and D. Slater and F. Tonkiss, *Market Society: Markets and Modern Social Theory* (Cambridge: Polity, 2001).

8   E. Buck, "The Flow of Experiencing in Anarchic Economies," in R. Amster, A. DeLeon, L.A Fernandez, A. J. Nocella II, and D. Shannon, *Contemporary Anarchist Studies: An Introductory Anthology of Anarchy in the Academy* (New York: Routledge, 2009), 57. Emphasis added.

9   F. Jameson, *The Seeds of Time* (New York: Columbia University Press, 1994), xii.

10 C. C. Williams, *A Commodified World? Mapping the Limits of Capitalism* (London: Zed, 2005), 23.

11 For example, see Byrne et al., "Imagining and Enacting"; Community Economies Collective "Imagining and Enacting Noncapitalist Futures," *Socialist Review* 28 (2001): 93–135; J. K. Gibson-Graham, "Poststructural Interventions," in *A Companion to Economic Geography*, ed. E. Sheppard and T. J. Barnes (Oxford: Blackwell, 2003); J. K. Gibson-Graham, *Post-Capitalist Politics* (Minneapolis: University of Minnesota Press, 2006); Gibson-Graham, *The End of Capitalism*; and C. C. Williams, *A Commodified World? Mapping the Limits of Capitalism* (London: Zed, 2005).

12 See, for example, J. Derrida, *Of Grammatology* (Baltimore: Johns Hopkins University Press, 1967).

13 See Gibson-Graham, "Poststructural Interventions."

14 M. Foucalt, "Governmentality," *Ideology and Consciousness*, 6 (1991): 5–21.

15 A. Escobar, *Encountering Development: The Making and Unmaking of the Third World* (Princeton, NJ: Princeton University Press, 1995).

16 Ibid., 17–18.

17 Ibid., 19.

18 See J. K. Gibson-Graham, *The End of Capitalism*.

19 Ibid: 5.

20 F. Braudel, *The Perspective of the World* (London: William Collins Sons, 1985), 630.

21 J. K. Gibson-Graham, "A Diverse Economy: Rethinking Economy and Economic

Representation," www.communityeconomies.org/papers/ rethink/rethink7diverse. pdf (accessed January 5, 2010), 1.

22   Byrne et al., "Imagining and Enacting," 16.

23   A. Amin, A. Cameron, and R. Hudson, *Placing the Social Economy* (London: Routledge, 2002), 60.

24   Castree et al., *Spaces of Work*, 16.

25   K. Polanyi, *The Great Transformation* (Boston: Beacon Press, 1944), 43.

26   K. P. Levitt, "The Great Transformation from the 1920s to the 1990s" in *Polanyi in Vienna: The Contemporary Significance of The Great Transformation*, Karl McRobbie and K. P. Levitt (London: Black Rose Books, 2000), 10.

27   For a more extended critique, see R. J. White and C. C. Williams, "Re-thinking Monetary Exchange: Some Lessons from England," *Review of Social Economy* (2009): 1470–1162.

28   D. Harvey, *The Limits to Capital* (Oxford: Blackwell, 1982), 373.

29   V. A. Zelizer, *The Social Meaning of Money: Pin Money, Paychecks, Poor Relief, and Other Currencies* (Chichester: Princeton University Press, 1997): 1.

30   See S. S. Soiffer and G. M. Hermann, "Visions of Power: Ideology and Practice in the American Garage Sale," *Sociological Review* 35 (1987): 48–83.

31   See N. Gregson and L. Crewe, *Second-Hand Worlds* (London: Routledge, 2002).

32   See L. Crewe, N. Gregson, and K. Brooks, "The Space of Creative Work: Retailers and the Production of the Alternative," in *Alternative Economic Spaces*, A. Leyshon, R. Lee, and C.C. Williams (London: Sage, 2001); and C. C. Williams and C. Paddock, "The Meanings of Informal and Second-Hand Retail Channels: Some Evidence from Leicester," *International Review of Retail, Distribution and Consumer Research* 13, no.3 (2003): 317–336.

33   For example, see E. Cahn, *No More Throw-Away People: The Co-operative Imperative* (Washington DC: Essential Books, 2000); R. Lee, "Moral Money? LETS and the Social Construction of Economic Geographies in Southeast England," *Environment and Planning* A 28 (1996): 1377–94; P. North, "LETS: A Tool for Empowerment in the Inner City?," *Local Economy* 11, (no. 3) (1996): 284–293; and C. C. Williams, T. Aldridge, R. Lee, A. Leyshon, N. Thrift, and J. Tooke, *Bridges into Work? An Evaluation of Local Exchange and Trading Schemes (LETS)* (Bristol: The Policy Press, 2001).

34   V. A. Zelizer, *The Social Meaning of Money: Pin Money, Paychecks, Poor Relief, and Other Currencies*: 18.

35   Ibid, 19.

36   See Williams, *A Commodified World?*

37   L. M. Salamon, and W. Sokolowski, "Volunteering in Cross-National Perspective:

Evidence From 24 Countries," Working Papers of the Johns Hopkins Comparative Nonprofit Sector Project, no. 40, Baltimore, Johns Hopkins Center for Civil Society Studies, 2001.

38   Ibid., 3.

39   See Gibson-Graham, *The End of Capitalism*; R. Lee, "Shelter from the Storm? Geographies of Regard in the Worlds of Horticultural Consumption and Production," *Geoforum* 31 (2000): 137–157; P. O'Neill and J. K. Gibson-Graham, "Enterprise Discourse and Executive Talk: Stories that Destabilize the Company," *Transactions of the Institute of British Geographers*, 24 (1999): 11–22; E. Schoenberger, "Discourse and Practice in Human Geography," *Progress in Human Geography* 22 (1998): 1–14; Williams, *A Commodified World?*; and M. Zafirovski, "Probing into the Social Layers of Entrepreneurship: Outlines of the Sociology of Enterprise," *Entrepreneurship and Regional Development* 11 (1999): 351–371.

40   O'Neill and Gibson-Graham, "Enterprise Discourse and Executive Talk," 11.

41   Ibid., 20.

42   For example, see M. Castells and A. Portes, "World Underneath: The Origins, Dynamics and Effects of the Informal Economy," in *The Informal Economy: Studies in Advanced and Less Developing Countries*, ed. A. Portes, M. Castells, and L. A. Benton (Baltimore: Johns Hopkins University Press, 1989); R. Lee, "Production," in *Introducing Human Geographies*, ed. P. Cloke, P. Crang, and M. Goodwin (London: Arnold, 1999); and A. Portes, "The Informal Economy and Its Paradoxes," in *The Handbook of Economic Sociology*, ed. N. J. Smelser and R. Swedberg (Princeton NJ: Princeton University Press, 1994).

43   For example, see Williams, *A Commodified World?*; and C. C. Williams and J. Windebank, *Poverty and the Third Way* (London: Routledge, 2003).

44   Cahill, "Co-operatives and Anarchism" in *For Anarchism, History, Theory and Practice*, ed. D. Goodway (London: Routledge, 1989), 240.

45   See Byrne et al., "Imagining and Enacting Non-Capitalist Futures, Rethinking Economy Project Working Paper no.1," Community Economies Collective "Imagining and Enacting Noncapitalist Futures"; P. Crang, "Displacement, Consumption and Identity," *Environment and Planning*, A 28 (1996): 47–67; L. Crewe and N. Gregson, "Tales of the Unexpected: Exploring Car Boot Sales as Marginal Spaces of Contemporary Consumption," *Transactions of the Institute of British Geographers* 23 (1998): 39–54; J. Davies, *Exchange* (Milton Keynes: Open University Press, 1992); Lee, "Shelter"; and V. A. Zelizer, *The Social Meaning of Money* (New York: Basic Books, 1994).

46   D. Harvey, *Spaces of Hope* (Edinburgh: Edinburgh University Press, 2000).

47   See also R. J. White, "Explaining Why the Non-Commodified Sphere of Mutual

Aid Is So Pervasive in the Advance Economies: Some Case Study Evidence from an English City," *International Journal of Sociology and Social Policy* 29, nos. 9/10, (2009): 457–472.

48   Cited in Cahill, "Co-operatives and Anarchism," 236.

49   N. Chomsky, *Noam Chomsky: The Common Good*, (Chicago: Odonian Press, 1999), 139.

50   P. Kropotkin, *Mutual Aid: A Factor of Evolution* (UK: Freedom Press, 1902 [1998]), 73.

51   J. K. Gibson-Graham, *The End of Capitalism* (Minneapolis: University of Minnesota Press, 2006), xii.

Part 3
Critique

"We are free, truly free, when we don't need to rent our arms to anybody in order to be able to lift a piece of bread to our mouths."—Ricardo Flores Magón

Globalized Contradictions of Capitalism and the Imperative for Epochal Change

John Asimakopoulos

According to the Congressional Budget Office, as of summer 2009 the United States has approved $787 billion in "stimulus spending" with trillions in additional commitments and calls for a second package to save capitalism for/from the capitalist lords on the backs of neo-serf taxpayers. Now that we face a new globalized Great Collapse, the time has come to show objectively why all of this was easy to predict and why capitalism must be replaced by a new socioeconomic system. This new egalitarian system is not assured based on deterministic-mechanistic Marxist economic theory. It is possible for capitalism to survive regardless of the global catastrophe required to save it given the use of state violence to protect it. Thus, the question becomes: do we accept the perpetual downgrading of working-class living standards or do we resist? Before asking people to resist, we must first demonstrate why things simply will not get better with objective analysis. Then we must demonstrate what would be a superior system and how it would work. Finally we need to show people how to resist in order to usher in a new epoch of social justice, love, and brotherhood and sisterhood. This must be part of anarchist economic analysis if we are going to argue convincingly for the need and, importantly, *possibilities* for system change. This chapter focuses on why capitalism is destined to collapse repeatedly.

According to Social Structures of Accumulation (SSA) theory, multiple social and historical factors, rather than mechanistic economics, determine economic growth. Specifically, capitalists invest on expectations of return that are shaped by external economic, as well as political and ideological, conditions. This external environment is referred to as the SSA, which determines economic expansion and the class distribution of economic gains. Important features of the institutional environment are the system of money and credit, the pattern of state involvement in the economy, and the structure of class conflict.[1]

The structure of class conflict is of particular importance because it determines the shape of institutional arrangements and whether they will be conducive to investment. SSA also holds that expansionary periods eventually end due to institutional relations becoming ossified, relative to the demands of new economic realities.[2] This is the Marxist argument of the relations of production (institutional relations) becoming fetters to the forces of production (industrial capacity).[3] Lastly, this approach views the development, internal dynamics, and decline of each SSA as historically contingent.

It is argued that a global SSA is forming based on the solidifying regimes of financialization, neoliberal trade, and a new global segmentation of labor resulting from, and intensifying, the defeat of developed nation working classes. But as the historical process of capital concentration is intensifying, occurring at the international versus national level, the fundamental mechanics of capitalism remain unchanged. However, this presents a *qualitative* break from the past in that corporations have severed the flow of a national business cycle by outsourcing *production* to nations with authoritarian labor and civil rights conditions for cheap disciplined workers while depending on market-based *consumption* in advanced nations. This leads to reductions in purchasing power without a mechanism to restore income flows back to the worker-consumers of developed nations. Consequently, the class contradictions of the new system have resulted, and will continue to result, in global economic stagnation, if not collapse. The reason is that the new regime of global production lacks a corresponding regime for consumption. Inevitably this will cause stagnation due to the classic contradiction of overproduction and underconsumption emanating from capitalist private property relations. Therefore, a structural solution is not reform, but altering property relations toward libertarian socialist/anarchist forms of societal organization, allowing for the uninterrupted flow of production-consumption.

Components of the Global SSA

Given the declining rate of profit since the 1970s within developed nations, capitalism has pursued surplus value through globalization. As a result, we are witnessing the formation of a new US-led global SSA based on three emerging regimes. The first is the financial regime based on the World Bank and International Monetary Fund (IMF) functioning as (de)regulatory institutions for the global economy.[4] The second is a neoliberal trade regime expressed by the World Trade Organization (WTO) and free trade agreements (FTAs).[5] The third involves globally segmented labor markets made possible by, and intensifying, the defeat of national working classes. The origins of these regimes can be traced back to developed nations, in particular the hegemonic United States and to a lesser degree the European Union.

The financial regime

The formation of the new financial regime centered on the IMF, World Bank, and transnational banks can be traced to the 1980s. Its creation came out of the collapse of the Bretton Woods regime in the 1970s. At that time transnational banks were forming, providing offshore tax havens without controls on capital flows for transnational corporations. The banks accumulated massive reserves from corporate accounts which were then lent to developing nations creating the foundation for the 1980s debt crises. These developments and corporate behavior were also a major cause for the demise of the Bretton Woods regime (which had institutionalized the old colonial relations) and financial deregulation (e.g., of capital flows and currency exchange rates, causing the Mexican currency crisis in 1994 and Asian in 1997). In the wake of the 1980s debt crises which followed, the role of the World Bank and IMF changed *qualitatively* by adopting neoliberal principles leading to the formation of new financial and trade regimes. The adoption of neoliberal ideology by these institutions was assured given that the United States has 16.79 percent of the vote at the IMF and 16.38 percent at the World Bank—shares multiple times more than that of any other single nation; the United States and European Union have 48.88 percent of the vote at the IMF and 44.94 percent at the World Bank; and traditionally the World Bank is headed by an American and the IMF by a European.[6]

Panitch and Gindin argue that the financial regime is not new.[7] Rather, it is a continuation of forces dating to the formation of Bretton Woods when the financial sector was requesting policies associated today with neoliberalism such as free capital flows. That financial or any other capital was opposed to regulation that it did not control should not be surprising. What is important is that at the end of the day Bretton Woods did not include these demands. Therefore the liberalization of capital flows is more properly dated to the 1980s although it has its origins in the prior system. Interestingly, Panitch and Gindin seem to acknowledge this qualitative shift: "The impact on American financial institutions of inflation, low real interest rates, and stagnant profits in the 1970s accelerated the *qualitative transformations* [italics added] of these years, which increasingly ran up against the old New Deal banking regulations....This was what prompted the global 'financial services revolution.'"[8]

Specifically, the first major shift occurred when in its *World Development Report 1980*, the World Bank changed the definition of development from "nationally managed economic growth" to "participation in the world market."[9] This was a move away from what in essence was nationally managed economic growth practiced by developing nations toward neoliberal global trade (meaning capital mobility) controlled by and privileging transnational corporations. Second, the World Bank and IMF went from providing project loans to reorganizing the economies of poor nations in crisis through policy/structural adjustment loans. For example, when poor nations are forced to seek help from the IMF (as a lender of last resort) they must agree to neoliberal reorganization of their economy—especially privatization—before obtaining assistance from the World Bank and transnational banks. In addition to privatization of state resources, these measures, which reflect the 1980s Thatcher-Reaganite ideology, include severe reductions in public spending, currency devaluation, and wage reductions to attract "foreign investment" as a result of decreased export prices.

Therefore, the emerging financial regime is designed to facilitate global capital mobility in search of profits via cheap labor. The importance of capital mobility and privatization is that it makes possible the financing of production and ownership of national resources in developing regions. This is demonstrated by the record level of net foreign direct investment (FDI) inflows to China which have intensified upon its WTO entry in 2001.[10] In fact, the implementation of such policies has been followed by intensification in FDI flows to extremely poor nations given no restrictions on profit repatriation. Prior to such liberalization, nations imposed restrictions on the levels of FDI flows and foreign ownership of domestic industries to maintain control over their economy. However, this made it difficult for transnational corporations to engage in their investment strategies. More important than rock-bottom prices for national resources, the regime secures the repatriation of profits from production in developing nations.

In terms of interstate rivalries, the financial regime is the most stable out of the three which constitute the emerging SSA. This is true because it institutionalizes US global financial interests tying the economies of other nations to it. According to Panitch and Gindin, "the globalization of finance has included the *Americanization* of finance, and the deepening and extension of financial markets has become more than ever fundamental to the reproduction and universalization of American power."[11] However, this was not sufficient to stabilize the global system of which financialization is but only a component. More specifically, as argued by Frank:

> financial instruments have been ever further compounding already compounded interest on the real properties in which their stake and debts are based, which has contributed to the spectacular growth of this financial world. Nonetheless, the financial pyramid that we see in all its splendour and brilliance... still sits on top of a real world producer-merchant-consumer base, even if the financial one also provides credit for these real world transactions. ...As world consumer of last resort...Uncle Sam performs this important function in the present-day global political-economic division of labour. Everybody else produces and needs to export while Uncle Sam consumes and needs to import....[a significant reduction in US consumption] may involve a wholesale reorganisation of the world political economy presently run by Uncle Sam.[12]

Therefore, the Achilles' heel of the system remains consumption. This is true even if nations such as China and Japan have no choice but to participate in the financial regime through purchases of T-bills to prop up the value of the dollar and thus US consumption/imports. In other words, even a global financial regime is dependent on a balance between production and consumption leading us back to purchasing power and aggregate demand.

The neoliberal trade regime

While the financial regime secures capital mobility, the global trade regime centered on the WTO and FTAs is needed to secure mobility of production. The blueprint was the 1994 North American Free Trade Agreement (NAFTA). NAFTA allowed the free flow of goods and investment *but not of people* between an industrialized high-wage region and a developing one with extremely low wages. Furthermore, NAFTA did not include any labor or environmental standards, leading to a race to the bottom.[13] It was predicted by proponents that NAFTA would lead to a US trade surplus with Mexico. Instead, from 1993 to 2004, it rapidly led to a $107.3 billion trade deficit and a loss of 1,015,291 US jobs.[14]

The establishment of the WTO in 1995 extended these dynamics to a global scale. For example, the US trade deficit with pre-WTO China averaged $9 billion per year from 1997 to 2001 (Scott 2007). When China entered the WTO in 2001, the deficit began to average $38 billion per year from 2001 to 2006. As a result of these investment flows, Robert Scott reports,

> The rise in the U.S. trade deficit with China between 1997 and 2006 has displaced production that could have supported 2,166,000 U.S. jobs. Most of these jobs (1.8 million) have been lost since China entered the WTO in 2001. Between 1997 and 2001, growing trade deficits displaced an average of 101,000 jobs per year…. Since China entered the WTO in 2001, job losses increased to an average of 441,000 per year.[15]

Furthermore, between 1948 and 1970 there were only six FTAs, thirty-four from 1971 to 1991, but after the establishment of the WTO in 1995 the number of FTAs reached 181 by 2002, spreading neoliberal trade far and wide.[16]

This neoliberal trade regime allows corporations to safely move production around the globe in search of low labor costs and financial incentives without fear of tariffs or barriers in order to boost historically declining profits. In addition to lowering transaction costs for globalized production, FTAs also guarantee that once the goods are produced in low-wage regions they can be exported unhindered into developed nations like the United States for market-based consumption. Barriers to trade would have made this unprofitable, thus limiting the extent of globalization.

Moreover, FTA rules are typically designed in secret by corporations and their governments, often with little to no participation of any citizen, environmental, or labor groups. A prime example of this is the WTO proceedings.[17] Not surprisingly, the trading rules disproportionately privilege capitalist interests, which pit high-income workers of developed regions against those of underdeveloped regions through outsourcing and export processing zones (EPZs).[18] For example, Mexican real wages have remained flat despite NAFTA's promises as employment increased in EPZ's or maquiladoras together with declines in US jobs and real wages.[19]

Globally segmented labor markets

These policies shift national labor market segmentation, a concept developed by Gordon et al. to a new artificially created *global segmentation of labor* without corresponding limitations on capital flows.[20] The origins of the new labor regime can be traced back to the 1980s when the United States had to contain inflation to stem capital outflows and balance the international financial system. At the time, taming inflation meant increasing interest rates through the Volcker shock (by reducing the money supply and later increasing federal rates) and containing wage-led inflation from a US labor and civil rights movement on its last gasp. The latter was achieved by crushing what remained of the labor movement exemplified by Reagan's firing of the air traffic controllers. This cleared the way for financial capital to expand its global outreach (by securing international confidence in the value of the dollar) and its merging with production capital.[21]

Although the new labor accord had been initiated by Reagan defeating US workers in the 1980s, it could not be fully developed into globally segmented labor markets without first the financial regime to secure capital mobility (1980s) and, second, the neoliberal free trade regime (1995) to secure mobility of production but not of people. For this reason the emergence of globally segmented labor markets can be dated to 1994–1995 with the establishment of NAFTA and the WTO, the final element in the equation. In essence neoliberal globalization, and the emergence of globally segmented labor markets, re-institutionalizes the old Bretton Woods core-periphery relations, which it had institutionalized in turn from the pre–world war colonial system. Effectively, the world's poor are trapped in regions of absolute-poverty wages, creating a modern serfdom.

More importantly, global segmentation of labor markets presents a *qualitative* change in that it institutionalizes and intensifies a 1970s labor accord based on defeated national working classes by updating the traditional core-periphery divide of colonialism and neo-colonialism. This creates high-income regions (figure 1) of *democratic market-based consumption*, where consumers are given greater sovereignty and consumption opportunities. However, as workers, they experience flat real wages, increasing inequality, and the erosion of social safety nets such as pensions, health-care benefits, and job security.[22] Low-income regions of *authoritarian production* such as China are also created where the great majority of people remain subsistence-wage consumers. For example, "it has been estimated that wages in China would be forty-seven to eighty-five percent higher in the absence of labor repression."[23] According to the National Labor Committee (NLC) these workers experience flat and extremely low incomes, violations of basic human and labor rights, and sweatshop conditions while independent monitors and the media are prohibited in such factories and EPZs.[24]

Furthermore, although the Bureau of Labor Statistics does not track Chinese wages, it estimated the hourly factory compensation in China to be sixty-four cents including wages, benefits, and social insurance.[25] By contrast, in 2004 the hourly factory compensation in Mexico and Brazil was $2.50 and $3.03 respectively, compared to $21.90 in Japan, $23.17 in the US, $23.89 in France, $24.71 in the UK, and $32.53 in Germany.[26] In addition, wages for China, Mexico, and Brazil have remained relatively flat since the 1990s as other parts of the world have been able to offer even cheaper labor. For example, the average hourly wage for apparel workers in Guatemala is thirty-seven to fifty cents, twenty to thirty cents in India, ten cents in Indonesia, with Bangladesh coming in at a mere one cent.[27]

In general, the macroeconomic picture that the three regimes are painting is very clear. The role of the IMF and World Bank changed to that of facilitators of capital mobility by the 1980s with the collapse of the Bretton Woods accord. In the 1990s, the neoliberal trade regime began to solidify with the transformation of GATT into the WTO (1995) and the formation of NAFTA (1994) a year earlier. Once the basic neoliberal trade structure was established, it set the stage for the formation of additional FTAs.

Having secured the mobility of capital and goods through the trade and financial regimes, corporations then began to outsource investment into developing nations for extremely low labor costs while suppressing workers at home. This explains why from 1993 to 1998 the top three recipients of FDI among developing nations were China (25.7 percent), Brazil (7.6 percent), and Mexico (6.5 percent), with India also gaining in recent years.[28] The preceding nations all have very large labor pools in absolute poverty combined with relatively stable political structures. As a result, 2004 net FDI inflows to China reached record levels at $53 billion, while net FDI outflows from the United States exceeded $145 billion compared to previous net FDI inflows of $11.3 billion in 1990.[29]

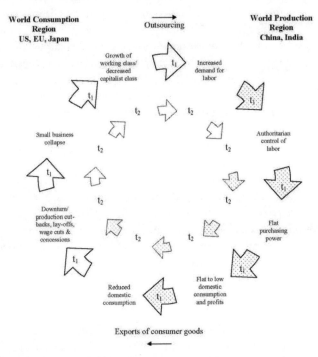

Figure 1. The Global Production-Consumption Model

As FDI inflows to low-wage regions reached record levels, so did America's trade deficit as corporations shipped back the output of outsourced production to developed regions for consumption. For example, the US trade deficit with China reached $201 billion in 2005, compared to the pre-WTO levels of $10.4 billion in 1990 and $6 billion in 1985.[30] The declining growth rates of real GDP per capita in developed nations is the mirror image of these trade deficits as corporations relocate production (and now services) to developing ones, with the most significant drop after the 1990s when the emerging regimes began to solidify (table

1). Panitch and Gindin argue that theoretically the privileged position of the US in the global system could allow it to experience perpetual trade deficits that nations like China have no choice but to accept.[31] This is possible given that the international reserve and trade currency is the US dollar. Thus, the United States can purchase global goods denominated in its own currency by printing money at a cost of a few cents for paper and ink.[32] Panitch and Gindin, though, ignore that these deficits have real consequence for US workers. According to Scott:

> Growth in trade deficits with China has reduced demand for goods produced in every region of the United States.... Workers displaced by trade from the manufacturing sector have been shown to have particular difficulty in securing comparable employment elsewhere in the economy. More than one-third of workers displaced from manufacturing drop out of the labor force.... Average wages of those who secured re-employment fell 11% to 13%. Trade-related job displacement pushes many workers out of good jobs in manufacturing and other trade-related industries, often into lower-paying industries and frequently out of the labor market.[33]

Such outsourcing has contributed to flat and even reduced real wages for the US working class as incomes of the upper class rise, leading to growing inequality. For example, the Gini ratios for US households in America were .397 in 1967, .419 in 1985, .450 in 1995, and .466 in 2004.[34] Furthermore, these shifts lead to reduced purchasing power and hence, aggregate demand.

	1960–9	1970–9	1980–9	1990–9	2000–8
US	3.33	2.53	2.49	1.99	1.21
UK	2.25	2.31	2.8	2.11	1.86
France	4.56	3.3	1.83	1.36	0.97
Germany*	3.46	2.8	1.79	1.54	1.22
Japan	9.13	3.44	3.23	0.81	1.2

Table 1. Average Yearly Percent Growth of Real GDP per Capita (using PPP in 2002 dollars) Author's calculations based on data from the US Department of Labor, 2009. .(*Data for Germany for years before 1991 pertain to the former West Germany)

In other words, globalization has constructed a finely tuned system that focuses on the efficiency of SSAs related to production. But economic activity is based on a production-consumption model and it is consumption that globalization is undermining. In the typical workings of a national business cycle, capitalist accumulation is equivalent to a *siphoning* of surplus value, and thus purchasing power, away from the working class into the pockets of the capitalists. But unless the capitalists invest that wealth in activities that generate jobs *and* adequate income, the economy will stagnate due to overproduction-underconsumption.

As figure 1 demonstrates, globalization is short-circuiting the income flow in the developed regions between production and consumption more so than nationally based business cycles. Thus, globalization with its combination of an SSA for democratic market-based mass consumption (upon which it depends) and the SSA of authoritarian organization of production is siphoning purchasing power from producers and consumers in the developed regions at a greater rate. According to Kotz "the result tends to be a high profit/stagnant wage expansion [for developed nations] that faces a contradiction between the conditions for creation of surplus value and those necessary for its realization."[35]

Toward Collapse: A Global SSA without Income?

If consumers' purchasing power is insufficient to clear markets, then stagnation is inevitable. Therefore the new global SSA could not sustain an expansionary period.[36] This is supported by the data on declining or flat GDP growth rates for the world's five largest economies prior to the Great Collapse of 2008 (table 1). This is true because the mode of capitalist accumulation and thus economic growth depends on market-based consumption, described by Marxist critiques of overproduction and underconsumption.[37] Specifically, most global goods and services are consumed by the wealthiest nations. This implies that the production of the new global SSA depends on consumption primarily by the United States, as Frank argues,[38] followed by the EU and Japan. Thus, although the financial system may be stable according to Panitch and Gindin, the overall global SSA, of which it is a component, is not, given a severely defeated US working class.[39]

Could high US consumption needed by the global system be derived from shared productivity gains between capital and labor? The answer is *no*; businesses have kept virtually all of the productivity gains.[40] What is even more troubling is that the gains themselves were derived not by technologically induced productivity growth, but by corporate savings, compliments of flat wages and a disciplined contingent labor force due to neoliberal restructuring of the economy.[41] Thus by definition it would be impossible to talk of shared productivity gains between labor and capital when they are derived at the expense of the former. Therefore, the historical trend of shared productivity gains that was expressed in the past Fordist expansionary SSA is no longer operative. But how did Americans continue to consume at high levels while real wages declined before the Great Collapse of 2008–2009?

The answer is debt. Harrison and Bluestone had argued that the growth of the 1980s and 1990s was fueled in large part by consumer credit/debt and government deficit spending.[42] Leicht and Fitzgerald also show how the disappearing US middle class continued to maintain its high consumption levels through debt.[43] They argue that as real wages started to stagnate from the 1970s, credit became easier to obtain. According to Kotz, growth in the mid-1990s was fueled partially by the wealth effect of the stock market bubble, especially in technologies.[44] Most of the growth, though, was accounted for by consumer spending due to low interest rates making borrowing more affordable. For example, in 2003 the real average credit card debt per household reached $9,000, up from $4,000 in 1990.[45] Once consumers maxed-out their credit cards at historic levels, new sources of debt continued to emerge, such as home equity loans that also reached historic levels.

In 2001 a severe recession was avoided thanks to continued strength in consumer spending. Kotz explains this was partially due to the temporary effect of the Bush tax cuts, which benefited some middle- and upper-middle-income households. He found most of the consumer spending, however, was accounted for by still-growing household debt.[46] From 2003 to 2007, the US economy has been driven by a continued rise in consumer spending despite flat incomes. This spending had been financed by historically low interest rates given the glut of liquidity/credit by the Fed's easy monetary policy, contributing to the housing bubble. The illusion of wealth generated by the housing bubble coupled with low interest rates and flat incomes led to an explosion of home equity loans. For example, home equity loans in 1990 amounted to $150 billion versus over $300 billion in 1998 and

$439 billion in 2006, while overall household debt (including credit cards and mortgages) as a percentage of after-tax income went from thirty percent in 1950 to over ninety percent in 2000 and 120 percent by 2005.[47] Thus, the middle layer of the working class has treated debt as income to continue an unsustainable level of consumption while the lower sections of the working class depended on debt to get by, given stagnant and even declining real income. Therefore, the question remains how goods and services produced under globalization are going to be consumed now that US consumer debt is maxed-out, the equity bubble burst, and interest rates after the housing meltdown of 2007–09 finally bottoms out. Consequently, globalization and the Great Collapse of 2008–2009 are the realization of the classic problem of overproduction and underconsumption.

Reform versus Structural Solutions to Boom and Bust

The problem is that globalization is developing the forces of production beyond the limits of the existing relations of production.[48] Therefore the current relations of production are becoming "fetters" to the full realization of the new productive forces. Stated differently, the emerging global SSA (unlike the Fordist model) lacks the necessary mechanism for consumption that can result in severe economic downturns. One solution would be to apply Keynesian stimulus policies on a global scale. Ironically, this does not seem feasible because the neoliberal ideology behind globalization includes privatization, minimal government spending, and tax cuts. These policies result in undermining the fiscal ability of states to engage in large-scale Keynesian spending. Even if this were possible, it would not resolve the class contradictions inherent in the capitalist mode of production as it relates to distribution and purchasing power.

Another alternative proposed by theorists is to promote re-regulation of national economies. For example, Harrison and Bluestone argued that "red-hot" growth would be the best way to reduce inequality.[49] They proposed a "Main Street" versus Wall Street model of Keynesian high-wage, pro-union, and anti-poverty programs to stimulate aggregate demand. They also advocated new growth theory, favoring supply-side growth through technological innovation to spur productivity growth. This, though, is not possible for the same reasons that prohibit a global Keynesian strategy. In addition, technologically driven productivity growth has not worked either.[50] As mentioned earlier, growth in the 1990s and early 2000 was driven by savings from a low-paid and disciplined contingency workforce made possible by outsourcing and anti-labor neoliberal policies.

Wolfson proposed a re-regulation of the economy by government to balance the power between capital and labor.[51] His suggestion was based on the observation that stagnation was caused when either capital or labor obtained an upper hand. In periods when capital had the advantage, it led to low wages and a flexible workforce, causing stagnation due to inadequate aggregate demand. In periods when labor had the advantage, it led to higher wages, lower profit margins, and stagnation due to a profit squeeze. However, anarchists would point out that government is part of the problem and cannot "solve" the contradictions inherent in capitalism as the state itself represents a classing of society that works in its own interests. In addition, it must be tacitly acknowledged that capital will always have a built-in advantage under capitalism in that it owns the means of production. And although not overtly stated by Wolfson, it is implied that private productive property is the problem.

Another important fact is underscored by Wolfson's argument of a profit squeeze. Even if labor obtains an upper hand through revitalized movements and pro-labor government policies, it still would not provide a solution. Instead this would lead to a temporary illusion of prosperity and ephemeral gains. Such an arrangement would inevitably result in a profit squeeze—thus recession and a realignment of class power anew. Such a seesaw between inadequate aggregate demand and a profit squeeze will continue as long as class conflict takes place within a capitalist framework.

Thus, all of the suggestions by various theorists are ultimately unworkable in that they do not state what is clear: stagnation is caused structurally by private ownership of the means of production. Therefore, their policy suggestions are aimed at softening the natural outcomes of capitalism's class contradictions, while maintaining the capitalist mode of production. This point becomes more so important if this new capitalism includes the normalization of ever deeper crises and growing domestic and global inequalities, which Panitch and Gindin argue should be accepted as here to stay.[52] Either way, all this makes the need for structural change rather than a cycle of crisis–reform–crisis imperative.

The alternative must be to create new economic models. But to create new models of production, distribution, and consumption, one would have to alter the fundamental relations in both production and consumption so as to allow a mechanism through which global output can be consumed. How can these relations be altered to achieve market clearing? This is where libertarian socialist/anarchist forms of societal organization have a solution: alter the relations of production in t_1 through direct action to achieve self-organization, self-direction, and private productive property elimination, ushering in a new epoch versus a new capitalist stage in t_2 (figure 2).

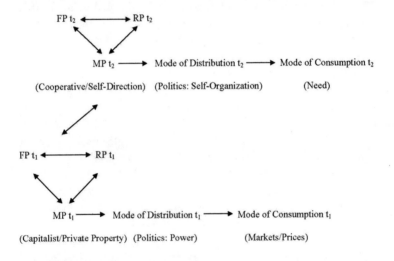

Mode of Production (MP); Relations of Production (RP); Forces of Production (FP)

Figure 2. Dialectical Change

Such a fundamental restructuring of national and global socioeconomic organization will not occur from impending collapse as Panitch and Gindin correctly pointed out, although I argue collapse is highly probable.[53] The reason is that brutal oppressive regimes that are better armed than a national citizenry have proven capable of staying in power many years despite running their economies into grinding poverty as demonstrated by many African dictatorships such as Zimbabwe's.

Therefore, direct action by a renewed transnational working-class movement will be required for fundamental structural changes. If labor can obtain hegemony and accept the cataclysmic social changes ushered in by the forces of globalization based on human needs considerations instead (figure 2), we could experience not a dystopia but a renewed golden age of social and scientific evolution resulting from a historic epochal change in the mode of production-consumption.

Today workers in developed nations (particularly the United States as the hegemonic power) must demand initial structural changes that can eventually evolve into deeper socioeconomic changes leading to a new global model. Such demands can only be met by challenging the dominant ideology with a radical *counter-ideology*; creating mass support and solidarity through *societal education* disseminated by worker-owned and-operated media; and engaging in *direct action* with civil disobedience, militant resistance, and even full-scale revolts.[54] These strategies are based on my prior analysis of US labor and civil rights history showing that this was how workers and people of color obtained most, if not all, their fundamental gains. Such actions, though, would require a renewed and militant labor movement with actual blueprints for an alternative form of socioeconomic organization (or as Gramsci called it a *counter-hegemony*).

This is why counter-ideology and societal education are needed to offer a new model of society to be achieved with militant direct action fueled by global solidarity and independent worker institutions, e.g., media, schools/universities, and activist political organizations.[55] In conclusion, things are getting worse for the "workers of the world." However, resistance is possible based on the classic call for "workers of the world to unite" and challenge the legitimacy of the existing system. We need to reassert ourselves and not be intimidated into accepting an emperor with "new clothes" every time capitalism goes through a transformation.

ENDNOTES

1   See David M. Gordon, Richard Edwards, and Michael Reich, *Segmented Work, Divided Workers: The Historical Transformation of Labor in the United States* (Cambridge: Cambridge University Press, 1982).

2   See David M. Kotz, Terrence McDonough, and Michael Reich, ed., *Social Structures of Accumulation* (Cambridge: Cambridge University Press, 1994).

3   See Karl Marx and Frederick Engels, "Manifesto of the Communist Party," in *Marx-Engels Reader*, ed. Robert C. Tucker (New York: W. W. Norton, 1978), 469–500.

4   See Phillip Anthony O'Hara, "Recent Changes to the IMF, WTO and FSP: An Emerging Global Monetary-Trade-Production Social Structure of Accumulation for Long Wave Upswing?" (paper presented at the conference of the Association for Social Economics, New Orleans, January 5, 2001); and Jamie Peck, "Labor, Zapped/Growth, Restored? Three Moments of Neoliberal Restructuring in the American Labor Market," *Journal of Economic Geography* [2, no. 2] (2002): 179–220.

5   See Philip McMichael, *Development and Social Change* (Thousand Oaks: Pine Forge Press, 2008).

6   IMF, "IMF Members' Quotas and Voting Power, and IMF Board of Governors," 2007, http://www.imf.org/external/np/sec/memdir/members.htm#1 (accessed November 10, 2010); and World Bank, "Voting Powers," 2007, http://go.worldbank.org/GC8OQ79ES0 (accessed November 10, 2010).

7   See Leo Panitch and Sam Gindin, "Finance and American Empire," in *The Empire Reloaded: Socialist Register 2005*, ed. Leo Panitch and Colin Leys (New York: Monthly Review Press, 2005), 46–81.

8   Panitch and Gindin, "Finance and American Empire," 57.

9   See McMichael, *Development and Social Change*.

10   US Census Bureau, "Foreign Trade Statistics, Foreign Trade in Goods (Imports, Exports and Trade Balance) with China," 2006, http://www.census.gov/foreign-trade/balance/c5700.html (accessed November 10, 2010).

11   Panitch and Gindin, "Finance and American Empire," 47.

12   André Gunder Frank, "Meet Uncle Sam—Without Clothes—Parading Around China and the World," *Critical Sociology* 32, (no. 1) (2006): 17–44.

13   See Robert E. Scott, Carlos Salas, and Bruce Campbell, *Revisiting NAFTA: Still Not Working for North America's Workers* (Washington DC: Economic Policy Institute, 2006).

14   Ibid., 5.

15   Robert E. Scott, *Costly Trade with China: Millions of U.S. Jobs Displaced with Net Job Loss in Every State* (Washington DC: Economic Policy Institute, 2007), 1.

16   Global Policy Forum, "Total Number of Regional Free Trade Agreements 1948–2002," http://www.globalpolicy.org/socecon/trade/tables/rta (accessed November 10, 2010).

17   See Phillip Anthony O'Hara, "A New Transnational Corporate Social Structure of Accumulation for Long-Wave Upswing in the World Economy?," *Review of Radical Political Economics* 36, (no. 3) (2001): 328–335.

18 See ibid. and McMichael, *Development and Social Change*.

19 See Scott et al., *Revisiting NAFTA*.

20 See Gordon et al., *Segmented Work, Divided Workers*.

21 See Panitch and Gindin, "Finance and American Empire."

22 See Peck, "Labor, Zapped/Growth, Restored?," US Census Bureau, "Historical Income Tables-Households. Table H-4. Gini Ratios for Households, by Race and Hispanic Origin of Householder: 1967 to 2005," 2006, http://www.census.gov/hhes/www/income/histinc/h04.html (accessed November 10, 2010); and US Census Bureau, "Historical Income Tables-Households. Table H-2. Share of Aggregate Income Received by Each Fifth and Top 5 Percent of Households All Races: 1967 to 2003," 2006, http://www.census.gov/hhes/income/histinc/h02ar.html (accessed November 10, 2010).

23 Scott, *Costly Trade with China*, 1.

24 National Labor Committee (NLC), reports (2000–06), http://www.nlcnet.org/live (accessed November 10, 2010).

25 Judith Banister, *Manufacturing Employment and Compensation in China*, http://www.bls.gov/fls/chinareport.pdf (accessed November 10, 2010).

26 US Department of Labor, Bureau of Labor Statistics, "Table 2. Hourly Compensation Costs in U.S. Dollars for Production Workers in Manufacturing, 32 Countries or Areas and Selected Economic Groups, Selected Years, 1975–2004," 2006, URL http://www.bls.gov/news.release/ichcc.t02.htm (accessed November 10, 2010).

27 NLC, reports (2000–06).

28 Global Policy Forum, "Total Number of Regional Free Trade Agreements 1948–2002."

29 Organization for Economic Co-operation and Development (OECD), *International Investment Perspectives* (OECD publishing, 2005), 12, 17, 46–47.

30 US Census Bureau, "Foreign Trade Statistics."

31 See Panitch and Gindin, "Finance and American Empire."

32 See Frank, "Meet Uncle Sam."

33 Scott, *Costly Trade with China*, 5.

34 US Census Bureau, "Historical Income Tables-Households. Table H-4. Gini Ratios for Households."

35 See David M. Kotz, "Contradictions of Economic Growth in the Neoliberal Era: Accumulation and Crisis in the Contemporary U.S. Economy," paper presented at a session sponsored by the Union for Radical Political Economics at the Allied Social Sciences Associations Convention, Boston, January 8, 2006.

36 See Kotz, "Contradictions"; O'Hara, "Recent Changes"; and O'Hara, "A New Transnational."

37   See Karl Marx, "Capital, Volume One," in *Marx-Engels Reader*, ed. Robert C. Tucker, 294–438 (New York: W. W. Norton, 1978) and Karl Marx, "Theories of Surplus Value," in *Marx-Engels Reader*, ed. Robert C. Tucker, 443–465 (New York: W. W. Norton, 1978).

38   See Frank, "Meet Uncle Sam."

39   See Panitch and Gindin, "Finance and American Empire."

40   See Kotz, "Contradictions"; and Kevin T. Leicht and Scott T. Fitzgerald, *Post Industrial Peasants: The Illusion of Middle-Class Prosperity* (New York: Worth Publishers, 2007).

41   See Frank, "Meet Uncle Sam"; Kotz, "Contradictions"; and Peck, "Labor, Zapped."

42   See Peck, "Labor, Zapped."

43   See Leicht and Fitzgerald, *Post Industrial Peasants.*

44   See Kotz, "Contradictions."

45   Leicht and Fitzgerald, *Post Industrial Peasants*, 58.

46   See Kotz, "Contradictions."

47   Christopher Conkey, "Home-Equity Loans Level Off," *Wall Street Journal*, March 11, A6; Leicht and Fitzgerald, *Post Industrial Peasants*, 58, 93; and Kotz, "Contradictions," 11.

48   See Marx, "Capital, Volume One"; and Marx, "Theories of Surplus Value."

49   As cited in Peck, "Labor, Zapped."

50   See Frank, "Meet Uncle Sam"; Kotz, "Contradictions"; and Peck, "Labor, Zapped."

51   See Martin H. Wolfson, "Neoliberalism and the Social Structure of Accumulation," *Review of Radical Political Economics* 35, (no. 3) (2003): 255–262.

52   See Panitch and Gindin, "Finance and American Empire."

53   Ibid.

54   See John Asimakopoulos, "Societal Education, Direct Action, and Working-Class Gains," *Journal of Poverty* 11, (no. 2): 1–22.

55   Ibid.

The Economic Crisis and Libertarian Socialists

Robin Hahnel

This chapter is based on an invited speech given by Robin Hahnel at the Anti-Authoritarian B-fest in Athens, Greece, on May 27, 2010. The talk addressed the origins of the global economic crisis that struck in the fall of 2008, and critically evaluated early responses by ruling elites in the United States and Europe. However, a great deal has happened since then. Rather than rewrite a speech which stands well on its own through May 2010, a short addendum follows, updating analysis through May 2011.

Why Libertarian Socialists Reject Capitalism

Libertarian socialists reject capitalism because it is authoritarian and exploitative not only in bad times but in good times as well. Libertarian socialists know that ordinary people are perfectly capable of managing and coordinating our own economic activities without self-serving elites to tell us what to do. Libertarian socialists who are more than armchair critics work tirelessly to replace the economics of competition and greed with the economics of equitable cooperation. Some work creating pockets of equitable cooperation wherever possible even while capitalism persists. Other libertarian socialists organize politically to build mass movements necessary to replace the capitalist system with an entirely different economic system in which workers and consumers manage their own economic affairs without bosses or commissars, and autonomous worker and consumer councils coordinate their interrelated activities themselves, through participatory planning, without recourse to markets or bureaucratic planning.

But if libertarian socialists did not need the worst financial and economic crisis in over eighty years to teach us that capitalism is an albatross around our necks, why is the current economic crisis of any particular importance to us? Why should libertarian socialists say or do anything differently than we were before the crisis struck?

The answer is very simple: *Because we are too few* … and the crisis opens important new opportunities for us to convince others of things we know—provided we can get them to listen.

The Problem Libertarian Socialists Must Solve

All too often libertarian socialists focus on *other* people's problems rather than our own. Too many libertarian socialists think *other* people's problem is that they fail to listen to and join us. Wrong! *Our* problem is that too few listen to us, much less join us. We need to remember in everything we do that this is *our* problem, which *we* must solve.

Our vision of a better world is thoroughly democratic. It is a vision that is much more deeply participatory and democratic than has even occurred to most people. But an important implication of a profoundly democratic goal that too many libertarian socialists conveniently ignore is that before our goal can be achieved a substantial majority of people must be ready to abandon the economics of competition and greed and embrace the possibility of an economics of equitable cooperation. So until we solve *our recruiting problem* there is little point in arguing over other issues, such as how to topple capitalist governments or defeat reactionary forces who will maneuver to maintain elite rule even when a majority of the population is ready to free themselves from all masters.

We will not solve *our* problem by yelling at people: See, we told you so—capitalism sucks! See, we told you so—mainstream politicians have betrayed you again! We will certainly not convince people that workers and consumers can manage their own affairs and organize and coordinate an efficient and equitable division of labor among themselves by simply repeating that we believe this is possible. We have been repeating that people can live better through self-government and free association for close to 200 years. Why should we expect more people to believe us if we offer no more compelling arguments than we have in the past? Why should we expect to recruit more people if we do no better job of addressing people's doubts about how self-managing, autonomous councils of workers and consumers can actually solve real problems that will arise once capitalist overlords and market forces have been banished? Leftists will never recruit enough people to support our vision as long as libertarian socialism remains a faith-based initiative.

Rhetorical flourishes about the virtues of free association that fail to go beyond what great libertarian socialist forebears preached a hundred years ago begin to sound hollow when unaccompanied by concrete solutions to problems sensible people know will arise. We need to learn to communicate in ways designed to convince those who are not already anti-capitalist rather than please ourselves. Too much of our discourse is designed to make us feel good. Too often we preach to our own small choir and ignore the fact that by doing so we further alienate those whose minds we must change and whose trust we must earn. This is why we must go beyond assuming our conclusions when we explain what is wrong with the economy today and why it is not working. This is why we must be much more concrete than we have been in the past, and present our case remembering that our primary audience are people who do not already agree with us and who paid us no heed in the past, but just maybe, due to recent events, may now lend us an ear.

Explaining *This* Crisis

When leftists explain this crisis as a predictable crisis of capitalism we convince nobody who was not already convinced that capitalism is prone to crisis. If we want to make people sit up and take notice of what we have to say we have to offer more insightful explanations than others do of exactly how such a terrible event—which does not occur every day—could have happened. In many ways the financial crisis of 2008 is a truly astounding story of greed and incompetence beyond anything even the most hardened critics of capitalist finance imagined. Leftists who learn to tell this story well will find ears that continue to listen.

The principal causes of the "perfect economic storm" that broke in the fall of 2008 were (1) the dramatic increases in economic inequality which made the system less stable as well as less fair, and (2) the reckless deregulation of the financial sector. In the United States both trends began in earnest with President Reagan in 1980, continued under Bush I and Clinton, and accelerated during Bush II. These trends were the result of a steady increase in corporate power, and the power of mega financial corporations in particular, and a dramatic decrease in the countervailing power of workers, consumers, and governments.

But it is important to add more detail because there are important lessons we need to help people relearn. I say relearn because many of these lessons were learned once before in the aftermath of the Great Depression of the 1930s, but unfortunately were *un*learned by the economics profession, the major media, and politicians, who then conspired to ensure that the general public forgot important, hard-learned lessons as well.

1. The financial crisis today is not simply the result of some mortgage loans that should never have been made. Less than 20 percent of mortgages were in arrears when the financial crisis broke, which means that 80 percent of mortgagees were current with their payments. *Only* because prudent regulation of the banking industry dating back to the Great Depression was systematically dismantled by politicians in both the Republican and Democratic parties under pressure from the financial industry, *only* because people like Larry Summers and Timothy Geithner intervened on numerous occasions in the past to prevent regulation of highly speculative Wall Street investment banks and hedge funds, *only* because lack of competent regulation created opportunities for financial players to make huge profits in socially dangerous ways, and *only* because European banks and the US government prevailed on European governments to imitate these disastrous trends was it possible for the worst financial crisis in eighty years to unravel when a housing bubble in the US—which had to come to an end at some point—finally did.

A short list of a few of the perverse incentives incompetent deregulation permitted—and continues to permit—is enough to boggle the mind.

(a) Local banks no longer hold the mortgages whose applications they approve. Instead, they immediately sell those mortgages to large banks and institutional investors. Clearly this leaves little incentive for local banks processing mortgage applications to care if applicants are really credit-worthy or not.

(b) Wall Street banks created securities composed of tiny fractions of the monthly payments due from thousands of different home mortgages, which they sold to institutional investors and also kept on their own books as assets. However, the agencies responsible for rating these *mortgage-based securities* are paid by the banks whose securities they are rating. The pressure on rating agencies to routinely stamp securities as triple-A for their paymasters, i.e., rate them of high quality and low risk, should be obvious to anyone.

(c) Securitization is not primarily a way to spread risk, as its creators assured us. More importantly it is a way to hide risk from outside detection, allowing banks to pass off low-quality securities as if they were high quality. However, since prospective buyers could not distinguish low-quality from high-quality mortgage-based securities, once mortgages started to fall in arrears, the market for *all* mortgage-based securities, even the good ones, dried up. Those are the so-called toxic assets we hear so much about on the books of the big Wall Street banks, and that is why the banks discovered, to their surprise, they could not sell even the good ones for more than a song once the housing bubble burst.

(d) CEOs' pay is often linked to the value of their company stock in the short-run. But CEOs have many ways to manipulate the price of their company stock in the short run to their advantage, even if by doing so they weaken the company and endanger the economy.

(e) When a financial institution is so important that its failure might trigger a financial panic, it creates a perverse incentive known as *moral hazard*. An institution that is "too big to fail" can engage in risky behavior knowing it will reap high rewards from risky investments when they prove profitable, but be rescued by the government with taxpayer dollars whenever they prove otherwise. Wall Street is the best example of "lemon socialism" the capitalist world has ever seen. When things go well Wall Street wins. When things go badly the taxpayer, not Wall Street, loses.

(f) And of course, last but not least: More leverage, i.e., playing with more of other people's money and less of its own, means higher rates of profit for any financial institution. But it also means greater financial fragility for the system as a whole, and a bigger collapse when a crisis materializes. Every attempt to restrict leverage for financial institutions that were "too big to fail" was defeated by the industry and its defenders, like Larry Summers.

Lesson 1: Unregulated, freemarket finance is an accident waiting to happen.
   If the credit system is going to be left in private hands, not only must regulations over traditional financial institutions be restored

and strengthened, but the new financial sector of Wall Street investment banks and hedge funds that grew up outside the old regulatory structures must be subjected to regulations that prohibit behavior that has proven detrimental to the public interest. A public takeover of the financial sector is the best option, not only to prevent further crises, but also to steer investment into energy conservation and developing renewable energy sources necessary to make our economies carbon neutral by mid-century, rather than into more unproductive asset bubbles. But short of nationalization, prudent regulation is an absolute necessity.

2. Large inequalities of income and wealth are not only unfair, they also increase the likelihood of economic crises for the simple reason that more of the income of the wealthy is not automatically turned into consumption demand. The poorer you are, the more likely you are to spend what little income you have relatively quickly, and thereby provide adequate demand for all that was produced. The richer you are, the more likely you are *not* to consume all your income. Unless the savings of the wealthy are successfully channeled into spending on goods and services by someone else, the demand for goods in general will fall short of the supply. When this happens, businesses unable to sell all they are producing cut back on production and lay off workers, which of course, further aggravates the problem. This self-reinforcing, downward spiral is what we are now experiencing, more strongly than at any time since the Great Depression eighty years ago.

Lesson 2: We need a massive fiscal stimulus because there is no other way to stem the recessionary slide that has become the overriding economic problem.

Household income is falling, few have any equity left in their homes they can borrow against, and most people's credit cards are maxed out. Clearly the increased spending needed right now is not going to come from the household sector. Nor will it come from the business sector since businesses are not going to invest in new plants and machinery when they cannot sell all they are making already. For now the only way to stem the downward recessionary spiral is for government to spend more than it collects in taxes—a lot more!

Yes, this means we need a big government budget deficit right now. *Bigger deficit now, good. Smaller deficit now, bad.* Even if all one cares about is minimizing the size of the national debt five years from now, the best policy is to run a larger deficit now. The logic is simple enough: nothing increases the national debt more than a recession because tax receipts go down when income goes down—which is what a recession is, falling production and incomes.

3. However, the underlying problem that created the conditions for the macroeconomic imbalance and also make it difficult to reverse is the dramatic growth of inequality over the previous decades, leaving too little purchasing power in the hands of those who use it fully and quickly. This problem must be rectified as well.

Lesson 3: Wages must keep pace with productivity increases or the economy will not only become more unfair it will also become more unstable.

What can be done to protect wages immediately? In the United States passage of the Employee Free Choice Act—which was stalled in 2007 by a Republican filibuster in the US Senate—would remove barriers preventing workers from forming unions, eliminate incentives for employers to stall negotiations over a first contract, and increase penalties for employers who break the law during union organizing campaigns. Eliminating tax breaks for companies that outsource jobs abroad and insisting on adequate and enforceable labor standards in all international trade agreements would help reduce downward pressure on US wages and working conditions. The Trade Reform, Accountability, Development and Employment Act of 2009 (HR 3012) would move us in the right direction.

Of course, passage of these bills would only be a beginning. Much more is needed to increase income equality. But new legislation to empower unions, new legislation to undo the damage wreaked by neoliberal international economic treaties, increasing the minimum wage, and strengthening the social safety net through funding increases for unemployment insurance, social security, and welfare programs are all necessary steps that would increase income equality and make economic crises like this one less likely in the future.

Explaining the Abysmal Response

The worst economic crisis in over eighty years has generated many words but few concrete actions that will improve matters. All we have to do is review the list of what needs to be done to realize how little our leaders have accomplished.

• Either take over or regulate the financial sector.

Instead the approach taken by the Obama administration was to continue the Bush administration policy of having taxpayers pay much more than the going market price for as many toxic assets as the banks told us they needed to sell off before they felt they could begin lending again. Before leaving as treasury secretary, Hank Paulson got Congress to pass TARP I, which gave the Treasury $700 billion of taxpayer money to use to purchase toxic assets through a "reverse auction" that was so hampered by perverse information asymmetries and conflicts of interest that Paulson could not achieve liftoff for his plan before leaving office. In TARP II Geithner and Ben Bernanke disguised and expanded the subsidy in the form of "private public partnerships" where the Federal Deposit Insurance Corporation and Federal Reserve Bank provide free insurance against downside risk to induce private party participation and continue to subsidize the banking industry by lending them as much as they want at effectively a zero rate of interest. In other words, Obama fully endorsed the "No Banker Left Behind" approach of his predecessor in the White House: keep applying ever larger doses of taxpayer bailout funds to banks deemed too big to fail even when those banks refuse to begin lending again in earnest, and stonewall pressure to renegotiate terms of mortgages that are unpayable.

Now we are hearing speeches from Obama and Democrats in Congress designed to assuage a furious public, followed by legislation designed to please their paymasters on Wall Street. When all is said and done, whether the Democrats do or do not pass their pathetic financial reform bill, the big holding banks will be even bigger and therefore less likely to be permitted to fail; commercial and investment banking will still be tied at the hip; trading in highly profitable, esoteric financial products, that have no social value whatsoever but put the financial system at great risk, will continue; and regulatory powers will be more concentrated in the hands of the Federal Reserve Bank, which Wall Street captured long ago. In short, financial reform will be a fig leaf in the United States, leaving the financial system just as prone to crisis as it was before September 2008. The only question will be what the next asset bubble looks like, and how long it will take to grow and burst.

• Launch a massive fiscal stimulus emphasizing spending increases over tax cuts, and spending on education, healthcare, and green jobs because these are not only the most socially useful investments but also provide more jobs per stimulus dollar.

Instead of implementing the single most important lesson Lord Keynes taught the world eighty years ago, the conservative government in Germany is tragically committed to a penny-wise and pound-foolish notion of "fiscal responsibility" for itself and for others; the Republican opposition in the United States is fanning the flames of concern over the national debt in a deliberate and cynical attempt to prolong the recession to reap short-run political gain in the congressional elections of 2010 and the presidential election of 2012; Obama's economic advisors, Laurence Summers and Timothy Geithner, have also stirred up deficit fears, and are responsible for preventing the administration from shooting for a larger fiscal stimulus in 2009, and killing any chance for a second stimulus in 2010. The Japanese government has done better on this score but cannot sufficiently stimulate the global economy on its own. Meanwhile, governments of smaller economies like Greece, Ireland, Portugal, Spain, Latvia, and all the smaller Third World countries have no choice but to practice fiscal austerity, because instead of protecting their ability to borrow on reasonable terms, those running the neoliberal international financial system have thrown the smaller economies to speculator dogs who jack up the interest premiums on their borrowing whenever their budget deficits increase.

In a global economy where new business investment may follow but certainly will not lead us out of recession, and where consumers in all the advanced economies are tapped out, there is nobody left except governments to prime the proverbial pump. Unfortunately, more than eighteen months into the recession the needed fiscal stimulus is still not forthcoming, and consequently we are headed for a jobless recovery at best, but more likely for a double dip as recessionary dynamics take root again.

•Reverse the trend toward greater inequality of income and wealth.

Instead the neoliberal trend continues unabated as inequality of income and wealth increase during the economic decline and Obama presidency, just as it did during the asset booms that preceded it and the presidencies of Reagan, Bush I, Clinton, and Bush II. The only sector of the US economy to have "recovered" is the financial sector whose profits are swollen again thanks to an open-ended bailout at US taxpayer expense, with none of the "conditionalities" demanding changes in behavior the IMF requires of its Third World clients in exchange for their bailouts.

An early indication that Obama was not going to do anything to change the balance of power in America came when he reneged on his promise to organized labor to prioritize the Employee Free Choice Act to begin to even the playing field for labor organizers. Labor helped Obama beat first Hillary Clinton in the Democratic primaries, and then John McCain in the general election. Hillary Clinton had the early advantage with organized labor during the primary campaign. A surprising number of unions came out for Obama over Clinton because he promised to champion the Employee Free Choice Act and they did not trust that Clinton would follow through no matter what she promised. During the general election Obama reaffirmed his pledge in return for all-out support from all of organized labor, and organized labor delivered. But the Employee Free Choice Act was the first piece of legislation Obama abandoned after being elected. Obama slapped organized labor in the face even before he told single-payer health advocates that their proposal was not worthy of consideration, and had guards turn Congressman John Conyers and a delegation of AMA doctors supporting single-payer away at the White House door when they tried to attend a meeting to discuss health-care reform being attended by CEOs from the insurance and pharmaceutical industries. Ironically, the feeble excuse he offered was that because of the severity of the economic crisis there were more important pieces of legislation he had to prioritize than the Employee Free Choice Act. Organized labor was "had" and knows it.

The reason for the abysmal failure to respond to the economic crisis effectively is that those responsible for creating the crisis are still in charge of the response. Politicians and political parties beholden to corporate interests and neoliberal ideology have not been replaced. And as a result, necessary financial reforms have been stonewalled, fiscal stimulus to stem the recessionary slide has been obstructed, worker, consumer, and citizen counterweight to corporate power continues to weaken, and consequently the economic crisis festers and worsens.

While the initial crisis was a tragedy caused by thirty years of brazen neoliberalism, the abysmal response to the crisis is a second human-made tragedy. Instead of choosing from a long list of distinguished economic advisors who warned against financial deregulation and the bankruptcy of trickledown economics, and who have excellent ideas about how to put our economic house back in order, President Obama instead chose as his advisors the very people responsible for the policies that brought on the economic crisis in the first place.

The advice of economists such as Dean Baker, Jamie Galbraith, Jane D'Arista, Robert Pollin, and Marc Weisbrot—not to speak of Nobel Laureates Joseph Stiglitz and Paul Krugman—is still being ignored. Instead, President Obama has unwisely chosen Lawrence Summers as his chief economic advisor and Timothy Geithner as his secretary of the treasury, neither of whom has a Nobel Prize to his name, and both of whom were key sponsors of the disastrous policies which got us into the mess we now find ourselves in. A very wise man once said: "We can't solve problems by using the same kind of thinking we used when we created them." President Obama had better hope that Albert Einstein was wrong, because so far he has chosen to follow the advice of a team of economists with close personal ties to Wall Street whose discredited ideas bear a major responsibility for creating the perfect economic storm that is by no means over. Lawrence Summers is not change; he is Clinton redux. Timothy Geithner is not change; he is a shill for Wall Street. And Ben Bernanke who Obama renominated and the Democratic Congress just confirmed for another term as chair of the Federal Reserve Bank bears much of the responsibility for the policies that led to the greatest financial crisis in over eighty years we are still suffering from.

Of course, the underlying question is why Obama chose the economic advisors he did, and why he continues to listen to them despite overwhelming evidence that their advice has failed to produce desirable economic results and has now revitalized a Republican Party that was in hopeless disarray only fifteen months ago. I am not particularly inclined to speculate about motives, but I suspect the answer to that question lies in where Obama has gotten his campaign finance support in the past, and continues to plan to raise money in the future. The answer lies in a political strategy that came to be known in the Clinton administration as "triangulation." And the answer lies in the fact that Obama personally *is* a centrist and not a progressive, and Obama *is* cautious not audacious—even though present circumstances would reward boldness and will punish timidity. Finally, people I trust who have taken the time to examine his career carefully tell me Obama always "talks the talk" but seldom "walks the walk."

In sum, two years into the crisis, insiders have only been replaced by other insiders who were equally culpable, and nowhere in the world have "insiders" yet been replaced by outsiders. Leftists who learn how to explain why the response of discredited leaders is woefully inadequate, and what governments should be doing instead, will find even more ears willing to keep listening.

Greece and the European Union

While I am much more familiar with the crisis in the United States and the status of our failed response than I am with the situation in Europe, I feel sufficiently informed to make a few observations about the crisis in Greece and problems unique to the European Union. Aeschylus, Sophocles, and Euripides created tragedy for the stage thousands of years ago, and now modern Greece is living through a real tragedy. The popular image of Greeks as unproductive, lazy workers who brought on this crisis by trying to live beyond their means is pure nonsense and a blatant attempt to blame the victims in order to exonerate those who are truly guilty.

The list of real villains begins with international financial speculators who have made it much more expensive and difficult for the Greek government to roll over its debt than it should be, and greatly magnified the size of the bailout package the European Commission and IMF had to put together. Banks and hedge funds that trade credit default swaps, currency traders, and rating agencies have perfected a speculative game that is extremely profitable for them but extremely detrimental to attempts to solve the Greek debt crisis and protect the euro. Libertarian socialists here in Greece would do well to learn to tell this story well to those they organize and work with.

First, Goldman Sachs advised the right-wing government that preceded PASOK how to hide its true debt from view so it could continue to borrow more and at lower interest rates than it would otherwise have been able to. Most of that hidden debt went to pay for corporate welfare and enable massive tax evasion by wealthy Greek supporters of the government. Then Goldman Sachs, knowing full well that Greek debt was higher than it appeared, began to play what former general counsel of Long-Term Capital Management Hedge Fund James Rickards calls the Whack the Piñata Game, and other players were soon to follow:

> Greece's travails are often measured by reference to the market in credit default swaps (CDS), a kind of insurance against default by Greece. As with any insurance, greater risks entail higher prices to buy the protection. But what happens if the price of insurance is no longer anchored to the underlying risk? When we look behind CDS prices, we don't see an objective measure of the public finances of Greece, but something very different. Sellers are typically pension funds looking to earn an insurance premium and buyers are often hedge funds looking to make a quick turn. In the middle you have Goldman Sachs or another large bank booking a fat spread. Now the piñata party begins. Banks grab their sticks and start pounding thinly traded Greek bonds and pushing out the spread between Greek and the benchmark German CDS price. Step two is a call on the pension funds to put up more margin, or security, as the price has moved in favor of the buyer. The margin money is shoveled to the hedge funds, which enjoy the cash and paper profits and the 20 percent performance fees that follow. How convenient when this happens in December in time for the annual accounts, as was recently the case. Eventually the money flow will be reversed, when a bail-out is announced, but in the meantime pension funds earn premiums, banks earn spreads, hedge funds earn fees, and everyone's a winner—except the hapless hedge fund investors, who suffer the fees on fleeting performance, and the unfortunate inhabitants of the piñata. What does any of this have to do with Greece? Very little. It is not much more than a floating craps game in an alley off Wall Street.[1]

The unfortunate inhabitants of the Greek piñata include the PASOK government, which, because it can no longer roll over the debt at the interest rates now demanded by buyers of Greek government bonds, must convince the European Commission, the European Bank, and IMF to be its underwriters and provide emergency loans. It includes the citizens and taxpayers in the EU who must assume risk they should not have had to bear as underwriters of new Greek borrowing. But most importantly, because those who run the global economy refuse to stop ridiculously counterproductive financial market shenanigans and force banks to write off unpayable debt, and instead impose increasingly draconian austerity measures in exchange for their financial backing, the most unfortunate inhabitants of the Greek piñata are ordinary Greeks who are being asked to suffer through ten years of depression conditions.

You here in Greece don't need me to tell you what those austerity measures consist of and how they will affect people. But perhaps I can be of some help by reassuring you (1) that the claim that workers are to blame because they are too lazy and too greedy is patently absurd; (2) that the austerity measures the European Commission and IMF has imposed and PASOK has agreed to administer will be completely for naught; and (3) that there is a much better and fairer response to the crisis.

Some Greek workers have longer vacations than some German workers. And some Greek workers can retire sooner than some German workers. All available evidence indicates that Greeks have made the right choice and Germans have made the wrong choice. We have long known that leisure is kinder to the environment than more consumption. So the Greek choice is the environmentally responsible choice. And new research suggests that once basic needs are satisfied, increases in average consumption have little positive effect on how satisfied and happy people are. So the Greek choice of leisure over more consumption is the wise choice as well.

However, because they are less well-equipped, Greek workers are less productive than German workers on average. This is certainly not the fault of Greek workers. If it is anyone's fault, it is the fault of their employers who fail to provide state-of-the-art equipment and working conditions. In any case, the solution is to prioritize improving the circumstances Greeks work in so their productivity increases. Unfortunately the PASOK austerity program will have the opposite effect.

Meanwhile, in the short run there are only two ways to prevent differences in Greek and German productivity from producing an unsustainable trade deficit between the two countries. PASOK has chosen to administer the first—drive down Greek wages. By agreeing to share a common currency with Germany, the second, better way, currency devaluation, was eliminated. Why is currency, or external devaluation, preferable to wage repression, euphemistically called internal devaluation? It can be done more quickly without causing domestic strife. And more importantly, it solves the trade problem with Germany without increasing income inequality within Greece. Devaluation means all Greeks must pay more for German imports. Wage repression means that Greek workers must pay more for German imports *and* also pay more for domestically produced goods, while wealthy Greeks pay no more for German imports than they did before; wealthy Greeks pay even less for domestically produced goods as lower labor costs lower domestic prices somewhat, and Greek employers are rewarded for failing to provide their employees with state-of-the-art equipment by getting away with paying their workers even less.

And what will be accomplished if Greek workers agree to shoulder the entire burden of solving the Greek debt problem? According to the projections of the same economists working for the European Bank, European Commission, and IMF who negotiated the agreement to provide up to $960 billion of support for the so-called PIGS in exchange for the austerity program PASOK will now administer in Greece, *even if the program works exactly as planned*—and no bailout program ever has—Greece's debt will *rise* from 115 percent of GDP today to 149 percent in 2013. In other words, the best that can be hoped for is that after three years of horrific sacrifice Greece will face an even worse debt crisis three years from now. Moreover the economy will be mired in a much deeper depression, giving employers even less incentive to upgrade equipment in Greek factories.

There Are Much Better Options

(1) There are both advantages and disadvantages to being inside the euro zone. For a country like Greece it is becoming more and more apparent that the disadvantages outweigh the advantages. But even if the advantages outweighed the disadvantages, it is better to leave the euro now rather than agree to damage the economy severely for

three years and have to leave the euro zone in any case—which is what current policies will lead to. If the EU/IMF will not offer Greece a way to *grow out of the crisis*, Greece is better off leaving the euro zone. Argentina tried what PASOK is trying—internal devaluation—from 1998 to 2001 only to drive half its country into poverty. After defaulting and devaluing, Argentine GDP dropped for one more quarter and then climbed 63 percent over the next six years.

(2) There are both advantages and disadvantages to defaulting on sovereign debt. But in the immortal words of former US treasury secretary Hank Paulson, who told the US Congress in October 2008 that they had no choice but to approve his $700 billion bailout request for US banks because Congress was "already on the hook," this time Greece had the stronger countries in the euro zone "on the hook" and needed to take more advantage of its leverage. Much of Greek debt is owed to banks from other European countries, Germany in particular. And as everyone knows, the euro would take a serious hit if Greece defaulted. After incompetent delays which multiplied the size of the necessary bailout several times, Germany finally agreed to save its own banks and protect its precious euro—certainly not to help Greek workers, who German newspapers slander as lazy and greedy. Had PASOK hung tough and defended the Greek economy against demands for greater austerity, it could have gotten financial backing on much better terms than it did. PASOK was a lousy negotiator on behalf of Greek citizens and deserves to be fired for incompetence as well as for siding with Greek capitalists against Greek workers who must tighten their belt.

(3) Instead of imposing wage freezes, reducing vacation and retirement benefits, and laying off public employees providing useful services and public goods, taxes should be raised on the wealthy and on financial corporations doing business in Greece. Raising the value-added tax is highly regressive. Going after taxi drivers for tax evasion is small change and petty. Tax evasion by wealthy Greeks is notorious and that is where fiscal austerity should begin—and end!

(4) Greece needs fiscal stimulus not fiscal austerity to pull its economy out of the recession. Moreover, the world needs fiscal stimulus not fiscal austerity to end the Great Recession. Governments everywhere, including Greece, should engage in aggressive fiscal stimulus. Greece has every reason to be angry at Germany for not engaging in more fiscal

stimulus, while Germany has no reason to criticize Greece for running a budget deficit, since it should be. All the PIGS should unite and refuse to accede to counterproductive demands that they engage in useless fiscal austerity, and demand that the stronger European economies like Germany launch even stronger fiscal stimuli. Otherwise Europe and the world will suffer through a decade like the "Lost Decade" Japan suffered through in the 1990s, or worse. If all the governments in Europe do this, and the larger countries back up the debts of the PIGS when the financial markets try to smash their piñatas, what are international lenders going to do? They can't make money if they make no loans. The only way to save the EU is if the EU learns to act like a government, and uses its considerable powers to do what its citizens need it to do to engineer an economic recovery. The EU has the power to stare down financial markets. What it lacks is the will to do this. The reason it lacks the will is because so far EU governing institutions are more beholden to those financial interests than they are to their citizens.

Greeks who say no to austerity today are right. They are doing no more than insisting that their government serve their interests and not continue to serve the interests of global capital instead. The more loudly, longer, and more powerfully that Greeks say no, the better off they and the rest of the world will be. Portuguese, Irish, Italian, and Spanish workers are watching, and I hope will start to say no as well. Who knows, maybe even the American people will eventually wake up from our lethargy and make our silver-tongued president, who asked us to vote for change, deliver the change he promised.

Hasta la Victoria Siempre

Addendum: Recent Events

It has been exactly one year since I gave the above lecture in Athens and time has certainly not stood still. The most important and most surprising development is the Arab uprising, which has the potential to move history forward in an important region of the world long locked in brutal stalemate by imperial machinations. But while the power of majoritarian protests refusing to accept corrupt and inept authoritarian rule in one Arab country after another serves as a catalyst for protests against ruling elites in Europe and even the United States, it is otherwise unrelated to the issues I addressed in Athens a year ago, so I will say no more on that subject.

Important developments during the last year in the United States include: (1) The *Citizens United* decision by the Supreme Court which undermines progressive electoral tactics by opening the floodgates to secret, corporate money in US elections; (2) the rise of the Tea Party and Republican electoral victories in the fall of 2010; (3) the defeat of all progressive legislation, on every subject, at the federal level; (4) Republican-led campaigns to cut vital services and destroy unions representing public employees in many states, as tax revenues continue to plummet; and (5) President Obama's decision to vacillate, triangulate, and sell out all the progressive constituencies who backed him in 2008 in a desperate attempt to secure his own reelection no matter how meaningless this becomes. As a result progressive forces and the overwhelming majority of Americans have been left to fend for ourselves with no end to massive unemployment and home foreclosures in sight. The question, of course, is to what extent the kind of mass protests which began in Wisconsin over the winter will grow and spread.

In Europe nineteenth-century economic fallacies now reign supreme as all Keynesian wisdom is abandoned by European ruling elites, and one country after another is subjected to draconian fiscal austerity that is not only obscenely unjust and inhumane, but counterproductive even in regards to achieving the narrow goal of debt reduction. Greece has just demonstrated the futility of fiscal austerity in exchange for bailouts, which are too stingy for anyone who cares to see. As of last week the Greek government was being forced to pay 16.8 percent interest on ten-year bonds, and as a result it has had to return to the EC for help less than a year after its first bailout. Yet the European Central Bank, European Commission, and IMF persist in meting out even larger doses of the same austerity medicine to Ireland, Portugal, and Spain. Unlike phantom political terrorists, against whom the US government wages war, real economic terrorists—those Nobel Laureate Paul Krugman calls "the bond vigilantes"—are left free to roam the globe, wreaking havoc on one small country's economy after another while nobody thinks to raise a finger. Global financial capital is even more powerful than a year ago, and politicians from all major political parties in Europe—whether center-right, as in Germany, France, and England, or center-left as in Greece and Spain—are even more subservient to its interests.

The political fallout has taken two forms. On the one hand we see the crumbling of electoral support for centrist political parties and the rise of opposition parties on both the left and right. In Canada the long-dominant Liberal Party has virtually collapsed, leaving the more solidly social democratic NDP as the official opposition party to Harper's Conservative Party government. In Finland the right-wing True Finn Party recently made significant electoral gains. In Spain and Greece social democratic governments which agreed to administer austerity programs have lost considerable political support while groups to their left and right compete to win the allegiance of growing numbers of the disaffected. On the other hand we see the rise of a youth rebellion that is distrustful of all establishment political parties calling not only for sane economic policies but for much deeper social changes as well. In Greece, Spain, and France anti-authoritarian groups have as much influence as anyone among young Europeans who are increasingly taking to the streets. Meanwhile European ruling elites persist in aggravating economic conditions, and older European progressives seem unable to stop them.

May 27, 2011

ENDNOTES

1   James Rickards, "How Markets Attacked the Greek Piñata," *Financial Times*, February 12, 2010, http://www.ft.com/ (accessed November 22, 2011).

Education's Diminishing Returns and Revolutionary Potential in the United States and Beyond

William T. Armaline and William D. Armaline

Time Travel

The following chapter was completed in May 2011. Since then, the world has seen sparks burst into flames in the now infamous Arab Spring. Former regimes have begun to buckle and fall, and rulers in Syria continue to slaughter civilians in the streets with military snipers, vowing to crush democratic grassroots resistance by force. In Europe, the anti-austerity movement continues with student and union support in France, Spain, Italy, England, and (in particular) Greece—where at least partial default on national debt now seems unavoidable. Fears of an EU collapse and a "double dip recession" continue to shake financial markets on a weekly basis. As we pen this sentence the Occupy Wall Street (OWS) movement has officially globalized (Japan, England, Spain, Italy, and so forth) after having already spread to cities all over the United States OWS, in the words of the movement, represents "the 99%" responding to record wealth disparity on national and global levels, particularly as a result of the recent recession and policy norms of working-class austerity and owning-class bailouts (read: wealthfare on steroids, the largest upward distribution of wealth by the state in the entirety of human history).

Accurate and honest historical accounts will almost certainly record the primary engine of these movements as youth and young adults, who almost universally face relatively poor economic prospects—even if they have "worked hard and played by the rules." People the world over are voicing their rage in the streets over, among other things, the diminishing returns on the schooling and wage slavery available to them (if any), and their lack of voice in decisions that most affect their lives. In their actions they demonstrate the revolutionary potential we describe below.

Introduction

The historical role of public education in the United States is a contested terrain, described both as a cultural institution with the potential to enable and liberate, and as a state institution that ordinarily operates to (re)produce power and resource inequalities along lines of class, race, gender, sexuality, ethnicity, and citizenship status. Whether public education as an institution and process of socialization and knowledge creation/dissemination (or later, "schooling") is ultimately empowering or oppressive across history or in potential is arguably among questions at the center of critical educational scholarship over the last century.

Such reflections on public institutions and the state are especially relevant in times of social rupture, when one is forced to reflect on previous practices and seek sustainable paths forward. The recent global recession, placed in the context of free market capitalism's fall from infallible grace and impending ecological crises, seems to be such a point of rupture. It is an opportunity for us to reflect on what has been done and how we might move toward political-economic sustainability and social justice in our local and global communities. How we come to understand the past and our collective futures—perhaps the essence of "education"—will determine our mutual paths in this regard.

In the United States, we presently observe the slashing of primary, secondary, and higher public education as states struggle with massive budget shortfalls and economic decline. Current and emergent university students face historically high debt loads and low prospects for sustainable employment in return for their educational credentials. Universities in the United States and other global communities have recently seen waves of student resistance to decreasing opportunities for work, the use of public moneys to bail out large corporations and banks, and public spending on war and state terror in Afghanistan, Iraq, and occupied Palestine.[1] In short, for many students (including the so-called "middle class") a university diploma no longer ensures sustainable employment. What happens when new generations question the value of formal education in the capitalist context? What opportunities do such ruptures in collective consciousness and institutional function present for those interested in fundamental social change? In other words, what opportunities for social justice are created when public education is decimated, and the "false promise" of schooling is laid bare?[2]

The "Crises" Continue

Though we mean to speak here to global conditions and possibilities, there is a great deal to be learned from the US context concerning education and recent political economic developments. Though the United States does not reflect the global experience in its totality, it serves as an important example here due to its role as an international hub for university education, and its still hegemonic, though declining, role in the global capitalist system. We hesitate to agree with his statement literally, but Bookchin had a point when he suggested in the late 1960s that, "we need a cohesive, revolutionary approach to American social problems. Anyone who is a revolutionary in the US is *necessarily* an internationalist by virtue of America's world position."[3] As with many global social problems (nuclear and military proliferation, for example) the global economic recession (particularly concerning the mortgage and credit markets) was an American export by most accounts. Though the effects of the crises are shared globally, those companies most responsible for the crash(es) were American and western European financial, corporate, and insurance firms.[4] Where the state responded to the plight of large corporations and banks with an orgy of corporate welfare—"bail outs"—the plight of working people has been met with cuts to social services, employment, credit, and education, even in the face of domestic "stimulus" funding. Similar patterns of policy and discourse are reflected in much of the EU, China, and Japan (particularly including recent natural and human-made disasters), for example, where the global recession damaged trade markets and shrank state revenues. We might better understand the generational position of all new workers and students under the current global recession by looking at the raw financial losses suffered by American households, the rise in individual debt, and the condition of public institutions currently under siege in the United States.

The global economic recession has been utterly devastating for working, underemployed, and unemployed people. As reported by the *Wall Street Journal*, the wealth of American families fell by 18 percent in 2008. The net worth of US households fell by a total of $11 trillion, "a decline in a single year that equals the combined annual output of Germany, Japan, and the UK."[5] Banks cut off credit to small businesses and large corporations (especially those without powerful contacts in the US Federal Reserve and Treasury), who then cut workers' jobs, wages, benefits, and so forth[6]. The new generation of workers, young adults, and graduates face a difficult economic climate—all amidst rising costs for education, credit, general costs of living, and record levels of national debt. As it seems, many will enter the employment market carrying significant debt in comparison to previous generations.

Where less than half of all graduates from four-year colleges in the US carried student debt before 1993, nearly two thirds (66.4 percent) carried student debt by 2004. In terms of amount, average student debt loads have doubled over the past decade to between $20K and $25K in the US and £13K ($25K) in the UK.[7] In addition, nearly half of college students in the US carry significant credit card ($1000 or more) and commercial debt to cover gaps between diminishing earnings and skyrocketing university and housing costs.[8] Two relevant works, *Strapped*[9] and *Generation Debt*,[10] detail the generationally unique characteristics of young adults in the United States: record lows in total savings, record highs in student and commercial debt, and record highs in education and living costs. Adolescents and young adults now face unprecedented levels of unemployment in the United States—rates over the past three years hovered at or above 10 percent, with an effective rate (including, for example, those who have stopped looking for work and/or dropped off unemployment rolls) at approximately 20 percent.[11] In sum, today's young adults face very difficult circumstances in the job, housing, and credit markets.

Contrary to dominant ideology that would assume one's socioeconomic condition depends on one's individual choices and ability to "compete" in various markets, young adults and their broader global generation are not to blame for their increasingly difficult situation(s). They've largely inherited truly unfortunate social and ecological circumstances, and on the whole show great promise in their tolerance and reflection of diversity, their political activism and civil engagement, and ability to avoid the police state (drops in arrests, imprisonment, drug overdose deaths, violent crime, and so on).[12] In fact, given the urgency of ecological challenges such as those caused by global warming, the fate of several species—including our own—depends on the luck or savvy of those very folks. For that reason, we might be concerned with the diminishing opportunities and returns for formal schooling and young adults' reactions to current political economic conditions.

The shrinking opportunities offered by formal schooling are possibly best illustrated by the current condition of the world's eighth-largest economy: California. California faced a state budget shortfall of $24.3 billion in 2009. The state administration and legislature decided to gut public education as part of an attempt to balance the books. California public schools (K–12) were forced to cut over $13.3 billion from their budgets, with another $4 billion planned for 2010.[13] The cuts manifested in average classroom sizes edging toward forty per classroom in public schools, the end of summer school and extra-curricular programs (including athletics) as we know them, and massive teacher layoffs—2,250 in Los Anegeles county alone.[14] In terms of higher education, the California State University (CSU) system, largely serving the state's working class, was forced to cut $586 million (following already deep cuts made in 2008) with similar quality and labor effects for employees and stakeholders.[15] Two years later in 2011, CA public schools and universities face even larger cuts in public support and students of the CSU and UC systems face another 30 percent tuition increase, after similar increases in tuition and student fees over the two previous years.[16]

California, where the effects of foreclosure and unemployment are evident, serves to illustrate our contemporary economic condition: as capitalists and modern financiers are saved from themselves at public cost, public resources are completely and utterly decimated. As has long been argued by Marxists and anarchists, during times of capitalist "crisis," we see owners and rulers employing their resources to protect their interests and prevent the full redistribution of wealth and power. Our point, however, is that such conditions provide an opportunity for class consciousness, especially for young people facing what has been called the "false promises" of education in bourgeois democracies.[17] New generations of workers and workers returning for further training are encouraged to conform to, compete in, and pay for schooling that will provide a credential—supposedly the key to gainful employment and class mobility. Under the conditions previously discussed, it's increasingly difficult to convince people that conformity to the systems of schooling or work has the payoffs promised in dominant capitalist ideology and discourse—especially as young and/or working people are also forced to fight unpopular wars to gain similarly vague and questionable rewards. As seen in Paris in 1968, a realization of such false promises can lead to mass movements and the revolutionary moments required for fundamental social change.[18]

The False Promises of School and Work

Early political economic critiques present the history of public schooling in the United States as a litany of parallel efforts at educating for social control and "productive citizenry," typically and narrowly defined in terms of the knowledge, skills, attitudes, and values that will promote a productive, efficient, and compliant workforce. This critical history, beginning with the revisionist work of Callahan and extended through Katz, Carnoy, Spring, and Bowles and Gintis, is well known and documented.[19] Many of these (and other) structural analyses suggested the role of schooling in "reproducing" inequalities along lines of race, class, and gender. Today we find similar, though more theoretically and analytically sophisticated critiques of No Child Left Behind (NCLB) and the standardization movement,[20] dominant (read: largely capitalist, racist, patriarchal, and xenophobic) curricula,[21] pedagogical practices,[22] and so forth. Though an exhaustive discussion of critical educational scholarship is far beyond the scope of this piece, we mean only to point out a central theme in historical and contemporary research. That is, in the maintenance and perpetuation of global capitalism, public education is often a mechanism to produce new generations of workers socialized for their inclusion, typically as wage slaves, in the larger political economy. This process might be seen as one distinct from that of creative self-discovery, intellectual and cultural growth, or grounded historical or scientific exploration.

In much of his recent work, Stanley Aronowitz addresses the class reproductive features of public schools in the conceptual distinction between "schooling" and "education."[23] Returning to the central question of how to define public education as an institution, Aronowitz makes a convincing argument that through the hidden curriculum, inequitable funding, the corporatization of schools,[24] and the standardization movement (NCLB and "Race to the Top"), a vast majority of activity in schools is the socialization process of "schooling." Specifically, "schooling" refers to a system of training through a disciplinary (in the direct and Foucauldian senses) credentialing system that "contrary to [its] democratic pretensions, teach(es) conformity to the social, cultural, and occupational hierarchy" rather than critical independent thought necessary for personal autonomy and democratic societies.[25]

In comparison, "education" is conceptualized as something outside of and beyond this coercive credentialing system.[26] "Education may be defined as the collective and individual reflection[27] on the totality of life experiences: what we learn from peers, parents (and the socially situated cultures of which they are a part), media, and schools."[28] Education is something that happens in all contexts: our homes, neighborhoods, cultural centers (public squares, churches, markets, and so forth), workplaces, and sites of leisure. Where in the system of schooling "legitimate" knowledge is determined by state standards (i.e., what's on the test), the concept of education places all people in the position of creating knowledge and history, and the importance of any particular idea or body of research is determined through shared struggle and survival in real contexts. We might think of these concepts in relation to early Marxist notions of alienated labor: standardized schooling alienates people from the creation (process of labor) and use (products of labor) of knowledge and ideas, reducing learning and creative processes (to Marx, the heart of the human "species being"[29]) to a soul sucking process of regurgitating empty, detached information. When taken out of this oppressive context, learning (here "education") can be a fulfilling process where we explore our shared social and natural world through tangible struggles and socio-cultural contexts.

The conceptual distinction between education and schooling allows for the consideration of fundamental change in how we go about creating and passing on knowledge and culture, rather than liberal reformism. It allows for a departure from typical liberal narratives on "equal access" to credentialing—asking instead, "access to what?" Aronowitz suggests that these typical liberal perspectives promote "the idea that class deficits can be overcome by equalizing access to school opportunities without questioning what those opportunities have to do with genuine education."[30] Here we might return to the "false promises" made to new generations of students and workers—that their investments of time, money, and energy will ultimately be rewarded with gainful employment and a path for improving one's quality of life and opportunity structure(s). People are promised education and upward mobility, but actually experience schooling, wage slavery, and the near certainty of class *immobility*. As research has shown over the past thirty years, wealth disparity and the centralization of capital in the US and global economies rise steadily, while the share of wealth and resources by working people continue to shrink. Class mobility for working and unemployed populations in the United States is a myth, where "the greatest source of individual wealth is inheritance. If you are not rich, it is probably because you lacked the initiative to pick the right parents at birth."[31] Realizing the "false promises" of educational credentialing is to realize the difference between education and schooling, and to realize that the meritocracies of school and work don't actually play out as Horatio Alger fables and more contemporary fictions might lead us to believe.

At the same time, educational credentialing is typically a necessary step for socio-economic survival and empowerment—especially for members of marginalized populations such as the poor, people of color, and migrant workers. Accepted hiring practices for jobs offering a living wage require some level of higher education in the "post-industrial" service economies. For some populations in the United States, the threats of not attaining basic educational credentials are quite severe. By 1999, approximately one in nine white high school dropouts would experience prison by their thirties.[32] However, the threat of incarceration is *far* greater for African Americans, who currently account for just under half of the 2.2 million people imprisoned in the United States, and suffer an incarceration rate nearly twenty-five times that of whites. Bruce Western's research on punishment in the United States demonstrates that, "incredibly, a black male dropout, born in the late 1960s had nearly a 60% chance of serving time in prison by the end of the 1990s. At the close of the decade (2000), prison time had indeed become modal for young black men who failed to graduate from high school."[33] Many poor students and students of color effectively choose between schoolhouses that bore, dispirit, and ultimately fail to deliver; prisons that brutalize and dehumanize their occupants; and increasingly dangerous military service.[34] But what happens when people actively question schooling, or refuse to play along? Working-class and minority students in particular have demonstrated various forms of resistance to formal schooling, as seen in ethnographic research on student resistance dating back to the 1970s in the United States and United Kingdom.

Early Studies of Resistance to Schooling

Drawing its origins from the "new sociology of education" in the UK,[35] "resistance theory" focused on micro-level analyses of the social construction of knowledge,[36] the forms that knowledge takes, the various meanings made, and the resultant distribution of that knowledge and those meanings. The intersection of such phenomenological studies with critical reproduction accounts of schooling gave rise to a series of ethnographic studies of schooling in the United States and United

Kingdom,[37] which helped to explain that working-class students are not passive, but play active roles in the producing of culture anew (albeit in line with older patterns of power and control) with each generation.[38]

These ethnographies document how working-class students see school as either completely irrelevant to "real life,"[39] or only relevant as a credentialing agent.[40] There is little if any inherent good in what schools have to offer in the eyes of students central to these studies. For example, in reveling in their masculinist and racist approach to life and work, Willis' white, working-class "lads" rejected the mental/feminine labor of schools long enough to solidify their positions in the shop-floor culture of their fathers and brothers. The cruel irony at work is that in refusing to play along in school, the lads appear to have chosen their place in society—pigeonholed into manual wage labor. They took an active role in their own ultimate economic and social subjugation, appearing to have entered freely into an unfree situation. What is important here is that these studies show that students are not merely passive victims in the process of cultural and economic reproduction. Their awareness is apparent and their resistance, albeit self-defeating, is active.

While Willis represents the beginning of a series of powerful ethnographies in industrial settings,[41] Weis is the first to extend that ethnographic approach to analyzing the role of schooling in deindustrializing contexts and documents what happens when factory jobs are no longer available.[42] In brief, given deindustrialization, young working-class kids come to realize that they must become credentialed in order to be considered for non-factory work, and they strike an implicit agreement with school personnel to attend to the tasks or "form" of schooling but not the content or "substance" of the curriculum.[43] As a result, the actual preparation for higher education and, by extension, well-paying jobs is lacking, as these students never really master the curricular content that might enable them to attend and complete college. Again, student insight into the changing political economy of deindustrialization is accurate as far as it goes. But their "chosen" path of action, a focus on the credential alone, is ultimately self-defeating.

Both Willis and Weis find in their subjects' experiences the potential for critical awareness and more radical political consciousness. In both cases, however, schools do not facilitate a deeper political awareness, but rather act to derail such understanding, both through the overt curriculum and through formal and informal institutional practices.[44] One example in Willis's work is the school's attempt to "reintegrate" potentially disenchanted students into the formal schooling process through more "relevant" (read: vocational, non-college prep) curricula and career education. The history of public education in the United States is replete with other examples of such efforts as well.[45]

It is interesting and distressing that current education proposals from the Obama administration parallel these reintegration efforts. Recognizing the huge social and economic impact of high dropout rates, especially in poor and nonwhite populations, coupled with the rising cost of a traditional four-year college education, the US government is trying to pump billions of dollars into two-year colleges that offer preparation in technological and service occupations as a way to encourage predominantly working-class kids to complete high school and seek post-secondary education for work. These same institutions are primary sites for retraining unemployed and displaced workers. Recent reports highlighted one such proposal to allocate $12 billion to "better prepare students for the changing job market."[46] While an expansion of opportunities for post-secondary education is not necessarily a bad thing, the focus on two-year colleges attracting low-income students merely reinforces an already tiered and tracked schooling system in the United States that has served to perpetuate historical positions of social and economic privilege and subjugation. The most recent policy appears to be no different from its nineteenth- and twentieth-century predecessors' focus on what Aronowitz and others characterized as "schooling" as opposed to "education." Further, like wage slavery, it's offered as a threat rather than a choice: dropping out as an alternative only increases the likelihood of incarceration faced by those who can't or won't play along with schools for a credential. Will contemporary students, and their unemployed and displaced brothers, sisters, and elders see through this ruse? If they do, will their "chosen" alternative move us all toward a more humane and sustainable future, or will it parallel past self-defeating forms of resistance?

As seen in previous research, the insights of working-class kids in industrial and deindustrialized contexts reflected a double-edged sword. While the students rightly perceived that schools and the economic structures those schools were designed to support work better for some than for others, their resistance only allowed for them being easily disciplined and coerced through the police state and wage work. Our contemporary challenge is to use this insight, dissatisfaction, and resistance to forge new coalitions and collective political action.

Resistance and Reform by Schools

Present national education policy may not bode well for efforts to revolutionize schooling from within. At the K–12 level, rather than taking seriously the inadequacy of public schooling to address the need for students to develop the knowledge, skills, and dispositions of critical citizenry, reforms are typically rehashed proposals for newly standardized curricula, high-stakes testing, and accountability measures for individual schools and teachers.[47] No serious effort is made to rethink what we actually do in/with schools in the first place. The effects of school reform in the aftermath of No Child Left Behind are to publicly identify inadequate schools (defined by test scores) and threaten them with a loss of funding should they continue to "underperform." The schools then do what they can to improve test scores, often misusing and even falsifying data[48] to remove themselves from the scrutiny of the press.[49] In the best of circumstances, horrible schools may get less horrible, but the educational experience and resultant life chances of our most vulnerable students remain woefully inadequate. These same students are then afforded the "opportunity" to attend community colleges to prepare for jobs that may or may not actually materialize, due to the fact that increasing the schooling attainment of working-class kids as a group does not create jobs for them. It only ups the ante to secure whatever jobs happen to become available. The political economic structure, certainty of wage slavery, and the position of the owning class remain the same.

NCLB was the centerpiece of the G. W. Bush administration's approach to reforming schools. The Obama administration, faced with the choice of either renewing or replacing NCLB as it considered the reauthorization of the Elementary and Secondary Education Act (ESEA), decided to create its own reform initiative, "Race to the Top" (RTTT). Where NCLB focused on restructuring or ultimately closing the most underperforming schools (read, "schools with the lowest standardized test scores"), the approach of RTTT was to reward schools and school districts that took the lead in developing rigorous curricula and transforming structural features of schooling, including the evaluation of teacher and administrator performance and connecting that evaluation to their pay (and ultimately to their ability to keep their jobs). On the surface, Obama and his education secretary Arne Duncan appeared to be challenging schools to be the best they could be, yet RTTT is really only the flip side of NCLB. The assessment and evaluation of student performance is still primarily tied to standardized test scores. The evaluation of teachers, schools, and districts is also determined by these same test scores, with a variety of metrics devised around both absolute test score achievement and "value added" approaches that consider where students start the year and where they finish, seeing the difference as the relative growth produced by the teachers and schools. This "value added" model was the basis of Duncan's school reform project in Chicago (Renaissance 2010) when he was the CEO of the Chicago Public Schools. There is no evidence the model worked in Chicago, and much to suggest that it did not.[50] Yet it has been used as a central feature of the Obama reform agenda.

Under both NCLB and RTTT, when schools fail to meet their targeted performance measures, a variety of reform models can be applied to "restructure" the building. Those models tend to focus on removing a significant proportion of the teaching force as well as the principal and other top administrators. Ultimately, if the changes do not lead to sufficiently improved performance, the school can be closed. Even if the school is not closed, students can transfer out to other local schools or to charter schools, taking their state subsidy money with them.

In both NCLB and RTTT, charter schools are seen as appropriate "choices" to replace the "failing" schools. Often, these charter schools, ostensibly public in nature, receive public funds but are run by for-profit management groups and are also exempt from many of the performance requirements set for regular public schools. Just as with the "value added" teacher assessment model, the evidence on charter school performance indicates that they do no better and often do worse than the public schools they replace.[51] Yet the RTTT reformers, along with many newly elected governors such as John Kasich in Ohio and Scott Walker in Wisconsin, continue to call for increasing the number of charter schools in their respective states.

One important lesson we derive from this NCLB/RTTT continuum is that the G. W. Bush administration and the Obama Administration really do not view schooling much differently. They both buy into the dominant, corporate ideology of schooling efficacy. They both see the problem of lower school performance as the fault of the students, their parents, and teachers and not the extension of larger social, political, economic, and cultural forces. Further, they see the poor school performance as contributing to the economic downturn and the difficulty of turning the economy around, rather than the opposite.

Fortunately, some schools, scholars, and activists have designed productive alternatives to dominant schooling models. Dominant trends aside, there are public schools across the US that have transformed and organized themselves to unpack the complexities of post-industrial society such that students can come away with a more critical and radically informed understanding of their positions and roles in the political economy.[52] Further, as indicated in the conceptual differences between "education" and "schooling," schools are not the only option for developing critical intellectual, political, and cultural understandings. Home, work, and community contexts offer rich opportunities that may not presently be afforded by schools. We will return to this point shortly.

What appears to "work" in progressive and transformative educational reform, both in the United States and abroad, is the process of developing schools and other educational settings that grow organically from a local context. This should be no surprise to those informed by forms of (broadly) libertarian socialist theory, where emergent anarchist pedagogy is based on such horizontal, community-based, democratic models.[53] Interested and committed educators connect with parents, local activists, and grassroots community organizations to develop schools that reflect and build on the strengths of the local community.[54] Typically those efforts begin with a view of education that seeks a more just, productive, and humane existence coupled with a structural critique of dominant schooling and the "opportunities" afforded by wage work. In other words, these efforts operate to critique the process of formal schooling and, in doing so, help students to question and understand, among other things, the false promises of school and work. From this dialogue, we might establish the fertile grounds for class consciousness and revolutionary educational moments.

The danger lies in larger entities (city schooling systems, the Gates Foundation, and so on) entering the picture to "systematize" or "replicate" features of particular schools they find attractive. The power of the small, organically generated schools comes from the connection with the community, the people who created them. Once that is lost, which is what typically happens when small local efforts are corporatized and systematized, the efficacy of the school to grow out of and reflect community life is often lost. What *is* exportable, however, is the *process* of creating the small schools in the first place. If and when larger public entities like school systems come to rely on the process (of education) more than particular products (e.g., an obedient workforce); or when our institutions come to rely on the vibrancy and intellect of local communities and organizations connected with dedicated and committed educators broadly conceived, there might be some hope for them to transform in more fundamental ways. Regardless of whether that can or will occur, we can draw from the experience of creating small, community-based and culturally responsive schools to develop our own approaches to education (as opposed to schooling) in and out of schools, linked to a more sustainable and humane social, economic, and political order.

Contemporary Student Resistance and Possibilities for Broad Social Change

Where earlier we discussed the resistance strategies of high school students to public schooling, we now see a pattern of resistance, civil disobedience, and direct action among young adults and students facing dire educational and socio-economic forecasts. As White reports, there were more than thirty student-led occupations on university campuses in the US and UK in response to decreasing educational and employment opportunities, increasing costs of education and housing, and the use of university resources to promote various military agendas in the first three months of 2009 alone.[55] As one specific example,

> New York University students barricaded themselves inside a campus cafeteria and demanded greater budget transparency [2/18/09], tuition stabilization and divestment from Israel. Although the occupation ended in failure, defeat turned to victory when the retaliatory suspension of 18 students galvanized campus support. The subsequent protests forced the administration to reverse their punitive measures.[56]

Such occupations and student protests in the United Kingdom were relatively sustained through 2010,[57] and student resistance in the United States has since expanded to address the educational rights of immigrants. In response to draconian legislation subjecting Latino/a and indigenous populations to racial profiling and unequal treatment under the law (SB 1070), and to the cutting of "ethnic studies" programs across Arizona, students continue an aggressive campaign of civil disobedience—including the occupation of school board meetings in Tucson[58]—to demand equal access to culturally relevant public education. In the already discussed state of California, students continue to join faculty and staff unions to protest skyrocketing tuitions, shrinking enrollment, department faculty/instructor/staff layoffs, increasing classroom size, ballooning administrative pay and growth, and a refusal by state officials across the board to seek revenues from (for example) oil extraction, as done in many other states to fund public higher education.[59] These and other observations suggest that the emerging generation of workers and students are less than fond of their current predicaments, and are willing to resist their own school and state administrations to affect policy. Rather than a collection of random events, we might consider this primarily student-led resistance as part of the larger global movement against imposed austerity programs, where, as in fiscally unstable countries of the EU, young people join those near retirement in protesting massive cuts to public education, retirement pensions, public health care, and public sector employment. The false promises of education (sustainable employment with the imagined quality of life to boot) meet the false promises of wage slavery (retirement) in the post-Fordist West to create interesting and potentially powerful lines of solidarity.

Spain and Greece offer perfect illustrations of this solidarity in action. Political analysts in Greece have reported that people's future aspirations across socio-economic status have dropped to all-time lows, along with studies from the Foundation for Economic and Industrial Research suggesting that economic indices have never been so low since they began reporting in 1981.[60] Kaimaki describes the conditions of what is now being called the "700 Euro Generation," who recently participated in the country's anarchist and labor inspired uprisings, resulting in the municipal takeover of several cities, and what is a sustained movement against capitalism and the Greek police state:

> This united front is led by a generation of the very young. There is a reason for this: daily life for most young Greeks is dominated by intensive schooling aimed at securing a university place. Selection is tough and children focus hard on it from the age of 12. But once the lucky ones get there, they soon discover the reality of life after university: at best, a job at 700 Euros ($1000) a month.[61]

Youth in Greece, along with other sections of Greek labor, came to realize the false promises of school and work in their particular context. This, along with an explosive movement against the Greek police state (a point of controversy, especially for immigrant populations for some time) sparked by the murder of a young anarchist by Greek police forces, might be seen as a revolutionary moment led by the resistance of students and young adults.

As we write the final revision of this chapter (May 2011) tens of thousands of students, unemployed, and underemployed have taken to the streets in major Spanish cities (in the *Puerta del Sol* in Madrid in particular), partly under the leadership of the self-described "Youth Without a Future," to protest the settling of state budgets on the backs of workers rather than on the backs of the banks, politicians, and financiers behind the financial "crisis."[62] With the EU's highest unemployment rate (approximately 21 percent), Spain also joins Greece and Portugal as the EU's most financially unstable members. As a result, Spanish politicians are increasingly pressured by other EU members to balance national budgets on the backs of the people to avoid "instability" in the EU, and to frame discourse around the global recession as the fault of greedy taxpayers and public employees rather than fraudulent and tyrannical bankers, investors, and politicians. Facing the obvious false promises of school and work in Spain and Greece, perhaps the complete dissolution of anything resembling a social contract, it should be no surprise that the young join the under/unemployed to protest their conditions and the people and policies that created them. They realize, simultaneously, that they did not create these crises, and that they have some agency in reframing the public conversation and conflicts over finite resources that affect their lives so acutely.

The lessons? As they realize the false promises of school and work, emerging generations of students and workers (along with older workers in potential solidarity) are clearly able and willing to resist the constructed authority of school and state administrations to affect policy and practice in their communities. However, as we have learned from previous research on student resistance, there is some question as to how we take advantage of this opportunity for mass consciousness and action in such a way that results in social change rather than the eventual co-optation and appropriation of those who resist.

Though a full discussion of social movement strategies is beyond the scope of this piece, we would like to conclude with relevant suggestions to take advantage of current opportunities to organize and resist in a time of social and political-economic rupture. Unfortunately, we would like to break the hearts of educational entrepreneurs the world over in recognizing that our collective approach to education (particularly if differentiated from schooling) is not subject to quick fixes, particularly from "free trade" models that wish to privatize education and employ systems of private and "charter" schools to replace public educational spaces and resources. That said, we might consider the following in our steps forward:

1) First and foremost, radical public educators should seek to "accompany" current labor (perhaps through public employee unions for those employed by public universities/schools) and student protests seeking to stop forced austerity programs that immediately threaten the survival and opportunity structure of both the new and retiring generations of workers. This should be seen as a relevant social movement strategy that opens the door to affective practices of shared struggle—particularly direct action. It should also be seen as a mechanism to establish solidarity and tangible networks between otherwise rarely connected populations of the working class. It is a way for public intellectuals to help create and promote "communities of struggle"[63] across age, area of employment, race, ethnicity, and gender.[64]

2) Rather than returning funding to public institutions that continue to school but fail to educate, we need to reconceptualize and fundamentally change our schools, universities, and libraries into institutions of equal access that respond directly to the needs of the communities served. This typically involves a certain level of decentralization and democratization of schools, school districts, school boards, and

universities. Such a process typically requires both forms of resistance and forms of more liberal-style "building from within." In terms of resistance from within educational institutions, we might look to strategies of sabotage, direct action, and mutual aid that might be employed by school or university staff, community members, students, teachers/professors, and even administrators within their employing institutions.[65] We see resistance from outside of educational institutions in the point above and the illustrations previously discussed in this section. Wonderful examples of building from within educational institutions can be found in the organic (as opposed to corporate- and Gates-inspired) small schools movement discussed by Klonsky and Klonsky, and others.[66]

Further, we might look to alternative measures to create and disseminate knowledge horizontally, outside of formal schooling. Scholars such as Murray Bookchin have for some time argued that, "Education ... is the top 'priority' for a radicalization of our time ... the *study* group, not only the 'affinity group,' is the indispensable form for this time—especially in view of the appalling intellectual and cultural degradation that marks our era."[67] The development of radical reading and study groups across age, race, ethnicity, gender, trade, and student/worker divides simultaneously provides an opportunity for class-consciousness building and education beyond the walls of formal schooling (not to mention without state censorship). Many organizations, such as the Radical Autonomous Communities (RAC) of southern California, have employed study groups and (online) list-servs successfully for these very purposes. In terms of building educational institutions outside of conventional schooling, one might look to the emerging Transformative Studies Institute (TSI).[68] The TSI seeks to become one of the country's only graduate "free schools," and currently offers its own independent academic press, radio show, interviews, scholarly journal, resources for social justice scholars and activists, and a growing body of faculty/scholars. Likewise, counter-institutions that have become staples on the libertarian left like the Institute for Anarchist Studies or the Z Institute should be supported by forward-looking anti-authoritarians, as should projects like the Anarchist Studies Network (http://anarchist-studies-network.org.uk) in Europe and the North American Anarchist Studies Network (www.naasn.org).

3) As noted previously, we need to rethink our notions of educational reform that stop at issues of access. We need to ask "access to what?" and change the curriculum or substance of public education accordingly. One of the greatest contemporary threats to working-class students is their being robbed of their history, and the general capability to critically interpret current events within a reasonable historical framework that reaches beyond last weekend. New workers are easy slaves to the extent that they depend on their rulers and owners to understand their own history and the realities and choices that face them in the present and future.

We need to recapture our own collective understanding of history that would include political philosoph(ies), local and global histories of non-elites that go beyond the history of wars and nation-states, and methods of civic engagement. This is an agenda that must be fought on several fronts. In terms of school curriculum, such changes require the entrance of radical scholars and workers into schools and universities (and vice versa), where strategies of resistance might be employed in classrooms, offices, and shop floors. Such resistance might first take aim at programs like NCLB and RTTT that steer curricula away from critical history and social science, toward "value free" skills in mathematics, vocabulary, syntax, and analytical reasoning.

As a second front, we can enter and engage with the larger public domain and news media. Radical and/or critical scholars must gather the courage and stomach to engage with news media that rank-and-file students and workers actually read/watch/listen to (i.e., not academic journals and specialty zines or blogs speaking only to their "choir"). In this sense we suggest public intellectuals actually engage their public in order to compete with the paid stooges and entertainers of the corporate owning class that tend to dominate mainstream news sources. To be effective, such engagement must happen consistently and from a large network of intellectuals—not simply the handful of "divas" on the left who currently rotate as predictable talking heads for large speaking fees and book sales (you know who you are, and so do the rest of us).

As we attempt to infiltrate mainstream news media, we might also turn to projects such as the "Media Carta" and "culture jamming" campaigns organized by writers/readers/supporters of the Canadian magazine *Adbusters* to release public discourse from the death grip of corporations.[69] Such campaigns employ legal (lawsuits and legislative reform) and extralegal (civil disobedience and sabotage) means to "reclaiming the mental environment": in short, take the major means of communication (television, radio, billboards, newspapers, and so forth) away from private companies and advertisers, providing space for public and community discourse, dialogue, expression, and journalism.

Final Reflection

Here we've attempted to outline global capitalism's effects on one of the world's largest institutional programs—public schooling. Studies of political economy, in order to be holistic and effective, must include analyses that go beyond quantitative market models, both to point out the disturbing relationships between capitalism and public institutions, and to suggest paths moving forward that create more sustainable and less hierarchical societies. Ultimately it will require a mass movement to democratize and redefine public education and to end the rule of elites in all political economic and social life—but these efforts are likely one and the same to a great extent. In order to build such a movement, we can and must begin in institutions such as schools, where much of our individual and collective "knowledge" is created, communicated, and deemed (il)legitimate. We wish to join radical students, workers, teachers, scholars, and activists in the battles ahead to rip the processes of knowledge and meaning making from the hands of rulers. We urge those interested in radical social change to take advantage of periods of social rupture to reconceptualize "education" and its place in forming sustainable non-hierarchical communities in the United States and beyond.

ENDNOTES

1   See M. White, "Campus Uprising," *Adbusters* 17 (no. 3), (2009), n.p., and M. Wainwright, "Student Occupations Expected to Increase," *Guardian*, November 28, 2010, http://www.guardian.co.uk/education/2010/nov/28/student-occupations-increase-sit-ins (accessed May 1, 2011).

2   See S. Aronowitz, *False Promises: The Shaping of American Working Class Consciousness* (Durham, NC: Duke University Press, 1992).

3   M. Bookchin, *Post-Scarcity Anarchism* (Oakland, CA: AK Press, 2004), xvi.

4   See M. Taibbi, "The Big Takeover," *Rolling Stone*, no. 1075 (March 2009).

5   S. M. Kalita, "Americans See 18% of Wealth Vanish," *Wall Street Journal*, March 13, 2009, A-1.

6   The automotive industry serves as an obvious example here.

7   R. Popescu, "Gen Y Struggles with ABC's" *New York Times*, Business—Your Money, May 5, 2006, www.nytimes.com/2006/05/05/your-money (accessed June 15, 2009); and Project on Student Debt, 2009, www.projectonstudentdebt.org (accessed June 15, 2009).

8   Project on Student Debt, 2009.

9   T. Draut, *Strapped: Why America's 20- and 30-Somethings Can't Get Ahead* (Norwell, MA: Anchor Press, 2007).

10   A. Kamenetz, *Generation Debt: Why Now Is a Terrible Time to Be Young* (New York: Riverhead Books, 2006).

11   Bureau of Labor Statistics, 2009, 2011, www.bls.gov/bls/unemployment.htm (accessed February 1, 2011).

12   See M. Males, *Framing Youth: Ten Myths about the Next Generation* (Monroe, ME: Common Courage Press, 2002) and Youthfacts, *Youthfacts*, website by the Youth Truth Institute, www.youthfacts.org (accessed February 1, 2011).

13   California Department of Education (CDA), "News Release: State Schools Chief Jack O'Connell Highlights Impact of Budget Cuts to Education," June 3, 2009, www.cde.ca.gov/nr/ne/yr09 (accessed June 15, 2009).

14   Ibid.

15   California Faculty Association (CFA), "FAQ on Possible Furloughs," 2009, www.calfac.org (accessed March 12, 2009).

16   Ibid.

17   See Aronowitz, *False Promises*.

18   Ultimately the fundamental changes sought by the participants of the Parisian uprising were effectively halted by the French ruling elite. How might we otherwise sustain such revolutionary moments and movements? As we will continue to argue here, a consistent and persistent overhaul of our educational institutions—indeed, how we come to see "education" in general—may be required.

19   See R. Callahan, *Education and the Cult of Efficiency* (Chicago: University of Chicago Press, 1962); M. Katz, *Class, Bureaucracy and Schools: The Illusion of Educational Change in America* (New York: Praeger, 1971); M. Carnoy, *Education as Cultural Imperialism* (New York: McKay, 1974); J. Spring, *The Sorting Machine: National Educational Policy since 1945* (New York: McKay, 1976); and S. Bowles and H. Gintis, *Schooling in Capitalist America: Educational Reform and the Contradictions of Economic Life* (New York: Basic Books, 1976).

20   See W. T. Armaline and D. Levy, "No Child Left Behind: Flowers Don't Grow in the Desert," *Race and Society* 7, (no. 1) (2004): 31–62; D. Hursh, "Assessing No Child Left Behind and the Rise of Neoliberal Education Policies, *American*

Educational Research Journal 44, (2007): 493-518; and D. Hursh, *High Stakes Testing and the Decline of Teaching and Learning: The Real Crisis in Education* (Lanham, MD: Rowman and Littlefield, 2008).

21   See M. Apple, *The State and the Politics of Knowledge* (New York: Routledge/ Falmer, 2003); and M. Apple, *Ideology and Curriculum* (New York: Routledge, 2004).

22   See P. McLaren, *Capitalists and Conquerors: A Critical Pedagogy against Empire* (Lanham, MD: Rowman and Littlefield, 2005); and P. McLaren and J. Kincheloe eds., *Critical Pedagogy: Where Are We Now?* (New York: Peter Lang Publishing, 2007).

23   See S. Aronowitz, "Against Schooling: Education and Social Class," *Social Text* 22, (no. 2) (2004): 13–15; and S. Aronowitz, *Against Schooling: For an Education That Matters* (New York: Paradigm Publishers, 2008).

24   See Callahan, *Education*; J. Spring, *Education and the Rise of the Corporate State* (Boston: Beacon Press, 1972); and J. Spring, *Education and the Rise of the Global Economy* (Mahwah, NJ: Lawrence Erlbaum, 1998).

25   Aronowitz, "Against Schooling: Education and Social Class," 20.

26   Such systems "test" one's ability to reflect dominant cultural capital and conform to standard hierarchical arrangements, while presenting themselves as objective meritocracies.

27   As Aronowitz (Aronowitz, "Against Schooling: Education and Social Class," 21) explains, "by reflection I mean the transformation of experience into a multitude of concepts that constitute the abstractions we call 'knowledge.'"

28   Aronowitz, "Against Schooling: Education and Social Class," 21.

29   We are referring here to the writings of early Marx (K. Marx, *Economic and Philosophic Manuscripts of 1844* (NY: International Publishers, 1964)) on alienation; specifically, alienation from the product of one's labor, the process of labor, and from the fundamental capacity of humans to apply creative energies—what it is, to Marx, to be human.

30   Aronowitz, "Against Schooling: Education and Social Class," 15.

31   M. Parenti, *Democracy for the Few* (New York: Wadsworth, 2007), 9.

32   B. Western, *Punishment and Inequality in America* (New York: Russell Sage Foundation, 2006), 26.

33   Ibid.

34   See A. Davis, *Are Prisons Obsolete?* (New York: Seven Stories Press, 2003).

35   See M. Young, *Knowledge and Control: New Directions for the Sociology of Education* (London: Collier-Macmillan, 1971); and J. Karable and A. H. Halsey, ed., *Power and Ideology in Education* (New York: Oxford University Press, 1977).

36   See P. L. Berger and T. Luckman, *The Social Construction of Reality: A Treatise in the Sociology of Knowledge* (New York: Anchor Doubleday, 1967).

37   See, for example, Carnoy, *Education*; and Bowles and Gintis, *Schooling in Capitalist America.*

38   See P. Willis, *Learning to Labour: How Working Class Kids Get Working Class Jobs* (Westmead, UK: Saxon House, 1977); L. Weis, *Working Class without Work: High School Students in a De-industrializing Economy* (New York: Routledge, 1990); and A. McRobbie, "Working Class Girls and the Culture of Femininity," in *Women Take Issue: Aspects of Women's Subordination*, 96–108, Women's Study Group, Center for Contemporary Cultural Studies, ed. (London: Hutchinson, 1978).

39   See Willis, *Learning to Labour*; and McRobbie, "Working Class Girls."

40   See Weis, *Working Class without Work.*

41   See Willis, *Learning to Labour.*

42   See Weis, *Working Class without Work.*

43   Ibid., 36.

44   For a more detailed account see W. D. Armaline and K. Farber, "Working Class Students and School, Life and Work: A Look Back at Willis and Weis," *Educational Studies* 30, (no. 2), (1999): 161–68.

45   See J. Spring, *The American School: 1642–1996* (New York: McGraw-Hill, 1996); and Spring, *Education and the Rise of the Global Economy.*

46   T. Lewin, "A Boon to 2-Year Colleges, Affirming Their Value," July 14, 2009, *New York Times,* www.nytimes.com/ (accessed May 1, 2010).

47   See Armaline and Levy "No Child Left Behind"; and Aronowitz, *Against Schooling: For an Education That Matters.*

48   See the "Texas Miracle" headed by then-superintendent of the Houston schools and former secretary of education Rod Paige and then-governor George W. Bush. See W. Haney, "The Myth of the Texas Miracle in Education," *Educational Policy Analysis Archives* 8, (no. 41), (August 2000), http://epaa.asu.edu/epaa/v8n41 (accessed May 19, 2011). More recently a similar cheating scandal plagued the DC schools; see J. Gillum and M. Bello, "When Standardized Test Scores Soared in D.C., Were the Gains Real?" 2011, http://www.usatoday.com/ (accessed May 19, 2011); and one involving data manipulation in the New York City schools under Joel Klein, see G. Schmidt, "Ravitch in Huffington Post Renews Critique of Obama and Duncan's 'Race to the Top,'" http://www.substancenews.net/articles.php?page=1575 (accessed May 19, 2011), both of whom relied extensively on tying teacher and administrator pay to student standardized test scores.

49   See Haney, "The Myth"; and S. Klein, L. Hamilton, D. McCaffrey, and B. Stecher, "What Do Test Scores in Texas Tell Us?" *Educational Policy Analysis Archives* 8, (no.

49) (October, 2000), http://epaa.asu.edu/epaa/v8n49 (accessed May 19, 2011).

50   For example, see S. Glazerman and A. Seifullah, "An Evaluation of the Teacher
      Advancement Program (TAP) in Chicago: Year Two Impact Report," Washing-
      ton, DC: Mathematica Policy Research, 2010, http://www.mathematica-mpr.
      com/publications/pdfs/education/TAP_rpt.pdf (accessed February 1, 2011).

51   For example, see Center for Research on Education Outcomes (CREDO), "Mul-
      tiple Choice: Charter School Performance in 16 States," Stanford University,
      Stanford, CA, 2009, http://credo.stanford.edu/reports/MULTIPLE_CHOICE_
      CREDO.pdf (accessed May 1, 2010).

52   See M. Klonsky and S. Klonsky, *Small Schools: Public School Reform Meets the Own-
      ership Society* (New York: Routledge, 2008); and Small Schools Workshop, 2009,
      www.smallschoolsworkshop.org (accessed May 1, 2010).

53   See A. DeLeon, "Oh No, Not the 'A' Word! Proposing an 'Anarchism' for Educa-
      tion, *Educational Studies* 44, (no. 2) (2008): 122–141; *W. T. Armaline*, "Thoughts
      on Anarchist Pedagogy and Epistemology," in *Contemporary Anarchist Studies: An
      Introductory Anthology of Anarchy in the Academy*, ed. L. Fernandez, A. Nocella, R.
      Amster, A. DeLeon, and D. Shannon, 136–146 (NY: Routledge, 2009); and N.
      Chomsky, *Chomsky on Democracy and Education*, ed. P. Otero (New York: Rout-
      ledge and Falmer, 2003).

54   For examples, see the Small Schools Workshop(s) in Chicago, active since 1991:
      www.smallschoolsworkshop.org.

55   White, "Campus Uprising."

56   Ibid.

57   For example, see Wainwright, "Student Occupations."

58   See www.saveethnicstudies.org for links to print and video coverage of the protests
      and their aftermath.

59   California Faculty Association (CFA) Website, "CFA Statement on Governor 's
      May Budget Revision," 2011 www.calfac.org (accessed May 16, 2011); and CFA,
      "FAQ on Possible Furloughs."

60   V. Kaimaki, "Bailouts for the Banks, Bullets for the People: Mass Uprising of
      Greece's Youth," Jan. 2009, *Le Monde Diplomatique* (English edition), www.
      mondediplo.com/2009/01/06greece (accessed March 17, 2009).

61   Ibid.

62   S. Poggoli "Youth Protests Sweep Spain as Unemployment Soars," National Public
      Radio, 2011, http://www.npr.org/2011/05/26/136683688/youth-protests-sweep-
      spain-as-unemployment-soars (accessed May 27, 2011).

63   A. Grubacic, "Introduction: Libertarian Socialism for the Twenty-First Century,"
      in ed. A. Grubacic, *From Here to There: The Staughton Lynd Reader* (Oakland, CA:

PM Press, 2010), 16.

64   For an excellent discussion of these principles and strategies for organizing and revolutionary action, see Grubacic, "Introduction: Libertarian Socialism for the Twenty-First Century."

65   See DeLeon, "Oh No."

66   See Klonsky and S. Klonsky, *Small Schools*; D. Meier, *The Power of their Ideas: Lessons from a Small School in Harlem* (Boston: Beacon Press, 1995); and E. Levine, *One Kid at a Time: Big Lessons from a Small School* (New York: Teachers College Press, 2002).

67   M. Bookchin, *Post-Scarcity Anarchism* (Oakland, CA: AK Press, 2004), xxvi.

68   See www.transformativestudies.org.

69   See www.adbusters.org for information, materials—including lesson plans, and current activities.

Part 4
Practice

"What I believe is a process rather than a finality. Finalities are for gods and governments, not for the human intellect."
—Emma Goldman

Anarchist Economics in Practice
Uri Gordon

It cannot be enough to criticize capitalism, even from a distinctly anarchist point of view. Nor will it do to merely construct models of free and equal economic arrangements, no matter how inspiring and realistic. In addition to these, the discussion of anarchist economics must also involve a look at ways of getting from here to there. In other words, it requires that we examine anarchist economics in terms of concrete, present-day practices and assess their role within the more general context of anarchist revolutionary strategy.

In this chapter I attempt to initiate such a discussion by surveying and examining the significance of the actual economic practices undertaken by anarchists and their allies today. In what ways are anarchists organizing to engage in economic practices that depart from the conventional, profit-oriented capitalist economy? What challenges and opportunities do anarchist economies confront in the contemporary landscape of social struggle? And to what degree do they serve as a meaningful contribution to revolutionizing society and replacing capitalism with non-hierarchical, unalienated forms of production and exchange?

In what follows, I begin by examining various economic practices that anarchists display in their everyday organizing, which can be meaningfully understood as a form of resistance to capitalism. I then attempt to situate these practices within the context of several key contemporary terms in anarchist revolutionary thought: direct action, propaganda by the deed, and the politics of collapse. To be sure, most anarchists also regularly participate in the conventional economy—working for wages, purchasing goods, and paying for services. Yet what interests us here are the kinds of practices that anarchists undertake against these prevalent modes of production, consumption, and exchange.

Before turning to a survey of the various types of economic practice in which anarchists engage, there is a preliminary point to be made about the broad choice of examples. Some readers may object to the inclusion of certain examples, which, they may argue, do not in fact qualify as anarchist. Alternative currencies and workers' cooperatives, for example, would receive criticism from anarcho-communists since they retain, respectively, the use of symbolic means of exchange and the payment of wages. Thus they are not only islands inside capitalism, but also not sufficiently prefigurative of an anarchist-communist society—one in which there are no wages, and products are not exchanged but distributed according to need. Similarly, anarchists who strongly endorse the primitivist critique of civilization would almost certainly object to most of the examples given here, since they continue to be anchored in domestication and rationality.

There is certainly substance to these objections. Nevertheless, I have chosen to keep the tent as wide as possible, if only for the reason that readers new to anarchism and less familiar with its internal controversies deserve to be introduced to the entire variety of practices that broadly fall within its sphere and left to make up their own minds. More generally, however, I would like to emphasize that the entire discussion of anarchist economics in practice must take place under the lens of imperfection and experimentation. This has to do with the distinction that Terry Leahy makes between purist and hybrid strategies, that is, between strategies that completely embody anarchist ideals and ones which continue to rely on aspects of capitalism.[1] Hybrid strategies have always been part of the anarchist repertoire of social resistance; yet the relevant question is whether hybrid strategies are viewed as already embodying the end point of desired social change (that is, a reformed capitalist system), or as necessary but temporary compromises with the ubiquity of capitalist social relations, a stepping-stone towards more comprehensive social change. As Leahy argues,

> To an extent hybrid strategies are symbiotic with capitalism. They can be seen as productive for the capitalist class in ameliorating some of capitalism's excesses. Yet they are also antithetical to the culture and economy of capitalism as a system. Given enough time and enough proliferation they will replace capitalism with something completely different....For those who ultimately want nothing but the best that an anarchist utopia can offer, the thing to do is to be mobile and seize opportunities for hybrids as they arise and move on as they grow stale.[2]

It is in this inclusive and experimental spirit that I offer the following examples. While limitations of space mean that the discussion is necessarily cursory, I have referenced some relevant literature throughout the exposition, and the reader is invited to consult it for further information and analysis.

Varieties of Anarchist Economic Practice

Withdrawal

Perhaps better defined as a "non-practice" than as a practice, the term "withdrawal" here indicates the various ways in which anarchists may abstain from participation in central institutions of the capitalist economy—primarily the wage system and the consumption of purchased goods. The goal of such a strategy is to weaken capitalism by sapping its energy, reducing its inputs in terms of both human labor and cultural legitimation. To be sure, the ubiquity of capitalist relations means that the options for withdrawal remain partial at best. Most of us must work for someone else to survive, and buy necessities that are not otherwise available for acquisition. Nevertheless, there are ways in which participation in capitalism can be significantly reduced, or undertaken on its qualitatively different margins. Rather than seeking full employment and aspiring to a lifelong career, anarchists can choose to work part-time or itinerantly, earning enough to supply their basic needs but not dedicating more time to waged work than is absolutely necessary—perhaps on the way towards the abolition of work as compulsory, alienated production.[3] In the area of housing, squatting a living space rather than renting one also abstains from participation in capitalism, though this option is less sustainable in most countries since it will almost certainly end in eviction. Anarchists may also reduce their participation in the moneyed circulation of commodities by reusing and recycling durable goods, and by scavenging or growing some of their own food rather than purchasing it from the supermarket.[4] Such practices can never by themselves destroy capitalism, since in the final analysis they remain confined to the level of personal lifestyle and rely on capitalism's continued existence in order to inhabit its margins and consume its surpluses. Nevertheless, strategies of withdrawal do complement other practices in carving out a separate space from capitalism, as well as in expressing a rejection of its ideologies of dedication to the workplace and of consumption as the road to happiness.

Anarchist unions

For the majority of us who cannot escape wage labor, joining an anarchist union can be a useful way to defend our rights and struggle for improved conditions within the capitalist workplace. The largest anarchist labor unions today are in Spain (CNT, CGT) and France (CNT-AIT). In English-speaking countries the Industrial Workers of the World (IWW) is the most prominent one, with about 2,000 members, most of them in the United States but also in Canada, Britain, and Australia.[5] Though very small compared to its heyday a century ago, the IWW is very active in several small and mid-sized firms—primarily in the printing, recycling, retail, and social services sectors. In the last decade, it has gained prominence through organizing immigrant warehouse workers in New York City as well as the struggles of its affiliated baristas in the Starbucks chain of coffee shops. Anarchist unions, in the view of their members, are not merely organizations that struggle on workers' behalf within the capitalist system, but rather part of the radical social movement that seeks its abolition. As the Preamble to the IWW constitution states, the struggle between the working and the employing classes "must go on until the workers of the world organize as a class, take possession of the means of production, abolish the wage system, and live in harmony with the earth."[6] This is the strategy of anarcho-syndicalism,[7] which strives to get the majority of workers in all sectors of the economy to join militant workplace organizations, weakening capitalism through their organized force and building up to a general strike. At this point the workers would not only halt production to negotiate better conditions, but seize the factories and land to establish an anarchist society with the same workers' unions now running the economy through democratic planning along with communities.

Workplace and university occupations

Another tactic related to syndicalism in its realization of action "at the point of production" is the workplace occupation. In such actions, workers lock themselves into the factory—either a means of resisting layoffs, or during a strike to prevent the employment of strikebreakers, or, under conditions of more widespread economic crisis and social revolt, in order to take over manufacturing and manage it themselves. Waves of workplace occupations have occurred throughout the past century, most prominently during the 1920 "hot summer" in Italy,[8] the May 1968 events in France,[9] and the Argentine rebellion of 2002.[10] Most recently, in the wake of the current financial crisis, a number of factory occupations have already taken place in response to layoffs and plant closures—including the Visteon car factories (formerly Ford) in Britain and Northern Ireland, the Aradco auto parts supplier in Canada, and the Republic Windows and Doors factory in Chicago. While these occupations ended in agreements with management to provide the workers with improved severance packages, they also displayed a powerful example of solidarity and indicate a rise in workers' militancy, which can be expected to expand.

Extending the logic of the workplace occupation to the "knowledge factory,"[11] occupations of universities can also be seen as a form of anarchist economic practice in their resistance to the corporate takeover of higher education and their practices of self-management. University occupations have characterized periods of large-scale protest, as with the May 1968 events in France and the Greek riots of winter 2008.[12] In 2008, the New School in New York City was occupied in protest of the reorganization policies of its president, and in the UK over thirty universities were occupied in protest of the Israeli army's attack on Gaza. Most recently, British students staged occupations around the country in response to rising tuition fees and cuts to teaching budgets.

Cooperatives and communes

Cooperatives are democratically run associations which can be established for production, consumption, or housing. Thus workers' cooperatives are businesses that are owned and managed by their workers. Unlike normal private firms where decisions on production, spending, and pay are made authoritatively by the managers and dictated to the workers, in cooperatives such decisions are made democratically, in meetings where each worker has an equal say. A consumer cooperative is a group of people that comes together to regularly purchase goods (most typically food) in bulk, and thus at reduced cost, later distributing them among the members. Housing cooperatives will typically own a building, with members occupying bedrooms and sharing the communal resources. Cooperatives usually adhere to a set of principles similar to the seven "Rochdale Principles," adopted in 1844 by the Rochdale Society of Equitable Pioneers, an early consumer cooperative in England. In one contemporary version these are: open and voluntary membership; equal control among members; limited returns on investment as interest or dividends; fair distribution of profits among members; educational and social objectives in addition to commercial ones; cooperation with other cooperatives; and concern for the community.[13] Communes can be viewed as intentional communities that combine the three types of cooperative in one arrangement. Members live together in one house or in separate units in a village, jointly own their productive resources (which can include agricultural land and workshops as well as collectively owned service businesses or tourist facilities), and collectively manage their consumption. Communes are thus perhaps the most ambitious variant of anarchist economics, since they are settings in which anarchist economics can be practiced comprehensively, in all aspects of daily life, rather than as a specialized activity.

Local currencies

Voluntary, self-managed networks through which participants exchange goods and services without profit or the use of standard national currency have proliferated worldwide in the last two decades. The Complementary Currency Resource Center currently lists 152 such systems in thirty-two countries, with a total membership of close to 338,000 people and a yearly volume of trade exceeding 56 million.[14] Instead of their national legal tender, such systems use various forms of local currency and credit as an independent means of exchange. These credits, vouchers, or notes may be equivalent to the national currency or they may account for a different standard such as a working hour. In English-speaking countries the most common variety is the Local Exchange Trading Scheme (LETS). Each year the members of a LETS receive a directory in which they all advertise the skills and services they offer and their contact details. Each new member receives a number of "credits," normally equivalent to a working hour, which they can spend or earn by receiving and giving services to other members. Local currencies encourage the consumption of local produce and thus keep wealth circulating within the community rather than being taken away by large corporations. The exchange networks created can also serve to build solidarity and mutual aid in the community. Although such systems are usually not explicitly anti-capitalist and are promoted as complementary to the standard economy rather than as an all-out alternative, anarchists do initiate and participate in such systems as a hybrid strategy.

Food Not Bombs

In organized Food Not Bombs events, practiced most widely in the United States, anarchists cook nutritious vegan food and distribute it for free in a public space. The first FNB group was founded in Cambridge, Massachusetts, in 1980 to accompany a campaign against nuclear and other weapons. The practice rapidly proliferated, with over 400 groups active today worldwide. Explicitly presented as an act of protest rather than charity, FNB events promote the idea of food as a basic human entitlement, detached from ability to pay, while at the same time publicly opposing the massive funding of the military and the arms industry at the expense of social needs. According to the movement's handbook, "the major contribution to stopping bombs is our withdrawal from the economic and political structures of the death culture. As individuals, many of us engage in war-tax resistance; as an organization, we operate outside the dominant economic paradigm. We do not operate for a profit; in fact, we operate with very little money compared with the value of the food we distribute."[15] Despite their entirely nonviolent nature, FNB events are often subject to repression and arrests, reflecting many municipalities' hostility to the poor and homeless. In addition to regular events, FNB groups have also supplied food for activist gatherings and protest camps, and have been some of the first to appear on the ground and offer food to the survivors of major disasters such as the San Francisco earthquake and in Hurricane Katrina. The network has also been one of the major contributors to popularizing the practice of decision-making by consensus in activist groups.

Free shops and "really, really free markets"

These are permanent or temporary spaces where goods such as clothes, books, tools, and household items—as well as services from bicycle repair to tarot reading—can be given and taken without the use of money. Free shops are permanent spaces, usually located in squats and social centers, whereas "really, really free markets" are regular events, usually taking place the last weekend of each month. Both of these initiatives—as well as Food not Bombs—manifest and propagate the idea of a gift economy. Gift economies have been widely studied by anthropologists in the context of tribal and traditional societies, but they are also easily discerned within any family or friendship network.[16] In gift economies, individuals freely give goods or services to one another without immediately receiving anything in return. Yet by maintaining through their actions the practice of gift giving, they too can expect to receive gifts themselves as part of a generalized culture of reciprocity. In attempting to launch an entirely different culture of exchange, anarchist practices of gift economy are the most distant from capitalism and do the least to partake in its structures.

DIY cultural production

Anarchism has a long history of association with artistic and countercultural movements, from Dada and abstract expressionism to beat poetry and science fiction.[17] In more recent decades, a prominent aspect of anarchist involvement in visual arts, theater and music has been the promotion of a do-it-yourself ethos of cultural production. This is an approach to the creation of art and culture as a popular and nonprofessional activity, independent of corporate interests and the pressures of the capitalist culture industry. As an economic practice, the DIY ethic displays anarchist values of accessibility, community, autonomy, and self-sufficiency in cultural production. As a political practice, it is most often accompanied by anarchist messages and social critique, and has been a major inspiration for the rise of contemporary anarchist activism.[18] Perhaps the most important field in which this approach was developed was the punk movement. Most punk bands start their way by producing their own self-recorded music on independent labels and putting on shows in homes and garages rather than commercial venues. Among punk fans, DIY culture has created a steady stream of amateur fan magazines (known as fanzines or simply zines), which contain reviews of records and shows alongside poetry, comics, articles, and recipes, all produced using photocopied and collaged images and a combination of hand-scrawled and typewritten texts.[19] Apart from punk music, the DIY ethic is clearly on display in the work of street theater troupes performing in public spaces, anarchist art collectives that put on exhibitions in squatted venues, and collaborative web design projects online.

The electronic commons

Though not by itself an anarchist initiative, commentators have drawn attention to the Internet's libertarian and communitarian features, particularly "its nonhierarchical structure, low transaction costs, global reach, scalability, rapid response time, and disruption-overcoming (hence censorship-foiling) alternative routing."[20] Though there is another side to this coin (e-consumerism, surveillance, and social isolation), the decentralized structure of the Internet has given rise to a free informational economy online, based on "commons-based peer production" and "group generalized exchange."[21] Contributors to projects such as the GNU/Linux operating system and Wikipedia produce and manipulate information without monetary compensation, motivated instead both by social recognition and the intrinsic enjoyment of their work associated with the "hacker ethic."[22] Many anarchists are active participants in contributing to the development of the electronic commons, and in Europe there is also a developed network of Hack-Labs—community spaces housing self-assembled computers that offer free Internet access and training in programming.

Anarchist Economics and Revolutionary Strategy

Having looked at some concrete examples of anarchist economics as they are practiced today, I move to the second stage of discussion: in what way can such examples be tied to broader anarchist revolutionary goals, and what opportunities and challenges do they face in this context? In order to clarify these questions, I would like to offer three different strategic outlooks under which we can interpret these practices: constructive direct action, propaganda by the deed, and the politics of collapse.

The ethos of direct action, central to anarchist politics, is too often recognized only in its destructive or preventative guise. Thus, for example, anarchists who object to the clear-cutting of an ancient forest will take direct action by chaining themselves to the trees, blockading the bulldozers, or sabotaging their operation. This sense of direct action is often invoked in opposition to other courses of action, such as petitioning politicians or mounting legal challenges through the courts—a "politics of demand" that extends symbolic legitimacy to the same institutions that anarchists oppose by appealing to them to rectify injustices. Yet direct action also has a creative and constructive aspect, manifest in the practice of anarchist economics in the present tense. Constructive direct action means that anarchists who seek a world based on different social relations undertake their construction by themselves. On such an account, for social change to be successful, the modes of organization that will replace capitalism, the state, patriarchy, and so on must be prepared and developed alongside (though not instead of) the attack on present institutions. Therefore, the cooperatives, DIY cultures, and gift economies that anarchists practice today can be seen as the groundwork for the realities that will replace capitalism or, to use the familiar Wobbly slogan, as "forming the structure of the new society within the shell of the old."[23]

The insight that anarchist economic practices ultimately function within rather than outside capitalism is important in this context. As we have seen in the survey above, most forms of anarchist economic practice are by no means entirely detached from the capitalist economy. Most of them, in fact, can be seen as islands that operate within capitalism, albeit with a different internal logic, and in a constant attempt to eat away at the prevailing system from the inside by propagating and proliferating alternative social relations among people. Contamination is the name of the game, yet the attempt to contaminate capitalism also carries the risk of being contaminated in return, a process of cooptation or, to use the Situationist term, recuperation. Can anarchist economic practices avoid becoming just another form of business enterprise, wherein the financial sustainability of the project gradually comes to take precedence over its political significance? This is not an easy question to answer. Yet as Andy Robinson comments,

> to remain anarchist, an anarchist business operates as a means, as the tool of a flow leading out of the system, never as an end in itself. It may, in a certain sense, be working inside the system, using dominant forms and means; but it should remain outside on the level of intentionality and desire, never reducible to these forms and means, always treating them as strategic choices, as means to be used for a purpose and discarded should they fail to serve it. To be sure, the tightrope of the danger of recuperation

is not taken away by conceiving it in such terms…but it is possible to negotiate this risk in more or less creative ways, in ways that are more or less effective in sustaining the insurgent desire in exteriority.[24]

These comments on recuperation occasion two further remarks. The first is to mention that alongside the strategic dimension, anarchist economic practices should be related to the broader ethical commitment among anarchists to a "prefigurative politics"—that is, to using political means that are by themselves an embryonic representation of an anarchist social future. Thus anarchist values are expressed in everyday activities and practices, stressing the realization of egalitarian social relations within the fold of the movement itself, rather than expecting them to only become relevant "after the revolution."[25] The second remark is that an individualist anarchist motivation can be seen at work within constructive direct action, quite separately from its strategic and ethical dimensions. From an individualist point of view, activists participate in anarchist economic practices not only in order to change society, but also simply out of the desire to inhabit such different social relations, and live equally among their comrades rather than conforming to the expectations of capitalist society.

Returning, however, to the strategic dimension, a question immediately presents itself: if the construction of a new society is to be the work of anarchists themselves, then the small number of participants surely means that this is a hopeless prospect. Without transforming current anarchist economic practices into the stuff of a mass movement, they will remain inspiring but insignificant efforts. Can this be overcome?

This brings us to the second prism under which we can view the practice of anarchist economics—that of propaganda by the deed. Despite the ill repute gained by this term, which became narrowly associated with bombings and assassinations in the last decades of the nineteenth century, propaganda by the deed can also be understood more broadly as pointing to the potentially exemplary nature of all anarchist action. On such an account, the most effective form of anarchist propaganda is the actual implementation and display of anarchist social relations. The practice of anarchist economics in publicly visible manner serves to demonstrate the possibility and desirability of alternative economic arrangements to a wide audience. The living practices of resource and income sharing, gift economies, and so on may directly inspire people by way of example, and encourage them to take up these practices by themselves. It is easier for people to engage with the idea that people can exist without bosses or leaders when such existence is displayed, if on a limited scale, in actual practice rather than merely argued for on paper. Thus Gandhi's assertion that "a reformer's business is to make the impossible possible by giving an ocular demonstration of the possibility in his own conduct."[26] Or, in the words of a commentator on the practice of "really, really free markets":

> Long-term participation in 'Free Markets dispels the materialist programming that makes people covet useless items by denying access to them, and demonstrates just how possible and fulfilling the anarchist alternative is. It also presents a point of departure for further struggles: if this is what we can do with the scanty resources we're able to get our hands on now, what could we do with the entire wealth of this society?[27]

At the same time, all of these strategies seem to have some inherent limitations. After all, the various anarchist economic practices discussed in this chapter have had a continuous presence in Western societies for the past forty years. Still, they do not seem to have precipitated anything like the large-scale social transformation intended. On the one hand, the anarchist movement is so small that even its most consistent and visible efforts are but a drop in the ocean. On the other hand, political elites have proven themselves extremely proficient at pulling the ground from under movements for social change, be it through direct repression and demonization of the activists, diversion of public attention to security and nationalist agendas, or, at best, minimal concessions that ameliorate the most exploitative aspects of capitalism while contributing to the resilience of the system as a whole. It would seem that ethical commitments to social justice and the enhancement of human freedom can only serve as a motivation for a comparatively small number of people, and that without the presence of genuine material interests among large sections of the population there is little hope for a mass movement to emerge that would herald the departure from existing social, economic, and political arrangements.

And here we come to the final point: fortunately or unfortunately, the conditions for such motivations seem to be rapidly emerging. The converging crises of the twenty-first century—climate change, financial meltdown, and the imminent peak in oil production—may be the only hope for large-scale social transformation. As capitalism becomes literally impossible to maintain under conditions of dwindling energy reserves and climate instability, the populations to which the anarchist minority in the West is appealing may finally conclude that a break with the system is in their material interest. Rather than a gradual and piecemeal social change, then, it may be that the tasks of anarchists and their allies is to create the kinds of initiatives that will allow populations to revolutionize the process of industrial collapse. The successful result of such efforts would be neither a continuation of hierarchical social relations in more locally self-sufficient forms (perhaps resembling feudalism more than capitalism), nor yet the deterioration into a *Mad Max* scenario of barbarity and gang warfare, but rather the emergence of qualitatively different societies in those places where people will have managed both to carve out a significant degree of autonomy and to use that autonomy in order to reconstruct the way they live. Yet there is no guarantee for any of this. The crystal ball remains murky.

ENDNOTES

1   T. Leahy, *Anarchist and Hybrid Strategies,* The Gift Economy, Anarchism and Strategies for Change http://www.gifteconomy.org.au/page25.html (accessed September 24, 2011).

2   Ibid.

3   Compare B. Black, *The Abolition of Work and Other Essays* (Port Townsend, WA: Loompanics, 1986).

4   See J. Shantz, "One Person's Garbage…Another Person's Treasure: Dumpster Diving, Freeganism and Anarchy," *Verb* 3, no. 1 (2005).

5   F. S. Lee and J. Bekken, introduction to *Radical Economics and Labor,* ed. F. S. Lee and J. Bekken (London: Routledge, 2009).

6   See Industrial Workers of the World, *Preamble & Constitution of the Industrial Workers of the World* (Cincinnati, OH: IWW, 2009).

7   See R. Rocker, *Anarcho-Syndicalism* (London: Pluto, 1989).

8   See P. Spriano, *The Occupation of the Factories* (London: Pluto, 1975).

9   See R. Gregorie and F. Perlman, *Worker-Student Action Committees: France, May '68* (Detroit: Black & Red, 1970).

10   See J. A. Gutiérrez, "Workers Without Bosses," *Red and Black Revolution* 8 (2004) http://www.struggle.ws/wsm/rbr/rbr8/argentina.html (accessed September 24, 2011).

11   See S. Aronowitz, *The Knowledge Factory: Dismantling the Corporate University and Creating True Higher Learning* (Boston: Beacon, 2001).

12   Inoperative Committee, ed., *University Occupations: France, Greece, NYC* (2009) http://zinelibrary.info/files/university%20occupations.pdf. (accessed September 24, 2011).

13   Radical Routes, *How to Set Up a Workers' Co-op* (2008), http://www.radicalroutes. org.uk/publicdownloads/wc.pdf. (accessed September 24, 2011).

14   CCRC, *Online Database of Complementary Currencies Worldwide* (2009) http:// www.complementarycurrency.org/ccDatabase/ (accessed September 24, 2011).

15   C. T. Butler and K. McHenry, *Food Not Bombs: How to Feed the Hungry and Build Community* (Tucson, AZ: See Sharp Press, 2000), http://www.foodnotbombs.net/ bookindex.html (accessed September 24, 2011).

16   See M. Maus, *The Gift* (London: Routledge, 1969), and J. Carrier, "Gifts, Commodities, and Social Relations: A Maussian View of Exchange," *Sociological Forum* 6 (1991): 119–136.

17   See A. Antliff, *Anarchy and Art: From the Paris Commune to the Fall of the Berlin Wall* (Vancouver: Arsenal Pulp Press, 2007); and J. MacPhee and E. Reuland, *Realizing the Impossible: Art against Authority* (Oakland: AK Press, 2007).

18   See G. McKay, *DiY Culture: Party & Protest in Nineties Britain* (London: Verso, 1998).

19   See T. Triggs, "Scissors and Glue: Punk Fanzines and the Creation of a DIY Aesthetic," *Journal of Design History* 19 (2006):69–83; and S. Duncombe, *Notes from Underground: Zines and the Politics of Alternative Culture* (London: Verso, 2008).

20   See R. Hurwitz, "Who Needs Politics? Who Needs People? The Ironies of Democracy in Cyberspace," *Contemporary Sociology* 28 (1999): 655–661.

21   See Y. Benkler, "Coase's Penguin, or, Linux and *The Nature of the Firm*," *Yale Law Journal* 112 (2002):369–446; and T. Yamagishi and K. Cook, "Generalized Exchange and Social Dilemmas," *Social Psychology Quarterly* 56 (1993): 235–248.

22   See P. Himanen, *The Hacker Ethic and the Spirit of the Information Age* (New York: Random House, 2001).

23   Industrial Workers of the World, *Preamble*.

24   A. Robinson, "Thinking from the Outside: Avoiding Recuperation," *Anarchy: A Journal of Desire Armed* 64 (2007): 37–49.

25   Compare E. Goldman, afterword to *My Disillusionment in Russia* (New York: Doubleday, 1923).

26   M. K. Gandhi, "On Another's Land," *Young India*, February 5, 1925, 68.

27   See CrimethInc, "The Really Really Free Market: Instituting the Gift Economy,"
     Rolling Thunder 4 (2009): 34–42.

Currency and Café Anarchy: Do-It-Yourself Economics and Participatory Resistance to Global Capitalism

Caroline K. Kaltefleiter

> "No dictatorship can have any other aim but that of self-perpetuation, and it can beget only slavery in the people tolerating it; freedom can be created only by freedom, that is, by a universal rebellion on the part of the people and free organization of the toiling masses from the bottom up."
> —Mikhail Bakunin, *Statism and Anarchism*

The recent global economic crisis continues to leave many people worried about their future, as 2009 brought news of higher unemployment rates, plant closings, falling house prices, and lower levels in consumer confidence. The gloom-and-doom discourse bantered about in the mainstream press fueled collective fear by posing questions like, "What happens if the US economy collapses? How will we survive? Can we as citizens and a national state thrive?"[1] The notion of an economic apocalypse is epitomized in an advertisement for a book titled *The Ultimate Depression Survival Guide*. The image for the ad is that of an atomic blast with the signifier of a dollar going up in smoke, symbolizing the annihilation of the American Dream. My initial reaction to this advertisement was similar to perhaps many who viewed it—"times are tough and boy are we as a society, especially young people, screwed." A few seconds later, I read the image differently as I realized the system was imploding, that a revolution was taking place inside/outside the system. I saw a politics of agency (re)emerging into a dominant sphere, embracing those who had been fooled by capitalism for far too long, allowing them to reconsider their place in society and actively to combat rampant globalization, ecological destruction, and economic inequalities inherent in an explosive global economy.

My analysis is grounded within the framework of cultural studies scholar Stuart Hall, whose work on encoding and decoding texts offers us a way of looking at competing readings in/out of a text and by extension scenarios of representation in contemporary society. Hall emphasizes that texts, through every moment in the process of communication, allow for active message composition (encoding) and message reception (decoding).[2] "The message continuum, from the original composition of the message/code (encoding) to the point at which it is read and understood (decoding), has its own determinants and conditions of existence."[3] Hall identifies three primary positions of decoding messages and signs, including the dominant position or "preferred" reading, the "negotiated" position, and the "oppositional" position/reading. He suggests that oppositional readings entail that the reader/viewer understands the preferred reading being constructed, but (re)interprets the message within an alternative frame of reference and social critique.

In the case of the economic crisis, readers/viewers whose social situations, particularly social class, align with the dominant scenario of representation have encoded in their consciousness protecting one's property, job, family, or, perhaps most importantly, status in society. On the surface, the dominant narrative of citizens "losing ground" in the face of an economic catastrophe is reinforced through daily media reports, images, and propaganda used to keep the national consciousness tied to capitalism. However, the current economic crisis offers oppositional readings and actions to achieve a fulfilling life. This paradigm shift calls upon citizens to reject the narrow "possessive individualism" imposed by capitalism as a means to transform global consciousness. A reshuffling of the dominant narrative related to global economic conditions entails drawing upon an anarchist(ic) culture that is self-organizing, self-reflective, and citizen-driven—and allows us to note possibilities within this culture for an anarchist economics. Indeed, anarchist economics might give us means by which to establish counter discussions and oppositional readings of both the market and the state so as to foster a dialogue that eliminates a culture of coercion and creates a vision of a free society.

In this essay, I situate myself not as an economist, though I hope to help develop *anarchist* economics here as its own unique (and holistic) form of economics, not simply focused on the rationalized and instrumental processes most often studied by economists. Surely others have much to say about the realities of prevailing wages, gross national product figures, or market trends—including anarchists. My analysis, however, is grounded in media and cultural studies' intersections with anarchist economics and seeks to examine capitalism and the phenomenon of globalization by deconstructing the ideas of spectacle, consumption, and exchange value. At the heart of this discussion is an interrogation of the concept of money and how in one's everyday life we might rethink the value of a state-issued currency over community-produced currencies. The very essence of opting for alternative currencies over a state issued monetary system represents a continuum of anarchist practices that allows for the gradual weaning, or deprogramming if you will, from a (pre)disposition to capitalism while, at the same charting new ways of (un)doing business and revolution. Anarchist theory and praxis present opportunities to (re)appropriate public spaces from enclosure and incorporation of globalization. The final portion of my essay demonstrates sites of resistance wherein everyday citizens participate in alternative currency exchanges, café collectives, and street actions to reclaim not only their communities, but purpose in their lives.

Global Economic Chaos and Uniform Distlanceless

> "The danger is that people are not aware of the danger. Everybody talks about the global financial markets as if they were irreversible. But that is a misconception."—George Soros[4]

Globalization is a ubiquitous concept readily discussed in the halls of academia and via broadcast outlets around the world. Scholars such as Waters and Held et al. divide theories of globalization into political, economic, and cultural globalization and conceptualize each factor accordingly.[5] The transient nature of a global economy is intrinsically tied to the individuals who participate in such transactions. I am interested in social and cultural issues related to global capitalism, and how one might (re)negotiate a politics of understanding and agency that would allow for a rethinking of concepts such as money, exchange value, and commodity fetishism. In his text *The Consequences of Modernity*, Giddens defines globalization as "the intensification of world-wide social relations, which link distant localities in such a way that local happenings are shaped by events occurring many miles away and vice versa."[6] German philosopher Martin Heidegger is often criticized for his fascist sympathies, however, his work on spatial analysis offers insights that foreshadowed contemporary debates about globalization. Heidegger not only described the "abolition of distance" as a constitutive feature of our contemporary condition, but he linked recent shifts in spatial experience to no-less-fundamental alterations in the temporality of human activity: "All distances in time and space are shrinking."[7]

In his analysis, the compression of space increasingly meant that from the perspective of human experience "everything is equally far and equally near." Instead of opening up new possibilities for rich and multifaceted interaction with events once distant from the purview of most individuals, the abolition of distance generates a "uniform distanceless" in which fundamentally distinct objects (subjects) became part of a bland homogeneous experiential mass.[8] The loss of any meaningful distinction between "nearness" and "distance" contributes to a leveling down of human experience, which in turn spawns an indifference that renders human experience monotonous and one-dimensional. This idea is effectively demonstrated in news reports of the 2008 global financial crisis. The economic meltdown first reported on Wall Street quickly reverberated in countries around the world including China and Japan, illustrating the interconnectedness of a global market collapse of local and national markets. Peter Gumbel of *Time* magazine reported the impact of bank failures in the United States. According to Gumbel, "On September 29, 2008, governments from Germany to Iceland rushed to five ailing financial institutions with huge cash infusions or full-blown nationalization, making it one of the grimmest days in the history of European finance."[9]

No Future: Globalization and Capitalism

While the mass media tend to report about the global economy and its financial crises in terms of dollars and cents or pounds and pence, we must acknowledge that globalization is about the socio-spatial relations between billions of individuals and that below any economic base is a lively interaction of people adding and subtracting value exchanged through an animated process of exchange.[10] In his text *The Philosophy of Value*, Georg Simmel notes, "The fact of economic exchange confers upon the value of things something super-individual."[11] Today's capitalist market is predicated on the notion that economic value is never inherent in the object itself, but rather is created through a politics of desirability or as Simmel put it, the practicality of economic value is "conferred upon an object not merely by its own desirability, but by the desirability of another object."[12]

Value then is created when men, women, and, now even more pressing, when children establish a personal and societal style. Today marketing consultants, branding gurus, and "cool" hunters seek out ways to market teen spirit—teen "cool"—to kids in the mainstream by co-opting the style, fashion, language, music, and culture of the margins—aboveground and belowground. Such cultural co-optation is not new. Consider the early punk movement. Many of the youth involved in that movement were from working-class families; were working low-paying jobs, unemployed, or students with little money to spare. A song, "No Future," by the British punk band the Sex Pistols articulates the despair of youth in Great Britain. As a result, they sought to find ways to fight class domination and societal repression through personal style and do-it-yourself (DIY) actions.

The legacy of cultural subversion and the DIY ethic of Punk can be traced back to the Situationist International (SI) that formed in 1957. The SI was a collective of avant-garde artists in Europe, including French theorist and artist Guy Debord. Julia Downes notes, "The SI revolted against the dominant discourses, images and ideas of capitalist consumer culture known as the *Spectacle* and sought to incite revolution by employing cultural tactics that exposed contradiction and openly critiqued society."[13] The SI encouraged others to express their frustrations through doing their own forms of cultural subversion in their everyday lives.

Like their British counterparts, punk youth in the United States opposed society-sanctioned wardrobes and capitalist clothing companies by creating their own retail resistance, reinventing everyday items and secondhand clothing. Utilitarian items such as safety pins and electric extension cords used by punks in the early days of the American punk movement provide two examples. Safety pins were used as jewelry and badges of courage—as punks elected to pierce unconventional body parts such as cheeks, lips, eyebrows, chests, and elsewhere. Electric extension cords were adapted as belts—used to hold up thrift store pants that were several sizes too big. The connector ends of extension cords were used as belt fasteners. As a participant of the punk scene in Athens, Georgia, I shopped at the Potter's House, a thrift store that sold clothing by the bag for as little as one dollar. As a working-class student at the University of Georgia, I had little money and often purchased men's suit trousers that were several sizes too big to make both a fashion and political statement. Belts were hard to find in the piles of clothing; however, there were boxes of discarded appliances and extension cords. The most unusual cords were those from 1950s appliances that were encased with fabric with speckles and dots around the wiring. Voila, one had an instant belt that was functional and stylish—not to mention the shock factor as people often stared at my belts as I walked down the street. The cords created a symbolic connection between cultures of the past and present but more importantly, a retrocritique of affluence and gender connoted by the fabrics and designs of tailored men's trousers.

Such fashion accessories would soon become a style that suburban kids, known as "posers" by many punks, would clamor for and argue with their bourgeois parents to obtain. In response to this "emerging market," US-based chain stores found in suburban shopping malls, such as Claire's Boutique and Hot Topic began to sell mass produced safety pin jewelry in primary colors and "extension cord" belts with a twisted-coil jelly rubber design in rainbow colors. Hence, the market co-opts styles of necessity and turns them into styles of desirability by collapsing the domains of individual expression and need into a uniformed distant commodity that is abstract from the cultural ethos and revolutionary politics that emerges as part of everyday life experience. The independent band Cake critiqued poser culture and capitalist exchange in the song "Rock n-Roll Lifestlye" (from 1995's *Motorcade of Generosity*):

> Your CD collection looks shiny and costly…And how much did you pay for your black leather jacket…Is it you or your parents in that income tax bracket. How much did you pay for a chunk of his guitar…And how much will he pay for a new guitar, And how long will the workers keep building him new ones…As long as their soda cans are red, white, and blue ones.

Cake's song explores the concepts of commodity fetishism and alienated labor, cornerstones of capitalist ideology that Karl Marx wrote about over a century ago. Marx argued that the working class was the victim of an illusion that he referred to as commodity fetishism. As Heath and Potter note, "Rather than perceiving the economy as a set of essential social relationships between individuals, the market gives an appearance of natural laws. Losing your job seemed to be a matter of bad luck. The ups and downs were determined by forces completely outside anyone's control."[14] Such objectification of social relations leads to the cultivation of a false consciousness wherein workers are alienated from their own work and see their labor as merely a means to the attainment of other ends/material goods. In other words, individuals participate in their own alienation and oppression through a false understanding of a need to compete with others for limited goods.

The recent global financial crisis offers an example of the competition cycle, and its unwitting impact on society. Workers queued up to spend cash on consumer goods that they desired—but didn't need or ultimately couldn't afford. High on debt and with easy access to credit, the workers are alienated from their labor; their actions inadvertently serve to drive up production and force companies to find new ways of producing more goods with less people. Ironically, the result is workers eliminating their own jobs or solidifying their place in the production line with few, if any, opportunities for autonomy.

Capitalism (re)distributes necessary labor and creates a value system cloaked in commodity fetishism that serves to obscure the reality of exploitative social relations and a culture of oppression. As Georg Simmel wrote, "The economic system of the world is assuredly founded upon an abstraction that is between sacrifice and gain."[15] Simmel's analysis suggests that we as citizens understand such abstractions and take direct action to counter capitalist practices, including co-optation, by creating alternative value systems, local currencies, and community-driven exchanges for goods and services.

Ithaca Baby: Dollars and Hours

"We need not wait for the government or a central bank to save us during this economic crisis: we can set this system up ourselves. It bypasses greedy banks and recharges local economics and gives local businesses an advantage over multinational corporations."—George Monbiot, 2009[16]

Economists note that economics is an inexact science. The economic roller coaster of the past two years has prominent experts scratching their heads as to what the markets will do next. Some economists give us reason to hope that the job market will improve and that the stock market will continue to tick upward. Yet mainstream media reports suggest otherwise. Watching the New York Stock Exchange trading graphics on CNBC in real time is like watching the roulette wheel spin around in Las Vegas and other casinos around the world. However, what happens to capital exchanged in Vegas doesn't stay in Vegas. The profits taken in at casinos from ordinary citizens are rarely reinvested in the local landscape. The gambling adrenaline rush is played out in everyday life through competitive consumption and it all starts with the illusion of money.

Popular and scholarly understandings of money tend to share some common traits found in narratives of globalization and modernity dyads. Cultural anthropologist Faidra Papavasiliou argues that money is a "fact," a reality that almost assumes the status of an agent, an agent that is increasingly unified and uniform across sociocultural, political, and economic boundaries. "The notion of net worth is a standard of measure of economic and social viability. While money is primarily a token denoting value, under current global capitalism it takes on the guise of a commodity, becoming an object of value itself. In this sense, it is also fetishized."[17] She notes that what emerges is the uncomfortable space between economic abstraction and lived experience, the two seemingly irreconcilable aspects of materiality as defined by modern money.[18] The spatial existence between economic abstraction and everyday life is in a Heideggarian sense a uniform distance where desire is reconfigured as utility that fuels consumption. In his essay titled "Home of the Brave," Steinsvold writes, "We Americans love our freedom; yet we have allowed the use of money to completely dominate our way of life. Indeed, we are no longer a free people. We are trillions of dollars in debt. We live in fear of depression, inflation, inadequate medical coverage, and losing our jobs."[19] Steinsvold advocates the complete dissolution of money to regain individual freedom. While a complete disavowal of money may seem extreme, some communities are embracing alternative currencies as a means to wean citizens off an economy backed by national currencies and to raise awareness that traditional money systems create serious social problems that devastate our local economies by removing money from local communities and transferring it to large corporations and financial centers. Local currency or "scrip" monetary systems became popular during the Great Depression. George Monbiot of the *Guardian* newspaper writes, "Businesses in the Unites States issued rabbit tails, seashells, and wooden discs as currency. The medium of exchange could be anything as long as everyone who uses it trusts that everyone else will recognize its value."[20] Corner Exchange, for example, is a sustainable community currency based in the Pacific Northwest where participants elect to use local currency over state issued currency for their economic exchanges.

Decisions to use local currencies are actions of resistance to a globalized economy wherein new possibilities for rich and multifaceted local interactions are actualized. My own experience with alternative currencies began over seven years ago when I moved to upstate New York. I live in Tompkins County near the town of Ithaca, home to the local currency Ithaca HOURS. Local residents sometimes refer to HOURS as "that other money." Ithaca's commitment to localism is often cited as one of the key reasons why the HOURS monetary system endures. The HOURS currency emerged during a period when the regional economy of upstate New York was going through tumultuous times, as factories shut down, businesses closed, and consumer spending declined—a shockingly similar situation to the current global financial crisis.

From its inception in 1991, one HOUR was set to be the equivalent of $10 US as this was the mean hourly wage for Tompkins County at the time. The currency calculation "evoked the principle of a living wage and demonstrated the system's commitment to social equity and justice."[21] Today a number of local businesses participate in HOURS systems. The farmers' market remains at the heart of the system. In her ethnography on alternative currencies, Papavasilio explores the social meaning of HOURS through narratives of local citizens,

> There is trust and relationships. You feel like you have a link with the other person, a common belief in community. What HOURS represent... is an acknowledgement, honoring time... One time I had about $150 in HOURS and I needed plumbing

work. So I looked for someone who took HOURS and met this new person [and] we had a long philosophical discussion about HOURS, and value, and money and work that you wouldn't otherwise [have] had with a regular plumber.[22]

Like many Ithacans, I too shop with HOURS and have established friendships and relationships with area merchants, be it Green Star, the local co-op or the farmers' market. My use of HOURS now goes beyond food purchases and home repairs to include medical services. Last year, my eight-year-old daughter was having difficulty seeing and reading in school. After an initial eye examination it was clear that my daughter not only needed glasses, but also vision therapy to help address her disability. I was pleased to find a pediatric optometrist who accepts Ithaca HOURS. I paid portions of my bill with HOURS as the total exceeded what I currently had in my HOURS reserve. Needless to say, this experience made me realize that the HOURS currency surpassed a novel system of exchange and was becoming integrated into mainstream culture. Through everyday experiences—a trip to the local co-op, art frame shop, or the eye doctor, citizens use alternative money systems such as Ithaca HOURS and challenge the way in which we have come to understand materialism and exchange value.

In short, everyday citizens who use Ithaca HOURS are social entrepreneurs who recognize that traditional money contributes to the creation of social conditions that devastate communities by removing money locally and transferring wealth to large corporations. Such actions leave people without a medium of exchange in their community. In response, using local currencies is investment in one's community and its future, intentional actions that counter global capitalism by supporting local economic activity, encouraging fairness and social equity, and promoting environmental education and sustainability.

Café Capital: Coffee, Communication, and Possibility

"There is a silver lining emerging from a declining economy. We're remembering something more important than money, which [is] each other in community. I'm optimistic that this, of infinite value, will grow. This is what will provide us with

the right foundation for building a new 'economy.'"—Trena
Gravem, 2009, NPR comments[23]

The capitalist agenda contributes to what Heidegger referred to as the loss of any meaningful distinction between "nearness" and "distance" and contributes to a leveling down of human experience, which in turn spawns an indifference that renders human experience monotonous and one-dimensional.[24] It is within this space of one-dimensionality that a sense of community is lost unless local citizens take responsibilities for charting their own forms of social change. The recent downturn in the economy has affected both business relations and social relations in many communities. In the northern village of Ellsworth, Michigan, a town of 500, the unemployment rate is nearly 16 percent, with vacant storefronts everywhere. Bob Felton, an Ellsworth resident, recounted the demise of his community. "It was depressing. We needed a place in Ellsworth where neighbors could catch up with each other, preferably over a cup of coffee and a cheap meal."[25] Last fall, the people of Ellsworth mobilized to create their own café called the Front Porch Café. The café grew out of discussions residents at area churches had about finding a place for people to come together, share a meal, and exchange ideas on improving life in the town.

The café cultural experience in Michigan bears a striking resemblance to the startup of the local cooperative café in my village of Dryden, New York. The Dryden Café was founded in 2007, not only in response to a declining economy in upstate New York, but also to a call to action to create a space of communication and exchange for local residents. With most residents commuting out of town for full-time employment, Main Street, the heart of the village, was grinding to a halt. Like Ellsworth, Michigan, several businesses closed or relocated out of town, leaving a roadway of vacant buildings and empty storefronts void of personal interactions. Residents were strangers as they passed each other going divergent directions to work, shop, and even get a decent cup of coffee. The idea for the café started in October 2006. Dryden resident and community leader Wendy Martin is often credited starting the café movement in the village. Martin notes that Eliot Spitzer, a 2006 New York gubernatorial candidate, used the mainstreet of Dryden as part of an advertising campaign to turn around the economy in upstate New York. The Spitzer campaign showcased a "For Rent" sign in Charlie's Diner which had been the town's local eatery. Yet after Spitzer's successful election, the landscape of Dryden remained desolate and unchanged. In an online interview with me, Martin recalls the collective despair of the town: "I walked through our village and looked at the FOR RENT sign. I was saddened by the message the empty store front sent to the thousands of people who pass through our village every day on their way to larger towns and cities."[26] Talking with friends and other residents, Martin envisioned the possibility of reconfiguring the old diner space into a café that would be cooperatively run. She recalls, "I spent the next few months talking to various friends and community members about the idea of a co-op style venture and as the conversations progressed, the idea of the café as it is today was formulated."[27]

A communication action plan for the space was drawn up, "flyers were sent to everyone in the village explaining the concept [and] announcing the date of the first public meeting to gather input for the project."[28] Outreach communication included taking down the "For Rent" sign and replacing it with a neon orange poster that read, "Interested in Starting a Local Café. Are You In? Meeting 7PM August 18, 2006, Village Hall." I remember seeing the sign in the diner window and thinking, "I'm in." Other local residents heeded an invitation to participate in a conversation to start a café and eighty people turned up to hear about the idea of a locally owned, locally operated café. Martin remembers the optimism of people coming together to change their community, already present the night of the first meeting.

> I believe what brought people together was the naïve optimism that we could do this. We were fearless. My feeling was we had nothing to lose and everything to gain. In fact the night of the meeting, I told everyone even if we are only open one month—in that time, friendships would be formed and thus we would have already succeeded. It was exciting to see people together and share their ideas.[29]

The creation of the Dryden Café also facilitated communication among local residents. As Wendy Martin put it, "There were a lot of people who felt isolated and wanted to be connected to something." Those involved with the café are inspired by a commitment to community.

The greatest success for me and I believe everyone is when you take a moment, sit still and look around. You see people quietly chatting, children playing, and friends greeting one another, but most importantly friendships forming. The number of people who have formed lasting friendships continues to thrill me.[30]

In all, the participation in the cafe is based on the ethical values of honesty, openness, social responsibility, and taking care of others, and sends a message to even the youngest patrons of the café: take responsibility for one's community and take care of others in need. The Dryden Café cooperative is an example of community anarchism wherein cooperative values of self-help responsibility, democracy, equality, equity, and solidarity are lived out every day as volunteers serve homemade meals, using fresh produce from local farms and original recipes of village residents. All of the baking at the café is done by volunteers. Food and baked goods from the café are often donated to local food banks. The café features artwork by local artists and live music on Friday nights—genres so far include folk, celtic, jazz, zydeco, and even punk.

My own experience with the Dryden Café certainly attests to creating new friendships and experiences that chart new roots of sustainability, exchange and in participatory economics—or as Michael Albert puts it, "parecon: life after capitalism."[31] Recently I attended the annual Dryden Dairy parade that showcases the work of organic farmers and milk producers. I was pleased to see Main Street thriving. Later, at the local festival, members of the café had their own booth where we made do-it-yourself Father's Day gifts. Most of the activities at the park were free and those for profit went to benefit area organizations. At the end of an exhausting day, it occurred to me that no matter what economic struggles lie ahead, this community would rally in its own space and create its course of resistance to globalization with sustainable goods from the fields, organic dairy farms, artist workshops, and even fair trade coffee at the Dryden Café.

Conclusion: Another World Is Possible

"I must have dreamed a thousand dreams. They're moving into the streets. This is the world we live in. These are the hands we're given…Use them and let's start trying to make it a place worth living in."—"Land of Confusion," *Invisible Touch*, Genesis, 1986

Driving home from Ithaca to Dryden the other day, I became entranced listening to the *Genesis* tune "Land of Confusion" on the radio. The lyrics offered a text of possibility in situating the work that goes on everyday as anarchists undertake actions such as alternative currency exchanges, café collectives, and street actions, including the Reclaim the Streets (RTS) movement. RTS is both an organization and a grassroots tactic. Its direct action strategies are a deliberate rejection of mainstream mediated politics and culture. Giorrel Curran suggests that RTS establishes sites of resistance by creating "unity between means and ends."[32] RTS anarchist actions (re)situate Heidegger's notion of space, that every experience is equally far and equally near. The RTS movement challenges capitalist encroachments and opens up new possibilities of multifaceted interaction at events by creating "temporary autonomous zones (TAZ) and showcasing a 'politics of pleasure' that celebrates identity, creativity, and autonomy."[33] RTS employs Situationist strategies and ideas. RTS activists embrace carnival actions as a political theatre of autonomy theorized by Mikhail Bakhtin.[34] According to Bakhtin, "Carnival does not acknowledge any distinction between actors and spectator. Carnival is not a spectacle seen by people; they are in it, and everyone participates because its very idea embraces all people."[35] The street party is a DIY event whose success is determined by those involved in the event. As Stephen Duncombe notes,

> Reclaim the Streets is a protest that only works if everyone participates. This is true not only for the organizers but for those who just show up on the day of the protest in costumes, with radios, drums or fire-breathing apparatus, and ready to dance… what happens at the action depends upon what people bring with them and what they do once they are there.[36]

Recently, community members and RTS activists in Galway, Ireland came together to rename their Main Street, Anti-Shop Street. Activists boycotted and blockaded big box stores and multinational retailers. RTS activists stated,

> we are here to take back our space from the capitalist, consumer-
> ist culture which has taken it over, with its bizarre ideas of a life
> dedicated to shopping, spending, buying and profit, so that we
> could share an experience of another world, where everything
> is free, people share and give food, fun, stuff and life, simply
> because they can and it just feels good![37]

Activists poured into the street chanting, "free food, free stuff,
free social interaction, and a free world for everyone."[38] Chanting
"Feck Money!" a "really really free market" was set up in the street,
with clothes, videos, cards, and other goods organized on tables to be
taken by citizens for free. As one activist reports, "Some people were
confused by the idea of free stuff—asking 'what's the catch'? Our reply
was there is none, just a group of people who believe in a better world
where gifts can be given freely and the only profit sought is making
others happy."[39] The event included Galway's Food Not Bombs group
that shared vegetarian food and messages for peace and a better society and "distributed vegetarian soup, bread and vegan cookies at the
REAL recession busting price of no euros and no cents."[40] The carnival atmosphere of the Galway protest situates spaces of resistance by
blurring the lines between the demonstrators and spectators. Through
their own curiosity, economic fury, and creative fervor, individuals located on/off the street engage in an economy of outrage that embraces
all people in the creation of a just economic world.

The global spatial expansion of capitalism is created by capitalist
consumption that includes not only the colonization of land spaces,
exchange space, and monetary spaces, but also the lifeworld interactions of individuals. Returning to Heidegger's notion of uniform
distanceless, the compression of space increasingly means that from
the perspective of human experience "everything is equally far and
equally near" and therefore reduced to a unidimensionality that creates
a homogenous mass of consumers who appear to be at the mercy of
corporations and the state. However, the recent global downturn presents oppositional readings of the event by creating existential spaces
wherein individuals and social groups are refusing and resisting the
clarion call of capitalism, opting instead for local forms of anarchy
highlighted in community currencies, café culture, and street actions.
Here individuals construct their own self-identities and self-economies

that open new possibilities for rich and multifaceted interaction and exchange. In all of these sites of resistance, participants create spaces of engagement that serve to critique global capitalism and to underscore actions of change by letting people know another world is possible. These spaces, however, exist within the cracks of capitalism and often succumb to its pressures. As I mentioned before, there is a tendency towards co-optation under capitalism and even the most reflective attempts at creating anarchist(ic) spaces can be rendered harmless through commodification. However, a radical politics that does not engage in everyday practices is an empty gesture. After all, radical politics—anarchist politics—should aim at nothing less than the restructuring of the whole of society. These attempts (community currencies, café culture, and street actions), then, can function as a necessary part of a revolutionary movement allowing us spaces in the here and now to experiment and refine anarchist ideals and lead us closer to an economy of democracy, participation, and sustainability.

ENDNOTES

1   See N. Ferguson, "The End of Prosperity," *Time*, vol. 172, no. 15 (2008): 16–21.

2   See S. Hall, "Encoding and Decoding," *Culture, Media, Language Working Papers in Cultural Studies* (London: Hutchinson, 1980).

3   Ibid., 129.

4   D. Boyle, *The Money Changers* (London: Earthscan, 2002), 81.

5   See Malcolm Waters, *Globalization* (London: Routledge, 1995); and D. Held, A. McGrew, D. Goldblatt, and J. Perraton, *Global Transformations* (Cambridge: Polity Press, 1999).

6   A Giddens, *The Consequence of Modernity* (Cambridge, MA: Polity Press, 1990), 64.

7   M. Heidegger, "The Thing," in *Poetry, Language and Thought* (New York: Harper and Row, 1971), 165.

8   Ibid., 166.

9   P. Gumbel, "Europe's Bank Scare" *Time Magazine*, vol. 172, no. 15 (2008): 26–27.

10 R. Fernandez, "George Simmel, Global capitalism and Anarchy," in *An American Fusion: Race, Ethnicity, Immigration, Sociology and Social Change*, 2009, http://blog.ronaldfernandez.com/2009/05/03/georg-simmel-global-capitalism-and-anarchy-3.aspx.

11 G. Simmel, "A Chapter in the Philosophy of Value," *American Journal of Sociology* 5 (1900): 577.

12 Ibid.

13   J. Downes, "Riot Grrrl: The Legacy and Contemporary Landscape of DIY Femi-
     nist Cultural Activism," in *Riot Grrrl: Revolution Girl Style Now* (London: Black-
     dog Publishing, 2007), 13.

14   J. Heath, and A. Potter, *Nation of Rebels: Why Counter Culture Became Consumer
     Culture* (New York: HarperCollins, 2004), 20.

15   G. Simmel, "A Chapter in the Philosophy of Value," *American Journal of Sociology*
     5 (1900): 3.

16   G. Monbiot, "If the State Can't Save Us, We Need a License to Print Our Own
     Money," *Guardian*, January 20, 2009, http://www.guardian.co.uk/commentis-
     free/2009/jan/20/george-monbiot-recession-currencies (accessed September 5,
     2011).

17   F. Papavasiliou, "The Political Economy of Local Currency: Alternative Money,
     Alternative Development, and Collective Action in the Age of Globalization," dis-
     sertation, Emory University, 2008, 30.

18   Ibid.

19   J. Steinsvold, "Home of the Brave? An Alternative to Capitalism," *American Daily*,
     March 14, 2006, 2.

20   Ibid.

21   Papavasiliou, "The Political Economy," 90.

22   Ibid., 209.

23   T. Gravem, comments to NPR story, "A Door Opens... To Pie, Coffee, and Pos-
     sibility," *Morning Edition*, National Public Radio, June 2, 2009.

24   Heidegger, "The Thing," 166.

25   J. Guerra, "A Door Opens... To Pie, Coffee, and Possibility," Morning Edition,
     radio program, National Public Radio, June 2, 2009.

26   W. Martin, online interview conducted by Caroline Kaltefletier, June 17, 2009.

27   Ibid.

28   Ibid.

29   Ibid.

30   Ibid.

31   See M. Albert, *Parecon: Life after Capitalism* (London: Verso, 2004).

32   G. Curren, *21st Century Dissent: Anarchism, Anti-Globalization and Environmental-
     ism* (New York: Palgrave Macmillan, 2006), 180.

33   Ibid.

34   See M. Bakhtin, *Rabelais and His World* (Bloomington: Indiana University Press,
     1984).

35   Notes from Nowhere, *We Are Everywhere: The Irresistible Rise of Global Capitalism*
     (London: Verso, 2003), 178.

36   S. Duncombe, "Stepping Off the Sidewalk: Reclaim the Streets NYC ," in ed. B. Shepard and R. Hayduk, *From ACT UP to WTO: Urban Protest and Community Building in the Era of Globalization* (London: Verso, 2002), 220.

37   "Galwegians Are Reclaiming Galway's Streets," *IndyMedia Ireland*, May 19, 2009, http://www.indymedia.ie/article/92362 (accessed May 30, 2009).

38   Ibid.

39   Ibid.

40   Ibid.

Part 5

Resistance

"The great are only great because we are on our knees. Let us rise!"—Pierre-Joseph Proudhon

Occupy, Resist, Produce!
Lessons from Latin America's Occupied Factories

Marie Trigona

Latin America's occupied factory movement has built an expansive system of workers' self-management through direct action and the expropriation of the means of production. The worker occupations lend insight to workers around the world, demonstrating that direct actions at the workplace can lead to revolutionary practices, self-determination, and worker control—three essential elements of a free society, and an essential component for an anarchist economics if we are to study what self-management might look like in a post-capitalist future. In Argentina, more than 13,000 people work in occupied factories and businesses, otherwise known as recuperated enterprises. The sites, which number more than 200, range from hotels to ceramics factories, balloon manufacturers, suit factories, printing shops, and transport companies, as well as many other trades. And these sites provide examples in embryonic form of what anarchist economics might mean applied to our experiences of work.

The working class has occupied factories since the onset of the industrial revolution as a strategy for workers to defend themselves against deplorable work conditions, unsafe workplaces, and retaliation. Recently in Latin America, workers occupied the workplace not only to make demands heard, but also to put worker self-management into practice. In Argentina, and other nations throughout South America such as Brazil, Uruguay, and Venezuela, workers rediscovered the factory occupations starting in 2000. Occupations spread in Argentina as the region faced a financial crisis in 2001 in which thousands of factories closed and businesses bankrupted. Growing unemployment, capital flight, and deindustrialization served as the backdrop for the factory takeovers in 2000.

Even though worker-recuperated enterprises have created jobs, fostered community projects, and improved working conditions for thousands, these sites face legal uncertainty and state attacks that have forced them to resolve problems autonomous from government intervention. The Argentine experiment in self-management has essentially questioned the very logic of capitalism. This may be why government representatives, industry representatives, and factory owners have remained silent and often times reacted with hostility on this issue; they are afraid of these sites multiplying and the example they have set. These experiences potentially could replace capitalism.

In anarchist writer Voltairine de Cleyre's text "Direct Action," she writes that capitalists' possession of the means of production is absolutely worthless without workers' activity and labor. Argentina's recuperated enterprises reaffirm the notion that workers do not need bosses to produce. When workers expropriate land, factories, businesses, or housing, they provide solutions to their own problems without the intervention of the state or other authoritarian institutions. This is what governments and capitalists find unacceptable— that workers are proving that the foundation of the capitalist model and the supposed "need" for state management is a farce. Nearly a century after Voltairine de Cleyre published "Direct Action," the text still proves relevant. As capitalism falls into an irreversible crisis now, workers throughout the world are employing factory occupations as a viable direct action to defend workers' rights and transform social relations.

Along with the birth of industrial capitalism, the working class commenced the dream of freeing themselves from exploitation, destroying the capitalist system through direct action, and re-appropriating the means of production. As historians and writers long noted, the aspiration for direct worker management of production has culminated in many worker takeovers through the greater part of the twentieth century—Russia (1917), Italy (1920), Spain (1936), Chile (1972), and Argentina (2001).

Industrial capitalism brought the employment of wage labor and, with wage labor, revolutionized the means of production igniting class struggle. Capitalist owners, since they owned the means of production, could then control labor, accumulating capital from the labor of the workers, in a concept which Karl Marx termed "surplus value." Given the very nature of capitalism, class relations have remained antagonistic throughout the course of modern society and the expansion of globalized industrial capitalism.

Since capitalists extract their profits from the productive process, they want the lowest wages possible for their workers and the least amount of costs in production (even at the expense of workplace safety and the environment). The objective of this cycle of exploitation is selling their products back to the masses at the highest price possible. Bosses have long sought to suppress the bargaining power of workers through economic and political manipulation. Throughout history they have sought to do so by any means necessary—including forceful, violent coercion. The state has unleashed violence on workers who decided to defend their rights in numerous attacks in the past 200 years (e.g., the Homestead Massacre in Pittsburgh 1892; Ludlow Massacre 1914; Memorial Day Massacre in Chicago 1937; and Argentina's own 1976–1983 military dictatorship, which targeted union organizing and "disappeared" 30,000 people).

Within capitalism, workers have no other choice than to sell their labor. In order to survive, workers needs a wage or they starve. Of course, this system has led to a conflict of interests between the working class and capitalist class. Through direct action, workers throughout history hoped not only to make their demands heard for a shorter workday, better working conditions, and higher salaries, but also transformed their own consciousness to understand that another system of production is possible.

Argentina offers one of the longest-lived experiences of direct worker management of this century. As such, the experiences of self-management in Latin America provide an example of new working-class subjectivities, self-determination, and working culture while they fight against dominant institutions, including the state and capitalist bosses. Their struggles provide a liberatory vision by sowing the seeds for a new society today, challenging market systems of domination, and questioning the legitimacy of private property.

Many anarchist traditions have been interwoven into the resistance strategies of Latin America's autonomous social movements, which includes the worker-controlled factory movement. In many cases, the worker occupations transformed class struggle into a collectivized system of self-management through direct action, essentially changing the entire premise of production within a capitalist society. No longer do workers produce under the exploitive supervision of bosses who appropriate their surplus capital. The workers themselves, after occupying their workplace and appropriating the means of production from their bosses, transformed the workplace into a space for liberation and cooperation.

"All co-operative experiments are essentially direct action" —Voltairine de Cleyre, "Direct Action"

The occupied factory movement carries to its core the ideals and practices of class struggle—not only in the way they have adopted the factory occupation as a legitimate tool for workers around the world, but also in the way they have resolved their problems autonomously from state intervention and put into practice workers' self-management.

The sites that have fostered systems of worker self-management first began with a worker occupation or some direct action at the point of production. The context and circumstance of each of the sites vary, but almost all share the commonality of the occupation. Many of Argentina's recuperated enterprises borrowed the slogan "Occupy, Resist, Produce" from Brazil's Landless Workers' Movement (MST), which for nearly a quarter of a century has built a massive movement of over one million families and taken over nearly thirty-five million acres from large land owners. Like MST in Brazil, Argentina's worker-controlled factories were occupied to find a solution to joblessness autonomously from the state, which was unwilling to intervene.

First the workers occupied their workplace, in a number of different circumstances, widely in the context of a bankruptcy. Then they had to defend the occupation and resist forceful eviction attempts. Production was frequently started when the workers were resisting and fighting for legality. Often actions such as highway blockades, street protests, and even threatening to destroy the sites of production accompanied the occupations.

Breaking Chains

One of the most emblematic actions was the workers' decision at various locations to cut off a lock to the factory or workplace with the lock symbolizing the protection of private property. Workers break the chain, putting their legitimate claim to jobs with dignity over the sanctity of private property.

"The most important factor, and most subversive, is that the recuperated enterprises confirm that businesses don't need bosses to produce," says Fabio Resino from the BAUEN Hotel. The nineteen-story, 180-room hotel has been operational since workers took it over in 2003. It operates despite a court-ordered eviction notice and void of legal recognition. The hotel has been a launch pad for the new occupied factories; many of the workers from the new take-overs have come to the BAUEN Hotel seeking advice and support.

The BAUEN Hotel had closed in December 2001. The alleged owners, Grupo Solari, acquired the hotel in 1997 and filed bankruptcy in 2001. Leading up to the hotel's closure, the hotel's rooms and facilities deteriorated, and the bosses began laying off workers. The remaining workers were fired in December 2001. The bosses abandoned the hotel located on a major avenue in downtown Buenos Aires, boarding it up and allowing it to become an eyesore, reminding the city of the impending financial crisis and widespread unemployment the nation faced.

The decision to occupy came in 2003, two years after the initial closure. Nearly thirty workers, along with supporters from other occupied factories and workers' movements, participated in the action. The workers first held an assembly at Chilavert, a printing press collectively run by its workers since 2002. There the workers voted to occupy the hotel.

Arminda Palacios worked as a seamstress at the hotel for over twenty years and played a key role in the occupation. Her account of the occupation rings with emotion, which she describes as a turning point in her life as a worker. The occupiers entered through an adjacent hotel on the block. When they got to the gate that connected the two hotels in the basement they made a pivotal decision to break in. "There was a small lock. We cut it off and we walked in," said Palacios giving the impression that the owners were assured that the private property was so sacred that no one would question the fraudulent bankruptcy. Immediately afterward, the workers went to the reception area and huddled together in tears when they realized what they had accomplished: saving their jobs and recovering their dignity.

Since the workers' occupation, the space has transformed into a modern-day commune, a far cry from the origins of the hotel with ties to the nation's bloody military dictatorship—which forcefully "disappeared" 30,000 workers, activists, and students. Hotel BAUEN was built in 1978 with loans from the military junta which dictated the nation from 1976–1983. Argentina's national soccer team took the 1978 World Cup and the military used the world championship as a media campaign to cover up the gruesome human rights abuses occurring at the time. Guests at the hotel, among whom were high-profile military and government reps, chanted a counter-human-rights slogan: "Somos derechos y humanos!" (We are right and human!) They cheered with the Argentine flag in hand, as thousands of women and men cried in terror while undergoing indescribable torture sessions; as the military drugged prisoners and then dropped their bodies into the Atlantic Ocean in the *vuelos de muerte,* or death flights. "This hotel was a symbol of the dictatorship: of the repression and looting that this country endured," said Raúl Godoy, a worker from the Zanon ceramics plant, the largest recuperated factory in Argentina in the Patagonian province of Neuquén. "Now this hotel is a symbol of the workers, the workers that are beginning to recover from 30,000 disappearances and take back what was stolen from us."

Hotel BAUEN's original owner, Marcelo Iurcovich, received more than 5 million to construct the BAUEN, with a government loan from the National Development Bank (BANADE). Iurcovich never held the hotel up to safety inspection codes, and never paid back state loans. He ran up debts and committed tax evasion while making millions of dollars in profits and acquiring two more hotels. Throughout the '90s the hotel became the emblematic symbol of neoliberalism, serving as the election bunker for former president Carlos Menem (1989–1999), who, ironically, has been blamed for ruining the nation's economy through privatization and reactionary free market policies.

In 2008, Victoria Donda, a national deputy whose mother and father were disappeared by the military dictatorship, sponsored an expropriation law in the national congress that would give the BAUEN legality. "The purpose of the bill is for the hotel to be expropriated by the State and for the workers to manage it. We are fighting for a law to declare this workplace, which already belongs to the community in Buenos Aires and the people, to declare it public domain." Donda's past was also clouded by the terror of the military junta. She was born at the ESMA (Military Navy Mechanics School), the nation's largest clandestine detention center, while her mother was in captivity. She is one of the 500 children born and kidnapped by the military and by people with connections to the military from 1976–1983.[1]

Nearly thirty workers occupied the BAUEN when it was first taken over in 2003. Today the cooperative employs more than 150. The BAUEN cooperative has proven that workers can efficiently manage hotel services, but also demonstrated creativity in opening this space to the cultural and social movements in the city. On a local level,

BAUEN Hotel has participated in efforts at coalition building and the development of a broad mutual support network. In the midst of legal struggles and successfully running a prominent hotel, the cooperative's members haven't forgotten their roots. The worker-run hotel has become a political center for movement organizing.

Direct action led to the BAUEN collective redefining the workplace on three fronts: struggle, culture, and work. Hotel BAUEN serves as a meeting place for worker, human rights, and environmental justice organizations. Subway delegates who have been organizing an autonomous, independent union use the BAUEN as a meeting space and venue for press conferences when announcing wildcat strikes. Human rights organizations like the Mothers of Plaza de Mayo, HIJOS, and international intellectuals such as Noam Chomsky, Immanuel Wallerstein, and Michael Albert have expressed their support of the Hotel BAUEN's commitment to worker control. Nora Cortinas, president of the Mothers of Plaza de Mayo's founding chapter, has confirmed her commitment to defending the BAUEN Hotel. When asked how she would defend the BAUEN she said, "Like this," while striking a boxer's pose ready to deliver the knockout punch.

On the cultural front, the Hotel BAUEN has held numerous street festivals in defense of workers' control. Thousands attended a street festival in November 2008 for a national expropriation law for Hotel BAUEN where Argentine rock legend, Leon Gieco, performed. Inside the hotel, many collectives have performed fundraising shows for the BAUEN and other social movements.

In order to survive, the BAUEN cooperative has resisted legal attacks and an uncertain future. Despite numerous eviction orders and lack of legal support, the BAUEN cooperative has continued to operate successful hotel services, convinced that they have a legitimate right to work without a boss. The global economic crisis has brought negative consequences for business at the hotel as tourism continues to drop. Many of the occupied factories have had to forge autonomous solutions to legal and market challenges. State representatives have been reluctant to put into motion an eviction attempt, sensing that because of the BAUEN Hotel's strategic location and ability to rally support, efforts at eviction would result in a costly bloodbath. Subway workers have threatened a total city transport shutdown if the courts were to sanction a police operation to evict the hotel collective.

The BAUEN Hotel has demonstrated that through direct action workers can avenge their historic exploitation by expropriating symbols of neoliberalism and oppression for the benefit of the community and working class. Since the workers broke the chains protecting private property, their lives and the workplace have transformed into a liberatory space. Whereas the hotel had been a dark symbol of the nation's state repression and neoliberal policies, today it symbolizes working-class resistance and culture.

Hide-and-Seek Capitalism

A number of factors set off each of the occupations in Argentina. When asked why the workers made the decision to occupy, 77 percent answered that the bosses owed the workers unpaid salaries; 41 percent answered that the company went bankrupt; 35 percent said that the company attempted to liquidate assets/empty out the factory; 29 percent pointed out work instability as a significant factor; 29 percent answered that they were expecting impending firing; and 18 percent answered that the boss or owner had abandoned the workplace.[2]

Most of the worker takeovers were actions to guarantee that the owners wouldn't be able to liquidate assets before filing bankruptcy to avoid paying workers indemnities and back salaries. Workers' demands steadily grew from measures to safeguard their jobs to the idea of implementing a system of self-management. With little hope that bosses would ever return to pay workers what they owed, they devised plans to start up production with no boss or owner whatsoever.

Bosses abandoning their workplaces were a common impetus for the workers' occupations. This was the case of La Nueva Esperanza cooperative, a balloon company formerly known as Global, which employed more than eighty workers in the 1980s. At the time of the factory's closure, the plant only employed forty workers. When the workers came to work on a Monday in 2004, to their surprise the factory's gate was closed with a sign reading, "closed until further notice." They jumped the fence to find that the factory's machinery had been taken away—essentially the workers found the plant ransacked. "We didn't know what to do. The first idea we had was to set off the factory's security alarm so the owner would show his face," said Claudia, a young worker with nearly ten years at the plant. The owner, Jorge

Sasinsky, never showed up, having owed taxes, four years in unpaid salaries, contributions to workers' social security funds, unpaid vacation time, and cash to suppliers.

Neighbors living next to the plant in a residential neighborhood in Buenos Aires informed the workers that on Friday after they finished their shifts at 5 p.m., they saw moving trucks and men removing machinery from the plant. The balloon workers interviewed said that they immediately set out on an independent investigation to find out where the boss took the machinery. They discovered that the boss had transferred the balloon manufacturing equipment to a warehouse in a nearby suburban city outside of the capital, in an industrial belt, but they didn't know exactly where. "There are a lot of factories in that area; factory owners get suspicious if they see a group of workers knocking on factory doors and asking questions. But we kept looking," said Nereo, a veteran worker at the factory. After days of searching, and losing what little hope they had left of finding the "factory," three workers persevered in their hunt.

Ready to give up, balloon producers saw a man sweeping the sidewalk outside of a factory and asked him if he had seen any sign of a factory opening. He tipped them off of a nearby deposit warehouse. It occurred to Nereo to open one of the garbage bags outside the warehouse. "Inside I found—the factory—I mean balloons."

Immediately the workers set up camp outside the warehouse to demand their jobs, unpaid salaries, or severance pay. The desperate situation dragged on for months. The workers rotated shifts at the sit-in. Judges from the labor courts and government representatives refused to hear the workers' claims. The trustee handling the workers' claims never met with the workers. Now jobless and broke, the workers relied on outside support to survive. "People who you don't even know bring you coffee, sugar, yerba mate. We couldn't believe the support that we got," said Eva, a worker at the factory for more than twenty years. The solidarity they received changed their perspectives and outlook. They also describe how uniting as workers while camping out gave them the courage to form a cooperative and take action. For more than eight months, eighteen workers maintained the sit-in outside the factory until they were violently attacked. According to the workers, following a news report that aired on television the boss sent lackeys to beat them. While two women were guarding the tent, a group of men attacked them, hitting one worker over the head with a bottle. That's when the workers decided: "Enough is enough."

Along with other social movements and workers from occupied factories, the ex-Global workers voted to expropriate the machinery and take it back to the original, but now abandoned plant. Workers from IMPA, a recovered metallurgical factory in Buenos Aires, provided trucks since they couldn't "rent" trucks to move equipment that legally didn't belong to the workers. Other activists from the recuperated enterprises, including the Chilavert printing shop, BAUEN Hotel, and Conforti, also participated in the expropriation. One worker describes how he packed up the truck until the last piece of machinery was loaded. Often times, workers from recuperated enterprises have decided to cease production at their workplace to participate in solidarity actions with other occupied sites—the idea being *si nos tocan a uno, nos tocan a todos*, (if they mess with one of us, they mess with all of us.)

Together they entered the plant in the suburbs, moved the machines onto trucks, and brought the machines back to the factory in the capital. When they were unloading the last truck the police showed up. They called for backup and five patrol cars came. The police told them they couldn't unload the truck, and the workers resisted until they were able to unload the last compressor. Video footage shows the workers, supporters, and other occupiers hurriedly locking the gate to prevent police from raiding the plant.

When the workers arrived at the plant, they found it in ruins and a part of the deposit area burn down. To assure that the workers wouldn't try to occupy it, the former owner set fire to the plant, according to the workers. Most of them had produced balloons for the company for at least several decades at the factory.

Another stage in the struggle implied the fight for legalization. The workers had to convince legislative representatives to support an expropriation bill to hand over the real estate and machinery to the cooperative. For five months, the workers occupied the factory illegally. On September 22, 2005, the city legislature granted the La Nueva Esperanza cooperative temporary expropriation and legal rights. "I never thought that I would be working in a cooperative; we feel as if the factory belongs to us and we're running it perhaps better than the former owner," said Claudia.

In many of the occupations, the bosses often played a game of hide-and-seek capitalism. Bosses have to hide because what they are doing is unethical, unfair, exploitive, and often times illegal. The postmodern theorist Michel Foucault posed the following question in his book *Discipline and Punish: The Birth of the Prison*: "Is it surprising that prisons resemble factories, schools, barracks, hospitals?" Given the nature of modern capitalism, it is not surprising—factories, in fact, resemble prisons in their layout and organization of time, as Foucault suggests. The factory in modern globalization serves as a location for manufacturing that can disappear and reappear across borders—spaces that are hidden from the gaze of society so they can exploit and control workers toiling inside with impunity. Many transnational manufacturing sites could be considered modern-day prisons—with workers laboring for nearly slave wages for unrestricted workdays and in deplorable conditions, bussed into extensive labyrinths of barbed wire and fences like the little media has shown viewers of maquiladoras in free trade zones. And many prisons have been transformed into modern-day factories with corporations paying inmates less than humane wages to manufacture products. In the case of Global balloons, the owner abandoned the old plant and workers to open a new factory with new workers willing to accept lower wages and higher production rates. The workers had to find their boss, who "disappeared" into thin air, to make their demands. The boss didn't count on the workers winning this game of hide-and-seek.

The workers, on the other hand, have opened their factories under worker control to the community. No longer do the sites have guards and gates to keep outsiders out—they have invited students, activists, and other workers to visit the factory to see what they have accomplished: creating jobs with dignity and building democratic workplaces. These sites have also fostered cultural spaces and community programs. More than twenty-three adult education programs operate in recuperated enterprises and the factory has now become a classroom for hundreds of adults. Chilavert printing shop, BAUEN Hotel, and Zanon ceramics factory regularly host schoolchildren who tour the sites to learn that workers can successfully run a business without a boss or owner, where all workers are equal—a concept children find inspiring and fascinating.

Syndicalism and Self-management

"Revolutionary syndicalism, basing itself on the class-war, aims at the union of all manual and intellectual workers in economic fighting organizations struggling for their emancipation from the yoke of wage slavery and from the oppression of the State. Its goal consists in the re-organization of social life on the basis of free Communism, by means of the revolutionary action of the working-class itself."—Rudolf Rocker

As the largest recuperated factory in Argentina, the Zanon ceramics factory has redefined the bases of production: without workers, production is impossible and without bosses, production flourishes. Zanon, still Latin America's largest ceramics manufacturer, is located in the Patagonian province of Neuquén, a region with rich working-class traditions and history. The workers officially declared the factory under worker control in October 2001 following a bosses' lockout.

In 2001, Zanon's owners had decided to close its doors and fire the workers without paying months of back pay or severance pay. Leading up to the massive layoffs and plant's closure, workers had gone on strike in 2000. The owner, Luis Zanon, with over $75 million in debt to public and private creditors (including the World Bank for over $20 million), fired most of the workers en masse and closed the factory in 2001—a bosses' lockout. In October 2001, workers declared the plant under worker control. The workers subsequently camped outside the factory for four months, pamphleteering and partially blocking a highway leading to the capital city of Neuquén. While the workers were camping outside the factory, a court ruled that the employees could sell off remaining stock. After the stock ran out, on March 2, 2002, the workers' assembly voted to start up production without a boss.

Since the occupation, the workers renamed the factory FASINPAT (Factory without a Boss). The Zanon workers have grown from a group of workers self-managing a union organization to a collective self-managing a factory under worker control. Omar Villablanca, a young worker, said that worker control wouldn't have been possible without the union organizing efforts previous to the occupation.

"Zanon is what it is today because the workers recuperated the factory's internal trade union. If we hadn't won back the union, Zanon wouldn't be functioning under worker control. The Zanon workers learned from the lessons of the internal union and listening to workers organizing in other factories."

Prior to the takeover in 2001, workers organized and won control of the ceramics union. A shop-floor movement won union representation elections inside the factory in late 1998, ousting the old union delegate tied to the bureaucracy and the employers. In 2000, delegates from the rank-and-file movement won the provincial-wide elections of the Neuquén Ceramists Union by a three-to-one margin. By 2007, having operated four years under worker control, Neuquén Ceramists Union assembly voted in favor of a new union statute reinventing the democratic principles and guidelines for the union inspired by the Spanish anarcho-syndicalist trade union, the General Confederation of Labor (or CGT).

Without support from the union, workers held a strike in 2000 following the death of Daniel Ferras, a twenty-two-year-old worker who died in the factory due to lack of emergency medical care and employer negligence. The eight-day work stoppage forced the company to provide an ambulance on site and form a joint commission of workers and managers to oversee production safety within the factory.

While FASINPAT includes a diverse array of political ideologies and backgrounds, in numerous public talks I have heard workers reference the historic example of anarcho-syndicalist organizations that organized self-managed work places during the Spanish Civil-War. The Zanon workers' experience of fighting for control of a mass union prior to the worker take-over at the plant helped create a precedent of collectively self-managing a struggle within capitalist society. It also helped to develop in the workers a sense of their power to run things. In this case, the sense of self-managing a union struggle led to the *autogestión* of a massive factory.

Central to the organization at FASINPAT is the notion of class struggle. At the factory, the workers transmit their identity as workers in social conflict with the capitalist and managerial classes with a perspective of emancipation for the working class. Beyond worker control at FASINPAT, the worker general assemblies held at the plant often discuss issues related to labor conflicts throughout Argentina.

The assembly has voted to contribute to numerous strike funds and to participate regularly and physically in protests in support of social movements locally and nationally.

The Zanon occupation took place in the context of an explosion of social movements and political organizing. Leading up to the popular rebellion in December 2001, in which former President Fernando de la Rúa was ousted, unemployed worker organizations were blocking highways throughout the nation to demand real jobs and a solution to the deepening economic crisis that left more than 50 percent of the population in dire poverty. The unemployed worker organizations, or *piqueteros,* were also building networks of popular movements based on the ideals of direct democracy, autonomy, and direct action. Popular neighborhood assemblies were appearing in neighborhoods in nearly all metropolitan areas, occupying banks and other abandoned spaces to provide autonomous solutions to local problems.

Many of the occupied factories have had to physically resist eviction attempts. At Zanon, the government has tried to evict the factory collective five times with massive police operations. Community support for Zanon has culminated to such a level that the government has had to back down. On April 8, 2003, more than 5,000 community members from Neuquén defended the factory, surrounding it, demonstrating their willingness to put their bodies on the line to defend a factory that "belongs to the people." The nearly 500 ceramics workers have sent a clear message to the government that the factory will not be taken back without a fight. "We have said that the factory belongs to the people, we are going to defend our factory. We are going to use the legitimate tools of defense that we have to successfully run this plant," said Raúl Godoy to a press conference prior to the April 2003 eviction attempt, appearing with activists from Mothers of Plaza de Mayo sitting behind him with their emblematic white handkerchiefs on their heads.

Zanon workers' prior experience in class-struggle syndicalism helped to catapult FASINPAT into the forefront of the occupied factory movement. Here they have proven that through direct democratic organization and class-based solidarity workers can develop successful experiences of worker control.

The workers will defend their factory regardless of the possible consequences, forging resistance to an unfavorable legal future. Rosa

Rivera, worker at Zanon for fifteen years, explains that Zanon is not only a struggle for the 470 workers inside the factory, but a struggle for the community and social revolution. "If factories are shut down and abandoned, workers have the right to occupy it, put it to work, and defend it with their lives."

A New Chapter in Working-Class History

When left with no other option, workers decided to take over factories and take charge of production themselves. Only later, when they had the support of the community and proved that they could run a factory did they demand legality. First came the occupation. "Occupy, resist and produce; production is the last stage," explains Candido Gonzalez, a veteran in the occupied factory movement from the recuperated Chilavert printing shop. "In order to produce you can't skip the two previous stages of occupying and resisting." Labor history suggests that without direct action, workers have little chance of winning. The stronger the action, the more likely they are to win their demands. The occupied factory movement embodies this logic with the slogan "Occupy, resist, produce!"

The state thus far has been unwilling to make changes to bankruptcy laws to protect workers from fraudulent lockouts and closures. In 2009, BAUEN has yet to gain full legal recognition although after nearly a decade of self-managing their workplaces, a forceful eviction is unlikely as long as the hotel can continue to rally support.

The workers at FASINPAT won a major legal victory in 2009. The provincial legislature voted in favor of expropriating the ceramics factory and handing it over to the workers' cooperative to manage legally and indefinitely. While Zanon now has legal standing, the cooperative will continue to defend workers' rights and self-management. This means these sites should stick to their roots as part of a worldwide network of working-class struggles.

We Can Write Our Own Futures!

Will direct actions like workplace occupations continue to grow as the world faces an economic crisis? From 2008 to 2010, Serbia, Turkey, France, Spain, South Africa, England, and Canada have seen worker occupations. The most well-known case in the United States has been the sit-down strike at the Chicago-based Republic Windows and

Doors plant where workers occupied their factory to demand severance pay and benefits after being abruptly fired. The occupations in Argentina continue to rise as the global crisis hits the South American nation. The Arrufat chocolate factory, Disco de Oro empanada (pastry) manufacturer, Febatex thread producer, and Lidercar meat packing plant joined the ranks of the worker-occupied factory movement from 2008 to 2009.

These sites in Latin America have developed a new model of organizing after learning the lesson that workers can't rely on governments, even "progressive" governments, and unresponsive unions to resolve the problems of unnecessary firings and joblessness. The worker occupations have proven that through the power of direct action, the reinvention of social relations, and producing for the benefit of the community and workers rather than greedy bosses, a factory can be transformed into a liberatory space. "Maybe one day our story will be included in a chapter in working-class history that a group of workers occupied a plant and began producing," said Adrian, from Arrufat chocolate occupied factory after lamenting the loss of his hand in the plant under capitalist supervision. And the occupied factories in Argentina are doing just that: writing a new future for working-class history and sending the message that workers can do what capitalists aren't interested in doing—creating jobs and dignity for workers.

ENDNOTES

1   Victoria Donda, *Mi Nombre es Victoria* (Buenos Aires: Sudamericana, 2009).

2   Julián Rebón, *La Empresa de la Autonomía: Trabajadores recuperando la producción* (Buenos Aires: Ediciones Picasso, 2007).

Call It an Uprising: People of Color and the Third World Organize against Capitalism

Ernesto Aguilar

Dignidad, Spanish for dignity, is a deceptively basic idea. Translated into the realm of political unrest, *dignidad* has become synonymous with the idea that poor people have a right to live without shame, hunger, want, or fear. Such an idea is so simple yet it cuts right to the chase to speak to the dreams and demands of the masses of disenfranchised people in the global South and around the world.

Today, ideas like *dignidad* are at the base of scores of popular crusades. The early part of the twenty-first century saw Nepal's masses, led by Maobadi rebels, overthrow a king, with memories of suffering prominent in the radical encounter. Evo Morales came to power on the strength of Bolivia's ethnic pluralities asserting themselves. Nigeria's civil society continues to campaign against oil conglomerates around the contention that its citizens should have the country's resources. Pakistan has seen a burgeoning anti-imperialist mainstream in response to US interventionism. In addition, the United States continues to have debates over race that play out through issues like immigration and disparities in the realms of health care and the criminal justice system. In each case, even if not so explicit, oppressed people in each land's minority sector and, more importantly, large numbers of those regarded as people of color by white majorities have taken considerable risks to challenge business and political leaders consorting with Western power and capital. Convulsions like these, whether in the streets, schools, or homes, require serious answers, implies István Mészáros:

> we cannot attribute the chronic problems of our social interchanges to more or less easily corrigible political contingencies. So much is at stake, and we have historically rather limited time at our disposal in order to redress, in a socially sustainable way, the all too obvious grievances of the structurally subordinated social classes. The question of why?—concerning substantive matters, and not simply the contingent personal failures, even when they happen to be serious, as the frequently highlighted

instances of widespread political corruption are—cannot be avoided indefinitely.[1]

In a period when the dominant line was for people to rest their fortunes on cooperation with multinational industry, how did notions of *dignidad* take hold? Moreover, why have these ideas captured imaginations so deeply? What can anti-imperialist First World tendencies, be they liberal, revolutionary, communist, or anarchist, learn?

Support for basic human rights as a cornerstone to political life is integral to populist and revolutionary politics in many Third World countries, especially in those that have seen dictatorships come to power, such as Paraguay, Uruguay, and Brazil. The repression people experience pervades the subconscious of the mainstream as well as the opposition. In the United States, memories of brutal expressions of racism remind millions, despite initiatives to obfuscate such history, that the United States is no exception. In addition, intense conflicts are giving way to equally intense contentions over power.

The planet is in the midst of a spate of rebellions, refusals, wars, and the kind of global conflicts signifying dissatisfaction with the current world order not seen since the anticolonial insurgencies of the twentieth century. That these pursuits have emanated primarily from the Third World—nations of postcolonial peoples fighting for existence in the shadow of US capitalism—as well as classes of oppressed people (people of color) in the First World should not be surprising. Many of these nations are seeing the harshest expressions of profiteering and their populations are resisting forces of international capital, which shows itself in the worst ways for these communities: land seizures, environmental devastation, and hopelessly troubled loan arrangements, to name just a few. Foreign projects force rural populations into urban centers and such relocations are often unsustainable; thus reinforcing immigration into the United States as the only viable alternative for many people in the Third World.

Colonial practices by Western powers against the Third World have manifested through the centuries to rest today in unequal allocations of property, power, and labor. Over the long march to national sovereignty, oppressed people have fought to establish a new vision that has broken them free of the imperialistic yoke, which employs such machinations as stealing local customs for integration into—and forcibly pushing loyalty for—a new, codified law. Modern influences such as the transnational flow of immigrants, the political muscle of emigrants abroad, and nongovernmental organizations with outside money and alliances influencing national destinies have all further muddied the political waters of self-determination and capital.

For these people, whose memories are long and whose resolve hinges on the fact that they have few political and economic opportunities, there is little option but to fight for a different world. One need only look back upon efforts like the Revolutionary Action Movement, a US-based black revolutionary nationalist formation; Mexico's Partido Democratico Popular Revolucionario (PDPR)/Ejercito Popular Revolucionario (EPR), which emerged during the recognition of police killings of indigenous peasants; and South Asia's myriad battles for cultural autonomy and economic justice as poignant examples. In these cases, the affected communities had little to lose, and the issues at hand were significant enough to warrant a diverse response.

C. L. R. James, in discussing the drive for Haitian independence in a speech published in *You Don't Play with Revolution: The Montreal Lectures of C. L. R. James*, suggests that these movements often find themselves underestimated by the ruling class:

> These people were backward, but as we learned…they had a certain integrity, a certain social consciousness of their own, which was developed apart from their masters. That was shown, not only in general and by observers who watched them closely, but also by what took place in the revolution. The revolution took place and, before long, they had made a clean sweep and were completely in charge of San Domingo.[2]

Whether people's strikes against the powerful in Oaxaca, the Naxalite rebellion against capital and secure economic zones in India, black communities defending undocumented immigrants in the United States, or Venezuela's fierce advocacy of the plight of the dispossessed, women, the indigenous population, and poor, the Third World is fighting back and igniting hope for other upturns in the process. Just as years before the Brown Berets were inspired by the Black Panthers who were inspired by the Chinese Revolution, solidarity has extended openly for generations. Even when, as in the Chinese experience, policies (in this case, toward Africa) were dismal, solidarity remained unwavering. Robin D. G. Kelly says in *Freedom Dreams: The Black Radical Imagination*:

> The status of the Chinese as people of color served as a powerful political tool in mobilizing support from Africans and African-descended people. In 1963, for example, Chinese delegates in Moshi, Tanzania, proclaimed that the Russians had no business in Africa because they were white. The Chinese, on the other hand, were not only part of the colored world but unlike Europeans they never took part in the slave trade. Of course, most of these claims serve to facilitate alliance building.[3]

Such solidarity is rooted in people who have a gut-level interest in challenging the current order to defend dignity and create better futures. While generally socialist in character, this kind of internationalism unfolding is a politics rooted in the view of the interconnectedness of oppressed people and their fights against fluid though evident exploitation. The exploitation in turn is rooted in the subjugation of oppressed people in scenarios of production and exchange.

It is here where ideas of *dignidad* were born. In these instances, almost exclusively impoverished and downtrodden ethnic and racial minorities have taken the lead in eruptions driven by complex experiences. Race and culture in turn shaped these experiences. Those new and subversive paradigms, however, understood that institutional discrimination and profiteering were not just matters influenced by race, but also the relationship of exchange. Many such intrusions into business as usual have constituted what Amilcar Cabral called an advance-guard in international barrages, providing guidance, political theory, practice, inspiration, and hope to those with dreams of social justice, freedom, and equality.

This chapter will explore resistance to capitalism by people of color, or, broadly, oppressed-class people in the Third World and oppressed-nation First World people of color, and the characteristics that have defined desires to dismantle power relationships as well as the practices behind them. In addition, the chapter will examine globalization's impact on class composition and people of color. Finally, where will these revolts of people of color rebelling against capitalist exploitation go?

While specters of the administration of US President Richard Nixon's attempts at equating "Black Power" with the ability to own a business, buy a home, and shop still loom in the popular imagination as part of capital's endless attempts at co-optation, noteworthy elements could challenge that process.

As a movement that aims for libertarian socialism, anarchism must account for the experiences of people of color because of their unique role in (sometimes forcibly) building modern capitalism, as well as maintaining it. Further, as a movement that aims to abolish all hierarchical authority, anarchism requires an analysis of colonialism, imperialism, and white supremacy in order to live up to its own aims. Unfortunately, in much anarchist theorizing and movement building this is notably absent. For an anarchist economics, this means we need an analysis of the resistance of people of color to capitalism, as well as an analysis of the complex processes of globalization and how they have affected people of color generally, and the global South specifically, as staging grounds for economic colonialism and imperialism. This essay will contribute to the growing body of literature making such an analysis.

Globalization and the Reshaping of Race

In *The Darker Nations: A People's History of the Third World*, author Vijay Prashad suggests that the Third World is more than countries along the sidelines of the Cold War or throw-ins among the First and Second Worlds, but rather is a product of the fray against colonialism and the galvanization of internationalism. Prashad shows that the unifying experience of colonialism brought together divergent peoples and histories to such important breakthroughs as the founding of the League Against Imperialism in 1927, the 1955 Asian–African Conference in Bandung, Indonesia, and the Tricontinental Conference held in 1966 in Havana, Cuba. Nevertheless, there is a space to understand capitalism as national liberation victors betrayed the character of their revolutions by surrendering their economies to global corporations.

Globalization, shorthand for transnational capitalist exchange, has been in this period almost exclusively an initiative in which the majority-white First World exploits the majority-nonwhite Third World, paying a fraction of what First World labor would receive for harvest, work, production, and manufacture for First World consumers. In

the First World, where slavery nourished such arrangements generations before, globalization became acceptable as a model that implied
international cooperation and unity of purpose, and thus somehow
being better than the servitude that operated before. Globalization,
however, has come at heavy costs to the Third World and associated
pressures in the First World. Such practices have created a class of
oppressed people in the Third World as well as people domestic to the
First World, whose general role is labor, the result of which has been
a profound imbalance of wealth. Desperation and indignation in the
Third World and a sense of relative deprivation among people of color
in the First World are challenges to globalization, which implicitly
promised to erase inequalities through financial advancement, greater
consumer choices, buying power, and skilled trades.

Globalization is further a process inside imperialism that is shrinking the world and breaking down the cultures and autonomy of the
oppressed nations beyond what imperialism was able to do in its earlier
stages (which tended toward control through economic relations). Globalization has complicated race by sharpening contradictions. Transnational capital deploys *comprador* classes in the gutting of the Third
World. In the First World, as there has always traditionally been, a deep
tension exists over people of color and loyalty to betterment, democracy, and self-determination—values largely co-opted by imperialism.
In *Meditations on Frantz Fanon's "Wretched of the Earth": New Afrikan
Revolutionary Writings*, James Yaki Sayles refocuses the fissure:

> What does Fanon say, "There is no native who does not dream
> at least once a day of setting himself up in the settler's place."
> That is, the "native" that Fanon describes as "wanting to take the
> place of" the settler is not the ex-native the person who comes to
> believe it's not his skin or the settler's skin that matters, and that
> being in the settler's place will not change the inherent exploit-
> ative character of the system of colonialism, i.e. capitalism. Let's
> be clear: to merely want to be "in the settler's place" means that
> you really like the system—you support the system—and you
> just complain because you're not getting your "piece of the pie."[4]

There's a direct link between the "skin analysis" of the mid-1960s
and the reasons that "Black Power" went from a revolutionary slogan to

an accommodationist one, taken up even by the rulers of capital, and reshaped as "green power" and "black capitalism" and what we today know as "empowerment" or as a call for "a piece of the action." It's no accident that the mass consciousness today is heavily "racialized," and not revolutionary, just as "black nationalism" became "ethnic pluralism" and "cultural equality" in the form pushed by the rightist tendency of Afrocentricity. The real revolutionaries were disrupted and fell by the wayside, the bourgeois forces filled the vacuum, and today the people think that "racial feeling" is the same as revolutionary thought and practice.

However, in the Third World, such questions of loyalty are not so easy and affect people's everyday existence. Globalization has helped vastly perpetuate class divisions on a worldwide scale with the associated diversity in each class. Antagonisms most clearly seen through income distribution have kept oppressed people (people of color) and Third World countries in difficult straits and drawn racial lines starkly despite post-racial pretensions.

In Latin America, where the idea of *dignidad* first rose to prominence, indigenous mobilizations have turned to the Internet and other technology to broadcast their demands for recognition and land rights as well as opposing globalization, which most often threatens the resources on which they depend and their local economies. While the Zapatistas are the best-known insurgents, organizations of Quichua, Quechua, and Aymara-speaking peoples in the Andes; the Mapuche in Chile; and Mayan indigenous groups in Guatemala are important examples as well.

Perhaps no leader in the early twenty-first century has symbolized the rise of oppressed people's internationalism and that challenge to globalization as Hugo Chávez. Venezuela's revolution united the country's diverse ethnic poor and melded strands of socialism, nationalism, and the sort of Latin American solidarity advocated by Fidel Castro years before. By arguing for the idea of participatory democracy, Chávez has emboldened oppressed people in his country to see themselves, and not the corporations who vie for Venezuela's vast oil resources, as stakeholders in their own futures. No better example of this was the soaring literacy rate during constitutional revision under Bolivarian principles (criticisms of Chávez being a nationalist rather than a revolutionary anti-capitalist notwithstanding). Venezuela's economic power in the capitalist framework and its willingness to be intransigent with the established Western authorities by wielding its might for the disenfranchised has made it a leader on the world stage.

Venezuela's rise illustrates the limitations of some political arrangements, however. The press of US imperialism has united a range of forces in the country, but also ensured the debate has not provided proper audience to various radical forces. For example, anarchist organizers, critical of the dominant sides vying for state power, struggle for footing in the shadow of Chávez and Venezuela's political elite. In 2010, instances of similar processes were visible in China, which saw a spontaneous workers' movement explode outside of established Communist Party apparatuses and as a challenge to private enterprise, and in the United States, where immigrant worker advocates mobilized nationally against regressive lawmaking supported by the political establishment. Anarchism is among the leading sets of ideas that offer an ideological break with the orders of the day, though lessons have yet to be gleaned from what a serious refutation of power *over* from all sides looks like. Regardless, even in cases where the people are putting community-oriented principles into practice, vigilance is required to ensure such aspirations are not lost in periods of compromise, revisionism, and expansion.

Whereas some have bemoaned the demise of the Third World, the energy the people of Venezuela and others offer anti-globalization forces hints at least at a reconception of what older opposition politics may have been. Whereas people of color before were thwarting the ambitions of capitalists and the attendant inequality, forced labor, and poverty that historically came with it, the push for *dignidad* signals a shift in oppressed-nation internationalist politics from such reaction to an action-oriented vision to which the majority-white First World has not been prepared to respond.

Oppressed nations going on the offensive with visions of better futures knocked the powerful off kilter and dependence on globalization hastened the decline of US political and economic power and created a crisis among US whites, whose hegemony went south, literally and figuratively. In 2009, the overwhelmingly white and conservative Tea Party movement became a mainstream media preoccupation. The Tea Party movement gained synergy with extremist white politicians apt to wage race war on countless fronts—including draconian laws against brown-skinned people while fighting undocumented immigration, banning the likes of Cesar Chávez from textbooks, and raising the specter of socialism when challenging politicians of color. The US working class, which has always enjoyed a relatively more privileged position within the global market, has historically fought solidarity with Third World workers and instead jockeyed for its own interests. Now white communities in the United States are seeing a painful set of contradictions, including internalizing middle and ruling-class interests in the name of financial security and competitive tensions with internal Third World counterparts (e.g., immigrant labor), who themselves organized mass rallies for greater inclusion in 2006 and 2010.

Far from being a surprise, the capitalist framework's need for stability requires clashes between different sectors of the working class (like white backlash to people of color) and the necessity to balance capital by marginalizing labor in the Third and First World. One need not read too far into history to find the manipulation of color and caste lines to maintain power, order, and the dominant class structure. In his essay "The Limits of Anti-Racism," Adolph Reed, Jr., points out how such issues nested insidiously:

> what the political scientist Preston Smith calls "racial democracy" came gradually to replace social democracy as a political goal— the redress of grievances that could be construed as specifically racial took precedence over the redistribution of wealth, and an individualized psychology replaced notions of reworking the material sphere. This dynamic intensified with the combination of popular demobilization in black politics and emergence of the post-segregation black political class in the 1970s and 1980s.
>
> We live under a regime now that is capable simultaneously of including black people and Latinos, even celebrating that inclusion as a fulfillment of democracy, while excluding poor people without a whimper of opposition. Of course, those most visible in the excluded class are disproportionately black and Latino, and that fact gives the lie to the celebration. Or does it really? From the standpoint of a neoliberal ideal of equality, in which classification by race, gender, sexual orientation or any other recognized ascriptive status (that is, status based on what one allegedly is rather than what one does) does not impose explicit, intrinsic or necessary limitations on one's participation and

aspirations in the society, this celebration of inclusion of blacks, Latinos and others is warranted.[5]

In the heat of this moment, fissures in class and race are forging political and economic opportunities for oppressed-nation capitalists. These participants are willing to serve dominant interests as well as splintering class in a way that tolerates Third World people internally, via undocumented immigration, for a utilitarian exchange of money to work, at little cost to capitalists (who might see a fine for hiring such workers, but no other recrimination).

The tolerance of undocumented workers, in spite of feigning the contrary, should make evident how white supremacy—which has driven much of the American project, from colonialism and racial inequality to basic teaching and socialization—is changing its hue, approach, and tenor in fundamental ways as the United States fights for its position in a changing world. Americans, who have built their fortunes on selling Americanness (cultural imperialism) to the world while, in the last generation or so, shedding key industries for cheaper consumption, no longer have work, and growing populations in the Third World and elsewhere are not interested in purchasing an American aesthetic. That the First World happens to be majority-white and its own exploited classes, as well as the Third World, happen to be majority-nonwhite, has forced critical structural changes. In this period overt racism is losing acceptability and countries traditionally thought of as Third World are rising as a result of Communist and/or socialist advances over decades in those lands.

Into this environment, the rise of Barack Obama as a politician and an icon of American leadership ushered in a new understanding for First World functionaries to ideas Third World organizers have long maintained as bitter lessons of capitalism and imperialism. The ascension of an oppressed-nation bourgeoisie may give globalization new clothes, from old-school visions of white supremacy to a business-school advocacy of dialogue, but the effects remain in essence the same. Whereas capitalism once flourished through slavery and colonialism, today developing contradictions between production, technology, the flow of transnational capital and class struggles have forged a new social order in the Third World, one that has resonating effects in the United States and First World.

Fighting Back against Capitalism

In exploring contemporary conflicts between people and capitalism, activists and scholars acknowledge how uniquely ethnicity, culture, and race play a central role in defining not only the conditions of people, but also the strategy and tactics employed in building mass operations and the revolutionary message itself. Writers like Fanon and organizers like Rameshwari Nehru and Claudia Jones helped define how issues of race, white supremacy, and the exploitation of oppressed people have reshaped our collective grasp of anti-capitalism. W. E. B. DuBois, for instance, postulated that there is a single capitalist ruling class in the United States, and that tumults such as the Civil War are therefore splits between different kinds of capitalists. Others, like poets Pablo Neruda and Khalil Gibran, tapped into the collective imaginations of the oppressed to bring about new ideas on identity, race, and politics.

Where radical white First World elements have reduced questions of race and nationality to simplistic terms—interpretations drawn from turn-of-the-twentieth-century Eastern Europe, mechanical dualities of assimilation or secession—people of color have developed anti-capitalist practice that considers cultural autonomy and community control. These efforts to challenge people of color to see themselves differently, to grasp their identities with an acknowledgement of racism while refusing to be reduced by it, have been important in emboldening forces for change.

Central to oppressed-nation and Third World fights against capitalism has been a demand to understand pertinent issues in a way outside of established Anglo models. The revolutions of the 1960s in places like Ghana, led by Kwame Nkrumah, Guinea, led by Sekou Toure, and Cuba, with Fidel Castro and Che Guevara, among others, would prove a powerful influence on oppressed people in the United States, both in terms of seeing people of color leading advancements, but also in terms of advocating alternative economic models. Even for elements that may reject the outcomes of the political visions by some of the leaders noted, as many anarchists do, learning from their successes and failures is important. In the United States, the black liberation movement presented the most important theory and practice in such a regard. As Huey Newton wrote in *To Die for the People*, initial revolutionary shocks raise consciousness long term by empowering people to meet their daily needs and helping them survive. Note the idea of survival, as opposed to the language of white capitalists of the time: economic opportunity, and the privilege of access to resources. Community survival conjures images of self-sufficiency in a unified, collective way. Newton's Black Panther Party sought to do that by launching dozens of "service to the people programs," from free plumbing and maintenance programs to land banks and child development centers. These models created work for people in the community that served a larger political purpose, while simultaneously meeting the needs of the community more generally. Further, they were an important contrast to established models that dictated people of color hustle to get loans, assimilate into the business world, amass money, learn English, and join the bourgeoisie.

Former Black Panther Party activist and anarchist community organizer Lorenzo Kom'boa Ervin is one of the more important revolutionary-left thinkers on counter-institutions. He dedicated much of his lifetime on work opposing racism and the criminal justice system, careful to point out its relationship to capitalism:

> The prison system is the armed fist of the State, and is a system for State slavery. It is not really for "criminals" or other "social deviants," and it does not exist for the "protection of society." It is for State social control and political repression. Thus, it must be opposed at every turn and ultimately destroyed altogether… Organizing against the enemy legal and penal system is both offensive and defensive. It is carried on with individuals, groups and among the masses in the community. We must inform the people on a large scale of the atrocities and inhumanity of the prisons, the righteousness of our struggle, and the necessity of their full participation and support. We must organize our communities to attack the prison system as a moral and social abomination, and we must fight to free all political/class war prisoners.[6]

Groups like Critical Resistance (CR) and Anarchist Black Cross note that prisons are tools of control. CR and the Jericho Movement have rallied thousands to fight capitalist expansions such as private prisons, super-maximum facilities, and more. In his 2010 political report to the African People's Socialist Party fifth congress, Omali

Yeshitela took it further, saying US laws are illegitimate because of the manner in which the country was founded and that dominant sections paint incarceration and settler-colonial justice in democratic terms rather than for the oppressive tactics they are.

While addressing US examples, it should also be noted in these efforts how people of color have actively fought capitalism by refuting assumptions among some sectors of the Left, which confuse white supremacy and the fundamentally reactive nature of white racial identity. Racism, for writers like Oliver Cox, is a social attitude among individuals that compliments the capitalist exploitation of people of color. Perceptions of white group power among individual whites give attitudinal racism much of its virulence. Kali Akuno is among a new generation with roots in the black liberation cause who are organizing and furthering theoretical frameworks most read in US political circles. Many new reviews of people of color–based anti-capitalism come with the understanding that the subjugation of black and all oppressed people is rooted in not merely the structures and needs of the US capitalist system, but in the privileges of ordinary whites. Simply renouncing whiteness, as some theorists advocate, avoids myriad social, political, and cultural histories and realities.

Some characteristics of anti-capitalism led by people of color which have retouched our understanding of the substance of these concerns include aggressive efforts to reeducate members and supporters about themselves and their relationship with the world. Mao Zedong, for example, suggested that restructuring society also meant remaking people to conceive of their relation to their world in new ways. The Young Lords Party, a Puerto Rican national liberation formation with bases most prominently in New York City and Chicago, organized men's groups to combat patriarchy, largely at the behest of women leaders in the organization like Iris Morales and Denise Oliver, and to retool the ways revolutionary men related to their female counterparts. Johanna Fernandez, writing about Oliver in *Want to Start a Revolution? Radical Women in the Black Freedom Struggle*, presents Oliver's viewpoint on the necessity for organizing within the community clearly:

> Responding to the feminist critique of nationalist women, the Young Lords emphasized that race and class cast a complexity on their oppression, which could not be understood or analyzed

by Anglo feminism. Oliver and others argued that these "right wing" women's groups, for example, did not take into account the exploited conditions of Third World women who, by virtue of race, were used as a cheap source of labor and paid significantly lower wages than white women.[7]

Globally, many of these outbreaks have openly condemned ideas of US exceptionalism and entitlement.

So much of US history avoids or obscures the forging of "democracy" in a way that explains the savagery, impunity, and sheer number of crimes committed against people of color in the United States. Historical events are taught and explained in a way that removes the event from context, while an ahistorical lens is applied to history itself. The slaughter of Native Americans, raw seizure of the Southwest United States, and chattel slavery of Blacks for cotton profiteering—all crimes without subsequent correction of injustice—are almost exclusively understood in shorthand. Roxanne Dunbar-Ortiz addresses the romanticism in "The Grid of History: Cowboys and Indians":

> Reconciling empire and liberty was a historic obsession of U.S. political thinkers and historians, in the twenty-first century openly being debated once again. Thomas Jefferson had hailed the United States as an "empire for liberty." Andrew Jackson coined the phrase "extending the area of freedom" to describe the process in which slavery had been introduced into Texas in violation of governing Mexican laws, to be quickly followed by a slaveholder's rebellion and U.S. annexation. The term "freedom" became a euphemism for the continental and worldwide expansion of the world's leading slave power. The contradictions, particularly since the initial rationalization for U.S. independence was anti-empire, are multiple.[8]

It should come as no surprise why many important Third World revolutionaries reject capitalist democracy as a model. Going still further, anti-authoritarians, and those comprising what may be regarded as an ultra-left wing, critique all power relationships. Such is presented oftentimes less as the necessity of no power at all (Jo Freeman, most popularly, reminds organizers that, in the absence of no one having power, the connected and cunning will rule), but more an issue of exploring new ways to guide our collective dreams.

In India, this has included a massive people's war, based among the country's poorest and most oppressed ethnic groups and aimed at dismantling the Indian government and its complicity with Western capitalism. The so-called Naxalites, christened after the state of Naxalbari, argue that economic advancement for the poor has meant ancestral lands are stolen and large tracts are literally given away to create factories which serve multinational corporations. Though their tactics are widely criticized, with people like Prashad condemning them in 2010, the Naxalites' takeovers of entire districts is indicative of wide support among oppressed people in India, but also other classes dissatisfied with how globalization and Western business has made powerful countries like China and India semi-colonial in many respects.

South America's many populist mutinies, which have demanded autonomy in resource control, provide a fresh understanding of colonialism's history and dynamics that are creating new realities. Globalization in Latin and South America is a product of market-driven neoliberal economic and political policies, many of which the International Monetary Fund (IMF) and World Bank (WB) enforced with First World support. In Mexico, *ejidos* (communal lands) once protected under the Constitution, were eliminated and the lands sold to corporations. Other issues bringing about conflicts, such as "structural readjustment," have meant eliminating aid for peasant farmers and poor people to buy food, privatized social services, an end to wage supports, and undermining of networks in Bolivia, Peru, and Nicaragua. IMF/WB dabbling coupled with the North American Free Trade Agreement for Mexico, and the corresponding Central American Free Trade Agreement, can be seen as the basis for explosive riseups that have taken off as a reaction to what many see as the sabotage of the subject country's autonomy for economic ends. In no other context could leaders like Ecuador's President Rafael Correa be so bold as to pledge the reexamination of debts in 2007 to determine their legitimacy, as well as to reject US trade agreements for the potential damage (and inflation) they would do to the poor in his country.

These exciting models are but a few of the many ways people of color are challenging capitalism and oppression. They are also creating alternative institutions intended for subsistence and options for oppressed peoples outside of the master-servant structure of capitalism, while likewise engaging in acts of courageous resistance to globalization, all efforts which face potential destruction internally and externally. Mobo Gao writes in *The Battle for China's Past: Mao and the Cultural Revolution* how China's current history is often told by and from the perspective of those whose privilege was threatened during the Cultural Revolution, those with Western patrons and others who were not direct beneficiaries of anti-capitalist reforms, namely peasants and the poor. Thus, rather than an engagement with impoverished communities to gain an understanding of their suffering and the land redistribution during this period for the majority's needs, in universities and Western flash-card historical reports a generation later, the narrative is solely of slave labor camps, torture, and hate. This is another example of the consequences of using ahistorical perspectives. Third World anti-capitalist victories, Gao implies, may ultimately be undone by people intent on serving the capitalist impulse:

> In the enterprise of constructing the past through the discourse of the present, remembering the Cultural Revolution as a nightmare identifies with the West, its values and its way of life, especially these of the United States. This is not surprising due to the hegemonic position of the West headed by the United States. The political, economic and military superiority can easily be translated as superiority in cultural and life value. These globally dominant values are therefore taken as universally and transcendentally true.[9]

Replace "Cultural Revolution" with any battle led by the oppressed and anyone can easily see why such observations raise the stakes for Third World anti-capitalism even higher—and how these historical narratives need to account for complexities that are currently ignored.

Interrogating the Future

People of color and the Third World will most assuredly continue to fight the impact transnational capitalism has had on oppressed communities. Examples of revolutionary resistance are prominent today, but the Third World has seen more reactionary responses, including xenophobia, retreats into patriotism, patriarchy, dictatorships, and militarism. Indeed, the questions for politics related to people of color and anti-capitalism are multifaceted.

Internationalism tends toward various fixed sciences and contradictions that are a part of the sum of history. However, Third World understandings (as well as the theory and praxis most associated with thinkers such as Gloria Anzaldua and Patricia Hill Collins) of race, ethnicity, and culture have helped to create a "subjectivity of oppression." Yet culture cannot be dissolved into economics, and race relations cannot be fetishized in a way that holds boundaries around racial identity categories as political objectives in themselves. How organizers of color integrate internationalism and intersectionality's recognition of multiple subjectivities will be monumental as political upheavals gel.

Radical white revolutionary tendencies such as First World socialism and anarchism have not adequately responded to the ways people of color and the Third World have taken on capitalism. Most tragically, tailism, practiced as an incorrect abstraction of Leninist or anti-authoritarian ideals, has taken hold in isolated quarters. Tailing oppressed-nation turbulence was most clearly expressed in US claims by people of color for national independence, a demand which has always been a marginal one among people of color, as it does not appear to offer a solution to capitalism and imperialism which are wrecking the Third World through transnational economic relationships. Worse, a profoundly conservative thrust argues that all revolutionaries should fall in line simply because oppressed-nation First World people or Third World forces make a call, without examining the aspirations, or possible consequences, of that call.

In the same breath, one of Marxism's most stunning failures, and a major obstacle to relevance beyond shorthand in the new millennium, has been a chronic inability to understand race and to dismiss racial oppression in favor of economism and reductionism. Such critiques paradoxically reduce race and gender to personal identity and competitors to class, thus missing their material basis and the ways they intersect with class. In what respects? Cultural norms, when used to divide labor into dominant groups and the Other, give the idea of internal colonization validity, particularly in the development of the US Empire. Likewise, the Communist International admirably stood at various points in time with national independence in the Third World, while denying cultural self-determination at a community level in its own project of Othering. That such an antiquated analysis (which was originally used to describe oppressed groups of the time such as the Polish people becoming a majority culture and economic power) is a default position stands as a glaring error that does not see the particularity of race in the United States, among other regions. Anarchists, however, need not, and should not, be limited by vulgar Marxism's stultifying reductionism.

To be fair, Third World and oppressed-nation fermentations have not had all the answers either. In truth, Third World liberation trends and oppressed-nation First World people of color can both look upon failures of their own revolutionary moments and turning points where eruptions were unable to respond to political, social, economic, and cultural conditions.

Theoretical tussles include how capitalism has shaped the most complex questions of various liberation movements' perceived goals and ideas of self-determination and autonomy. How do communities effectively address matters of privilege and power when those ascending the ladder are members of the oppressed-nation's bourgeoisie?

In Mexico, the release of the major-studio motion picture *Frida*, on the life of multiethnic artist and communist activist Frida Kahlo, brought on a dialogue. Culture and politics, writers articulated, must define identity rather than national origin and ethnicity. Globalization has exacerbated an interdependent but unequal relationship between the United States and Mexico, writes Isabel Molina-Guzmán in *Dangerous Curves: Latina Bodies in the Media*, and US-based representations of Latin American icons take on some gravity related to how culture and politics collide. Molina-Guzmán sums it up this way:

> Ethnic identity is not fixed; rather it is in a constant state of formation and reformulation as it responds to the ever-shifting terrain of post-colonial global culture…. By questioning how we are represented, we are provided the opportunity to redefine ourselves and in redefining ourselves critique dominant systems of social signification. Competing constructions of ethnic identity provide an opportunity to negotiate the symbolic colonization of Latinidad and open up more fluid understandings of the mediated performance of gendered Latinidad.[10]

However, much work in the political realm remains in process. How can those committed to the revolutionary project clarify these relationships further?

Akuno and others stress dialectical perceptions by people of color of anti-capitalism. Concerned people should look at the essence of every happening, separating out what is positive and revolutionary from what is negative and reactionary. Some storms, after a thorough analysis, are capitalist at their core, through the positions for which they speak in support.

Eric Mann, in discussing the 2001 World Conference against Racism hosted in Durban, South Africa, notes that an effective strategy would require organizers to understand openly the strengths and weaknesses of capitalism and imperialism.

> Whether under Republican or Democratic tactical leadership, the strategy of U.S imperialism is to rule the world. In a society in which big business is king, U.S. led monopoly capitalism relies on profits and superprofits from Third World nations. It achieves these objectives by "integrating" Third World nations into an international economy structurally dominated by the IMF, World Bank, WTO, NATO, and yes, the UN, which in turn, are controlled by the U.S. Under this totalitarian capitalist system, Third World nations are systematically underdeveloped through a global network that destroys their local industries, obliterates protective tariffs, penetrates their local markets, privatizes their national and natural resources, and impounds cash crops to feed Western banks. As Christian charities get rich exploiting pictures of emaciated Third World children, they exhibit a racist blind spot where they refuse to connect the dots between Third World poverty and first world wealth, between structural racism and U.S. imperialism.[11]

These issues are most certainly salient, and perhaps likely soon to be addressed.

In 1999, a host of Third World countries, including from the Caribbean and Asia, fought back against Western interests on key economic and trade issues. Solidarity by thousands of protesters in Seattle gave punch to the anti-globalization actions. Years later, the Third

World and oppressed-nation First World people of color keep fighting. Whether modern populism evolves into a genuinely anti-capitalist vision or one in which nationalist impulses will further divide internal classes is yet to be seen. However, it is the idea of dignity that the world can put off no longer.

ENDNOTES

1   "The Structural Crisis of Politics," *Monthly Review*, September 2006, http://monthlyreview.org/2006/09/01/the-structural-crisis-of-politics.

2   C. L. R. James, *You Don't Play With Revolution: The Montreal Lectures of C. L. R. James* (Oakland: AK Press, 2009), 56.

3   Robin D. G. Kelly, *Freedom Dreams: The Black Radical Imagination* (Boston: Beacon Press, 2002), 67.

4   James Yaki Sayles, *Meditations on Frantz Fanon's Wretched of the Earth: New Afrikan Revolutionary Writings* (Montreal: Kersplebedeb/Spear and Shield, 2010), 246–247.

5   Adolph Reed, Jr., "The Limits of Anti-Racism," http://www.leftbusinessobserver.com/Antiracism.html (accessed October 6, 2011).

6   Lorenzo Kom'boa Ervin, "Purpose of the Movement," in *A Draft Proposal for an Anarchist Black Cross Network*, http://www.spunk.org/texts/groups/abc/sp001498/purpose.html (accessed October 6, 2011).

7   Johanna Fernandez, *Want to Start a Revolution? Radical Women in the Black Freedom Struggle* (New York: New York University Press, 2009), 287.

8   Roxanne Dunbar-Ortiz, "The Grid of History: Cowboys and Indians," *Monthly Review*, July/August 2003, http://monthlyreview.org/2003/07/01/the-grid-of-history-cowboys-and-indians (accessed October 6, 2011).

9   Mobo Gao, *The Battle for China's Past: Mao and the Cultural Revolution* (London: Pluto Press, 2008), 37.

10 Isabel Molina-Guzmán, *Dangerous Curves: Latina Bodies in the Media* (New York: New York University Press, 2010), 117.

11 Eric Mann, "On to Durban: Putting the Heat on the U.S.," *Durban Dispatch #1*, http://www.frontlinespress.org.

Part 6
Vision

"The bourgeoisie may blast and burn its own world before it finally leaves the stage of history. We are not afraid of ruins. We who ploughed the prairies and built the cities can build again, only better next time. We carry a new world, here in our hearts. That world is growing this minute."—Buenaventura Durruti

Chopping Off the Invisible Hand: Internal Problems with Markets and Anarchist Theory, Strategy, and Vision[1]

Deric Shannon

With capitalism in crisis (again), people all over the world are looking for alternatives. It makes sense that people are, as it should be all but obvious to anyone by now that capitalism is prone to crises and that if we want a decent world, we need to organize it in some other way. Anarchists typically don't stop with wanting an end to the existing economy (or in the parlance of some, abolish "economy" altogether), but also argue generally against all forms of domination and various oppressions. The best of us realize that these different forms of domination intersect in complex ways throughout social life, and so our theories and strategies reflect that understanding.

One alternative among anarchists has been a market form of socialism called *mutualism*. This was both a strategic and visionary economic argument detailed first by Proudhon, which he modeled after what he experienced and observed among sections of workers in Lyon, France in the early nineteenth century.[2] Proudhon argued that worker-owned and managed firms could replace capitalist firms, abolish wage slavery, and create a world where every worker had access to his/her own means of production, either individually or collectively. Since capitalism rests on the ability of capitalists to pay workers a fraction of the value that they produce and keep the rest in profits by virtue of their ownership of the means of production, worker ownership and self-management would rid us of those social relations. Proudhon envisioned a world where these worker-owned and self-managed firms would compete in a stateless market—a socialist market that was regulated by a grand agro-industrial federation.

Proudhon initially made his arguments for mutualist strategy and vision (the two are always intimately tied) well over a century ago. But market forms of socialism have seen a rise in popularity, as we might expect as people begin to question the nature, logic, and "necessity" of capitalism. For example, Schweickart's work on what he calls "economic democracy" has been translated into multiple languages and enjoys wide support.[3] Mutualists write and agitate with groups like the Center for a Stateless Society and the Alliance of the Libertarian Left. Even UK Conservative Party member Francis Maude has suggested that public sector workers might form cooperatives.[4]

In this chapter, I'd like to lay out some broad critiques of market socialism generally, but specifically the anarchist current practiced by the workers of Lyon all those years ago and articulated by Proudhon and his contemporaries (this is, after all, a collection of writings on *anarchist* economics)—mutualism. I'm a libertarian communist, so many of my criticisms aren't going to be all that new to others of my anti-political persuasion, but I hope along the way I can at least say some old things in new and useful ways. There's also been a rise in interest in mutualism in the United States, with this newer form borrowing from some of American anarchism's tradition of individualists like Benjamin Tucker and Josiah Warren. And with interest in alternatives to capitalism on the rise, this might be a decent place for anarchist communists to intervene. So what follows is a brief critique of what I see as some of the theoretical and strategic shortcomings of mutualism, and particularly—perhaps most importantly—why we might want to reject markets as a part of any post-capitalist vision.

Theory

The state lies at the center of modern mutualist theory and I find myself agreeing with parts of how they analyze the state, but mostly disagreeing with their conclusions. One of the more intelligent and prolific mutualists, Carson, writes that "(a)s a mutualist anarchist, I believe that expropriation of surplus value—i.e., capitalism—cannot occur without state coercion to maintain the privilege of usurer, landlord, and capitalist."[5] So far so good.

Indeed, capitalist social relations require the state to manage the class antagonisms that arise as a result of the private ownership of productive property. Capitalists accrue surplus value from workers by paying them a portion of what they produce (i.e., wages) and stealing the rest in the form of profits. The state protects this arrangement with violence—absent the protection provided by the state, workers could just take the means of production and the full social product of our labors and do with it as we please. But the fiction of private property is reinforced by the fiction of the state—and these mythologies, these fundamentally *religious* and *mystical* features embedded in our social organization, allow the expropriation of surplus value. On this, we agree.

The problems arise when modern mutualists suggest that then "(i) t is statism that is at the root of all the exploitative features of capitalism."[6] Further, "it follows that it is sufficient to eliminate the statist props to capitalism."[7] This comes rather intuitively from the work of past American individualists who tended to reduce anarchism to anti-statism. Tucker, for example, defined anarchism as "*the doctrine that all the affairs of men should be managed by individuals or voluntary associations, and that the State should be abolished.*"[8] Thus, abolishing the state was "the fundamental article" of anarchism (here referring to anarchism as articulated by Proudhon and Warren)—"it is the doctrine which Proudhon named An-archism" and anarchists are reduced to "simply unterrified Jeffersonian Democrats."[9] Mutualists, then, trade the "primary contradiction" of vulgar economism with a new "root" for all social ills—in this case the state. This leads to sloppy and ill-considered theory (which of course leads to sloppy and ill-considered strategy and vision).

After all, the market isn't isolated from the rest of human experience. And, of course, with the help of the state, capitalism is embedded in our current market practices—but not just capitalism. We are, after all, anarchists—opposed to *all* relations of domination. Likewise embedded in market practices are patriarchy, assumptions of "normal" and "able" bodies, white supremacy, rigid and heavily policed categories for gender and sexuality—this list could get quite long. And these relations of domination, far from having a "root" that can be attacked to resolve the rest, intersect together in our institutional arrangements as well as our daily lives.

When mutualists propose that the state lies at the heart of our relations of ruling, where do we find these other forms of domination? Their theory treats the state as a root, ignoring the role of patriarchy, for example, in laying the foundations for primitive accumulation and the development of capitalism *and* the state.[10] Similarly, if we see the state as a first-order hierarchy, structuring the economy and the rest of our social relations that spring from it, it ignores an analysis of the role of white supremacy in the construction of the modern social order. Thus, historical developments from how the slave economy developed modern American capitalism, and by extension the global economy[11] to the role of different eras of white supremacy and their own economic hallmarks, such as Jim Crow in the United States or the strategic use of racial divisions in strike-breaking[12] are all reduced to "statism" in this formulation.

Now all of this isn't to suggest that the state does *not* buttress these institutional arrangements—it does. The state was used to codify slavery, implemented Jim Crow, and backed capital in its use of strike-breaking. But, at the same time, these other relations of domination buttress the state itself. That is, there is *no root* and our relations of ruling are intricately tied together. Further, to assume otherwise is to make all kinds of errors in theory and strategy, springing from those reductionist assumptions. Ackelsberg notes in her excellent book on the Mujeres Libres, a group of anarchist women formed during the Spanish Civil War, how historically many anarchists—and these anarchist women in particular—refused the class reductionism of parts of the syndicalist movement that saw capitalism as the primary contradiction.[13] This led to "many anarchists" treating "the issue of women's subordination as, at best, secondary to the emancipation of workers, a problem that would be resolved 'on the morrow of the revolution,'" an idea that the Mujeres Libres struggled against.[14] Unfortunately, mutualist theory makes the same mistake in regards to the state—the supposed "root" of capitalism, leaving the rest to be resolved after we first do away with the state.

Contemporarily, the question of reductionism and primary contradictions is perhaps best answered by black feminists and womanists who put forward the theory of intersectionality.[15] In response to debates in the movements of the '60s and '70s in the United States regarding the origin of oppression and exploitation, feminists began having internal discussions about how we might identify and attack this "root" of social oppression.[16] Following the Combahee River Collective statement,[17] many feminists stopped seeing a need for identifying a single source for domination. Rather, they argued that relations of domination intersect in complex ways and aren't reducible to a single foundation. To fight against any form of subjugation is to recognize the need to fight against them all. This lends itself nicely to anarchist analyses—particularly where feminists account for anarchist calls to demolish the state and capitalism.[18]

And reducing capitalism to this single origin compromises anarchist theory in some rather head-spinning ways. Some modern mutualists, for example, write and work alongside so-called "anarcho"-capitalists. After all, these capitalists oppose the state too. And if we can just work together with these defenders of wage labor, private property, and hired protection (because someone has to keep the workers' hands off of those productive assets somehow without the state around to help) we can end the state—and then capitalism falls? It's a rather interesting case of circular reasoning, even leading Carson at one point to refer to the likes of Murray Rothbard, who once bragged about capturing the word "libertarian" from his "enemies"[19] (i.e. anarchists) as "intellectually honest."[20]

But anarchism has always been socialist—and since the early twentieth century is typically *communist*. Anarchists oppose all forms of domination and exploitation and this includes capitalism—we always have. It is an insult to the memory of the thousands of anarchists who have died or been imprisoned fighting *against capitalism* to suggest otherwise. And it is a compromise beyond all strategic reasoning to suggest that we can unite with capitalists against the state in order to end capitalism. But not so for mutualists, who see the state as capitalism's root. Indeed, to end capitalism we will also need to bring an end to all relations of domination—as they mutually reinforce one another (this, of course, also means smashing capitalism).

I want to be clear that I'm not suggesting that we refuse to work in campaigns with supporters of capitalism—including those who oppose the state. Mass organizations and campaigns include folks with all sorts of ideas and we shouldn't require a litmus test to organize with people (although we might engage in some activities where it makes sense to limit it to people we have some basic agreements with). But we should make a few things clear in our movement activities. First, as mutualists correctly note, capitalism cannot exist without the state. There can be no stateless capitalism, so arguing for it is a dead end in and of itself. Secondly, anarchists are opposed to capitalism, as we are opposed to all relations of domination. We are opposed to wage labor—the ability for people to own productive property and expropriate the surplus value created by others who use it. There are no "anarcho"-capitalists.

A Few Words on Strategy

Theory, strategy, and vision are intimately connected, so I wanted to also say a few words on mutualist strategy. Again, much to the credit of mutualists, they recognize some fundamental necessities in strategy—particularly if we want an end to capitalism and not just buffers to make it kinder to working people:

> For labor to wage a successful class war, it must think in terms of war, not "rights" or "the law." The mainstream unions are psychologically addicted to the legacy of the New Deal "social compact." Their inability to think outside the limits of the NLRB process is a severe handicap. Labor must think in terms of war, using all the means at their disposal, limited only by srategy [*sic*] and by their own sense of justice, without regard to "established procedures."[21]

Indeed, here again we are agreed. But in the same document, Carson doesn't seem to be advocating for "war" elsewhere. For one, as we might expect from someone who sees the state as capitalism's "root," there is nothing there in his "political program for anarchists" on how to deal with patriarchy, white supremacy, heteronormativity, and so on. Again, anarchists—opposed to all relations of domination—should have *something* to say about those things. We've certainly not come to big agreements on how to deal with those hierarchical divisions, but we shouldn't ignore them. And putting them into this *mutualist* framework might be interesting (can the invisible hand strangle patriarchy, for example?). To be fair, I did see an attempt to account for some of these things when I looked over some of the material of the Alliance of the Libertarian Left, but capitalism wasn't roundly condemned in those materials (nor was its role in maintaining these other hierarchical divisions recognized).

Beyond that, much of Carson's strategy in his political program mirrors Proudhon's—mutual banking, the creation of cooperatives, the mutualization of public services, and so on. This is a reformist position in the classical sense—we hold off until that last possible moment for confrontation. We might learn here from Martin and Barrot's *communization*:

> Communization, on the contrary, will circulate goods without money, open the gate isolating a factory from its neighbourhood,

close down another factory where the work process is too alienating to be technically improved, do away with school as a specialized place which cuts off learning from doing for 15 odd years, pull
down walls that force people to imprison themselves in 3-room
family units—in short, it will tend to break all separations.[22]

Here there is no waiting, no markets, no cooperative islands in a sea
of capitalism, but the conscious creation of communism in our lives—
the expansion of that which exists into other spheres of life, breaking
those separations and opening wide those cracks of possibility in the
here and now. It is neither an admonition to wait for confrontation
or attack, nor is it a suggestion that we wait for a Great Revolutionary Event that ends history, but a suggestion that we intervene in our
daily lives now and take what belongs to us—everything. This means
we can attack and expropriate this moment and that confrontation
isn't some far-off wish while we create *infrastructure*—indeed, these
confrontations and expropriations *are* infrastructure.

The creation of alternative institutions figures high in mutualist
strategy and has done so since the time of Proudhon. Again, I would
agree that we need to create alternatives to replace the existing society
(at our best, in the process of destroying the old, we create the new—as
Bakunin noted over a century ago). And so Proudhon saw the creation of mutual aid societies, mutual credit and banking associations,
worker-owned and operated public services (taken from the purview
and direction of the state), and so on as steps out of the existing order. Similarly, and as we might expect from a *market* socialist, he saw
worker cooperatives as central to his strategy for slowly evolving us out
of capitalism. But cooperatives, as a demand under capitalism, suffer
from what Kay describes as *self-exploitation*:

> *Thus the problem is not how capital is managed, but that it is capital*,
> regardless of who manages it or how democratically they do
> so…the assets of a co-op do not cease being capital when votes
> are taken on how they are used within a society of generalised
> commodity production and wage labour. That is to say there
> remains an imperative to accumulate with all the drive to mi-
> nimise the labour time taken to do a task this requires, even in
> a co-op….A firm operating in a competitive market—as would

certainly be the case with firms *"about to go bust"*—must generate enough surplus to re-invest in expanding output and new technology to maintain or improve its market position relative to its rivals. That is to say the firm—as a concentration of capital—has a logic of its own. It needs to be nourished by surplus living labour or it will whither [*sic*] and perish. As dead labour, it must vampire-like suck life from the living, and lives the more, the more it sucks.[23]

In other words, market pressures come to bear on cooperatives as they do with any other business under capitalism (and would under competitive market socialism). Now, this doesn't mean that cooperatives are necessarily *bad* or that self-managed enterprises under capitalism cannot teach us any lessons. Indeed, even minimal decision-making and participation in our work lives under capitalism can point to alternatives to how we've organized our social world(s) (nearly completely *without* our participation, and certainly so in most of our lives at work). But cooperatives as a strategy out of capitalism contain their own internal problems, along with the markets that they assume. And these problems persist into mutualist post-capitalist vision.

Vision

Carson writes that a mutualist world would be "a world of decentralized, small-scale production for local use, owned and controlled by those who did the work—as different from our world as day from night, or freedom from slavery."[24] I agree. It would differ from our existing society vastly. But two questions arise for me. One, would such a world remain *socialist*? Secondly, is market socialism—retaining markets, competition among firms, negative externalities, production as a separate sphere of life (i.e., "work" and "jobs")—really *enough*?

I said before that I particularly objected to markets in terms of post-capitalist vision. A part of this is because it's hard for me to see societies that advocate for market socialism, as such, as remaining *socialist*. I do think that if we recognize a need for a *stateless* socialism that people will try all sorts of experiments along the way. Communism would be rather meaningless if it were forced onto workers (I'm comfortable forcing it onto our exploiters) and without a state to force a single vision onto people, post-capitalism will take on a lot of different forms in different areas. Workers will likely attempt market forms of socialism. They already are doing so *strategically* in the cooperative movement, though much of it has lost its socialist character or desire to move beyond capitalism (a reflection of what might come of market socialism without a push to go beyond it?). But arguing for markets as an end goal seems to me to be asking for a return to the same kinds of exploitative relations we have currently. Markets force pressures for profiting in the process of competition. And it's hard for me to see mutuality within this competitive sphere. When cooperative firms are able to accumulate at greater rates than others, how does this not lead to greater inequalities that form the basis for the kinds of accumulation that precedes capitalism?

This is a bit of a presumption, admittedly—none of us know what a post-capitalist society will look like (though we see glimpses when we live and observe these relations in embryonic form and attempt to embody the values we promote in struggle). Workers, having abolished themselves as a class, (are creating and) will create what that future society looks like. It won't be dictated by theorists, although I do think it's incumbent on anti-capitalists to put forward our best guesses (and to do so humbly and *as guesses* rather than certainties). And in our lives, for libertarian communists, that means creating the content of communism. Thus, rather than seeing the present as a set of what exists at a given moment, we might reorient to seeing it as sets of *becoming*—of emerging conditions in a historical process in which we, the dispossessed and exploited, are players and not passive spectators.

But, one might ask, why would you criticize market socialism as a post-capitalist vision—as a best guess as to where going beyond capitalism might lead us? Mainly because markets have internal problems that create inequality and because I think they tend to dissolve, rather than create, social solidarity.

First and foremost, markets are not participatory. That is, rather than planning our social lives (or, better yet, *living*), we leave those things to the proverbial "invisible hand." We "participate" inasmuch as we guess at what we should produce (actually, typically our bosses *calculate* what we produce, though presumably we would do so ourselves under market socialism) and we consume what we can create or what is made available to us through the market. We remove our selves from the process and replace them with the motive to profit.

Relatedly, market allocation has negative externalities attached to it. Things like air pollution, to name one (perhaps tired) example, aren't consented to by third parties outside of the exchange arrangements between a given producer and buyer of a good (say, a particularly gas-guzzling car, to stick with this example). In the process of market competition, these negative externalities are produced without the consent of third parties. So while "free trade" is typically seen as a consensual exchange of goods on a market, it says nothing about the consent of affected third parties. A society where we are free to create our own lives would be a society where we have a part in the decision-making process for those things that affect us to the degree that they do affect us. Markets are anathema to that kind of participation and active creation.

The biggest negative externality of markets, I think, is what they do (and what they would do under market socialism) to social solidarity. If worker-managed firms compete in the market, it means that the income of those workers is tied to how well their firm performs. Some groups of workers will have greater access to the social product as a result of how they manage their workplaces or what they have access to within it. Some will have better equipment, better capacities in the individuals of their workplace collectives, and so on.

This undermines social solidarity in that it pits workers against one another for greater access to the social product. It can generate unemployment, as self-managed firms can lower their expenses by ridding themselves of workers—in much the same way that companies "downsize" under capitalism. With workplaces competing for access to the social product through the market, the greater the firm can maximize its surplus, the greater the income of the workers becomes—thus, this access to added income incentivizes layoffs and unemployment if a firm can maintain output without the need for (perhaps less productive) parts of their workforce.

Similarly, market competition incentivizes negative externalities and can actually *de-incentivize* positive externalities. With income being tied to the success of a given firm, this provides a motivation for shifting social costs onto others. To return to the example of air pollution, equipment to minimize such pollution can be costly. In a market society, since the income of workers is tied to the success of the firm in market competition, polluting can increase the income of a given set of workers. Relatedly, if a given workplace cannot profit from a social *good*, it de-incentivizes those positive externalities (in this case, clean air).

And importantly, this kind of competition erodes the kinds of values that motivate most anarchists (even most mutualists). The self-interested profit-seeking of market allocation—even with the kinds of checks in place suggested by mutualists (such as Proudhon's agro-industrial federation or price fixing)—promotes an ethic of each against the rest. Under capitalism we are taught that ethic as *individuals*. Were we to compete in a market of self-managed firms, we would learn that ethic as collectivities.

Further, mutualism still assumes the workplace and job as spheres of life separated from the rest of human experience. Rather than ridding ourselves of this fundamental form of human alienation, it retains those separations. This means a couple of important things. One, markets would still serve as a primary source of socialization for children—for people. For example, if a firm can profit from making women feel like shit about their bodies and then produce a product to "fix" that problem, then it incentivizes heavily policed and impossible standards of beauty for women. Markets can create material incentives for the kinds of socialization processes where we are separated from inventing our sense of self outside of those pervasive market relations.

This also means that we've retained the workplace—that dreaded place where we waste our time, mostly bored out of our minds and pushed to grind harder and harder, chasing access to commodities (as the workplace is where we are tied to in order to access the social product through compulsory labor). We maintain the kinds of rational and calculable processes that govern capitalist social life. For libertarian communists, it is not enough that we share some measurable and calculable social product. We do not solely want a quantitative shift in how we allocate goods. We want a qualitative shift in how we organize our social world. What might society look like if, rather than being organized around profit, rational exchange, and calculated self-interest, we organized our world around fundamentally different values like pleasure, desire, or even adventure? What might the world look like if we weren't so concerned with questions like "How much?" but instead asked questions like "How well?" Does alienation and atomization that is self-managed sound like the kind of alternative we should be fighting for? I think we can, and should, ask for (and take) much more.

This might also lead us out of a productivist mind-set and into a world where we stop producing so much useless shit.

For the Accumulation of Freedom

I think that mutualists get some very basic things right. The private ownership of the means of production, expropriation of the surplus value produced by workers, the command structures in the workplace—all of these things are part and parcel of capitalism and mutualists rightly reject them. If we see the creation of communism as a process—as an activity of the dispossessed—then we are likely going to see experiments in market socialism along the way, as the idea resonates with many people. I do hope this critique is taken in the spirit in which I intend it—not to denounce mutualist economics or market socialism, but to explain why libertarian communists create different content in that process of making the future and why anarchists might reject a theory, strategy, and vision revolving around markets.

In their theory, I think mutualists are right to suggest that the state protects the social relations of capitalism. But I think they're wrong to suggest that it is the root of capitalism—as if dismantling the state alone can rid ourselves of the complex and intersecting relations of ruling we live under. Further, it confuses primitive accumulation and the creation of capitalism by ignoring the roles of other relations of domination in creating and supporting both capitalism *and* the state. This, of course, leads to ill-considered strategy.

Again the mutualist Kevin Carson is right to suggest that working people need to stop thinking in terms of social fictions like "rights" and make war with capital and the state. But in his program, no doubt due to seeing the state as a primary contradiction, he has nothing to say about non-class oppressions. And the mutualist strategy, centered on the market, of creating alternative institutions and reforming our way out of capitalism—particularly through mutual credit and cooperative business enterprises—bleeds into the visionary problems with mutualism.

Mutualists correctly assert that we must move beyond capitalism. But maintaining markets in a post-capitalist society maintains the atomization of any profit and competition-oriented system. Further, it incentivizes negative externalities and de-incentivizes positive externalities. It pits workers against one another in competition over access to the social product. And it maintains the workplace as a separate sphere of life and organizes our social world on the same rational, calculable controls that are part and parcel of capitalist alienation.

Libertarian communism, I would argue, is something we create the content for in our struggles and will often look different than that produced by market socialists, though we do have sentiments that we agree on. While we can't create a perfect world, I do think we can create a better one. And I believe that we should reach for the most utopian of possibilities while doing so. While guesses about what a future society might look like can provide us with some possibilities for inquisitive folks, ultimately the creation of post-capitalist society is the task of all of the dispossessed—not solely theorists. To me, this movement is communism and its future is yet unwritten, but is *becoming*.

ENDNOTES

1   I'd like to thank Matt Ignal, Zach Blue, Abbey Volcano, Tom Wetzel, John Asimakopoulos, and Bill Armaline for comments that helped me write this piece. I know none of you agree completely with my particular perspective, but your advice helped tremendously, though all errors, mistakes, and so on belong to me alone.

2   For an excellent contemporary collection of Proudhon's work, see Iain McKay, ed. *Property Is Theft!: A Pierre-Joseph Proudhon Anthology* (Oakland, CA: AK Press, 2011).

3   See David Schweickart, *Against Capitalism* (Cambridge: Cambridge University Press, 1996); and David Schweickart, *After Capitalism* (Lanham, MD: Rowman and Littlefield, 2002). For the interested reader, there are a few debates between Schweickart and Michael Albert, one of the minds behind "participatory economics," precisely over market socialism, cataloged in various places on the internet.

4   "Public Sector Workers Urged to Form Co-operatives," *Guardian*, November 17, 2010, http://www.guardian.co.uk/society/2010/nov/17/public-sector-workers-co-operatives (accessed June 15, 2011). He's certainly neither suggesting real cooperatives, nor market socialism. Rather, he is using the rising interest in alternatives to private ownership as a way to achieve a sort of verbal sleight-of-hand (see Anarcho, "Mutualism: Fake and Real," Anarchist Writers, Nov. 18, 2010, http://anarchism.pageabode.com/anarcho/mutualism-fake-real (accessed June 15, 2011).).

5   Kevin Carson, "The Iron Fist behind the Invisible Hand: Corporate Capitalism as a State-Guaranteed System of Privilege," mutualist.org, http://www.mutualist.org/id4.html (accessed June 15, 2011).

6   Kevin Carson, *Studies in Mutualist Political Economy*, http://www.lulu.com/items/volume_68/8968000/8968917/3/print/8968917.pdf (accessed June 15, 2011).

7   Carson, "The Iron Fist."

8   Benjamin Tucker, *Individual Liberty*, http://theanarchistlibrary.org/HTML/Benjamin_Tucker__Individual_Liberty.html (accessed July 5, 2011).

9   Ibid.

10 For example, see Sylvia Federici, *Caliban and the Witch: Women, the Body, and Primitive Accumulation* (Brooklyn, NY: Autonomedia, 2004); Maria Mies, *Patriarchy and Accumulation on a World Scale: Women in the International Division of Labor* (Atlantic Highlands, NJ: Zed Books, 1986); and Carole Pateman, *The Sexual Contract* (Stanford, CA: Stanford University Press, 1988).

11 See Joe R. Feagin, *Racist America: Roots, Current Realities, and Future Reparations* (New York: Routledge, 2010).

12 See Carter A. Wilson, *Racism: From Slavery to Advanced Capitalism* (Thousand Oaks, CA: Sage, 1996).

13 See Martha A. Ackelsberg, *The Free Women of Spain: Anarchism and the Struggle for the Emancipation of Women* (Oakland: AK Press, 2005).

14 Ibid., 38.

15 For example, see bell hooks, *Feminism is for Everybody: Passionate Politics* (Cambridge, MA: South End Press, 2000) and Patricia Hill Collins, *Black Feminist Thought: Knowledge, Consciousness, and the Politics of Empowerment* (New York: Routledge, 2000).

16 For example, see Lydia Sargent, *Women and Revolution* (Boston, MA: South End Press, 1981).

17 Combahee River Collective, "Combahee River Collective Statement," http://circuitous.org/scraps/combahee.html (accessed June 15, 2011).

18 For a piece linking anarchism with intersectionality, see Deric Shannon and J. Rogue, "Refusing to Wait: Anarchism and Intersectionality," http://theanarchistlibrary.org/HTML/Deric_Shannon_and_J._Rogue__Refusing_to_Wait__Anarchism_and_Intersectionality.html (accessed June 15, 2011).

19 See Anarcho, "Mutualism: Fake and Real."

20 See Carson, "The Iron Fist."

21 Anarcho, "Mutual Aid, Parecon, and the Right Stealing the Word 'Libertarian,'" http://anarchism.pageabode.com/anarcho/mutual-aid-parecon-right-stealing-libertarian (accessed June 15, 2011).

22 François Martin and Jean Barrot, *Eclipse and Re-emergence of the Communist Movement*, http://theanarchistlibrary.org/HTML/Francois_Martin_and_Jean_Barrot__AKA_Gilles_Dauve___Eclipse_and_Re-Emergence_of_the_Communist_

Movement.html (accessed June 22, 2011).

23   Joseph Kay, "On Co-ops, Conflicts, and Strawmen," http://libcom.org/library/co-ops-conflicts-straw-men (accessed June 14, 2011). I'm not sure I'd use the same terminology, as "exploitation" typically refers to an arrangement where one party expropriates the surplus value of another, but his points about cooperatives operating in a market are excellent. The entire exchange between him and Iain McKay over this issue is a great read, for those interested.

24   Carson, "The Iron Fist."

Ditching Class: The Praxis of Anarchist Communist Economics

Scott Nappalos

Libertarian Communism, the Aspiration of Classes in Struggle

Class relationships stand at the core of global societies in our time. The interlocking web of capitalist and state power relations are embedded and reproduced as class exploitation at every level in communities. The abolition of class exploitation is the foundation of any future socialist economy, one which I hope would lead to a society where all people and communities would be able to develop autonomously to their full capacities. During every struggle for liberation and autonomy, class has stood in the way of further developing our human potential. Class has provided the bedrock for counterrevolutions and, even more threatening to liberation, has been capitalism's ability to reproduce class relations even when the old actors, the capitalists, have fled the scene. New classes rise to take the place of the old ones, and the failure to do away with class altogether has led to some of the worst human tragedies, particularly in the former Soviet countries and various national liberation struggles.

Any group of people who seek to do away with class exploitation will run up against a problem. How is another form of economic activity possible? The easy answer is that capitalism is not eternal. Capitalism is realistically a marginal form of economic organization in human history, though one that spread from western Europe a few centuries ago to become wholly dominant, and has left a path of carnage (human and environmental) in its wake. Still, we don't want merely a different economy, but a better one, and ideally one that transcends the problems of tyranny, inequity, waste, and deprivation.

Libertarian communism is one such possibility, though there needs to be a disclaimer. None of the so-called "communist countries" had any semblance of communism. All had class systems with workers and managers, with wage systems, and where the workers neither owned nor controlled their work and its products. Thus, those countries resembled capitalism more closely than a society based on the abolition of remuneration in the form of wages and democratic control.[1]

Likewise most people identified with communism today only believed in communism after their own disclaimers. Marx, Lenin, and

292 The Accumulation of Freedom

most of their followers made a distinction between higher and lower stages of communism, where we would pass from lower to higher communism as the revolution unfolded, the proletarian state withered away, and so on. Many Marxists thought of this lower stage as socialism. For this reason whenever mainstream Marxist theory attempted to address the question of post-revolutionary society, the emphasis was placed on the lower phase of communism. The lower phase, following Marx's conception of a transition period, would bear some of the marks of the capitalist society which gave birth to it, including compulsion to work via a collectivist wage system—sometimes of labor vouchers, or at other times different wage schemes. For this reason, much of the Marxist communist economic literature isn't actually communist, but focused on collectivist economics. The higher stage of communism is left to be determined by the post-revolutionary working class, except for a few exploratory remarks in Marx's corpus.

Libertarian communist economics, however, have a few defining features:

1) A commitment to a future economy based on the praxis of the revolutionary working class and popular classes.

2) An economy based on the destruction of the wage system of labor, and a de-linking of the value of labor in production from the distribution of society's wealth to its members.

3) Collective control and management of the entire economy by the direct control of workers and community members united in a council system of direct democracy.

4) The abolition of intermediary institutions of power governing the economy.

The assets of libertarian communist economics are also some of its weaknesses, at least in regards to what is sometimes called prescriptive economics. Prescriptive economics attempts to lay out a vision, in our case, of a post-capitalist economic system based on some core values. Praxis is the concept of linking ideas and vision with concrete practices and struggles. Historically, it was the anarchist communists who generally took up the problem of the possibility of classless society, and even then only tempered by the necessary recognition of the leadership and innovation of everyday people to solve the problem concretely. The lack of materials on prescriptive economics can be traced in part to the strong commitment in anarchist and libertarian communist thought to the concept of praxis.

Praxis

Paulo Freire defined praxis as "reflection and action upon the world in order to transform it."[2] This is to say that we should seek to act as revolutionaries through a conscious program of uniting our thinking about our actions and the impact they have. Theory and practice should aim for a relationship of back and forth, testing and reassessing, and building theory collectively out of the concrete struggles of the oppressed classes in action. As Marx says in *The German Ideology*,

> Communism is for us not a *state of affairs* which is to be established, an *ideal* to which reality [will] have to adjust itself. We call communism the *real* movement which abolishes the present state of things. The conditions of this movement result from the premises now in existence.[3]

Libertarian communist prescriptive economics has then been shaped by belief in the potential leadership of the working class and popular classes, and the commitment to prescriptive economics reflecting both a strategy for achieving such an economy and a theory which reflects our experiences in struggle. The luminaries of libertarian communist economics come from periods of intense class struggle. Kropotkin, Berkman, Bordiga, the Impossibilist Socialists of the Second International, Socialisme au Barberie, De Jaques, theorists of the CNT, and Cafiero all address critical issues in prescriptive economics, and do so from the strengths and weaknesses of the revolutionary moments they participated in. For the English-speaking world, there is a familiar challenge. The overwhelming majority of prescriptive economics in the libertarian communist tradition came from Slavic, Romance, and East Asian regions. Until recently, few of these texts were translated. Many remain out of print, or only available in obscure journals. Some like Bordiga, have next to nothing in English, and can generally only be read in Italian and French, with less available even in Spanish. With this in mind, a project of study, translation, and debate around libertarian communist economics is an important part of the libertarian communist rebirth underway worldwide.

Lived Libertarian Communism

The experiences we have are limited to partial and momentary experiences in the revolutionary movements such as the Spanish revolution, the Hungarian workers councils in 1956, the Israeli kibbutzim, the Ukrainian communes during the Makhnovschina, and various libertarian endeavors today like autonomous Zapatista communities, the Argentinean factory seizures during the economic collapse of 2001, workers who broke with Allende's government to expropriate in Chile, and some more limited applications in open source, free software, libraries, occupied housing, and occupied collectivized health care and education. Starting with the Paris Commune, libertarian and authoritarian socialists alike drew from the lessons of revolutionary moments, and sought to extrapolate lessons for the future. Bakunin and Marx spent considerable work on the Commune, and it perhaps shifted some of the revolutionary thinking of the time. The aim of this work isn't to make such a study, but these historical exercises are useful and will partially be repeated here. That said, these experiences hardly warrant enough data to speak authoritatively on post-revolutionary society, but there are lessons which are worth reflecting on, and there are some broad conclusions we may draw. Seeing the seeds of libertarian communism as a lived body of activity demonstrates the potential for a future society beyond the shackles of present oppression and exploitation.

Peasant struggles across the world demonstrated glimpses of economic relations based on collective distribution and production. In Georgia during the 1905 Russian Revolution, anarchist communist peasants seized land and created a commune for a period with distribution without wages or money. The same would occur soon thereafter in the Ukraine, where a whole region of anarchist communist peasant and workers' councils would build the seeds of an anarchist communist economy, until it was surrounded and crushed by the Bolshevik armies. During the Mexican Revolution, insurgent communities organized with the resistance of Emiliano Zapata also ran land communally, as had been a part of indigenous traditions, and which spread under revolutionary leadership of peoples in arms.

Following World War I, Italy exploded in working-class resistance. Workers fought austerity through independent militant unions, the anarcho-syndicalist USI, and a system of workers' councils. At its height, general strikes led to factory occupations and workers' councils that approved social production before its repression. The railway union, for example, was one of the most militant and anarchist-influenced unions in Italy during the "Red Years" of 1919–1920. The railway union supported the occupations and workers' councils, and refused to transport troops to crush the councils. The union eventually extended this resistance from occupation towards communist production.

> As the rail union moved into a position of support for the occupation throughout the country, the workers on the Italian State Railways began switching freight cars to the factory sidings, providing fuel and raw materials and transport connections between the various factories under occupation. This action was essential in enabling the workers to continue production.[4]

In Hungary in 1956, a general insurrection swelled after protests led by student and clandestine left groups were violently repressed in an atmosphere of workers' resistance across the soviet bloc and repression by the USSR following Stalin's death. Workers shortly took the lead and created a system of workers councils to run society collectively, abolished the Communist Party in practice, and built soldier's councils for the defense of the revolution. The workers took the struggle beyond a military fight, stopped production, and actually began running the economy for the community's needs. While any revolutionary situation is rife with ambiguities and contradictions, we can see kernels of communist economics within the reorganized production and distribution experiments of the Hungarian workers in revolt. Nick Heath writes,

> Peasants and farm workers organised deliveries of food to the workers in the cities. They drove out the kolkhoz (State farm) managers. In some areas they redistributed land, while in others they kept the collectives going under their own management.[5]

Workers continued to produce in the collectively managed industries, while distribution was carried out on a communist basis in many instances. This was based on the needs of the community in the struggle, and without a system of wages or allocation according to the perceived value of their contribution. Heath quotes the *Observer* at the time:

> A fantastic aspect of the situation is that although the general strike is in being and there is no centrally organised industry, the workers are nevertheless taking upon themselves to keep essential services going for purposes which they determine and support. Workers councils in industrial districts have undertaken the distribution of essential goods and food to the population, in order to keep them alive. The coal miners are making daily allocations of just sufficient coal to keep the power stations going and supply hospitals in Budapest and other large towns. Railwaymen organise trains to go to approved destinations for approved purposes. It is self help in a setting of Anarchy.[6]

The Hungarian situation was cut short by its enforced isolation by the united Stalinist and capitalist powers fearing a spread of workers' democracy, and ultimately Russian tanks silenced the Hungary libertarian experiment. We can only speculate how the question of wages and community management would have played out, and if the workers' council system would have spread direct democracy beyond the workplace alone. Still, this experience, which has been repeated across history, reflects the potential for an economy run on collective control over distribution de-linked from the wage system and its corresponding distribution system.

History is filled with other experiences with many outside the workplace. In Italy during the '60s and '70s, workers and social movements rose up and took the struggle outside the factory walls. In occupied buildings, the women's movement and workers began to plan and organize collective buildings for community use on a non-monetary basis. Fare strikes saw the unity of transit riders operating without monetary exchange, and in some cases (as nearly fifty years before) transit workers redirecting transit for popular usage. Experiences in squats reorganizing and redeveloping space collectively is spread throughout Europe in Germany, Holland, Austria, Italy, France, and so on. Fare

strikes, collective expropriation and redistribution of groceries, and occupations are mere glimpses within non-revolutionary situations of a
communal economy run by the community on a needs basis.

The Spanish revolution, created by the popular resistance of the
peasants and working classes to a fascist coup in 1936, led to a broad
libertarian experiment unparalleled in its depth and breadth. Without
delving too deeply into its complex and contradictory experience, we
can see that the Spanish revolution demonstrated the potentials of
a communist economy. The Spanish economy and movements were
highly regionalized at the time. Likewise the advances of the revolution differed by region, its movements, ruling class, productive capacities, and so on. While in Catalonia the state was allowed to survive, in
Aragon anarchist militias and peasant organizations destroyed the rule
of the local ruling class and state. Gaston Leval, a Spanish anarchist
who took part in and studied the revolutionary collectives across Spain,
documented the experiences of the collectives and communes, which
abolished wages, money, and established social distribution de-linked
from productive value. Leval is worth quoting here at length:

> But—and this was the case especially in Aragon—where the
> State did not dominate, many original solutions had to be im-
> provised; and we mean "many," for each village or small locality
> introduced its own solution.
>
> At the beginning, then, there was no tacit agreement other
> than for the abolition of money, the expression and symbol of
> traditional injustice, social inequality, the crushing of the poor
> by the rich, the opulence of some at the expense of the poverty
> of others. For centuries, and from as far back as the complaints
> of the outcasts of fortune had been transmitted from genera-
> tion to generation, money had appeared as the greatest of all
> means of exploitation, and the hatred of the common people
> had built up against the cursed metal, against the paper money
> which the revolutionaries had set their minds on abolishing first
> and foremost.
>
> In Aragon they kept their word. Nevertheless, for all that
> the principle of the "prise au tas" or in economic terms free con-
> sumption, was not applied. Apart from access, without control,
> to existing goods available in great abundance, and which were

not the same in every village (here it was bread and wine, elsewhere vegetables, oil or fruit) some form of order was established from the first days when it was felt to be necessary, just as it was for the prosecution of work and production. *For the revolution was considered right from the beginning a very important constructive undertaking.* Especially in the countryside, there was no revolutionary orgy. The need to control and to foresee events was understood from the first day.[7]

Experiences varied with the praxis and conditions of struggle. In the village of Naval for example:

No money, not even local money, no rationing. Free consumption from the first day, but supervised consumption. Everybody could call at the "Antifascist Comite" which is advised, if necessary, by the local libertarian group. A cooperative for general distribution was improvised and it produced a book of coupons numbered 1 to 100, in which were marked from day to day the commodities handed over on demand, and the consumer's name.[8]

The accounting system was further simplified, and no excess or wasteful consumption was seen. This was a system created under wartime conditions by people who were not trained accountants, managers, or bureaucrats. Nor was distribution and production isolated to independent towns; these moneyless communist experiments sought to coordinate and federate their economies in the collective endeavor of fighting fascism and building libertarian communism.

So far as distribution was concerned, whatever the form or method adopted, the organising initiative was appearing all the time. In hundreds of villages, libretas de consumo (consumer books) in different sizes and colours were issued. Ration tables were appended, for one had to ration not only in the event of a reduction in the reserves and perhaps in production, but because it was also necessary to send food supplies to the front and the towns, which only too often appeared not to appreciate the gravity of the situation.[9]

The Spanish collectives in many cases reorganized production, increased output, and—with workers directing their own workplaces—improved upon a backward and ailing economy. Rather than chaos reigning, workers demonstrated the power of self-management and the potential of everyday people to transform an economy for profit into an economy for social need in relatively short periods of time, all while under a brutal foreign-supported war.

Attempts to broaden this communist economy were restricted by the political situation. The failure of the revolutionary working class to destroy institutions of power led to a tenuous situation in which the leadership of the CNT faltered and allowed the state and capital to reorganize and the Stalinist communist party to set about destroying the gains of the revolution. The villages of Aragon sought to expand their experiment across the rebel territories on the eve of the counterrevolution as the Stalinist armies marched on Barcelona, attacked the militia system, and effectively solidified the suppression of the popular revolt, which had failed to establish the hegemony of the people over its enemies on the left and the right early on. Leval is extremely lucid here, and lays out the foundations and genius of the libertarian communist concepts of praxis, and theory arising from the lessons of struggle.

> One can, nevertheless, come to the following conclusions: for the problem of distribution, which from certain points of view was greater than that of production itself, the Collectives demonstrated an innovatory spirit which by the multiplicity of its facets and its practical commonsense, compels our admiration. The collective genius of the rank and file militants succeeded in solving problems which a centralised governmental organisation would have neither been able nor known how to solve. If the pragmatic methods to which they had to have recourse may appear to be insufficient, and sometimes unsound in view of some contradictions which one observes here and there, the development tending to eliminate these contradictions was taking place rapidly (in eight months, or less, depending on the cases, structural resolutions had been taken) and progress was being rapidly made towards unifying and decisive improvements. During that time, in the part of the country where the official money

ruled, the peseta was continually being devalued because of the inability of the government to hold down prices, and speculation was getting under way and growing.[10]

These lessons of struggles show us some of the outlines of a libertarian communist economy, developed and run collectively by the exploited classes creating a new world through a reorganization of social relationships and a transformation of the economy. How that economy could function in a fleshed out sense requires us to move from the partial experiences we have to a theory of communism which grows out of them.

A Libertarian Communist Society

There are two broad spheres within the economy: how things are produced and how they are distributed. A number of different alternatives have been proposed on how communist distribution would function. Generally speaking, people agree on the idea of council democracy organized from the shop to the industry and federated by industry regionally and higher up globally. Directly democratic councils are democratic organs without representation. Workers and community members decide directly in open meetings how they want things to be. Above the mass assemblies, committees and councils of delegates coordinate between workplaces and neighborhoods. Delegates are given mandates and are expected to carry out the will of the assemblies. Likewise, delegates are immediately recallable if they overstep their bounds, and the decisions of delegates are either open to referendum or dependent upon approval of the assemblies. How exactly this functions, the mandates of the delegates, and so on, are questions which I think have both political and not merely technical content, and are best chosen through practice.

Neighborhood councils federated upward similarly would provide the means for deciding what to produce and how much, with workers deciding how to do so, and communities formulating the fairest and safest way to produce and deal with waste, pollution, and so on. Industries would not merely be collectivized as the present economy contains worthless industries and products, as well as patently destructive ones such as nuclear arms. This process would likely take some time to transform an economy organized for boom and bust based on private profit to an economy serving the needs of the community on a usage basis. Job classes and the worst work would need to be reorganized and shared equally. There would need to be a base minimum of socially necessary labor contributed to receive the benefits of society from those who are able.[11]

Considering distribution then, communist economic practice and thinkers have proposed a number of strategies for organizing the allocations of the wealth of society. Within the communist economic tradition there are two main frameworks: planned and what I call emergent. These are less theories than they are poles within the existing thought.

Planned communist economics, generally speaking, has advocated for the distribution of goods through planned production decided in mass assemblies federated in councils. All people in an area would get together on a regular basis to consider, based on an analysis of the amount of materials and labor available, what to produce and how to allocate the products based on the needs (rather than wages) of individuals and families. Producing then in a communist society would rely on two functions: measuring the desire of people for things, and producing both in a collective and accountable manner.

Given the present level of technology, it would be very simple to measure the actual consumption of people. In a communist society, we could readily automate the recording of statistics both of consumers and of resources in production. This could produce real-time data on how much of what is needed and any patterns of consumption, and give society a means for anticipating and allocating resources toward what people want. This would provide a democratic way for allocating resources between varying producers. As the UK Socialist Party States:

> For the purpose of planning the development of production, information could be brought together through the work of information centres, which could collate the appropriate statistics. Such information centres could exist on local, regional and world levels. On the smallest local scale, information centres could monitor the position of stocks and productive capacity to meet local needs. By collating these statistics, regional information centres would be in a position to know the complete picture throughout the region. This could be achieved by also monitoring

the position of stocks, productive capacity and needs among regional production units. A world information centre could collate regional statistics in a similar manner. This would be a connected but decentralised world information system providing any combination of information that people required.[12]

This isn't to say, however, that we should merely produce whatever happens to be consumed at one particular moment. While communism would do away with the artificially created hyper-consumptive needs of capitalism through elimination of profit and wealth inequities, we want to be able to build an economy and society that reflect our desire for a better world and not just passing fancies. There must then be a mechanism for linking these decisions about our social direction and our actual proclivities.

The usage schedules provide the data which can be debated in the communal councils that then would decide how to allocate resources to industries, save toward development for future production, and invest in opening up new production or furthering existing production. Presumably workers who want to create new industries and products would present their offers to the assemblies for consideration in adjudicating between using existing labor and materials. You could think of this as partial planning wherein resources are collectively allocated through considering, debating, and crafting a plan based on the priorities of the collectivity, and then become debated and changed through federations of councils moving upward, while the actual industries and products have the flexibility to adapt with actual usage. This is analogous to a form of popular budgeting where the wealth of the community is divided up into blocks for industries with earmarking based on popular proposals and coordinated through federations that would share data, revise proposals, and send back the budgeting for review by affected communities.[13]

Production schedules would be based on the collective priorities set in directly democratic councils and federated upward. This would provide a means for anticipating and coordinating various industries not based on wages, prices, and class inequity. Rather than price, communal priorities are the arbiter of what and how much is produced. Instead of wages, need is the basis for consumption. Decisions about society's produce would be conscious and collective, rather than the individualist produce-whatever-sells-come-what-may of capitalism. This was perhaps the position of Kropotkin's communist municipalities in *Conquest of Bread*. Participatory economics makes a proposal with councils of planning for an integrated global economy, which in theory could be modified to be communistic.[14]

Another position might argue for an economy that is emergent and adaptive.[15] This concept of communist distribution relies on intuitions and lessons from seeing society as an interdependent, living, and complex, organism-like body. The motivation for this position arises from two sources. First there is a suspicion here about our ability to plan successfully, consciously, and explicitly a full economy; and secondly *there is both support for and historical antecedents of a dynamic and evolving form of self-planning in a communist society*. During the Hungarian and Spanish revolutions, people were able to take over the economy and in some instances in a very rapid period of time convert existing production for private profit into a collectivized economy for common use. This occurred initially outside of any single unified planning apparatus. Distribution evolved out of countless actions of individuals and groups which came to unify and reorganize to meet the demands presented by the wars and communities. This isn't to say there wasn't organization, but to say there is a difference between organization that is structurally and historically open and has the ability to produce emergent and evolving structure, versus extensively planned organization that is predictive and fairly static. There is little evidence to point to people living under such conditions guiding their activities by adhering to such programs. We can understand the activity of an economy as emergent out of problem-solving at countless levels, and producing stability once equilibrium can be reached. This is a problem that is unfortunately hidden from these discussions: *how to obtain equilibrium in a revolutionary context is in many ways a more significant problem than that of abstract models of potential futures*. Surely part of this task involves principles and practice (revolutionary and libertarian content) beyond merely the form of a robust and adaptive economy.

There is good reason to question our ability to anticipate what we will want in the future.[16] Under capitalism desire is created, modified, and exploited. With profit eliminated, needs would become collective and organic. Still, needs are not fixed and predictable. If anything, human life is filled with fluctuations and unpredictable shifts. Moreover it's not clear that our conscious reflections about our own perceived consumption and desires are accurate. People often mischaracterize themselves based on how they like to see themselves versus how they act. Politicize the situation and generalize it over millions of people, and there is a significant structural weakness in creating an economy based on self-reflective projections. Cornelius Castoriadis raised similar objections while in Socialisme au Barberie during the 1960s and '70s.[17] Castoriadis rejects strict planning on a similar ground.

> The plan can't propose, as an ultimate target, a complete list of consumer goods or suggest in what proportions they should be produced. Such a proposal would not be democratic, for two reasons. Firstly, it could never be based on "full knowledge of the relevant facts," namely on a full knowledge of everybody's preferences. Secondly, it would be tantamount to a pointless tyranny of the majority over the minority. If 40% of the population wishes to consume a certain article, there is no reason why they should be deprived of it under pretext that the other 60% prefer something else. No preference or taste is more logical than any other. Moreover, consumer wishes are seldom incompatible with one another. Majority votes in this matter would amount to rationing, an absurd way of settling this kind of problem anywhere but in a besieged fortress. Planning decisions won't therefore relate to particular items, but to the general standard of living (the overall volume of consumption). They will not delve into the detailed composition of this consumption.[18]

Producing then in a communist society would rely on two functions: measuring the desire of people for things, and producing both in a collective and accountable manner. Participatory economics proposes to measure desire for goods through people's conscious guess of how much they want things. This proposal, however, would rely on a dialogue between people's actual usage of existing goods, and collective structures of decision making for development and deciding the direction of the economy.

For some goods for which there are absolute and intractable scarcity, we would need to find a fair system for distributing based on real needs. This is a real pressing question, which again many economic theorists ignore because they are creating blueprints not based in real praxis to address how we get from our present state to a revolutionary and later post-revolutionary society. The transition from existing production to social production will necessarily create shortages in the short run. In the long run, the use of our collective knowledge, mechanization of the worst work, and the elimination of useless production which consumes such a massive portion of the capitalist economy (finance, military, prisons, frivolities of the wealthy, and so on) will give us a bounty that can more than provide for the world. Indeed we already produce more than enough food to feed the whole world, but burn much of it in excess to keep prices high. Many anarchist communist thinkers put forward the concept of rationing for such goods. There is a time-honored practice in this regard, and it is the distribution form used in war time or organ transplants, for example. Alexander Berkman writes:

> When the social revolution attains the stage where it can produce sufficient for all, then is adopted the Anarchist principle of "to each according to his needs." In the more industrially developed and efficient countries that stage would naturally be reached sooner than in backward lands. But until it is reached, the system of equal sharing, equal distribution per capita, is imperative as the only just method. It goes without saying, of course, that special consideration must be given to the sick and the old, to children, and to women during and after pregnancy.[19]

This is of course different from, for example, the rationing in the Soviet Union, where the best and lion's share went to the party elite. Indeed with organs presently, there is an international organization which identifies the neediest and most qualified, and ranks them. Organ transplants occur on a communist basis in that it is need and availability that determines who gets organs, rather than price, their work, or perceived value. While rationing is to be avoided at all costs, we must recognize in times of hardship it may represent the only real equitable solution.

That said, Berkman's communist alternative of open usage with surplus fails to address how a society could plan and deliberate between issues where a decision must be made, such as with pollution or conflicting uses for the same materials. Any deconstruction of the world capitalist economy will face up to the gross global inequities and repressed development of large sections of the world. We need a method for consciously and collectively developing all of the world's communities' capacities, and addressing underlying ecological disasters presently existing (and unsustainability in the long term engendered by capitalism's search for expanded markets and increasing profits).

Only through community councils could we make those decisions. The solution is not a technical one, however. We cannot merely invent an economic scheme for settling, say, fights over where pollution will end up. The mechanism already exists in the above discussion for bringing to the table various proposals, but *with the political content for a community there can only be a political process within the community councils*. No assignment of value, arbitrary as that would be, will solve that point. Instead communities will have to come together, debate, compromise, and craft the best solution for all. Power and struggles concerning power can be mediated by structures, but structures are only the shell of a solution. They provide no guarantees, and ultimately such political problems require a material, social, and historical analysis of that situation. Inevitably we require more experiences, practice, and experimentation to address it beyond truism, vague generalities, and empty formalisms.

That said, while there is no guarantee that it will always go as we wish, unlike in capitalism there will be a structural pressure toward being principled, as any community will be in the same position throughout the various planning initiatives. We wouldn't want to burn others who would be in a position to burn us in the future. Unlike now, there would be no financial or political incentive to do so either. When real conflicts do arise, and they will, it will be a community struggle that will on occasions go beyond our models and formulas.

A Critique of the Wage System

Distribution, however, draws clear lines. With distribution, we have seen communist economics to be defined by an absence of a wage-system of work, distribution based on human needs and material stores rather than on the perceived value of individual labor, and the replacement of accumulated capital with production for human need. Collectivist economics, of which participatory economics shares all these features, is rather a system of compelling people to work for various wage schemes. Collectivist distribution is based on accumulated income earned as wages and distribution of such income given based on the perceived value of the individual's work. Collectivists have defined the value of labor under socialism in a variety of ways: amount produced, hours worked, difficulty of the work and effort in working (participatory economics), value of labor to society, and so on.

Communist economics rejects a wage system in part due to the experiences of revolutionary societies. If there is one thing we can see in the revolutionary experiences of Spain, Russia, China, Cuba, Hungary, Germany, and so on, it is that given the opportunity, capitalism can emerge out of its enemy. Class divisions and class inequities provide a launching ground for potential ruling classes. While a lesser opportunity than the proposal of a "proletarian" state, wage systems provide the ground for economic inequities, the accumulation of capital, and the material strength that could prefigure a new ruling class in ascendency. This is an essentially negative objection. On the positive side, communist economics provide additional alternatives and possibilities that are unavailable in economies that rely on the retention of inequity and wage labor. By abolishing the divisions both in work and in compensation, communism gives birth to fundamentally new social relations both between people and in production. A communist basis of distribution pushes the emergence and structuring of social production based on the real and lived needs of the community that benefits from the production. By rupturing the link between labor and consumption, communism offers an alternative method of living and working based on social need and human desire.

Moreover it is worth questioning on what basis a fair wage would be made. Under capitalism wages aren't fair. A wage is based on the market, and that's it. But socialist wages are all based on some perception of the value of someone's labor. For participatory economics this is a wage "for the effort or sacrifice they expend in contributing to the social product."[20] Various collectivist wages were proposed based on how many hours you work, how much you produce, the value of your contribution to production, and so on. There is a basic problem with all of these, though; they are arbitrary and inequitable.

In our time, production is largely social. The contribution of an individual is very difficult to isolate from the contributions of countless others that make that work possible. Simply put, social labor and capital are so intertwined in present society, the individual contribution in most instances is nearly impossible to measure apart from the labor of others and the social capital that allowed that individual to produce. Capitalism doesn't try; it just pays what people are forced to accept. Looking only at hours, we all know one person's hourly labor may be different from another; yet they receive the same wage. The value of someone's work then too is unfair because some people are naturally handicapped, and others shouldn't be able to get rich merely based on talents without exerting themselves much. If we judge based on effort and sacrifice, however, such a system is open again to arbitrariness. Having coworkers judge each other's work would turn the gossip and infighting at work presently from an annoyance into a system of power over wages. Value is not a neutral thing to assign; it is power-laden and a tool of coercion. Participatory economics and collectivists want to take a repressive-tool capitalism that mystifies real social labor that exists, and turn it into a tool of justice when disassociated from a profit system.

The difficulty assigning value to labor illustrates something more fundamental; we don't want an economy that prioritizes and rewards coerced labor *based on perceived value*. Both the danger of wealth inequities and the socially destructive pressure created by value assignments point to the more liberatory solution of an economy in which the value of labor is de-linked from consumption. This was traditionally formulated as "from each according to ability, to each according to need."[21]

Toward Communism

As a movement, we need to move beyond a role as the moral memory and model maker of the mass struggles of our times. A libertarian alternative needs to engage in the construction of praxis directly out of the movements we are immersed in, with our theory evolving alongside our practice. With Marx and Kropotkin, it is correct to see elements of communism already existing in present society. Gilles Dauve contributes to this dynamic and historical approach to communist economics with the concept of communization:

> Communism is not a set of measures to be put into practice after the seizure of power....All past movements were able to bring society to a standstill and waited for something to come out of this

universal stoppage. Communisation, on the contrary, will circulate goods without money...it will tend to break all separations.[22]

Presently existing communism doesn't mean functionally existing communism. Our task is not to set up islands of communism (which would almost certainly reproduce capitalist relations), nor to try to instantiate communism in present struggles. Capitalism is made up of relationships between people, not merely things and wealth. The real question of the development of a communist economy is about the development of revolutionary consciousness of the working class in mass struggle, and the development of communization and its practices. The defeat of capitalism isn't a theory, but a historical moment in our struggles, and it is one that requires working through the social relationships, organization, and consciousness of workers in struggle.

ENDNOTES

1   It's worth noting that Lenin and Leninists tended to identify capitalism with a lack of planning (the so-called anarchy of the market). Planning was seen then as a step toward socialism. In effect they created planned, state-run capitalism (or, if you disagree, a deformed version of such) using the tools of capitalist management theory such as Taylorism. Among the many mistakes, there is a misassessment of capitalism. Capitalism is often highly planned and well beyond the individual enterprise. History has shown us now that planning is far from neutral. These points are well developed in Raniero Panzieri's essay, "The Capitalist Use of Machinery: Marx Versus the Objectivists," http://libcom.org/library/capalist-use-machinery-raniero-panzieri.

2   Paolo Freire, *Pedagogy of the Oppressed*, http://marxists.anu.edu.au/subject/education/freire/pedagogy/ch01.htm (accessed May 25, 2010).

3   Karl Marx, *The German Ideology*, http://www.marxists.org/archive/marx/works/1845/german-ideology/ch01a.htm (accessed May 25, 2010).

4   Tom Wetzel, *Italy 1920*, http://workersolidarity.org/?p=122 (accessed June 16, 2010).

5   Nick Heath, *Hungary '56*, 1976, http://libcom.org/library/hungary-56-nick-heath (accessed June 16, 2010).

6   Ibid.

7   Gaston Leval, *The Anarchist Collectives*, http://libcom.org/library/collectives-leval-2#ch8 (accessed June 16, 2010).

8   Ibid.

9   Ibid.

10   Ibid.

11   There is much to be debated here, such as how work would be reorganized, the revolutionary process as we transition from the present economy to the future, environmental standards and choices, and the amount of necessary labor and how it would be maintained and regulated. These are general problems, unlike distribution, adequately discussed throughout the left libertarian tradition. I will for these reasons set it aside here.

12   Socialist Party of Great Britain, *Socialism as a Practical Alternative*, 1994, http://www.worldsocialism.org/spgb/pdf/saapa.pdf (accessed May 28, 2010).

13   Additionally there will need to be means for deciding between communities in conflict over proposals. This is not a technical problem, but a political one. Struggle is struggle. If conflicts arise, despite no profit or power being involved, and democratic means fail to solve these disagreements, that is a political conflict for which no formal means will solve. This is a larger discussion I lack the space for here unfortunately.

14   Purged of its wage system and promotion of inequities of income, we could imagine a similar integrated planned communist system whereby we moderate locales' planned needs with global production, development, and capabilities. I am not aware of any such theory, though it is possible. I think there's reason for its absence, which I will come to later.

15   Emergent economics arises from latent theory that has arisen both in revolutionary struggle and an understanding of contemporary science of living systems. Without taking too extensive a detour, anarchism and libertarian communist thought has had a strong current in complex systems thinking, and the experiences of revolutionary movements have deepened the lessons about the specificities of complex adaptive systems like human societies. Take a single cell in a living being. A cell is a unit made up of uncountable chemicals. Those chemicals in themselves have a number of properties. Within the organization of the cell, however, new properties and processes emerge like the production of proteins, reproduction, and the creation of a cell wall. The activity of the cell is such that we can find general rules and principles of its living, but it is probably impossible to trace the actions of the cell back to its constituent parts; activity within such a system is too complex and evolving to reduce merely by trying to grab a moment as an individual. Complex adaptive systems are systems in which there are non-linear relationships between the actors organized at various levels of organization. These relations produce actions that are in theory reducible to their parts, but act collectively through being mutually inter-defined and adaptive. This creates different laws and order

at different levels, and seemingly emergent properties that are not shared at lower levels. For example, I think, but my hair does not. It also shows us why top-down and hyper-engineered social programs ultimately fail. Imposing order at one level on a non-linear and complex level lower is unlikely to have direct causal impact. This is merely a theoretical way to make sense of Soviet planning, where higher-level planning was unable to anticipate and adapt to the reality on the ground and thereby created system failures. Moreover, complex adaptive systems give us a vocabulary for explaining and understanding revolutionary concepts developed in struggle. Decentralization, autonomy, diversity, and free association all are reinforced by understanding the way that order exists differently at different levels of organization, the emergence of properties out of lower levels, and the inability of centralized higher-level bodies to impose order on lower-level complex systems. While this vocabulary isn't necessary for libertarian communist thought, it is a useful tool, and one that unites it with an ever-increasing field of knowledge linking biology and living sciences with social theory.

16   While collectivist and participatory economic theory has significant objectionable content (wage inequities for example), this is an objection of a different order. It is worth considering how important prescriptive economic theory is, and what its ability is and isn't to bring about the change it theorizes. I suspect here most libertarian communists would differ too with such proposals.

17   Castoriadis proposed a lower-stage of communism (socialism) with wages paid for hours worked, though unlike participatory economics everyone would be paid the same wage. Not strictly a communist then, Castoriadoris puts forward a communistic proposal without wage differentials and contributed to communist theory.

18   Cornelius Castoriadoris, *Workers' Councils and the Economics of a Self-Managed Society*, http://www.lust-for-life.org/Lust-For-Life/WorkersCouncilsAndEconomics/WorkersCouncilsAndEconomics.htm#7._General_Problems_of_Socialist (accessed May 25, 2010). Originally published by Solidarity.

19   Alexander Berkman, *ABC of Anarchism*, chapter 12, 1929, http://www.lucyparsonsproject.org/anarchism/berkman_abc_of_anarchism.html (accessed May 28, 2010).

20   Michael Albert, *Life after Capitalism*, http://www.zcommunications.org/zparecon/pareconlac.html (accessed May 30, 2010).

21   There is a controversy over how to interpret this statement in terms of "from each." Some theorists argue that everyone would benefit from the goods of society without any compulsion to work in any form. Others require some minimum socially necessary labor (assuming one is able) to receive the right to the collective bounty of society's labor. The latter is the traditional answer which was dominant in the

312 The Accumulation of Freedom

CNT during the Spanish revolution, by Bertrand Russell, Chomsky, and many eminent theorists. It is my bias and one I will assume for this article.

22   Gilles Dauve, *Eclipse and Re-Emergence of the Communist Movement*, http://libcom.org/library/eclipse-re-emergence-communist-movement (accessed June 18, 2010).

The Anarchist Method: An Experimental Approach to Post-Capitalist Economies

Wayne Price

There are various opinions on the question of what a libertarian social-ist economy would look like. By "libertarian socialism," I include an-archism and libertarian Marxism, as well as related tendencies such as guild socialism and parecon—views which advocate a free, cooperative, self-managed, nonstatist economy once capitalism has been overthrown. Before directly discussing these programs, alternate visions of communal commonwealths, it is important to decide on the appropriate method. Historically, two methods have predominated, which I will call the *utopian-moral* approach and the *Marxist-determinist* approach (neither of these terms is meant to be pejorative). I will propose a third approach, which has been called the "method of anarchism" (or "of anarchy").

The utopian-moral method goes back to the earliest development of socialism, before either Marxism or Bakuninist anarchism developed. It was the method of Saint-Simon, Robert Owen, Fourier, Cabet, and later of Proudhon. A thinker starts with a set of moral values by which the present society may be condemned. Then the author moves on to envision social institutions which could embody these values. (These writers, pioneers of socialism, communism, and anarchism, did not call themselves "utopians," but saw themselves as "scientific" thinkers.)

A current example of utopian-moral methods is the program of "parecon" (short for "participatory economics"), originally developed by Michael Albert and Robin Hahnel.[1] Typically, in the first section of Albert's book, *Parecon*, he poses the key question, "What are our preferred values regarding economic outcomes and how do particu-lar economic institutions further or inhibit them?"[2] He works out a set of desirable values and then considers how an economy could be organized to carry them out.

The advantages of this method should be apparent. What Albert wants and why he wants it is transparent. It may be fairly argued for or against. Pareconists offer a yardstick by which to judge potential economies, as well as real ones, so that radicals do not claim to be for freedom but accept some totalitarian monstrosity.

However, there are also problems with the utopian-moral method. Various thinkers start with more or less the same values (e.g., freedom, cooperation, equality, democracy/self-management, and the development of each person's potentialities). Yet they propose quite different models of a new economy. How to decide among these models?

Also it could be argued that it is authoritarian for radicals today to make decisions about how other people will organize their lives in the future. The more precise and concrete the model, the more this is a problem. Not surprisingly, quite a number of historic utopian models were very undemocratic in structure (speaking of Owen, Fourier, Cabet, and Saint-Simon). This is not true of the parecon model, but a modern version is in B.F. Skinner's *Walden Two* (1976), an imagined socialist commune with a dictatorship by behavioral psychologists.

Finally there is a problem in that the utopian approach starts from values rather than from an analysis of how capitalist society functions. There is really no necessary connection between any particular model and the dynamics of capitalism (besides the moral critique). The visions of the possible futures do not point to any strategies for getting to these futures. Since they propose a drastic change in society, they may be seen as implying a social revolution. But it is certainly possible to adopt some utopian model and believe that it can be reached by gradual changes, such as building various alternative institutions until capitalism can be peacefully replaced—that is, by following a gradual, pacifistic, and reformist strategy. A program that does not say whether to be revolutionary or reformist is not much of a guide to action.

The main alternate method has been that of Marxist-determinism. Marx and Engels valued the preceding "utopian socialists" for various things, such as their criticism of capitalism and some of their proposals. But the original Marxists claimed that another method was needed. It was, they thought, necessary to analyze how capitalism was developing, including its main drive mechanism: the capital-labor relationship in production. This provided the basis of a strategy: the working-class revolution. It indicated the emergence of a new society out of that revolution. This relationship was their main interest. Marx and Engels only mentioned the nature of the new society in passing remarks, scattered throughout their writings—such as a few paragraphs in Marx's "Critique of the Gotha Program."[3]

In this work, Marx discussed the nature of communism, including at first paying workers with labor credits and later providing goods freely upon need. Yet such ideas were not advocated nor made as speculation, but stated as factual predictions. This is *what would happen*, he was saying; human choice seemed to be irrelevant. The goal of Marx and Engels was not to implement a new social system. It was to see that the working class overthrew the capitalist class and took power for itself. Once this happened, the historical process would take care of further social development.

In *State and Revolution*, Lenin regarded himself as praising Marx when he wrote, "Marx treated the question of communism in the same way as a naturalist would treat the question of the development of, say, a new biological variety, once he knew that it had originated in such and such a way and was changing in such and such a definite direction.... It has never entered the head of any socialist to 'promise' that the higher phase of the development of communism will arrive; ...[it is a] *forecast* that it will arrive."[4]

The Marxist-determinist method also has distinct advantages. It is tied to an economic theory. It has an analysis of what forces are moving in the direction of a new society and what ones are blocking them. It leads to a strategy that identifies a specific change agent (the working class, leading other oppressed groups). There are strands of autonomist Marxism which interpret Marxism in a libertarian, anti-statist fashion which overlaps with class struggle anarchism.

On the other hand, like a naturalist's study of an organism's development, there is no moral standard, just a "forecast" (even though, in fact, Marx's work is saturated with moral passion; but this is not the system). So when Marxist-led revolutions produce state-capitalist totalitarianisms that murder tens of millions of workers and peasants, very many Marxists support this as the result of the historical process which has created "actually existing socialism." Marx and Engels would undoubtedly have been horrified by what developed in the Soviet Union and other so-called communist countries. But a method without a moral standard made it difficult for Marxists to not support these states.

Both the utopian-moral and Marxist-determinist methods have advantages and weaknesses. Let me suggest an alternate approach to post-capitalist, post-revolutionary economic models. This has been raised by anarchists in the past. It starts from the doubt that every region and national culture will choose the same version of libertarian socialist society. It is unlikely that every industry, from the production of steel to the education of children, could be managed in precisely the same manner.

Kropotkin proposed a flexible society based on voluntary associations. These would create "an interwoven network, composed of an infinite variety of groups and federations of all sizes and degrees, local, regional, national, and international—temporary or more or less permanent—for all possible purposes: production, consumption and exchange, communications, sanitary arrangements…and so on."[5]

Perhaps the clearest statement of this flexible and experimental anarchist method was made by Errico Malatesta, the great Italian anarchist (1853–1932). To Malatesta, after a revolution, "probably every possible form of possession and utilization of the means of production and all ways of distribution of produce will be tried out at the same time in one or many regions, and they will combine and be modified in various ways until experience will indicate which form, or forms, is or are, the most suitable… *So long as one prevents the constitution and consolidation of new privilege*, there will be time to find the best solutions."[6] Malatesta continued, "For my part, I do not believe there is 'one solution' to the social problems, but a thousand different and changing solutions in the same way as social existence is different and varied in time and space."[7]

We cannot assume, he argued, that, even when the workers have agreed to overthrow capitalism, they would agree to create immediately a fully anarchist-communist society. What if small farmers insist on being paid for their crops in money? They may give up this opinion once it is obvious that industry will provide them with goods, but first they must not be coerced into giving up their crops under conditions they reject. In any case a compulsory libertarian communism is a contradiction in terms, as he pointed out.

"After the revolution, that is, after the defeat of the existing powers and the overwhelming victory of the forces of insurrection, what then? It is then that gradualism really comes into operation. We shall have to study all the practical problems of life: production, exchange, the means of communication, relations between anarchist groupings and those living under some kind of authority… And in every problem [anarchists] should prefer the solutions which not only are economically superior but which satisfy the need for justice and freedom and leave the way open for future improvements."[8]

Whatever solutions are tried, he is saying, they must be nonexploitative and nonoppressive. They must "prevent the constitution and consolidation of new privilege" and "leave the way open for future improvements." It is precisely this flexibility, pluralism, and experimentalism which characterizes anarchism in Malatesta's view and makes it a superior approach to the problems of life after capitalism.

"Only anarchy points the way along which they can find, by trial and error, that solution which best satisfies the dictates of science as well as the needs and wishes of everybody. How will children be educated? We don't know. So what will happen? Parents, pedagogues and all who are concerned with the future of the young generation will come together, will discuss, will agree or divide according to the views they hold, and will put into practice the methods which they think are the best. And with practice that method which in fact is the best will in the end be adopted. And similarly with all problems which present themselves."[9]

Others have pointed to the experimental approach as central to the anarchist program. For example, Paul Goodman, the most prominent anarchist of the '60s, wrote: "I am not proposing a system.... It is improbable that there could be a single appropriate style of organization or economy to fit all the functions of society..."[10] Or, as Kropotkin put it, an anarchist "society would represent nothing immutable.... Harmony would...result from an ever-changing adjustment and readjustment of equilibrium between the multitudes of forces and influences, and this adjustment would be the easier to obtain as none of the forces would enjoy a special protection from the state."[11]

Issues Raised by Differing Models of Post-Capitalism

There are a number of problems that post-capitalist visions have to address and the ways that they address these issues are what differentiate them. The approach I have raised does not insist on any one answer to each issue, but suggests that different answers may be tried in different regions at different times. However, the answers proposed by different models provide us with ideas of possible responses to these problems. That is, the utopian-moral and Marxist-determinist models may be treated as "thought experiments," providing suggestions that may be experimented with.

A key problem is *the method of coordination in the post-capitalist economy.* Three answers have been proposed: a market, central planning, and some sort of noncentralized planning.

First, there has been proposed what might be called "decentralized market socialism." It would be for an economy of democratically managed producer (worker-run) cooperatives, consumer cooperatives, family farms, municipal enterprises, and very small businesses that would compete in a market. Such a model has been advocated by various reform socialists who are concerned with the failures of state-managed economies.[12] It has been advocated by Right Greens, Catholic distributionists, nonsocialist decentralists, and others.[13] The Yugoslavian economy under Tito had something like this (under the overall dictatorship of the Communist Party).

In theory such a system would not be capitalist, because there is no capitalist class that owns the means of production and there is no proletariat that sells its ability to work to a separate capitalist class. But, however democratic each enterprise, the population cannot be said to actually manage the overall economy in a democratic way. It would really be run by the uncontrollable forces of the market. There are bound to be business cycles, unemployment, and a distinction between more prosperous and poorer enterprises and regions (effects which were seen in "communist" Yugoslavia).

An alternative would be some degree of central planning, as Marx seems to have assumed. In a nonstatist society, the central authority would be answerable to an association of popular councils and assemblies.[14] Castoriadis imagined that there could be a central "plan factory," which would create an overall plan.[15] Somehow, he believed, this could be consistent with libertarian socialism of self-managing workers' councils. Anarcho-syndicalists and guild socialists have also tended toward a centralized economy, managed by democratic unions. All sorts of representative institutions can be proposed for democratic central planning, although they all have the difficulty of important decisions being made outside of the direct control of the working population.

The third suggestion is that of a democratically planned, but not centralized, cooperative economy, "the idea that production could be directly coupled to individual and social need through democratic assemblies (or cybernetic networks) of workers and consumers."[16] Parecon is a model of such a nonmarket, noncentralized system. Planning would be carried out through cycles of back-and-forth negotiations among producer and consumer councils using the Internet.

In a pluralist, experimental, post-capitalist world, different regions might experiment with different types of economic coordination. Regions might try out mixtures of different models. For example, even in the parecon model there is an element of central planning in the "facilitation boards," which help to smooth along the planning process. Even in decentralized market socialism, presumably there would be some sort of overall regulation, as there is under capitalism, if not by a state then by some communal agency. Takis Fotopoulis proposes "a stateless, moneyless, and marketless economy" but one which includes "an artificial market" for a "non-basic needs sector...that balances demand and supply."[17]

A related issue is *the size of the economic unit*. While economic planning by capitalist states is on a national basis, revolutionary socialist-anarchists generally regard this as inappropriate to a post-capitalist economy. As internationalists, we are aware that the world is being knit together by imperialist globalization. At the same time we know that much of this worldwide centralization is not due to technical needs but to the need of capitalists to control natural resources, to dominate world markets, and to exploit the poorest workers in order to make the biggest profits. To end the rule of states and bureaucracies, anarchists want *as much as possible* of local, face-to-face democracy. This requires a degree of economic decentralization. Indeed, any sort of economic planning would be easier, and easier to make democratic, the smaller the units. Finally it would also be easier to keep production and consumption in balance with nature, the smaller the units are.[18]

Traditionally anarchists have sought to balance national and international association with the need for local community by advocating federations and networks. There can be no hard-and-fast rule about how centralized or decentralized an economy has to be. As Paul Goodman put it, "We are in a period of excessive centralization.... In many functions this style is economically inefficient, technologically unnecessary, and humanly damaging. Therefore we might adopt a political maxim: to decentralize where, how, and how much [as] is expedient. But where, how, and how much are empirical questions. They require research and experiment."[19]

Murray Bookchin advocated an economy based on communist communes similar to the Israeli kibbutzim. This was part of his "libertarian municipalist" model.[20] Another version is raised by Fotopoulos[21] and it is also discussed as "Scheme II" in Goodman and Goodman.[22] The community as a whole would be an enterprise and, through its town meetings, would make decisions about economic planning. This would not prevent communities from forming federations on a regional, national, and international level. They could coordinate their plans and exchange goods, services, and ideas.

Parecon has its own twist on this issue. Workplaces would be managed by workers' councils. Consumption would be organized through consumers' community councils. These are relatively small, face-to-face groupings. But the unit which is covered by the final plan is primarily the nation (which, in the case of the United States, if it still existed, would be much of a continent). In fact, Albert specifically rejects "green bioregionalism" and any notion of prioritizing small institutions or local "self-sufficiency."[23] (Actually decentralists do not advocate complete community self-sufficiency, but enough dependence on local and regional resources to be *relatively* self-reliant, within broader federations and networks).

The issue of size is directly related to that of *technology*. Just as is true of economic institutions, so productive technology would have to be flexible, pluralistic, and experimental. Machinery and the methodology of production have been organized by the processes of capitalism (and militarism) to serve its interests. Technology would have to be completely reorganized and redeveloped over time to meet the needs of a new society. Immediately after a revolution, the workers will need to begin to rework the process of production (machinery included) to do away with the distinction between order givers and order takers, to produce useful goods, to be in balance with the ecology, and to make a decentralized but productive economy possible.[24]

Just how these will be done would require a great deal of rethinking and trial and error.[25] The parecon model does not include any reconsideration of technology, but does call for the reorganization of work to create "balanced job complexes." Occupations would be broken down and reconfigured so that individual jobs would include both interesting and boring tasks, both decision-making and tedious aspects. (This has been described by Marxists and anarchists as the abolition of the division of labor between mental and manual labor).

This approach is distinct from either the technophobes, who want to reject all technology beyond that of hunter-gatherer society, and those who accept modern technology as capitalism has created it. Both these views overlook how flexible technology might be in a totally different society.

Another key question facing a post-capitalist economic economy is that of *reward for work*. There have been proposals for paying workers for their work in some sort of money or credit, which is used to acquire goods and services. Pareconists propose paying workers for the "intensity" and "duration" of their labor, that is, how hard and how long they work, as judged by coworkers. In *Walden Two*, the ruling psychologists were able to increase or decrease the amount of credits earned for any particular job to motivate members to do unpleasant tasks.[26]

By contrast, in a fully communist economy, work would be done only for the pleasure of doing it, or because people feel a duty, or because of social pressure (people do not want their neighbors to call them "lazy bums"). Consumption will be a right, based only on human need and unrelated to effort. Kropotkin is usually understood as advocating such a communist system after a revolution. Bookchin also proposed going straight to a free communist economy.

Various thinkers have proposed a split system. Almost every socialist system, including parecon, provides free goods for children, the ill, and retired older adults. Fotopoulos advocates a basic needs sector and a non–basic needs sector, the first to be treated as free communism and the second as having goods to be earned through work.[27] Similarly Paul and Percival Goodman propose dividing the economy into a basic economy, which provides a guaranteed minimum subsistence (food, clothing, shelter, medical care, and transportation), and a separate economy to take care of everything else.[28] Even if the non–basic needs sector was market-like, there would be no reserve army of the unemployed, since everyone would have at least the guaranteed minimum to live on.

This too is an area where different regions might try out different methods.

This leads to the question of whether to plan for *a transitional economy*, whether to expect two or more *stages of post-capitalist economic development*. In his "Critique of the Gotha Program," Marx wrote, "We are dealing here with a communist society, not as it has developed on its own foundations, but as it emerges from capitalist society…still stamped with the birthmarks of the old society."[29] He distinguished between this "first phase of communist society" and "a more advanced phase of communist society."[30] These are both communism, to Marx, because even the first phase is a "cooperative society based on common ownership of the means of production."[31] (For some reason, Lenin renamed the first phase "socialism" and only the final phase "communism").

In Marx's first phase, people would be rewarded for the number of hours worked with labor-time certificates which they could exchange for goods according to how many hours went into making each good. While vastly more just and equal than capitalism, this still has bourgeois limitations since workers have unequal capacities and unequal needs. When productivity has vastly expanded and human abilities are further developed, it will be possible to advance to the higher stage of communism, which will function according to the standard, "From each according to their abilities, to each according to their needs."

We can add that in poorer, less-industrialized nations, a post-revolutionary society would not be able to even reach the lower phase of communism (socialism) by itself. It would, however, be able to take steps toward socialism by such means as replacing the state with a council system and replacing corporations with self-managed cooperatives. Yet it might be unable to abolish money or it may have to make other compromises with capitalism. Meanwhile it would do all it could to help the revolution to spread internationally, especially to the industrialized, richer nations, in order to get economic aid for industrializing in its own way. (This concept was raised by Lenin and Trotsky;[32] I have "translated" it into libertarian socialism, so to speak.)

While Marx's views are well-known, less well-known are the similar views of Bakunin. According to his close comrade, James Guillaume, Bakunin believed, "We should, to the greatest extent possible, institute and be guided by the principle, *From each according to his* [sic] *ability, to each according to his need*. When thanks to the progress of scientific industry and agriculture, production comes to outstrip consumption...everyone will draw what he needs from the abundant social reserve of commodities. In the meantime each community will decide for itself during the transition period the method they deem best for the distribution of the products of associated labor."[33]

Even Kropotkin, author of anarchist-communism, believed that right after a revolution goods would not be free to all able-bodied adults but would only be guaranteed to those who were willing to work for a set amount of time. Only as productivity increased would it be possible to make goods available to all regardless of labor.[34]

The realism of a transitional approach should be obvious given that we would indeed be going into a cooperative, nonprofit economy straight from capitalism. Modern technology is potentially more productive than either Marx or Bakunin could have imagined. Yet a post-revolutionary generation would still have to develop the poorer majority of the world in a humane and ecological fashion. Also, they would have to rebuild the technology and cities of the industrialized countries in a self-managed and sustainable way. Therefore, I doubt that there could be an immediate leap into full communism.

However, the "transitional stage" concept has been used by Marxists to justify all sorts of horrors, making excuses for Stalinist totalitarianism. This is not what Bakunin, or even Marx, had in mind. It shows the need for a vision with moral values to judge a new society.

Neither Marx nor Bakunin/Guillaume proposed a mechanism for going from a transitional phase to full communism. One possibility might be to use the idea of a split economy (a basic communism and a non-basic needs sector). As productivity grows, the free communist sector might be deliberately expanded, until it gradually includes all (or most) of the economy.

Rather than a series of transitional periods, it may be most productive to think in terms of an experimental, pluralist, and decentralized society, in which different parts face the problems caused by the transition out of capitalism and deal with them in differing ways. A libertarian socialist society would always be "transitional" in that it would always be changing, always in transition to a more harmonious, freer, and more egalitarian society. It would never reach perfection, since that is not a human goal, but it would continually be changing, refining itself, readapting to new circumstances in a never-ending spiral of experimental improvement.

Endnotes

1   See Michael Albert, *Moving Forward: Program for a Participatory Economy* (San Francisco: AK Press, 2000); Michael Albert, *Parecon: Life after Capitalism* (London: Verso Books, 2003); and Robin Hahnel, *Economic Justice and Democracy: From Competition to Cooperation* (New York: Routledge, 2005).

2   Albert, *Parecon*, 28.

3   Karl Marx, "Critique of the Gotha Program," in *The First International and After: Political Writings*, vol. 3, ed. David Fernbach (London: Penguin Books, 1974), 339–359.

4   V. I. Lenin, *Selected Works in Three Volumes*, vol. 2 (Moscow: Progress Publishers, 1970), 348, 357–358. Lenin's emphasis.

5   Peter Kropotkin, *The Essential Kropotkin*, ed. E. Capouya and K. Tompkins (New York: Liveright, 1975), 108.

6   Errico Malatesta, *Errico Malatesta: His Life and Ideas*, ed. Vernon Richards (London: Freedom Press, 1984), 104. My emphasis.

7   Ibid., 151–152.

8   Ibid., 173.

9   Errico Malatesta, *Anarchy* (London: Freedom Press, 1974), 47.

10 Paul Goodman, *People or Personnel: Decentralizing and the Mixed System* (New York: Random House, 1965), 27.

11 Kropotkin, *The Essential Kropotkin*, 108.

12 See Frank Roosevelt and David Belkin, ed., *Why Market Socialism? Voices from Dissent* (Armonk, NY: M. E. Sharpe, 1994).

13 For example, see Robert A. Dahl, *A Preface to Economic Democracy* (Berkeley, CA: University of California Press, 1985).

14 See Wayne Price, *The Abolition of the State: Anarchist and Marxist Perspectives* (Bloomington, IN: AuthorHouse, 2007).

15 See Cornelius Castoriadis, *Political and Social Writings: Vol 2, 1955–1960*, ed. and trans. D. A. Curtis (Minneapolis: University of Minnesota, 1988).

16 David Belkin, "Why Market Socialism? From the Critique of Political Economy to Positive Political Economy," in *Why Market Socialism?*, ed. F. Roosevelt and D. Belkin (Armonk NY: M.E. Sharpe, 1994), 8.

17 Takis Fotopoulos, *Towards an Inclusive Democracy* (London/NY: Cassell, 1997), 256–257.

18 For a compendium of decentralist arguments, see Kirkpatrick Sale, *Human Scale* (New York: Coward, McCann & Geoghegan, 1980).

19 Goodman, *People or Personnel*, 27.

20 See Janet Biehl with Murray Bookchin, *The Politics of Social Ecology: Libertarian*

Municipalism (Montreal: Black Rose Books, 1998).

21   See Fotopoulos, *Towards*.

22   See Paul Goodman and Percival Goodman, *Communitas: Means of Livelihood and Ways of Life* (New York: Columbia University Press: 1960).

23   Albert, *Parecon*, 80–83.

24   See Castoriadis, *Political and Social Writings*.

25   For ideas, see Goodman and Goodman, *Communitas*; George McRobie, *Small Is Possible* (New York: Harper & Row, 1981); and E.F. Schumacher, *Small Is Beautiful: Economics as if People Mattered* (New York: Harper & Row, 1973).

26   See B. F. Skinner, *Walden Two* (New York: Macmillan, 1976).

27   See Fotopoulos, *Towards an Inclusive Democracy*.

28   See Goodman and Goodman, *Communitas*.

29   Marx, "Critique," 346.

30   Ibid., 347.

31   Ibid., 345.

32   See V. I. Lenin, "The Impending Catastrophe and How to Combat It," in *Selected Works in Three Volumes*, vol. 2 (Moscow; Progress Publishers, 1970) and Leon Trotsky, *The Permanent Revolution & Results and Prospects* (New York: Pathfinder Press, 1970).

33   James Guillaume, "On Building the New Social Order", in *Bakunin on Anarchism*, ed. Sam Dolgoff (Montreal: Black Rose Books, 1980), 362.

34   See Kropotkin, *The Essential Kropotkin*.

Porous Borders of Anarchist Vision and Strategy

Michael Albert

Any distinctive political perspective strongly favors particular visionary and strategic claims though people of contrary perspectives reject or at least largely doubt those claims.

I claim participatory economics and participatory society provide a worthy, viable, and even necessary and potentially sufficient anarchist revolutionary vision. I also claim that proposing anarchist strategy is a much more complex and delicate undertaking.

Along the way, I centerpiece two central anarchist themes: (1) the need to strategically plant the seeds of the future in the present, and (2) the seemingly contrary need to recognize that future people should freely and diversely decide their own future lives rather than today's activists arrogantly and intrusively deciding future peoples' lives for them.

Anarchist Vision

Anarchism is about reducing fixed hierarchies that systematically privilege some people over others to a minimum. Men should not enjoy advantages as compared to women, nor heterosexuals as compared to lesbians, gays, and bisexuals, nor members of any one racial, ethnic, or cultural community as compared to members of some other, nor members of any political party or group as compared to members of some other political party or group, nor members of any one economic class as compared to members of some other economic class.

Anarchism doesn't require that we all do the same things, which would be a ludicrously unattainable and boring condition. Nor does anarchism require that we all enjoy the same levels of happiness, which would be an impossibly intrusive and repressive condition. But anarchism does forbid society from systematically privileging some people materially or socially over others. In an anarchist society citizens should freely fulfill themselves without being systematically subordinate to or systematically superior to other citizens. We should each benefit from the same structural opportunities. We should each gain from the gains others enjoy.

Simultaneously, however, anarchism also favors future people deciding their own future lives. Some anarchists think this entails rejecting the idea of anarchist institutional vision. They feel anarchism should seek classlessness, solidarity, equity, justice, diversity, self-management, and other general values—but not specific institutional arrangements for attaining these values. Anarchism should recognize that all institutional choices are contextual so that future citizens will decide in a myriad of ways whatever they themselves determine.

In other words, some anarchists favor a "values yes, institutions no" approach to vision. They urge that no particular specific institutional aims are necessary to anarchism. Instead, anarchism asserts only that future citizens themselves, by whatever institutional means they choose, should diversely implement the values all anarchists favor. Let a thousand institutions bloom!

I believe that while a "values yes, institutions no" stance is well motivated and in considerable degree insightful, still it goes too far.

First, trivially, anarchism is not "anything goes." The freedom of anarchist future citizens should not include the freedom to own slaves or the freedom to hire wage slaves, as but two of countless conditions anarchism should obviously rule out.

But second, and more subtly, must anarchism rule anything in? Are there social components that a future society must incorporate to be deemed anarchist?

In other words, even as we want to currently advocate and aggressively seek only the most minimal array of future features lest we trample the freedom of future citizens to make their own choices, do we have to unrelentingly seek some centrally important visionary features right from the outset lest future citizens never enjoy that option? Are some features not merely contextual, but unavoidably central if there is to be freedom?

We shouldn't say, for example, that in the future people must eat these foods, wear those clothes, or settle on this size for workplaces or that mix of products to produce in amounts and patterns we prescribe—because for us to now make such determinations would manifest our current tastes, current preferences, and current thinking as developed in conditions we are currently familiar with but that will not pertain in the future—as well as because such choices of course would rarely be intrinsically and unavoidably essential to attaining the values of anarchism.

But while we can all rightly agree that blueprinting the future would inappropriately overreach, I do believe that enabling future citizens to freely, diversely, creatively, and knowledgeably decide their own social lives requires that we advocate some institutional vision. We can now know based on history's accumulated insights that future people will operate in accord with at least some social relations we can specify now or that future people will not operate freely. More, due to their being necessary for freedom, we should ourselves now begin seeking these particular centrally important social relations so that future people will be able to freely experiment with and make diverse choices about all other aspects of society and be free to adapt these central structures as they decide, as well.

In other words, current anarchist institutional vision should be limited to precisely those relatively few positive institutional commitments we are confident future people must enjoy if they are to have the information, circumstances, inclinations, opportunity, and even the responsibility to creatively and knowledgeably self-manage their own situations. Positive institutional vision should not extend further than that minimum, but neither should positive institutional vision stop short of that minimum.

Anarchists should strongly advocate and tirelessly seek the minimum necessary institutional vision to overcome cynicism, inspire hope and creativity, and inform strategy sufficiently to establish the basis for future self-managed outcomes—all without extending our claims and actions into domains that we can't know or that transcend our right to currently decide.

As an Example, Consider the Economy

When I claim that participatory economics (or parecon for short) is an anarchist economic vision, I mean parecon includes the minimum economic attributes a future economy must embody if future actors are to equitably self-manage their own lives, fulfill their own desires, mutually aid one another, and so on.

Pareconish self-management, for example, is the idea that people should have a say in decisions proportionate to the degree those decisions affect them. This is an ideal, of course, but in any event there should be no systematic and snowballing divergences. There should be no condition of some people enjoying more than proportionate say and of others suffering less, as a fixed or even steadily worsening condition, and thus of some people repeatedly and systematically dominating other people's life choices and conditions. It isn't that we should all always get our way, an obvious impossibility given the diversity of human interests. Rather, over time, it is that we should all have a just and fair say.

Equity, a second central value of parecon, is the idea that citizens should have a claim on society's economic product that increases if they do socially valued work longer, more intensely, or under worse conditions. We should not receive income for property, bargaining power, or even output, but we should receive income only for the intensity, duration, and onerousness of our socially valued labor.

This remunerative norm accords with anarchism's respect for human rights and responsibilities and its conception of solidarity. The norm promotes work that meets real needs even as it also establishes socially self-managed levels of labor and leisure.

Solidarity, parecon's third central value, is the idea that people should care about one another's well being rather than each of us trampling the rest or at the least turning the other cheek to others' difficulties.

Now "nice guys finish last" because society's institutions guarantee that economics is a war of each against all where callousness is a prerequisite for success. In an anarchist economy each of us succeeding should require that we each also aid others. Our own gains and other people's gains should be mutually supportive, not mutually exclusive.

Diversity, a fourth central parecon value, is the idea that people should have a wide range of options available and that when making choices, diverse paths forward should be kept available or experimented with. This provides unexpected benefits from paths we might otherwise have arrogantly ignored, as well as insurance against unexpected difficulties on paths we wrongly thought optimal.

Finally, as the fifth and sixth parecon values, environmental husbandry is the idea that humans and the rest of the environment ultimately constitute an entwined community in which humans have to take responsibility not only for the impact of our choices on ourselves but also on the rest of nature's domain—and, in turn, efficiency is the related idea that economic activity should produce what people seek for fulfillment and development without wasting assets we value, while furthering self-management, equity, solidarity, diversity, and husbandry.

Okay, why can't anarchist economic vision be that list of values—however modified, augmented, or refined—without proposing any specific institutions? Parecon's answer is twofold.

First, worthy economic values are essential but not alone convincing. People don't doubt the possibility of an alternative economic arrangement mainly because they doubt the morality of left values, but mainly because they doubt that those values can be implemented. Thus, we can fully dispel people's skepticism not solely by asserting worthy values, but only if we also describe institutions consistent with those preferred values.

And second, worthy values alone do not provide needed orientation for strategy and tactics. The distance between worthy values and well-conceived demands that we can productively struggle for, or between worthy values and well-conceived organizational structures we can usefully build, is very large. Demands and organization are conceived in light of institutional aims as well as worthy values. Institutional insights that move us toward effective strategic choices need to be shared and built upon, rather than each actor having to start over repeatedly as if no one had traveled similar ground before.

In light of the above, parecon proposes a minimalist institutional vision for establishing economic conditions that will permit future people to self manage their own economic lives while also being sufficient to overcome cynicism and inform strategy.

For example, if future people are to self-manage the economy, workers and consumers will need venues where they can meet, discuss, and finally decide their preferences and actions. These venues are workers' and consumers' councils, which are in turn federated at diverse levels and all use self-managing procedures.

Such self-managing councils can and should be part of our economic vision. On the other hand, the detailed arrangement of such councils and of their daily internal relations and their specific methods of dispersing and discussing information and of tallying preferences in different situations will be up to their participants and will take many forms in light of different contexts and desires. We certainly don't know enough to have strong attitudes about all these details, nor is it our right to decide such details for future folks in any case, nor, for that matter, is there only one right way to settle on details. Instead, the details of their own future implementations of self-managing councils are for those who are affected to decide contextually in the future. On the other hand, that we must generate self-managing councils in a new society if that new society is to be anarchist is a bare bones essential aim.

Okay, let's assume we develop worthy councils with self-managed decision-making procedures. Nonetheless, disparities in income and wealth could easily disrupt council members having a fair say over decisions affecting their lives. Given that possibility, we cannot have people earn income for their property, their bargaining power, or even for their output in our new workplaces since each of these means of earning income would introduce wide disparities in wealth which would in turn disrupt self-management. Instead, so that both moral and material conditions of freedom will exist, parecon proposes that remuneration should be for duration, intensity, and onerousness of socially valued work, with allowance for those who cannot work, of course.

But then how would we arrange equitable remuneration from industry to industry, given each industry's unique characteristics, and even from one workplace to the next, given different worker preferences? We can certainly offer guesses about various ways this might occur, but we don't and can't now know which patterns will prevail. Indeed, the details of future diverse implementations of equitable remuneration are relevant to us today at most insofar as we describe some possible choices that future people could make in order to demonstrate that equitable remuneration can indeed be achieved. Knowledge arising from future experimentation or emerging from as yet unknowable future preferences and circumstances in different countries, industries, and even in different firms within industries, will of course inform the choices of future people on how they wish to implement the equity norm, including, for example, how closely they will want to measure variables like duration and intensity, or what indices they want to collect and consult data about, and so on. However, when we say that the future is diverse, the diversity we have in mind doesn't include remuneration for property, power, or output—and it does include remuneration for duration, intensity, and onerousness of socially valued labor.

Continuing, if pareconish self-management and equity are to persist in a new economy, which they must if there is to be freedom and participation for all actors, it can't be that some actors are consistently and greatly empowered by their daily economic activities while other actors are consistently exhausted and disempowered by theirs, as is typical of corporate divisions of labor. The reason we can't have this disparity in the overall empowerment effects of work is because if the disparity exists, the set of people who have a relative monopoly on knowledge, skills, confidence, and energy for decision-making will dominate the people who lack those prerequisites of participation. To have freedom means we can't have that sort of class hierarchy, but then what must we seek in place of familiar corporate divisions of labor?

Consider a workplace. Suppose its workers institute democratic and even self-managed decision-making via a workers' council and associated teams and divisions that they define in their workplace. Also suppose its workers institute equitable remuneration for duration, intensity, and onerousness of socially valued work in a manner they choose as compatible with the technical and social character of their industry and workplace. However, along with those innovations, as typically occurs in many co-ops and occupied factories, suppose also that these workers also retain the old corporate division of labor in their workplace so that about one-fifth of the employees do all the empowering work, and the other four-fifths of employees do only the rote, repetitive, and in any event disempowering work.

In that case, despite their self-managing and equitable innovations, and despite each worker being formally granted equal democratic say in the council, the predictable, inexorable outcome of their choices, seen over and over in history as well as easily comprehensible by our knowledge of social interactions, is that in time the group doing all the empowering work (who I call the coordinator class) will set council meeting agendas, dominate council discussions and debate, overwhelmingly set workplace policies, and in time even decide to pay themselves more and allot themselves better conditions.

In short, their position in the old corporate division of labor will propel these empowered "coordinator class" members to dominate disempowered employees—which is to say, the working class–yielding, writ large, the economic class rule so common to what has been called twentieth-century socialism. The point of the observation is that the minimum conditions necessary for all future workers to be freely able to collectively diversely determine their own lives includes solving the problem that a persistent corporate division of labor will inexorably destroy such potentials.

So what alternative way of organizing work can workers' councils adopt in place of an old corporate division of labor to protect and even propel real participation and self-management? What minimalist structure regarding work apportionment can ensure freedom for future workers without impinging on future workers' rights to decide diversely their own social relations?

Parecon says the answer is "balanced job complexes," which means dividing up work so that each actor has a mix of overall tasks and responsibilities comparably empowering to the mix each other actor has.

But how does any particular workplace arrive at these new job complexes? We can usefully talk about some ways it can be done, or about some ways it has been done in some instances, to show both possibility and implications, but actually choosing among specific options of how best to generate and continually refine balanced job complexes in specific circumstances is a task for future people facing those circumstances. What can't be left to the future, however, supposing we want the future to be classless, is deciding that we want to eliminate the old division of labor and deciding that we want job complexes balanced for empowerment. The details are contextual, yes, certainly—but the basic need is a prerequisite for classlessness.

Parecon therefore claims that advocating and working to institute balanced job complexes, like advocating and working to institute self-managing councils or advocating and working to institute equitable remuneration, is essential to attaining the preconditions of full freedom. More, the claim isn't premised only on thinking about social relationships—though there is nothing wrong with applying our imaginations to complex problems. Rather, we also know from extensive practical experience of co-ops and twentieth-century socialist and anarchist endeavors just how deadly to self-management and equity the old division of labor is.

Now let's go one more step and suppose a future workplace institutes pareconish self-managed workers' councils, equitable remuneration, and also balanced job complexes. Is that the essence of desirable and anarchistic economics? Is the rest of what will constitute desirable economics a matter for future choice and not of current advocacy? Or is there still another economic aspect that is so essential for future freedom and classlessness that we must advocate it now, as part of our current vision, and that we must work to attain it starting now, lest not attaining it in turn prevents freedom from ever being attained?

Parecon says yes, there is another essential feature, called participatory planning. But why does parecon think we must choose participatory planning for economic allocation rather than just saying that future citizens, including some people opting for one way of allocating, and other people diversely opting for other ways of allocating, will decide allocation for themselves?

The first reason why putting off this choice, or being pluralist about it, isn't an option is technical. You can't usefully or even sensibly have an economy in which there are significantly different methods of settling on relative values and associated levels of output, duration of work, and so on. If there are two, three, or more different methods for allocating items, then the same items will have different and conflicting relative prices depending which method of allocation is consulted, and there will also be different and conflicting logic and associated implications for behavior operating as well, and the contradictions will more often than not disrupt viable operations.

However, the more interesting and informative second reason why multiple modes of allocation aren't an option is social. Both markets and central planning, which are the prevalently preferred options for allocation, each destroy self-management, equity, solidarity, diversity, and husbandry and each impose, albeit in different ways, the old division of labor and thus the familiar coordinator/worker class division and hierarchy. The derivative conclusion is that if we self-consciously, or even just inadvertently, include either markets or central planning or any combination of the two as our means of allocation in a future economy, these structures will subvert our other libertarian values and aspirations, just like including corporate divisions of labor would subvert our agendas, or including top-down rule would subvert our agendas, or including remuneration for property would subvert our agendas. An anarchist stance regarding the economy is for freedom and against class rule, and so it has to reject market and centrally planned allocation.

It would take more time than I have here to make a full case about markets and central planning, much less to demonstrate the worthiness and viability of their replacement, but parecon says what is needed if workers and consumers are to self-manage economic life is a mode of allocation that: (a) conveys relevant social, material, and environmental information to confident and knowledgeable workers and consumers, (b) gives workers and consumers the means to express their own desires and to learn other people's views and desires and to then together cooperatively adapt their desires into mutual accord, and (c) achieves all this in a way that properly accounts for the full social, material, and environmental costs and benefits of choices even while conveying to each actor self-managing say while smoothly arriving at viable and, in the sense we mentioned earlier, efficient choices.

Parecon makes a case that participatory planning, which is just parecon's name for cooperative negotiation of economic inputs and outputs by nested, self-managing workers' and consumers' councils, is what can and will accomplish these aims.

Do parecon's advocates—or anarchists who adopt parecon as an economic vision—have to describe this new mode of allocation fully, delving into its many details to the third or fourth or tenth decimal place of accuracy? Far from it. All that is necessary is to describe participatory planning's core elements sufficiently to demonstrate its viability and worthiness, including for dispelling cynicism and orienting strategic choices.

For that matter, will the information exchange, cooperative negotiation, and tallying of decisions of participatory planning have different specific local operational features in different countries, in different industries in one country, and even in different workplaces in one industry, and will its many diverse features also vary as people develop new understandings through their experiences as well as due to enjoying new technical possibilities? Of course.

To demonstrate the possibility and virtues of participatory planning we can and should talk about some possible specific structures for its implementation, but we should do so flexibly and always remembering that the full contours of this new mode of allocation will only emerge from real practice. Still, to have participatory planning as part of our goal, says the pareconist, even if we only broadly and flexibly specify its features, is essential if we are to dispel cynicism about there being a worthy alternative to markets and central planning, and if we are sensibly to orient our strategic choices.

So parecon is a proposed economic vision for attaining classlessness via workers' and consumers' self-managing councils, remuneration for duration, intensity, and onerousness of socially valued work, balanced job complexes, and participatory planning. It is minimalist in the sense of trying to broadly and loosely pinpoint only the defining institutional features we must attain to establish the conditions of freedom necessary for future people to determine diversely the rest of economic life.

Of course, however, life is not just about economics, and the same broad approach to vision can be usefully undertaken regarding other dimensions of life as well. For example, what are the values we aspire to for political adjudication, legislation, and collective implementation; for cultural identification and celebration of communities and their interrelations; for birthing, nurturing, and raising the next generation and conducting daily household and sexual relations; or for other domains of life? And then, given our values for polity, culture, kinship, and so on—what are the minimum institutional structures that we must attain to establish conditions permitting future people to live however they choose in those domains, by way of mutuality and self-management, and consistent with sought values?

When activists cautiously answer those questions without overextending, but also without saying too little to dispel cynicism or guide desirable strategy, we will have a flexible, continually adaptable, institutional vision to define our political and social commitments. I think, at that point, even while recognizing that new insights might of course still yield new commitments, anarchists could say that part of what being anarchist means is favoring this vision.

Anarchist Strategy

Now comes the hard part, in which, ironically, for some anarchists their attitude of eschewing visionary detail reverses itself at precisely the moment it ought not to do so. That is, whereas some anarchists in my view wrongly doubt the desirability of adopting even a minimalist institutional vision as part of what it means to be an anarchist—many anarchists do think it makes sense to deem a rather sharp and strong set of strategic attachments as being critical to being an anarchist. That is, some anarchists reject having a strong stance about elements of vision, where I think it makes sense to actually have such a stance, but then do have very strong strategic views they think are unbridgeably necessary to being anarchist, where I believe having such a stance is far more problematic.

Of course sharing strategic insights is generally good—and I am not questioning that. What I worry about, rather, is the extent to which some anarchists, like many people of other political stances, tend to think that momentary strategic commitments are matters of unbridgeable principle.

What can a strategic commitment mean?

Well, it could mean that I think democratic centralism, or the use of violence, or organizing inside unions, or rejecting electoral focus, or creating self-managing institutions of our own, or whatever other strategic commitment we might want to list, is essential as an anarchist organizing approach all the time and is thus a core part of being anarchist. Or it could mean I think democratic centralism or any of these other commitments is very likely to be essential, though there could be exceptions, so there is a high burden of proof on not using it. Or it could mean I think democratic centralism or any other commitment has horrible implications so it is very likely to be counterproductive and there is a high burden of proof on using it. Or it could mean that I think democratic centralism or any of the others is despicable and should never be used, period.

My view is that the first and fourth stances are both virtually always ill-conceived because there is virtually no such thing as a strategic commitment, positive or negative, that is a principled touchstone and therefore unbridgeable in all times and places, a priori. Rather, the most we can say in general about strategic commitments will almost always take the form of a burden of proof formulation.

To clarify, let's take a few examples that might arise for anarchists. For example, some anarchists will say presidential electoral campaigning is not just suspect, entailing a high burden of proof to justify emphasizing such activity as a strategic priority, say, which I would agree with, but that presidential politics is actually verboten for anarchists. These folks tend to argue that the downside of such activity is ubiquitous, immense, and unavoidable. If you are for an electoral focus, even only in some situations and not in others, they deduce that you are not really anarchist. There is no situation, they say, warranting a presidential electoral focus by an anarchist.

To me, unlike saying, say, that an anarchist vision must reject markets and include some type of cooperative negotiation of inputs and outputs and must reject a corporate division of labor and include some type of balanced job complexes, or, if not, then it isn't anarchist because it won't have classless relations—a comparable pronouncement to saying that an anarchist must totally reject all presidential electoral involvement by erecting a binding stop sign saying it is simply and always anti anarchist to prioritize such activity—makes no sense.

Yes, it certainly does make sense to point out the likely or even just possible debits of electoral work—of which there are many—and it also makes sense to have an understanding of those debits as part of the shared conceptual strategic agreement of anarchists.

But then, even having that broad understanding, it nonetheless makes sense and is in fact necessary to consider any specific proposal for prioritizing electoral activity to see if there aren't in its case mitigating factors which make the proposal desirable even for an anarchist agenda. To say it can never make anarchist sense to be involved in presidential electoral politics is not just inflexible and sectarian, it is also wrong.

For example, suppose that winning a presidential election would clearly create a context vastly more welcoming to and productive for all kinds of local and national anarchist activity, whereas losing the same election would curtail all that activism. Or imagine an even more peculiar—to an anarchist—situation. That is, imagine a national candidate for president who stands far to the anarchist side of the political spectrum and who is incredibly eager to use the presidency to propel the population toward consciousness and activism that will enhance popular power and participation, foster council formation and prioritization, overcome old local and state governmental structures, and finally also overcome even old national political structures. Could electing this person be problematic? Yes, maybe—for example, one might claim all those allegiances are lies, or that despite those allegiances the person will have no wiggle room, or that the process will subvert her sincere desires, and so on. But would someone thinking that such a campaign could be a positive and even high-priority part of anarchist social change despite those worries, due to thinking the potential problems could be surmounted and the benefits enormous, automatically mark that person as not anarchist, or not radical, or even as a supporter of the status quo? Of course not.

It is this ability to realize that people can sincerely differ about centrally important strategic matters without it indicating that one or the other of the disputants has sold out or has otherwise lost their libratory sense that political infighting often forgets. The truth is that leftists often disagree due to honest differences over complex circumstances and not solely due to one or the other being an enemy of change and an agent of reaction.

As another example, take implementing workers' control in workplaces. An anarchist might reasonably say, and I would agree, that in general this is a very high-priority goal. The anarchist might then add, however, going a step beyond what I would urge, that as a result of its importance, whenever instituting self-management can be done it ought to be done, forthrightly and rapidly, and that there can be no exception to this injunction. To waffle about implementing workers' self-management, this anarchist might say, is always anti-anarchist.

Of course, there is no doubt it could be true in a particular situation that waffling about implementing workers' self-management demonstrates anti-anarchist leanings. But the more interesting question is could there be a situation in which opposing self-management isn't anti-anarchist at all, and in which, instead, pursuing workers' self-management in some particular plant or industry would impede an overall anarchist agenda?

Oddly, the answer is yes. For example, consider a situation where in the early stages of a transition process seeking self-management throughout society, the easiest place to initiate massive rapid innovations is in a very large and wealthy oil industry, where the workers are already by far the best paid and most comfortable workers in the country, and where oil industry surpluses finance the country's innovations for other sectors and communities, and where oil workers self-managing their industry could lead to their taking more of the oil surplus for themselves at the expense of others. Oddly, in such a situation, if the oil workers' consciousness was not yet very advanced, enacting self-management in the largest industry in the country, oil, before establishing norms of equitable remuneration, could actually set back the overall project of attaining self-management throughout the whole society. Thus seeking self-management whenever and wherever you can would in this case be potentially counterproductive rather than absolutely essential.

Let's take an even more peculiar and ironic situation. Suppose a country is in a massive project to transform, with the federal government and various grassroots movements strongly on the side of change, but many old mayors and governors, and many old owners and media moguls as well as many local police forces still opposing, obstructing, and sabotaging efforts at change. Suppose, in fact, that in the case of those old police forces they are largely corrupt and are by their theft and violence creating a climate of fear that is in turn seriously impeding federal efforts to facilitate local creation of people's participatory communes and people's popular power. What should be done about the police?

Can you imagine an anarchist saying, in this unusual context, "well, since the army is steadfastly in favor of the revolutionary process, how about if we use the army to discipline and if need be to replace the police, thus removing the latter as an obstacle to change, eliminating the climate of fear that the police produce, and proceeding with transition. All of this accomplished as quickly and with as little violence as possible thanks to the army?" Of course, says the approach's anarchist advocate, I realize using the army domestically is a very dangerous choice for diverse reasons, but, that said, letting the police persist in their corruption and violence risks total disaster. More, given the work that has been done throughout the army to date, and the very serious community and organizational controls we can impose on the proposed military efforts, I think we can make this work.

My point is I can imagine an anarchist proposing that. In fact I can imagine me suggesting such a path as a possibility in Venezuela, say, where the described conditions do indeed exist—just as the conditions of the prior examples exist in Venezuela as well—and clearly my making such a suggestion, whether wise or not, would not mean I had thrown in with state power, or had abdicated my belief in grassroots self-management, or had become a fan of coercion, and so on, but instead it would mean only that in a rather unusual context, this approach seemed to me most likely to have the positive consequences that any anarchist advocate of real freedom would want to achieve, whereas other approaches would accomplish less, with even more risk.

The point of these strange examples, and many more that the reader can no doubt conceive, is first that in sum they are not in fact all that strange. Actual social struggle is very complex and diverse, with specific features arising that often make knee-jerk application of political beliefs very dangerous. All the above situations could plausibly exist in broadly similar form in other countries than Venezuela, even in my own, the

United States, at some future date. But second, for the same reasons, one thing we can certainly know is that there is no strategic injunction that is universally binding in all times, places, and situations.

Indeed, whereas I think it does make sense to say about a particular perspective such as anarchism that some view is essential to it regarding vision, so that anarchism should adopt a particular broadly conceived visionary goal where to forswear this goal is to reject anarchism, I think it does not make sense to say about a particular perspective such as anarchism that some particular strategic commitment is essential to it so if a person ever does anything that appears contrary to that commitment, the person has left behind anarchism.

Finally, let me give a reverse example. Anarchists typically reject democratic centralism as a means of making decisions in a revolutionary project. This could mean: (1) that anarchists think democratic centralism should never be employed and that to employ it is always a sign that one is a not an anarchist or even an anti-anarchist—or it could mean (2) that anarchists think democratic centralism typically has horrible by-products and a debilitating internal logic that together tend to subvert anarchist aims so that there is a very high burden of proof on utilizing such decision procedures.

To me, unless one nuances it tremendously, stance (1) is insupportable. Suppose, for example, that anarchists are having a demonstration that is going to feature a big rally and speeches, and then a march that spins off from the rally, and then a major building occupation, say, that spins off from the march. The target for the occupation is secret and, in fact, the wrong target has been leaked so that the police will occupy that building with all their attention, while the march ignores that destination and instead goes unobstructed to its real target. There is a need for flexibility as well as secrecy, so the movement chooses/elects a tactical leadership committee that is empowered to unilaterally decide as the march unfolds what actual target makes most sense to occupy and when to run for it, and so on.

Well, this is essentially a democratic centralist approach—but it is one which could in context further the anarchist agenda, and which, given that the tactical committee forms, acts, and then disbands, would have little in the way of negative lasting repercussions, though, yes, the mind-set involved is of concern and if the same people were always the tactical leaders whenever such a committee was needed, that would be a serious risk. So, would advocating this use of secret flexible leadership make one an anti-anarchist? Did making similar choices make Bakunin, among others, an anti-anarchist? Of course not.

So what's my point?

I think and hope that with further investigation anarchists will overwhelmingly agree that parecon/parsoc provides an economic vision and an emerging but still far from fully conceived social vision, each of which are compatible with and indeed also fulfill the aspirations of the long heritage called anarchism, but each of which also avoid overspecifying a future that we can't yet know and which, in any event, it is for future people and not us to determine.

I also think there are many strategic insights that anarchists can very reasonably share as part of their overall perspective, such as the need to plant seeds of the future in the present, such as balanced job complexes and self-managed decision making; the need to have demands, language, and organizational structure and procedures that not only meet current needs on behalf of suffering constituencies, but also propel escalating desires that lead toward preferred goals; the need to win currently sought reforms in ways that develop means of winning still more gains in the future; the need to measure success by assessing gains in consciousness, organization, and in circumstances and fulfillment; the high burden of proof on employing violence or on employing any long-term, top-down structures and methods such as persisting democratic centralism; and the criticality of overcoming not only capitalist, but also coordinator mentalities and structures in our own projects and in society writ large.

But more, to avoid sectarianism, arrogance, and knee-jerk calculations, as well as to be on track toward the better world we all desire, I think it is key to realize that having a minimalist but compelling and inspiring anarchist institutional vision is essential, whereas regarding strategy we need to prioritize understanding that there is no single virtuous or effective anarchist strategy such that one size fits all. Instead, there is need for sincere and well-meaning debate and disagreement, even about pivotal issues and possibilities, undertaken without casting aspersions on motives and values, and even trying to experiment with minority conceptions rather than only implementing those that are most favored.

Postscript: Toward the Occupation of Everyday Life

Deric Shannon, Anthony Nocella II, John Asimakopoulos

November 16, 2011

Over the last couple of months we've finished this book while watching a new global phenomenon evolve. Occupation isn't typically referred to as a movement, but a tactic. Yet people have begun referring to the "Occupy Movement"—a movement whose primary concerns are the inequalities that are endemic to capitalist society. That is, there has never been a historical moment under capitalism that has not been typified by the wealthy largely owning and operating the world at the expense of the rest of us and this series of attempts at taking (and keeping for periods of time) public space seem aimed against exactly those organizing principles. Anarchists argue that there is nothing new in these unequal arrangements—although in a time of capitalist crisis perhaps those large-scale inequalities are exacerbated, waking people up who were previously sleeping to new possibilities. Interestingly, this movement, which began in countries like Tunisia, Egypt, Greece, and Spain and was carried into the United States by a loose collection of folks dubbed by *Rolling Stone* "anarchists and radicals with nothing but sleeping bags," has gone global.

Within these various occupations one can see principles at work that are directly at odds with the present society. People come together into groups to discuss issues in assemblies where we usually remain alienated from one another—sometimes even frightened of strangers, our neighbors, and even at times our friends and loved ones. People are sharing resources within the encampments, freely distributing food, water, and other supplies where usually we are forced to purchase those things with money accessed through work. People are doing the "dirty work" of cleaning, cooking, and other menial tasks voluntarily and are acknowledged for their labor where we typically threaten a segment of society with starvation if they don't do this work or routinely ignore that it is, in fact, work for many people who clean homes, do laundry, cook, raise children, and so on. People are innovating—at Occupy Wall Street, after Bloomberg took the protesters' power generators, new generators were made from bicycles—and the reward for that innovation is the satisfaction of mutual aid where we are told that we need incentives in the form of wealth for innovation to exist.

But we also have seen other organizing principles at work.

Last weekend a number of the occupations were forcibly removed by the police. The reports of people being maced, beaten, stripped, searched, prodded—in a word, *governed*—are ubiquitous. The state has trashed thousands of dollars of tents, sleeping bags, cooking equipment, and perhaps most striking, thousands of *books* carefully organized into a library at Zucotti Park, bringing to mind scenes from Ray Bradbury's *Fahrenheit 451* (apparently ideas are dangerous after all). They've also destroyed those meeting points where people gathered to talk about ideas, debated the best ways forward, and engaged in the messy process of collective engagement in life without the state and capital as mediators within our social lives—even if the context was limited.

We might see this as a metaphor for our future lives. Anarchists argue that no amount of tinkering with capitalism is going to make it sustainable or bearable. No amount of toying with the mechanisms of the state are going to make it desirable. And there is no way that the diffuse and complex arrangements of domination in our institutions, culture, and our very selves can be overcome without also dismantling the state and capitalism.

So we might learn lessons from the occupation movement, whether it sustains, wanes, or changes form. First, capitalist austerity should demonstrate to everyone beyond the shadow of a doubt now that the state isn't going to regulate capitalism to our benefit. Even "gains" that we fight for in the form of demands on the state can be taken from us as quickly as they are granted by our rulers. We keep nothing that we cannot take ourselves and, importantly, defend (as the police batons around the world have shown time and time again, particularly over the course of the last few years as the crisis has set in and an increasing number of the dispossessed have risen up in response).

Second, there is radical potential in coming together to talk. This doesn't mean that we can talk domination away, but it does mean that capitalist society is alienating and isolating and a part of ending capitalism is ending our isolation. As we said in the introduction to this collection, "economics" presents a problem for anarchists and the relationship isn't easy—particularly as "economics" typically assumes the separation of production and consumption from the rest of social life as some specialized sphere. But clearly capitalism, and its attendant individualist ethos, creates an alienated and isolated social body. Experiences of community, and particularly communities of resistance standing up to the state and capital, contain possibilities for building new social forms on our own terms.

Finally, and perhaps most importantly, these social forms can stick if they're not left at the public assemblies, but are diffused throughout our everyday lives. This is already being experimented with by members of various occupations and is, perhaps, what most people mean when they refer to "occupation" as a tactic. Groups connected with local movements are beginning to help protect the homes of others with mortgages being foreclosed in places like Minneapolis, Cleveland, and New York City. In Chapel Hill, a local group took a downtown building for a short period of time, complete with possible plans for using the abandoned space for local shows, a free medical clinic, a library, and more before they were violently ejected by police. Similarly, on the coattails of a successful general strike in Oakland, a group attempted to take a vacant building but was fought back by the police. Workers in Oakland, during the general strike, took and shut down the local port. Likewise, over the last few years, occupations of school buildings have become common actions in disparate places such as Berkeley, Athens, Santiago, London, Paris, New York City.

So what if we refused to stop at meeting in assemblies and camping in public squares? What might it look like if we began occupying places within our daily lives—our homes, our workplaces, our schools? What if we began taking space and food and water and distributed them freely, refusing to allow the conventions of the economy to mediate those activities for us? Indeed, since anarchists argue that we don't need experts and bureaucrats to run our affairs and that we can create life on our own terms, the diffusion of these occupations into daily life can give us a glimpse of a world that *might be* and could possibly point to post-capitalist alternatives as a process *out of* capitalism and into a new and unwritten future.

We might look at these two different organizing methods as a crossroads. In one direction is the police truncheon, the tear gas, thousands of pairs of zip-tie handcuffs, police vans filled with the bodies of anyone with the audacity to challenge the power of the state and capital. In the other direction is an unwritten future being created in the present of assemblies, mutual aid, cooperation, and an end to the isolation and alienation that come from an economy and a social world built for working instead of *living*.

We have a world to win. For the occupation of daily life!

Contributor Biographies

Ernesto Aguilar, born and raised in Houston, is a media worker and organizer who has been active in many movements, including founding a variety of groups focusing on everything from reproductive rights to international solidarity movements and police accountability. In the early 1990s, Aguilar cofounded the Black Fist collective, which focused on issues of race in the anarchist movement and was allied with groups like the Federation of Black Community Partisans, the precursor to the black anarchist formation Black Autonomy International. The Black Fist collective convened with Lorenzo Kom'boa Ervin the Anti-Authoritarian Network of Community Organizers conference in Atlanta in 1994. Aguilar was also involved in the formation of the Anarchist Black Cross Network and in web development for the anarchist newspaper *Onward*. In 2001, he founded the Anarchist People of Color e-mail list and website, illegalvoices.org, from which emerged nearly a dozen autonomous regional US collectives identified as APOC. APOC supporters held a 2003 conference at Wayne State University in Detroit. Aguilar continues to organize with a variety of groups and is the founder and editor of People of Color Organize, a website on political activism, theory, and practice.

Michael Albert is a founder and current member of the staff of *Z Magazine* as well as System Operator of *Z Magazine*'s website: ZCom (www.zmag.org). Albert's radicalization occurred during the 1960s. His political involvements, starting then and continuing to the present, have ranged from local, regional, and national organizing projects and campaigns to cofounding South End Press, *Z Magazine*, the Z Media Institute, and ZNet, and to working on all these projects, writing for various publications and publishers, giving public talks, and so on. His personal interests, outside the political realm, focus on general science reading (with an emphasis on physics, math, and matters of evolution and cognitive science), computers, mystery and thriller/adventure novels, sea kayaking, and the more sedentary but no less challenging game of Go. Albert is also the author of numerous books. Most recently these include: *Remembering Tomorrow* (Seven Stories Press), *Realizing Hope* (Zed Press), and *Parecon: Life after Capitalism* (Verso). Many of Albert's articles are stored in ZCom and can be accessed there, along with hundreds of other *Z Magazine* and ZNet articles, essays, interviews, and other materials.

William D. Armaline was most recently a professor (now retired) of teaching and learning and the founding director of the Center for Innovative and Transformative Education at Bowling Green State University. Throughout his thirty-five-year career in education, he has been an activist/teacher/scholar working with colleagues in higher education, in the public schools, and in communities at large to reconceptualize schooling structures concomitantly with transforming pedagogical practices. His current work is a critical and personal reflection on schooling reform, replete with the dreams and ambitions of someone who saw (and to an extent still sees) education as a potential vehicle to liberation.

William T. Armaline is a multidisciplinary scholar in "Justice Studies" at San Jose State University. His recent research focuses on systemic racism and human rights abuses through the institutionalization and incarceration of marginalized populations. His scholarship also includes work on radical political economic theory, human rights theory and practice, and the development of critical pedagogies. Rather than making selective contributions as an "activist," William "puts in work" as a way of life.

John Asimakopoulos is executive director of the scholar-activist Transformative Studies Institute (TSI) and associate professor of sociology at the City University of New York, Bronx. He is also editor in chief of *Theory in Action*, an interdisciplinary, peer-reviewed journal, and is working with TSI to establish a new free and progressive university operated by scholar-activists. John's work focuses on labor, globalization, and social theory championing the formation of counter-ideology, independent working-class media and educational institutions, and direct action. John's interest in the working class stems from his parents, who obtained only third-grade educations. They worked as landless farmers in Greece and later as immigrant factory workers in the United States. Early on in life, John observed that his parents' hard work was never rewarded, which pushed him to think of social justice. Ever since, he has dedicated his life to promoting equality and social justice for all people.

D. T. Cochrane is a father, partner, and PhD student. His research interests are business history, theories of value and accumulation, and business disruption movements. His dissertation is on De Beers and the changing role of diamonds in the United States in the 1940s.

Uri Gordon is an Israeli activist and academic. He is the author of *Anarchy Alive! Anti-Authoritarian Politics from Practice to Theory* (Pluto Press). While completing his doctoral research at Oxford, he organized with community initiatives and anti-capitalist networks in the UK and Europe including Indymedia, Earth First, and Dissent. He now teaches environmental politics and ethics at the Arava Institute for Environmental Studies, and is active with the Negev COexistence Forum for Civil Equality and Anarchists Against the Wall. His research continues to focus on grassroots sustainability, radical peace-making, and anarchist politics. He is also active as a facilitator, trainer, and translator.

Robin Hahnel is visiting professor in the Department of Economics at Portland State University in Portland, Oregon, and professor emeritus at American University in Washington, DC. His most recent books are *Green Economics: Confronting the Ecological Crisis* (M.E. Sharpe 2011), *Economic Justice and Democracy: From Competition to Cooperation* (Routledge 2005), and *The ABCs of Political Economy: A Modern Approach* (Pluto 2002). With Michael Albert he is co-creator of an alternative to capitalism known as "participatory economics." Robin has been active in numerous progressive movements and organizations for over forty-five years.

Caroline Kaltefleiter is professor of communication studies and women's studies as well as a founding member of the Anarchist Studies Initiative (ASI) at the State University of New York, Cortland. She has written numerous articles and conference papers on anarchist studies, do-it-yourself culture and the riot grrrl movement. Recent works include: "Anarchy Grrrl Style Now: Riot Grrrl Actions and Practices," "Riot Grrrls and Bois: Gender Contestation in (Trans) Zines and Performance Sites of Resistance"; and "Juno and Diablo: Cinematic Riot Grrrls and the Cultivation of a Liberated Girlhood." Kaltefleiter calls herself an activist first then an academic. She was a member of the Riot Grrrl Washington DC chapter and remains committed to

Riot Grrrl through zines and correspondence. Her current research interests include youth culture capitalism, post-feminism, and popular culture. She is currently finishing a forthcoming academic text nearly two decades in the making on the Riot Grrrl movement, that privileges an inside/out perspective.

Ruth Kinna teaches political theory in the School of Social, Political and Geographical Sciences at Loughborough University, UK. She is co-editor, with Laurence Davis, of *Anarchism and Utopianism* (Manchester University Press, 2009), author of *The Beginner's Guide to Anarchism* (Oneworld, 2005 and 2009), and has written a number of articles on anarchist writers and activists. She is currently working on two anarchist projects: an edited collection, *Libertarian Socialism: Politics in Black and Red* with Dave Berry, Saku Pinta, and Alex Prichard (to be published by Palgrave), and a research companion to anarchism for Continuum Books. She is a member of the Anarchist Studies Network and editor of the journal *Anarchist Studies*.

An anarchist for over twenty years, **Iain McKay** has been involved in many anarchist groups in the UK. He is currently a member of the *Black Flag* editorial collective, Britain's leading (and longest-lasting) anarchist magazine. In addition, he has produced *An Anarchist FAQ*, which summarizes and explains anarchist ideas and history and an introduction to and evaluation of Kropotkin's ideas on mutual aid (both published by AK Press). He also writes on a host of issues for *Black Flag* and *Freedom*, as well as on websites (primarily *Anarchist Writers*). He has recently edited and written the introduction to *Property is Theft!*, the first comprehensive anthology of Pierre-Joseph Proudhon's writings (published by AK Press).

Jeff Monaghan is based in Ottawa, Canada. He does paid work for a small communications company and cares for a fleet of rusty bikes. He is a member of Ottawa's Exile Infoshop collective and Books to Prisoners-Ottawa. He plays drums in a couple of sloppy "punk rawk" bands and spends his spare time with his loving partner Ange and their kid.

Scott Nappalos is a registered nurse living in Miami, Florida. Scott has been active in movements against the war and for environmental justice, anti-racist and anti-sexist organizing, and popular media. An active member of the Industrial Workers of the World for ten years, Scott continues to work on autonomous workers struggle in healt care, and other industries. Scott has served as a trainer for the IWW's training program as well as a member of the Organizing Department Board and the International Solidarity Commission. Scott has worked on solidarity campaigns with popular and revolutionary movements in Iran, India, El Salvador, Mexico, and Haiti. Scott's writings have appeared in *The Industrial Worker, Anarcho-Syndicalist Review,* and *Turbulence.* Scott is a cofounder and a member of the editorial collective of *Recompositions: Notes for a New Workerism,* an online journal of autonomous workers' struggle and organization. Presently, he is completing a collection of his writings on political organization, popular struggles, the problem of revolutionary consciousness, complex systems theory as a methodology for revolutionaries, and revolutionary strategy. Scott is one of the founding members of Miami Autonomy and Solidarity, a revolutionary political organization founded in 2009 and active in popular movements and committed to building praxis and strategy for political struggle in our time.

Anthony J. Nocella, II, award-winning author, poet, community organizer, and educator, teaches at Hamline University as a visiting professor of urban education. Nocella focuses his attention on urban education, peace and conflict studies, inclusive social justice education, environmental education, disability pedagogy, queer pedagogy, feminist pedagogy, critical pedagogy, anarchist studies, critical animal studies, and hip-hop pedagogy. He has taught workshops in mediation, negotiation, and strategic social movement building, and has assisted a number of legal committees in North and South America. He has provided expressive and experiential education workshops to nongovernmental organizations, prisoners, incarcerated youth, and students in middle and high schools, representing organizations such as Alternative to Violence Program, Save the Kids, and American Friends Service Committee (AFSC), in hopes of increasing the peace and providing skills to revert violent conflicts to nonviolent transformation. He is on more than a dozen boards, including the AFSC, Center for Gender and Intercultural Studies (CGIS), Institute for Critical Animal Studies (ICAS), and the Central New York Peace Studies

Consortium. Nocella has written scholarly articles in more than two dozen publications, cofounded more than twenty active socio-political organizations, four academic journals, and is working on his fifteenth book on the subject of urban education. His latest publication is *Hollywood's Exploited: Public Pedagogy, Corporate Movies, and Cultural Crisis* (2010), coedited with Richard Van Heertum, Benjamin Frymer, and Tony Kashani.

Wayne Price has been involved in revolutionary socialist organizing and theoretical work for over forty years. He has evolved through anarchist-pacifism and dissident Trotskyism to revolutionary class-struggle anarchism, hopefully learning from his many mistakes. He worked as a special education teacher and as a school psychologist and earned a doctor of psychology degree. For years he was active in antiwar activities and in oppositions within the teachers' union. He writes regularly for www.Anarkismo.net. He has authored two books, *The Abolition of the State: Anarchist and Marxist Perspectives* and *Anarchism and Socialism: Reformism or Revolution?*

Deric Shannon is a US anarchist organizer who lives on the East Coast. He is a coeditor of *Contemporary Anarchist Studies* (Routledge 2009) and co-author of *Political Sociology: Oppression, Resistance, and the State* (Pine Forge 2010). When not writing and reading, he's playing music with friends or organizing for a livable future.

Chris Spannos is an activist, organizer, and anti-capitalist. He has worked as an embroidery machine operator, social service worker, sailor, and cook. From 2006 to 2011 Chris was full-time editor and system administrator at ZNet. He currently lives in Greenpoint, Brooklyn, New York City. He edited the anthology *Real Utopia: Participatory Society for the 21st Century* (AK Press 2008) and is interested in the theory and practice of autonomy. He is founder and editor of the online magazine the *New Significance* (thenewsignificance.com).

Marie Trigona is a writer, video maker, radio producer, and translator whose work has been inspired by international anarchist working-class history and anti-imperialist struggles. Her work focuses on labor, human rights, community media, and social movements in Latin America.

She has collaborated with the direct action and video collective Grupo Alavío. Trigona's writing has appeared in publications including *Z Magazine* and *ZNet*, *NACLA*, *Monthly Review*, *Canadian Dimension*, *The Buenos Aires Herald*, *Left Turn*, *Americas Program*, *Upsidedown World*, *Dollars and Sense*, and dozens of other media outlets. She is a correspondent at Pacifica's "Free Speech Radio News," a worker-run news program aired on nearly 100 stations in the United States. Currently Trigona studies at the Latin American School of Social Sciences (FLACSO) in Buenos Aires.

Dr. Richard J White is a senior lecturer of economic geography at Sheffield Hallam University, UK. To date, Richard's main areas of research have focused on rethinking "the economic" in economic geography, exploring the geographies of commodification, and mapping the limits of capitalism in contemporary society. As an anarchist geographer Richard is also actively engaged with anarchist praxis focused on harnessing post-capitalist/heterodox economic futures. Richard is also the editor-in-chief of the *Journal for Critical Animal Studies*, and is currently serving on the editorial boards of the *International Journal of Sociology and Social Policy* and *Theory in Action, The Journal of the Transformative Studies Institute*. He can be contacted at Richard.White@shu.ac.uk.

Colin Williams is professor of public policy in the Management School at the University of Sheffield in the UK. His interests are in re-representing and constructing alternative economic practices beyond the market economy. His recent books include *Informal Work in Developed Nations* (Routledge, 2010), *Re-thinking the Future of Work* (Routledge, 2007), *A Commodified World? Mapping the Limits of Capitalism* (Zed, 2005) and *Community Self-Help* (Palgrave-Macmillan, 2004). He can be contacted at: c.c.williams@sheffield.ac.uk .

Abbey Volcano, a member of the Workers Solidarity Alliance and Queers without Borders, currently lives in Connecticut. She is presently writing on reproductive freedom and normative violence. Abbey only loves a handful of things more than she loves graphic novels: organizing for a less boring and fucked-up world, kitties, her family, and fantasizing about moving to Madrid and becoming an oil painter.

Index

Support AK Press!

AK Press is one of the world's largest and most productive

anarchist publishing houses. We're entirely worker-run and democratically managed. We operate without a corporate structure—no boss, no managers, no bullshit. We publish close to twenty books every year, and distribute thousands of other titles published by other like-minded independent presses from around the globe.

The Friends of AK program is a way that you can directly contribute to the continued existence of AK Press, and ensure that we're able to keep publishing great books just like this one! Friends pay a minimum of $25 per month, for a minimum three month period, into our publishing account. In return, Friends automatically receive (for the duration of their membership), as they appear, one free copy of every new AK Press title. They're also entitled to a 20% discount on everything featured in the AK Press Distribution catalog and on the website, on any and every order. You or your organization can even sponsor an entire book if you should so choose!

There's great stuff in the works—so sign up now to become a Friend of AK Press, and let the presses roll!

Won't you be our friend? Email friendsofak@akpress.org for more info, or visit the Friends of AK Press website: http://www.akpress.org/programs/friendsofak